MW01063129

FINANCING NONPROFITS

FINANCING NONPROFITS

Putting Theory into Practice

Edited by

Dennis R. Young

NATIONAL CENTER ON NONPROFIT ENTERPRISE

AND

ALTAMIRA
PRESS

A Division of
ROWMAN AND LITTLEFIELD PUBLISHERS, INC.
Lanham • New York • Toronto • Plymouth, UK

ALTAMIRA PRESS
A Division of Rowman & Littlefield Publishers, Inc.
A wholly owned subsidiary of The Rowman & Littlefield Publishing Group, Inc.
4501 Forbes Boulevard, Suite 200
Lanham, MD 20706
www.altamirapress.com

Estover Road
Plymouth PL6 7PY
United Kingdom

Copyright © 2007 by National Center on Nonprofit Enterprise

All rights reserved. No part of this publication may be reproduced, stored in a retrieval
system, or transmitted in any form or by any means, electronic, mechanical,
photocopying, recording, or otherwise, without the prior permission
of the publisher.

British Library Cataloguing in Publication Information Available

Library of Congress Cataloging-in-Publication Data

Finacing nonprofits : putting theory into practice / edited by Dennis R. Young.
    p. cm.
  Why study nonprofit finance? / Dennis R. Young—Individual giving / Patrick
  Rooney—Institutional philanthropy / Joseph Cordes and Richard Sansing—
  Government funding of nonprofit organizations / Michael Rushton and Arthur
  Brooks—Fee income and commercial ventures / Estelle James and Dennis R. Young—
  Elizabeth Keating and Mark Hager—Volunteer resources / Anne Preston—
  Collaboration and barter / Renee Irvin—Gifts-in-kind and other illiquid assets /
  Charles M. Gray / Woods Bowman—Income portfolios / Kevin Kearns—Finanncial
  health / Janet Greenlee and Howard Tuckman—Towards a normative theory of
  nonprofit finance / Dennis R. Young
  Includes bibliographical references and index.
  ISBN-13: 978-0-7591-0988-9 (cloth : alk. paper)
  ISBN-13: 978-0-7591-0989-6 (pbk : alk. paper)
  ISBN-10: 0-7591-0988-5 (cloth : alk. paper)
  ISBN-10: 0-7591-0989-3 (pbk : alk. paper)
  1. Nonprofit organizations—Finance.   2. Nonprofit organizations—Management.
  I. Young, Dennis R., 1943-
  HG4027.65.F545 2006
  658.15—dc22   2006015227

Printed in the United States of America

Contents

V   Synthesis

List of Tables

List of Figures

List of Boxes

Foreword

I would like to share our story with you because I believe it illustrates and underscores the very important and best scholarly thinking and research outlined in this book. It also reflects the understandings I have come to realize through more than thirty-five years in the nonprofit sector, ten of which I have served as president of Boys & Girls Clubs of America.

Over the last decade, the financial revenues of Boys & Girls Clubs of America have grown dramatically. In 1995, the national organization raised and generated a total of $14 million from the private sector, barely enough revenue to cover our operating expenses. Most of this revenue came from two sources: corporations and foundations. In 2005, only ten years later, more than $100 million was raised from the private sector. In 2005, these private sector funds came from foundations, corporate foundations, corporate cause-related marketing projects, investment income, planned gifts, and earned income. The national organization also generated more than $15 million from government sources to support the work of the national organization and almost $100 million in federal and state funding for our local clubs. Additionally, the national organization provided more than $40 million in technology hardware and software for local clubs that was contributed by corporations and foundations. At the local level, in 1995, the combined revenue of our affiliates was $362 million. In 2005, the combined revenue of our local clubs exceeded $1.1 billion!

This increase in revenues, both at the national and local levels, enabled the Boys & Girls Club Movement to increase the number of Boys & Girls Clubs from 1,800 to 3,900 and to expand and enhance programs to include state of the art technology centers, educational enhancement programs, learning centers, and much more. In short, in ten years, the size of the movement more than doubled and our impact on individuals, communities, and the nation grew exponentially.

This dramatic increase in revenue did not come about by chance. It was the result of a clear understanding of the need for our services and a disciplined plan to respond to that need. The disciplined planning process began with a recommitment to our mission, the development of a vision, and a strategic plan to realize that vision. At the same time, the planning process called for a rigorous examination of our revenue streams and an understanding of our strengths, weaknesses, untapped potential, and the prospective interests of existing and new donors in our mission, vision, and plan.

It was clear from the beginning that our major revenue streams would come from external sources and not from our members or from our clubs. At the local level, we knew that increasing dues and fees for club members was not the right strategy for us simply because we serve primarily young people from disadvantaged communities. At the national level, we also made the decision that we would not burden our local clubs with large dues to the national organization. (Today, dues from local clubs amount to less than 6 percent of our annual budget.) We learned that significant increases in revenue would need to come from external sources and would require some significant changes in the way we did business.

At the national level we learned, for example, that while we were strong in corporate giving, there was much untapped potential in the developing area of corporate cause-related marketing that would require us to strengthen our brand. We also learned that our greatest weakness was in the area of individual giving and that developing strong relationships with individual donors—beginning with our own board—was the key to success. We also saw the potential to attract government dollars both at the federal and state levels and the need to educate Congress and state legislatures about the potential role we can play in addressing the widespread need for after school programs in America, especially in disadvantaged communities. Finally, we recognized the growing potential of earned income and the need to explore this area as well.

This journey over the last ten years was successful at the national and local levels for several reasons. First, we had a plan, one that was important to communities across America. Second, the plan resonated well with many funding constituencies whom we talked with in the process of developing the plan. Third, we understood that financing our ambitious plan would call on us to do business differently and also make some incremental investments in our infrastructure. The kind of changes I am referring to not only helped to attract donors but helped to strengthen the organization. All this was quite consistent with the concepts in this book that emphasize the connection between the benefits conferred by a nonprofit's programs and the sources from which it can successfully seek resource support.

The changes and investments we made in our infrastructure generated millions in incremental revenues at the national and local levels. We focused on strengthening our brand, which drove donor awareness of Boys & Girls Clubs and also heightened corporate interest in partnering with us on cause-related marketing projects. We expanded our government relations program to educate Congress and state legislatures on the value we bring to communities. We focused on building strong boards and actively engaging our board members in the development of the movement's plans. We launched an initiative on individual giving that started with the board and also one on planned giving that has created a pipeline of revenues for the future.

Specifically, at the national level, the increased board engagement led to a centennial campaign in which personal gifts from board members totaled almost $50 million. Nationally, we also began a search for a new facility and now have tenants providing significant earned income. We also established an investment committee of the board and recruited some top investment professionals to serve on that committee, which made a dramatic and positive impact on our endowment and investment income potential. In addition, we began the practice of ending the year with a small surplus that would help to build our reserves and our endowment. Finally, we successfully approached major corporations to support our technology initiative with significant in-kind state-of-the-art hardware and software for our local clubs.

At the local level, our clubs came to understand the importance of diversifying their revenue streams when it became clear that United Way contributions were going to continue to decline as a percent of their overall budgets. Led by the national organization, our clubs got involved in areas that were new to them. They began raising government funding from the states, focusing on individual giving, building their individual donor base, and implementing endowment and planned giving programs.

What has become clear in our experience is that increasing revenues is not an exercise in finance or development alone. Rather it is a comprehensive process that begins with a mission, a strategic plan, a financial plan, an organizational development strategy, and a board development plan. It is also a long-term proposition and organizations need to have clear strategies and plant important seeds that will take time before they bear fruit. We also learned that diverse funding streams not only generate more revenues, but provide protection if one or more revenue streams diminish or go away entirely, that the awareness of the brand is an integral part of successful fundraising, that a long-term view of an organization's finances is the correct perspective, and that thinking short term can undermine long-term financial stability.

As far as we have come, we have further to go. While many contemporary nonprofits, including Boys & Girls Clubs, share the challenge of attracting and maintaining sufficient resources, the scholarly thinking and research included in this book are critical to a full understanding of the potential to generate funds and manage them well. Our experience at BGCA confirms the basic principles of nonprofit finance developed in these pages: start with a mission; connect the nature of the benefits you are providing with the constituencies who care about these benefits and are willing to support them; diversify income sources to manage risk and to adequately reflect the multifaceted nature of your mission;

monitor your financial health; build endowments and other assets to support mission effectiveness and financial health; and integrate financial decisions into the basic strategic thinking for the organization. The contents of this book will no doubt stimulate the thought and the ideas that will enable nonprofits of all types and sizes to develop comprehensive plans to generate and manage the resources needed to fulfill their missions for years to come.

Roxanne Spillett
President
Boys and Girls Clubs of America
February 2006

Preface

This book emerges from a deliberative process over several years that involved discussions among dozens of scholars, nonprofit managers, and community leaders across the country. It was conceived, coordinated, and supported by the National Center on Nonprofit Enterprise (NCNE), an organization whose mission is to help nonprofit organizations develop and use their economic resources wisely. NCNE addresses its mission by bridging the world of research and scholarship to the arena of nonprofit management practice. This book clearly reflects that bridging, as it required substantial dialogue between the academic leaders who have contributed its chapters and many individuals on the front lines of managing and leading nonprofit organizations in their communities who have provided feedback and given generously of their experiences.

The project was inspired by the confluence of several important observations. First, it has been clear for many years now that nonprofit organizations often struggle to mobilize sufficient resources to maintain themselves and to effectively address their manifold and challenging social missions. Indeed, sustainability and capacity building have become overused buzzwords in today's nonprofit scene. Second, the complexity of nonprofit finance is salient and continues to grow. No other form of organization depends on so many different sources of income—gifts and grants, government funding, earned income, investment income, volunteer resources, gifts-in-kind, and so on. Moreover, these broad categories of income exhibit many variations within them and more seem to be invented year by year.

These two observations beg for some orderly way of thinking so that nonprofit managers are not lost in a thicket of confusing possibilities without some compass to find an appropriate pathway to their financing decisions. Fortunately, a third significant observation is that the body of economic and organizational scholarship concerned with, or at least relevant to, nonprofit organizations has grown considerably over the past thirty to forty years and contains within it many insights that can be helpful in defining this pathway. Theories and empirical research on public goods and markets, on risk and portfolio management, on the role of nonprofits in a market economy, and on the behavior of the nonprofit firm, all potentially contribute to a set of principles that can guide nonprofit leaders in their pursuit of the best combinations of income to address their particular circumstances.

These three general observations helped bring together an outstanding set of scholars to pool their efforts toward the common goal of a book that would bring all, or at least most, of the parts of nonprofit finance into a coherent whole, in a manner that would be conceptually illuminating and immediately useful in practice. The history of the project goes something like this: In 2003, NCNE responded to the opportunity of offering a colloquy session at the annual meeting of the Association for Nonprofit Organizations and Voluntary Action (ARNOVA) on the theme of nonprofit finance. Several scholars were invited to make remarks in a panel session, which was then opened for general discussion from the floor. The response was very enthusiastic, for the importance of the topic if not the preliminary ideas put forward about the appropriate place of different sources of income, such as gifts, earned income, and government funding. Based on this experience, NCNE embarked on a formal book project, asking leading scholars to consider writing papers on specific topics, roughly following the list of chapters of this book. On this voluntary basis, the project got underway and it soon became apparent that it would require a formal meeting of the authors to provide one another with guidance and to work out the details of the book. It was also clear that grounding the project in practitioner experience, to supplement the useful but mostly academic feedback received at ARNOVA, would be very important.

These considerations led to a conference in January 2004 in Cleveland, Ohio, cosponsored by three of NCNE's institutional partners: the Mandel Center for Nonprofit Organizations at Case Western Reserve University, the Center for Nonprofit Policy and Practice at Cleveland State University, and the Center for Nonprofit Excellence in Akron, Ohio. The two-day event enabled the authors to present their preliminary chapters to a diverse audience of nonprofit practitioners and to receive feedback from practitioner/discussants who read and commented on each chapter. The event also allowed the authors to deliberate among themselves on the structure and content of their drafts and the book as a whole.

The next opportunity for feedback came in November 2004 when a subset of the authors again offered a colloquy at ARNOVA, receiving additional helpful suggestions and feedback. Then in October 2005, another subgroup of the authors presented their findings to the annual Especially for Nonprofits conference held at Virginia Commonwealth University in Richmond, Virginia. This conference was hosted by the Especially for Nonprofits program funding partnership led by the Community Foundation Serving Richmond and Central Virginia. This event was yet another robust opportunity for feedback and testing of our ideas. Finally, the authors presented a synthesis of the book in a third colloquy at ARNOVA in November 2005, affording the chance for additional refinement as well as prepublication promotion!

This twisting and adventurous path to publication would not have been possible without lots of help along the way. At NCNE, Richard Brewster, Sarah Masters, Sonu Mulupuru, and Isabelle DuBois Wattles provided coordination and logistical support, including maintenance of a website that made it much easier for the authors to review each others' work and for the editor to keep track of things. Susan Eagan, Stuart Mendel, and Elaine Woloshyn, and the staff of their respective centers, including Avis Boyd and Ann Lucas, were instrumental in organizing the event in Cleveland, where Mario Morino got us off to a flying start with his opening remarks. Russ Cargo, NCNE's board chair, was responsible for bringing NCNE and Especially for Nonprofits together for the Richmond conference. The organizing committee for that event was chaired by Maureen Neal of the Virginia Society of Fund Raising Executives. Finally, Lisa Shepard, Eythan Clarke, LaToya Walker, Cara Brown, Charles Ford Jr., Gardner Neeley, and especially Shannon Omisore on the staff of the Andrew Young School of Policy Studies at Georgia State University provided the editor with able assistance in the final stages of this project.

Discussants of chapter drafts at the Cleveland and Richmond events were especially helpful. These included Mary Verdi Fletcher, Mitchell Balk, Lee Fisher, Ann Palmer, Robert Rensel, Harriet Fader, Richard Stahl, Reginald Gordon, Greta Harris, Maureen Denlea, Sheena MacKenzie, and Randy Wyckoff.

While there was never any core funding, several financial supporters were very important to this endeavor along the way. For the Cleveland event, these included the Morino Institute, Richard Pogue, the Mount Sinai Healthcare Foundation, Fifth Third Bank, and SS&G Financial Services. For the Richmond event, the Community Foundation Serving Richmond and Central Virginia was the principal funder and coordinator of the collaborative that provided the resources. Overall, financial supporters of the National Center on Nonprofit Enterprise, including our partner academic centers, the Rockefeller Brothers Fund and the W. K. Kellogg Foundation, allowed NCNE to provide the underlying support and guidance to carry the project forward to fruition. Finally, the staff of AltaMira Press did a wonderful job in expediting the publication process from start to finish.

The plan for the book is as follows. The introduction (chapter 1) describes a landscape of urgency and complexity surrounding contemporary nonprofit financial decision making and it argues for the development of a general conceptual framework through which this landscape can be understood and best grappled with as a practical matter. This chapter also provides a more detailed road map to the rest of the book. The second part of the book offers a piece by piece analysis of different potential components of nonprofit operating income, including individual and institutional philanthropy, government funding, fee and commercial income, membership dues, investment income, and volunteer services. The third part of the book focuses on special sources of capital for building programs and infrastructure, including barter and collaboration, gifts-in-kind, and borrowing and debt. That discussion leads easily into the fourth part, which examines portfolio issues, including portfolios of investments and portfolios of income sources, and to an overall consideration of nonprofit financial health, including measurement, governance, and developmental considerations. The final chapter puts things together into a new, synthesizing framework for nonprofit finance as a whole, combining considerations of the appropriate role for distinct sources of income with the financial health and risk-related considerations of portfolio management.

It is the hope of the authors, and the staff and board of the National Center on Nonprofit Enterprise, that this volume will become a useful resource in several ways: as a practical guide to financing strategies for executive directors, CFOs, and board members of nonprofit organizations in a wide variety of fields; as a text for graduate students in nonprofit finance; and as a source of ideas for researchers to continue to probe and illuminate the many subtle issues associated with finding the right mix of resources to support the important work of nonprofit organizations in our society.

Dennis R. Young
Bernard B. and Eugenia A. Ramsey
Professor of Private Enterprise
Andrew Young School of Policy Studies
Georgia State University
February 2006

I

INTRODUCTION

1

Why Study Nonprofit Finance?

Dennis R. Young

> *Finance*: 1. the management of (esp. public) money.
> 2. monetary support for an enterprise. 3. the money
> resources of a government, company or person.
>
> —*The Oxford Dictionary and Thesaurus, 1996*

Introduction

The concept of finance as it applies to government, business, or personal affairs is widely understood, and the methodologies for public, corporate, and personal finance are well developed. Finance has to do with managing the money necessary to support these various types of enterprises in efficient and appropriate ways. The mention of nonprofit, nongovernmental enterprises is visibly absent in the dictionary definition of finance. This is not surprising. After all, the nonprofit sector is substantially smaller than the business and government sectors by most economic measures, and perhaps not worthy of special attention in a dictionary definition. Moreover, it is not commonly perceived that nonprofits are so different from business or government that they deserve their own financial methodology. In this book we argue to the contrary.

Let's start with money. Yes, money is very important to the sustenance and success of nonprofit organizations. But other resources are also extremely important to these organizations. Most

3

prominently, the value of volunteer labor is estimated to be approximately one-third of the national income attributable to nonprofit organizations in the United States, a far greater percentage than for business or government (Weitzman et al., 2002). In addition, nonprofits are also sustained in important ways by in-kind resources such as contributions of equipment, supplies, or assets such as real estate and art collections.

Consider also the *kinds* of money that nonprofits utilize for operating purposes. Unlike business and government, which rely primarily on one general source of revenue—sales and taxes respectively (plus loans that are eventually repaid through sales and taxes)—nonprofits are distinctive in their dependence on several different sources of revenue and in many combinations of those sources. Broadly speaking, nonprofit sources of monetary income include charitable donations, fees, government funding, investment income, and in-kind gifts that are converted to cash. However, as this book makes clear, there are many variations within each source category. Charitable giving includes individual donations and institutional philanthropy through foundations and corporations; fee income includes sales revenues from pricing of core services, profits from commercial ventures, and membership income; investment income derives from a wide variety of securities or commercial projects in nonprofit fund portfolios; and convertible in-kind income includes real estate, artwork, used cars, and other material gifts. In addition, some forms of income crosscut these categories. For example, is museum membership to be considered fee revenue or a charitable contribution? Are charges reimbursed through a government insurance program (such as Medicare and Medicaid) to be counted as fees or government funding?

Moreover, nonprofits are far from uniform in their dependence on these different sources of income. For example, nonprofits in fields such as education are, on average, most heavily dependent on fees, while nonprofits in the arts depend almost as much on private giving as fee revenue. Nonprofit social service agencies rely mainly on government funding, while churches depend almost entirely on contributions (see Salamon, 1999a). These, of course, are just aggregate patterns. Within these broad fields of nonprofit service, wide variations exist. For example, the Museum of Contemporary Art (MOCA) in Cleveland relies on charitable contributions for almost 80 percent of its income while the Cleveland Play House, housed in the same building complex, relies on a much more balanced revenue portfolio of contributions, program fees, investment income, and government grants. Available research suggests that the vast majority of nonprofits have more than one source of revenue and that an organization's size and financial health are related to the diversification of its income portfolio (Chang and Tuckman, 1994).

It is not just the nature of operating income that distinguishes nonprofit finance, however. Nonprofits are distinct in the challenges and opportunities they face in securing capital. On the one hand, nonprofits are precluded, at least directly, from raising capital funds in the same ways that businesses and governments do. In particular, they cannot issue stock or impose taxes. On the other hand, they have numerous unique opportunities to raise capital in ways that business and government may not. For example, the tax laws give nonprofits advantages that they can convert into capital, and imaginative nonprofits can tap into equity markets, indirectly if not directly. Similarly, nonprofits face special problems in borrowing because of restrictions on the liquidity of their assets and difficulties in designating collateral, but they can sometimes exploit special opportunities for tax-exempt bond financing or borrowing from unique sources such as the Nonprofit Finance Fund. In general, businesses do not have to worry about restrictions on their assets, while nonprofits frequently do.

Like businesses, nonprofits can also accumulate operating surpluses that they can use for capital purposes. Unlike publicly traded corporations, nonprofits can accumulate very large endowments. Moreover, nonprofits have access to foundation funding which often takes the form of "social investment capital." Indeed, foundations must ponder their own options when they make both grant-making and investment decisions. For example, foundations can help nonprofits with their capital needs by making "program related investments" or loans, blurring the line between the investment and grant-making divisions of a foundation. Finally, nonprofits can acquire capital assets through gifts ranging from automobiles to buildings to works of art. Moreover, nonprofits often trade for the use of such assets outside the monetized economy. Still, in an economy driven by competitive returns to investment capital, it is fair to say that nonprofits are generally challenged to raise sufficient amounts of capital to finance their start-up, expansion, and infrastructure replacement needs.

All of the above factors make it very problematic to measure a nonprofit organization's financial performance. Governments judge their financial performance by whether they are able to balance their budgets while attending to the public service needs of their constituents. This of course, is not as simple as it sounds. Fiscal conservatives can emphasize financial integrity, low taxes, and a good credit rating to the neglect of public infrastructure and social needs. Advocates of public spending can ignore the implications of unbalanced budgets and tax disincentives. Indeed, in the last three decades, these political divisions have led to crises in the financing of government at all levels, seriously impacting the financial support of nonprofit organizations (Galaskiewicz and Bielefeld, 1998; Salamon, 1995). Nonetheless, well established ways of thinking about public finance, including the framework of cost-benefit analysis (Gramlich, 1981) and analyses of efficiency and equity effects of tax and expenditure policies in the allocation of public resources (Quigley, 1983), provide a common set of metrics in these debates.

The performance issue is substantially clearer for private business. Profitability is the bottom line and stock price reflects the ability of a company to produce future earnings. No such unambiguous criterion exists for nonprofits. While nonprofits are required to break even, surplus revenue is not necessarily a signal of success. Nor does bankruptcy serve as a clear indicator of failure since nonprofits cannot be forced into bankruptcy by their creditors. Multiple indicators may be needed to determine if nonprofits are both financially healthy and productive in addressing their social missions. Calculation of social returns on investment, or some form of cost-benefit analysis, may be required. Both equity (fairness) and economic efficiency are important considerations. And financial health indicators may need to include not only operating deficits or surpluses and a healthy balance sheet, but also some explicit indicators of vulnerability to risk—including measures of the diversification of income and special assets such as endowments that can serve as insurance against catastrophic contingencies.

In all, we make a case in this book that the financing of nonprofit organizations is a quite distinct and complex subject deserving its own theory and principles so that nonprofit leaders and managers can manage their scarce resources as effectively as possible. It simply does not suffice to beg and borrow from corporate and public finance in order to patch together, in an ad hoc manner, answers to the finance issues of nonprofit organizations. The central features of nonprofit finance are its diverse income sources, the equally diverse incentives and preferences of the consumers, donors, and government agencies that provide this income, and the need for each organization to find a strategy that will enable it to capture the income mix that best accomplishes its social mission.

Nonprofits in Fiscal Stress

It is not difficult to find stories of fiscal stress and failure among contemporary nonprofit organizations. Indeed, the actual number is probably vastly under-reported, given the tendency of nonprofits to fade away rather than officially go out of business. (A nonprofit organization may be dead or comatose for long periods of time without being removed from official records. See Bowen et al., 1994.) However, when more prominent nonprofits close their doors, it merits public attention and often reveals insights about the kinds of situations in which nonprofits are unable to maintain themselves and effectively address their missions. Here are a few recent vignettes:

Box 1.1. Roman Catholic Archdiocese of Brooklyn

In February 2005, the Roman Catholic Archdiocese of Brooklyn announced the closing of twenty-two of its schools in Brooklyn and Queens. Several factors led to the closings, including

---

increasing labor costs deriving from the shortage of priests and nuns, and increases in tuitions that contributed to a long-term trend of declining enrollments. In St. Theresa's, one of the schools to be closed, enrollments had declined from approximately 1,000 in 1964 to 176 in 2004, while tuitions rose from a nominal sum to approximately $4,000 (in 2004 dollars) during that period. In 2003, alumni donated $30,000 to help the school, and a $170,000 deal was made with the city to rent out the ground floor of St. Theresa's to a local public school. The parish also contributed $117,000. However, projections for 2004 and 2005 indicated that revenues would fall short of expenditures by more than $500,000 each year. (*New York Times*, 20 February 2005, p. 24.)

Box 1.2. Children's Express

In the summer of 2001, Children's Express, an award winning charity that trained children to be journalists, closed its doors in financial failure, having accumulated over $2 million in debt. Problems began in 1996 with the death of the charity's founder, Robert Clampitt, a visionary leader who had maintained a special relationship with the donor community. Despite its financial struggles, Children's Express continued to expand its staff and programming with the help of a major grant from the Kellogg Foundation. By the time of its closing, Kellogg money represented 95 percent of Children's Express's income. Meanwhile, the new CEO of Children's Express had opened a line of credit and ultimately ran up a debt of almost $400,000 exclusive of lease obligations. In fiscal year 2000, debt represented almost twice the organization's income. In the spring before it closed, Children's Express had $13 million in pending grant requests. In addition, fund-raising efforts tied to challenge grants from an anonymous donor and a member of the board failed in the spring prior to closing. (*The Chronicle of Philanthropy*, 9 August 2001, pp. 32–33.)

Box 1.3. The Bellevue Art Museum

In September 2003, the Bellevue Art Museum in Seattle, Washington, closed its doors as a result of financial failure, after having built a new building for itself just two years earlier. The building had exceeded original estimates and the board had cut plans for a separate endowment to support operating costs so that donations could be used for construction. After the opening, attendance was below projected estimates, contributing to a growing operating deficit. A line of credit was established to cover deficits in anticipation of the receipt of outstanding campaign pledges, which served as collateral. By 2002, $750,000 had been borrowed, adding substantial interest costs to operating costs. Cuts were made in staff and board members were asked for additional contributions. Ultimately, a major donor turned down a request for $500,000 leading to the decision to close. (*Seattle Times*, 16 November 2003.)

Box 1.4. The San Diego Symphony

In 1996, the San Diego Symphony declared bankruptcy and discontinued its performances. It had been playing an ambitious schedule of concerts but attendance was lagging and charitable contributions were slowing. Costs of its labor contract with musicians became unsustainable. There was only a small endowment, less than $1 million, generating only a modest stream of investment income. In 1998, the symphony reorganized under Chapter 11 and began a rebirth. A gift of $2 million from a local philanthropist and other new donations helped cancel much of its debt. Musicians agreed to accept only a small portion of the back pay they were owed. A refreshed concert program led to increased ticket sales. In fiscal year 2000, the orchestra posted a revenue surplus of $387,000. (*The Nonprofit Times: Financial Management Edition*, 15 February 2001, pp. 1–6.)

> **Box 1.5. National Conference for Community and Justice**
>
> After almost eighty years of distinguished service in the fight against prejudice, the National Conference for Community and Justice (formerly the National Conference of Christians and Jews) finds itself on the edge of financial insolvency. On a budget of $26 million it ran a deficit of more than $4 million in 2003. In 2003, it closed three local offices. In 2004, it closed eight more and cut its central office budget by $1 million. In all, twenty-three of the sixty regional offices that existed in 2003 will be closed. An endowment worth $22 million in the year 2000 dwindled to $4 million by 2004, with much of the money spent to cover deficits of its national and regional offices. Much of NCCJ's financial troubles can be traced to 11 September 2001 when its charitable revenues declined substantially and never fully recovered. NCCJ depends on charitable contributions for approximately half of its revenues, with the rest deriving from program service revenues (fees), government grants, and returns on investment. A consulting report has suggested that NCCJ's problems are attributable to its centralized structure which fails to hold regional offices accountable for their financial performance. Fundamental structural changes that would provide regional offices with greater autonomy and responsibility were suggested. Meanwhile, NCCJ could become insolvent by 2006. (*The Chronicle of Philanthropy*, 17 February 2005, pp. 24–25; Guidestar report, 21 April 2005.)

It is widely accepted that the turn of the millennium has been a period of exceptional financial distress for nonprofit organizations (Salamon and O'Sullivan, 2004). The confluence of traumatic events, pressures to reduce government funding, and an economy that has been slow to create or maintain employment for lower income workers, have caused nonprofit organizations to seek new sources of revenue and greater efficiency (Young, 2006b). Moreover, the public appears to have lost confidence in the ability of nonprofits to effectively manage the resources with which they are entrusted (Light, 2004).

While contemporary developments suggest a special urgency to the financial challenges of nonprofit organizations, the present period of stress and change is not unique. With respect to government funding in particular, the last twenty years have been eventful and unnerving, featuring not only severe contractions in government funding in some areas of nonprofit activity but also important structural changes in the forms of this support— especially a transition from supply side funding through grants and contracts to demand side subsidies through vouchers, reimbursements, and tax incentives (Grønbjerg and Salamon, 2002). Nonprofits have survived and adapted to periods of fiscal stress before, especially during the Reagan era of the 1980s (Salamon, 1995; Galaskiewicz and Bielefeld, 1998) and they will do so again. But they need to be better prepared. In particular, their sources of support are changing over time and they need to know what makes sense in designing new fiscal strategies for the future.

As the foregoing vignettes suggest, the real challenges come at the level of the individual organization. The broad aggregate trends mask the wide variety of nonprofit organizational circumstances that call for customized strategic solutions for each nonprofit organization. While these vignettes reveal some serious mistakes in basic financial planning and strategic management, they also suggest a lack of clarity about how to develop an appropriate resource base. Clearly Children's Express needed to diversify its revenue portfolio and attend to the connection between its revenues and the beneficiaries of its programming. The same could be said of the San Diego Symphony in its prebankruptcy phase, or for NCCJ in its current crisis. Both Children's Express and the Bellevue Art Museum relied too heavily on debt. The art museum and NCCJ needed a better handle on the role of endowment, while St. Theresa's and the Archdiocese of Brooklyn needed a greater understanding of St. Theresa's markets for earned income, both direct tuition and rentals of its facility, as well as the potential for donor support. In addition, St. Theresa's and perhaps NCCJ need to rethink how they will attract volunteer support or staff who will work for modest wages. For such challenges, nonprofit managers and leaders require a set of principles and guidelines grounded in the intrinsic character of their missions and the specific circumstances in which they operate.

Panaceas

In periods of fiscal stress especially, there is a tendency to search for panaceas. Historically, for example, *endowments* have often been thought of as magic bullets that would essentially solve for good the financial problems of a nonprofit organization fortunate enough to have one. As Woods Bowman discusses in chapter 12, endowments should certainly not be the first priority of a financially stressed nonprofit organization. And, indeed, endowments can be inappropriate for some financially sound nonprofit organizations as well: for example, when current priorities outweigh the importance of long-term future spending. Moreover, reasonably positioned nonprofit organizations can become very unhealthy by inappropriately depending on their endowments in times of stress. The near demise of the New-York Historical Society is a dramatic case in point (Guthrie, 1996). While other aspects of poor management contributed to this sad story, the misunderstanding of the role of endowment and the temptations to draw it down as a means of short-term survival demonstrated that a significant endowment per se is not sufficient to maintain fiscal health and organizational success. For one thing, expenditures must be managed within the constraints of investment income and in cognizance of restrictions that may be imposed by donors. For another, investment income too is subject to variation and decline and cannot serve as an absolute guarantor against other losses.

Perhaps the magic bullet that has attracted most attention in recent years is commercial income from profit-making ventures. Nonprofits have long included commercial income in their portfolios. One needs only to think about the long and venerable history of Girl Scout cookies or church bingo games and bake sales (see Crimmins and Keil, 1983). However, the more recently conceived notion of "social enterprise" has brought new attention to this source of income, suggesting to many nonprofits that they really ought to look to venture income as a way of bolstering their shaky finances. Recent institutional initiatives such as the Yale-Goldman Sachs nonprofit business plan competition and the Social Enterprise Alliance, and new social enterprise programs in many schools of business, have added to the momentum of this strategy. The broad thrust of discussion has been that earned income is a good thing and that all nonprofits ought to become more enterprising. But the social enterprise movement in the United States is beginning to generate a counter literature of skepticism and caution (Weisbrod, 2004; Foster and Bradach, 2005). Most thoughtful writers and consultants have been appropriately cautious in their recommendations for nonprofit commercial ventures (e.g., see Dees, 2004).

In this text, we offer a middle ground. As argued in chapter 5, commercial ventures, or even fee income more generally, are seen as appropriate in some circumstances and not others. In general, what makes nonprofit finance really special and interesting is the fact that different sources of income apply to different circumstances and that the *mix* of income sources is what nonprofits should be thinking about. As noted above, income portfolios vary widely across the sector and there is precious little literature to guide a nonprofit on its most appropriate mix. In order to develop such guidance, it is really necessary to go back to first principles and theory.

The Role and Use of Theory

Nonprofits often justify their need for additional funds by alluding to their costs and their inability to fund programs through ordinary means such as sales of services. In fact, many nonprofits do have cost structures that make it difficult to break even. In particular, many nonprofits in the fine arts, higher education, and health care have substantial physical plants that must be maintained. Other nonprofits, in social services and the performing arts, for example, must sustain substantial core staffing. These organizations have large fixed costs that must be paid even before the first client or customer is served. Often there is no market price that will cover total (fixed plus variable) costs, no matter what price is charged or how many people are served. The question for nonprofit finance is whether this circumstance justifies alternative financing.

Certainly, we would not accept the cost-based argument from a for-profit organization. Businesses that can't break even go out of business, and this is generally accepted as appropriate. Exceptions do occur when large for-profit employers in key industries such as defense are bailed out by government because they are felt to be too critical to be allowed to fail and or because their demise would create major economic dislocations. But generally, individual nonprofits do not occupy such crucial economic and security positions. Still, the precedent of occasional government assistance for failing for-profit industries provides a hint for how we should think about the finance of nonprofit organizations and why they justify assistance beyond their abilities to survive in the marketplace.

The cost-based argument for nonprofit subsidy doesn't wash because it asks people to assume that the nonprofit's mission is intrinsically valuable and worth preserving at all cost, and it positions the nonprofit as a supplicant for charitable or public dollar gifts. ("Please help. We do good work but we can't make ends meet!") The real issues are whether nonprofits that seek economic resources outside the marketplace are producing social benefits that cannot be generated in any other way and whether those benefits justify the additional costs. More specifically, are the benefits being produced of such value to the potential philanthropic and public sector constituencies from which the requested resources would be derived, such that a convincing argument can be made for their support?

The latter viewpoint reflects the essential approach taken in this volume. In particular, we examine each generic source of nonprofit income and inquire of the circumstances—the kinds of goods and services, the nature of the beneficiaries, the incentive effects that influence mission effectiveness and efficiency of resource use, the risks involved—under which it best serves those who would pay. Further, we examine sources of income in combination with one another, both particular mixes—such as fees subsidized by grant funding, and overall income portfolio issues—as they affect the ability of nonprofits to remain viable and to satisfy the constituencies who pay for their work.

In these analyses, our use of available theory is wide ranging but grounded in a core of ideas from microeconomics. Our objective is to pull relevant fragments of existing theory together in order to form a coherent overall conceptual framework for nonprofit finance. Notably, theories of "market and government failure" and "public and private goods" enter critically into our thinking about the role of charitable giving and government funding, and into the use of fee income and commercial ventures to support nonprofit operations. In these instances, the authors ask where collective benefits justify the argument for philanthropic and government support and where fee income can capture the private benefits of those who consume the services. The theory of markets underlies the analysis of fee and commercial income, volunteer services, and barter and collaboration. In these cases, the concept of "gains from trade" fuels the understanding of the circumstances under which these sources of income support are likely to be forthcoming. The concept of "transactions cost" is critical to the analysis of charitable fund-raising, institutional grant making, pricing strategies for fee income, barter and collaboration, and gifts-in-kind. Here, the issue is whether the costs associated with identifying and securing these resources justify the benefits received by each of the parties involved. In particular, in what circumstances are these resource strategies efficient ways of doing business?

Ideas from cost-benefit analysis, reflecting notions of collective benefits and costs to society and to particular groups within society over time, are especially relevant to analysis of foundation grant support, investment income and endowments, and borrowing and debt. In these cases, resource suppliers at one point in time design their investments so that desired benefits to targeted groups are received at another point in time. The timing issue is significant because it affects the terms of grants, investments, and loans, and the restrictions under which internal resources are held. An important adaptation of cost-benefit analysis applies to nonprofits because these organizations are often concerned with particular groups and not necessarily society as a whole. Thus, "mission-related" benefits (and beneficiaries) drive the rationale for particular forms of income and investment and how those benefits are valued by resource suppliers, for example by foundations interested in assisting particular underserved groups. Or, in the case of membership income, nonprofits may make distinctions in fee schedules and privileges among different classes of members considered more or less important to the mission of the organization.

The concept of "incentives" is fundamental to a theory of nonprofit finance, as well, because incentives influence how much particular resource suppliers are willing to support a nonprofit seeking to serve its intended beneficiaries. Incentives to overcome free-riding permeate consideration of charitable contributions. Incentives associated with taxation of private foundations influence decisions about how foundations make their grants. Government tax incentives influence charitable giving. Crowd-out effects between different sources of income reflect how the providers of one source of income are influenced by those of another. Incentives intrinsic to pricing of services influence the willingness of consumers to pay fee income to use the organization's services. Incentives associated with membership dues schedules influence who will join, and who will not join, a nonprofit organization. Valuable nonpecuniary incentives offered by nonprofit organizations help determine the level at which volunteer contributions will be forthcoming. And so on. Almost every aspect of nonprofit finance must consider the incentives associated with the efforts to secure particular resources and the propensities to supply them.

These various fragments of microeconomic theory allow the authors here to examine each potential nonprofit income stream, and to consider the circumstances where each is feasible and appropriate. Moreover, this approach also allows us to take the first cut toward analyzing the most critical and special issue of nonprofit finance—what *combinations* of income sources work best in alternative circumstances. In particular, by developing an understanding of the rationale for individual income sources, we also identify the basis for specific income mixes. For example, a nonprofit service such as inoculations for disease, which generates both private benefits (to the individual receiving the vaccination) and collective benefits to the community (diminished risk of contagion) calls for a combination of fee and grant revenue.

The microeconomic basis for particular income source combinations gives us a strong start to the broader issue of appropriate income portfolios. Specifically, this level of analysis allows us to demonstrate how income source combinations can be designed to match the service characteristics and benefits they are designed to support. However, in examining their income portfolios, nonprofits must also be concerned with broader issues of organizational health and stability. Hence we extend our analysis of nonprofit income portfolios in several ways. First, we apply additional microeconomic ideas such as elasticity of demand to the phenomena of interactions among income sources, namely, "crowd-out," to determine if marginal adjustments in the mix of income sources are warranted to increase income support. Second, we apply ideas from corporate finance and organization theory to understand how income portfolios can help with the management of risk and the pursuit of financial health. Specifically, we ask how diversification of income sources, the pursuit of particular (presumably stabilizing) income streams such as returns on investments (e.g., endowments), and the monitoring of particular financial ratios (among assets, liabilities, income and expenses, etc.) contribute to organizational stability and financial health.

Ultimately, the goal of our exercise in theory development is to formulate a normative conceptual framework that offers clear guidelines for practice, and helps answer the question: What combinations of income best support the performance of a nonprofit organization seeking to address a given social mission in a particular set of circumstances?

Plan of the Book

The foregoing theoretical framework forms a unifying thread throughout the book. An overall theory of nonprofit finance is our quest, though we can only achieve the rudiments of such a theory in this volume. The book is organized as follows.

Chapters 2 through 8 consider distinct sources of income that can support nonprofit operations, and the circumstances under which each is appropriate. We begin with charitable giving by individuals analyzed by Patrick Rooney, who clarifies the public goods rationale for contributed income and the challenges of overcoming free riding. The next chapter, by Joseph Cordes and Richard Sansing, considers the special role of institutional funders in supporting nonprofits in circumstances that offer leverage for foundations to achieve their own social mission and donor objectives. In chapter 4, Michael Rushton and Arthur Brooks analyze various forms of government support for nonprofits, including direct payments and tax incentives that provide resources in exchange for nonprofit provision of various kinds of government-defined public benefits. Estelle James and Dennis Young, in chapter 5, analyze fee and commercial income, taking the view that nonprofits frequently provide services of a largely private character for which beneficiaries can feasibly and appropriately be charged; however, considerations of externalities and distributional impacts shaped by the nonprofit's mission require modified pricing arrangements and often subsidies from other sources. In chapter 6, Richard Steinberg analyzes membership dues—which reflect elements of both fee and contributions income. Steinberg focuses on the connection between a nonprofit organization's particular objectives and the design of its dues policy, especially incentives that encourage certain kinds of members and which provide different combinations of organizational revenue and social benefit. In the next chapter, Woods Bowman, Elizabeth Keating, and Mark Hager analyze the role of returns on investment as a form of income unconnected to the organization's output and thus strategically positioned as a flexible source of reserve capacity as a hedge against risk. In organizations with large fixed costs, investment income is seen as an offsetting fixed income stream ("fixed" in the sense that it does not derive from the organization's output, not in the sense that it is guaranteed). Finally, in chapter 8, Anne Preston analyzes in-kind volunteer services "income" in the context of the markets for volunteer and paid labor. This allows her to consider desirable mixes of paid and volunteer workers in staffing various nonprofit functions, as well as the incentives and resources necessary to recruit, train, retain, and motivate volunteers.

Chapters 9 through 11 specifically focus on sources of capital for nonprofit organizational development and programming. In chapter 9, Renee Irvin considers how nonprofits can collaborate and barter their resources in order to achieve greater overall capacity and mission effectiveness. Issues of economies of scale and scope, gains from trade, and transactions costs associated with maintaining collaborative arrangements, lace this analysis. In chapter 10, Charles M. Gray considers specific instances where nonprofits acquire capital through donations of gifts-in-kind, such as real estate and art collections, as well as smaller material gifts that can add to the capital assets of a nonprofit or be cashed out. Tax incentives are critical to the analysis of circumstances that make it attractive for donors to provide nonprofits with these resources. In addition, the conditions in secondary markets influence how nonprofit organizations balance their asset portfolios by selling or retaining such gifts. In (an appropriately numbered) chapter 11, Robert Yetman analyzes the opportunities and pitfalls for nonprofits to meet their capital needs through debt, and the strategic role of debt in a nonprofit organization's capital structure. Yetman utilizes the framework of cost/benefit analysis to examine the merits of borrowing to finance various kinds of nonprofit projects.

The next section of the book takes a more comprehensive view of nonprofit finance by considering overall portfolio and performance issues. In chapter 12, Woods Bowman considers the issues associated with managing endowments and other nonprofit assets, observing that endowments serve particular roles in offsetting fixed costs and insuring against catastrophic risk, but also introduce inappropriate temptations to build slack or serve as stop gaps for current shortfalls. In chapter 13, Kevin Kearns develops a unique multiattribute utility framework to bring together the various considerations that enter nonprofit revenue portfolio decisions, including risk management, the interactions (such as crowd-out) between alternative sources of income, and matching of particular income streams to the mission benefits a nonprofit intends to provide. Kearns emphasizes the complexity of nonprofit decision making and the necessity of systematically aggregating multiple stakeholder viewpoints into decisions about income sources and mixes. In chapter 14, Janet Greenlee and Howard Tuckman consider how nonprofits can measure their financial health and vulnerability in a rigorous economic way, given their choices of strategies to customize their income and asset portfolios to fit their particular missions and constituencies. Especially important to this analysis is the recognition of three levels of risk facing nonprofit organizations—risk at the market, industry, and individual organization levels.

Finally, in chapter 15, Dennis Young offers a synthesis intended to bring the various dimensions of nonprofit finance theory as developed in chapters 2 through 14 into a common framework. As noted earlier, the key to this framework is the understanding that sources of income and capital support must be driven by the mutual interests of the receiving nonprofits and the motivations and requirements of the sources of those resources. While not all nonprofit resource transactions are strictly quid pro quo, the idea that resource flows supporting nonprofits must reflect the markets and quasi-markets for private, public, and charitable resources from which they derive is the basic piece of wisdom on which a practical theory of nonprofit finance can be constructed.

One feature of chapters throughout the book is a quest to derive practical advice and guidelines from theory so that the knowledge accumulated here can be immediately applied. The authors have addressed this objective in several ways. First, the book is written in an accessible style that should be comprehensible to anyone reasonably familiar with nonprofit organizations, whether or not they are economists or financial managers. Second, each chapter has been sprinkled liberally with examples and sometimes case studies to illustrate key points. Third, and perhaps most important, each chapter includes a set of *diagnostic questions* that practicing nonprofit managers can use to assess how the principles espoused in the chapter apply to their individual circumstances. In short, it is our belief that by asking the right questions, practitioners can be best prepared to find the right answers for their organizations, in the confusing, complex, and diverse universe of nonprofit finance.

II

SOURCES OF SUPPORT
FOR OPERATIONS

2

Individual Giving

Patrick Rooney[1]

Introduction

According to *Giving USA 2003*, individuals gave $184 billion in tax-deductible donations to nonprofits in the United States in the year 2002. When we add in another $18 billion from charitable bequests (i.e., gifts made to nonprofits in one's will—one's "final gift"), individuals contributed 84 percent of total giving that year. While overall giving (i.e., giving from all sources: households/individuals, charitable bequests, corporations, and foundations) constitutes only 20 percent of nonprofit revenues overall (O'Neill, 2002), donations are a critical component of nonprofit finance in many circumstances. Indeed, in some fields of nonprofit activity, charitable contributions are the dominant mode of financial support.

This chapter reports on important contemporary patterns and trends in individual giving in the United States and their significance for nonprofit organizations in various contexts. We also examine the practices in which nonprofits engage to secure and utilize this source of income. With this empirical backdrop, we then describe relevant strands of economic theory and nonprofit research that help us understand and explain the role of individual giving in sustaining nonprofit organizations, and hence guide the practice of fund-raising and nonprofit resource development planning. The review of theory and research also allows us to consider where further research is needed to advance our understanding of the role of individual giving in nonprofit organizations. Subsequently, we ask how practice in fund development and management can be improved, based on our present knowledge—including questions that nonprofit managers and leaders can ask themselves in order to make wise decisions about seeking support from individual donors. Finally, we conclude with some cautions about the role of philanthropy and the circumstances where this source of funds can be effective.

Patterns and Trends

As noted, individuals in the United States gave $184 billion to nonprofits in 2002 in inter vivos giving (i.e., gifts made during one's life) and another $18 billion in charitable bequests. Individual giving has averaged 1.9 percent of personal income for the past four decades (*Giving USA 2004*), ranging from a low of 1.5 percent in 1995 to 2.3 percent in 1963 and remaining at or above 2.0 percent since 1996. Personal giving as a percentage of personal income tends to be pro-cyclical, moving in the same direction as the business cycle, declining during difficult periods and rising with prosperity.

Individual giving also tends to increase with household income. According to Havens, O'Herlihy, and Schervish (2006), 86 percent of U.S. families earn less than $100,000. These families earn 48 percent of the total U.S. income and give almost 41 percent of all itemized gifts. The 13 percent of households earning between $100,000 and $1 million per year account for 38 percent of the income and 43 percent of itemized gifts. Few households earn more than $1 million per year (0.4 percent of population), but they earn 14 percent of total income and give 16 percent of total household donations. This skewed nature of income and giving is also demonstrated in the Center on Philanthropy Panel Study (COPPS), a philanthropy supplement to the University of Michigan's Panel Study of Income Dynamics (PSID). According to COPPS 2003 data, households earning at least $100,000 were almost twice as likely to be donors compared to those earning less than $100,000 (90.8 percent vs. 46.2 percent), and these higher-income households donate over three times as much ($3,630 vs. $1,164).

It has sometimes been erroneously reported that low-income and high-income households give much larger shares of their incomes than the middle class. This "U-curve" result arises when one examines only donors, because many low-income households give generously. However, because many low-income households don't give at all, the U-shaped curve flattens out when we include both donors and nondonors. Havens et al. (2006) demonstrate that giving as a percentage of income is relatively flat for a wide range of income earners (the 98 percent earning less than $300,000), varying from 1.7 percent to 3 percent, and averaging 2.3 percent. On the other hand, those 2 percent of households earning $300,000 or more give an average of 4.4 percent of their incomes and account for 37 percent of all gifts.

Wealth also plays an important role in giving, as documented in a *Giving USA Update Spring 2004* focused on wealth that reported a number of findings from Havens, Schervish, and O'Herlihy (2001) and COPPS. In particular, 47 percent of Americans are in low net worth households (under $75,000), which collectively contain only 2.4 percent of the total net worth in the nation; these households give only 11 percent of all gifts. By comparison, the top 7 percent of wealth holders have 63 percent of the total net worth and give 50 percent of all gifts. Moreover, giving grows fairly dramatically with increases in income at all wealth levels and increases with wealth at all income levels. Not surprisingly, there are stark differences in average giving between the lowest wealth holders (less than $300,000) who are also among the lowest income earners (less than $40,000), and those with high net worth (more than $1 million) and high income (more than $100,000). The former gave an average of $979 in 2000 compared to the latter who gave an average of $7,535, 7.7 times as much.

Generally, a wide range of studies have found inter vivos giving to be positively correlated with age (at least until retirement), income, educational attainment, and marital status (married persons give more than singles). (See Havens et al., 2006, and Rooney et al., 2004). Rooney et al. (2005) found that whites gave 41 percent more than minority households, but that these differences become statistically insignificant after controlling for income, educational attainment, and other factors. This suggests that the differences in the mean levels of giving are due to differences in income and educational attainment and not race or ethnicity. Conversely, Rooney et al. (2005) found that single men and women give similar amounts on average, but once one controls for income, education, and age, single women are significantly more likely to be donors and donate significantly more than single men.

Charitable bequest giving is also skewed toward large estates. For example, Havens, O'Herlihy, and Schervish (2006) report that final estates (i.e., the estate of the last-surviving spouse) with $20 million or more in assets comprised only 0.6 percent of all estates filed in 2000, but generated 44 percent of all charitable bequest dollars that year. Estates under $1 million form the vast majority of all estates (44 percent) but create only 6 percent of the dollar value of all charitable bequests.

There is also substantial regional variation in giving, especially individual giving. For example, according to *Giving USA Summer Update 2004*, individuals in thirteen states gave at least 5 percent more than the national average while those in twenty-seven states gave at least 5 percent less. After controlling for several socioeconomic-demographic factors, there were still several states at least 5 percent above (eleven states) or below (fifteen states) their expected giving levels (using national norms to predict for each state), although many of the "high" and "low" states are switched. For example, Georgia and Mississippi both went from giving over 10 percent *more* than the national average nominally to giving more than 5 percent *less* than the national average after controlling for demographics such as income, age, and religious affiliation, while Indiana, Minnesota, New Mexico, and Oregon went from being 5 percent or more *below* the national average in nominal terms to being 5 percent or more *above* average after controlling for the demographic variables (*Giving USA Summer Update 2004*).

Furthermore, when Brown and Rooney (2005) disaggregated total giving into religious and secular giving, they not only found significant differences in the amounts given by census regions, but also differences in the determinants of giving by region. For example, differences in wealth were an important determinant of religious giving in four of the nine census regions but income was not a significant predictor in those same regions. Conversely, income was a significant driver of religious giving in three of the remaining five census regions. While income was an important determinant of secular giving in all but one region, religious affiliation was a significant (negative) predictor of secular giving in only one census region.

In studies of giving in specific regions, researchers have found a noteworthy variation in both the sources and levels of giving, as well as the uses of giving. For example, in a study of philanthropy in Memphis, the Center on Philanthropy found much higher than average percentages of donations going to religious institutions (*Memphis Gives 2003*). Conversely, the Center on Philanthropy found giving in New Hampshire to be substantially less than the national averages (*New Hampshire Gives 2005*), which was essentially entirely due to lower than average religious giving. Furthermore, Wilhelm et al. (2004) found that even after controlling for income, wealth, home equity, race, and marital status, living in the South was associated with a significant increase in religious giving, but not in secular giving.

Recent studies of philanthropy in three regions conducted by the Center on Philanthropy (*Memphis Gives 2003; St. Louis Gives 2003; Indianapolis Gives 2005*) have found that most of the philanthropic dollars from households and individuals remain in these metro areas (82 percent in Memphis, 74 percent in St. Louis, and 79 percent in Indianapolis). Similarly, the vast majority of philanthropic dollars from all sources (households, corporations, and foundations) from these communities are given to nonprofits in these communities (80 percent in Memphis, 71 percent in St. Louis, and 78 percent in Indianapolis). These data suggest an important "propinquity effect" of which nonprofits must be aware in making their plans for charitable funding.

Private philanthropy plays an important role in most nonprofits, but as table 2.1 shows, the variation in reliance among subsectors is huge. As might be expected, religion and foundations receive the highest shares of their income from private philanthropy (90 percent each) and the lowest shares from the government (1 percent or less each). Internationally oriented

Table 2.1.   Funding for the Nonprofit Sector Ranked by Amounts Donated

Subsector	Donated to Subsector (in billions)	Share of Philanthropy (%)	Philanthropy's Share for That Subsector (%)	Government's Funding Share (%)
Religion	$84	35	90	1
Education	$32	13	20	10
Foundations	$22	9	90	0
Health	$19	8	1	45
Human Services	$19	8	15	60
Arts/Culture	$12	5	40	10
Public Benefit	$12	5	5	15
Environment/ Animals	$7	3	N/A	N/A
International	$4	2	60	20

Source: Columns 1 and 2 are from Giving USA (2003). Columns 3 and 4 are from O'Neill (2002).

nonprofits also attract a great deal of private support and relatively little governmental support. Arts and culture is fourth in its share of private philanthropy and also near the bottom with respect to governmental support. In education, health, and human services, philanthropy plays an important role in total dollars given, but represents a relatively small share of total revenues. Remaining revenues for nonprofits in these areas come substantially from earned income and governmental support.

Over the last forty years, total "formal" philanthropy, defined as tax deductible gifts to U.S.-based 501(C)(3) organizations, excluding informal philanthropy such as gifts to friends and neighbors, and excluding political contributions and gifts to foreign governments and organizations, has grown 205 percent in real (inflation-adjusted) dollars (Giving USA 2004). While individual (inter vivos) giving has grown an impressive 175 percent in real terms over the last forty years, it is in fact the slowest growing source of philanthropic revenue. Corporate giving (direct and from corporate foundations) has grown 286 percent; charitable bequests have grown 308 percent; and foundation giving has grown an incredible 433 percent (all adjusted for inflation, Giving USA 2004). As a result of its relatively slower (but still impressive) growth, individual giving's share of total giving has declined from 83 percent in 1963 to 75 percent in 2003. Even when we include charitable bequests, the share of giving from individuals (living and dead) has fallen from 89 percent in 1963 to 83.5 percent in 2003 (*Giving USA 2004*).

That trend, however, may be reversing. Havens and Schervish (1999) and Havens et al. (2006) estimate the impact of the imminent "trillion dollar transfer." As the baby boomer generation dies and leaves its accumulated wealth to children and favorite charities, Havens and Schervish project that charities will receive between $6.6 trillion (based on a scenario of 2 percent real economic growth per year) and $27.4 trillion (based on 4 percent real economic growth) in charitable bequests and between another $14.6 trillion (2 percent real growth) and $28 trillion (4 percent real growth) in inter vivos giving by individuals (see Havens et al., 2006, table 2.1).

The decline in the share of total giving by individuals over the past forty years is largely a result of the rapid growth in foundation giving (433 percent) and charitable bequest giving (308 percent). However, as the "trillion dollar transfer" proceeds, charitable bequests will play an increasingly important role in total giving, especially if the higher economic growth scenario in the Havens and Schervish estimates prevails. In the low growth scenario, charitable bequests will constitute about one-third of total individual giving over the 1998–2052 time period, but bequests would be almost one-half of the total contributions from living and dead individuals in the high economic growth (4 percent per year) scenario. In fact, one might argue that the differences in the relative growth rates of giving by the various sources over the past forty years reflect the early stages of the wealth transfer process projected by Havens and Schervish.

Despite the decline in the share of individual giving as a percentage of total giving over the last forty years, it is still by far the largest and most important source of private philanthropy in the United States (*Giving USA 2005*). A survey by the National Committee on Planned Giving (NCPG) (2001) found that, in some cases, people name in their wills nonprofit organizations with which they did not have a prior relationship. However, normally an ongoing process of cultivation and stewardship, including annual giving, takes place before donors make their final gifts to a given nonprofit or make a charitable bequest at all.

Current Practice

For many nonprofits, individual giving plays an extraordinarily important role in their ability to pay for overhead costs such as senior staff compensation and key activities such as accounting, budgeting, planning, and evaluation, as well as rent and utilities. However, many foundations and large donors restrict their gifts to programmatic expenses or limit the overhead rates severely. While it is quite understandable that these givers want to pay only for programmatic expenses, overhead costs must be paid in order for a nonprofit to survive and be effective in fulfilling its mission (see Wing et al., 2005a).

The nonprofit sector has a large number of very small nonprofits (whether measured by assets, revenues, expenses, or employees) and relatively few large ones. Boris (2006, figure 3) calculates that almost 41 percent of nonprofits had expenses of less than $100,000 in the year 2000 and accounted for less than one percent of all nonprofit expenses. Similarly, the next smallest group ($100,000–$499,999) accounted for 31 percent of all nonprofits but only 2 percent of expenses. Together these two groups comprise the majority of nonprofits (71 percent) but only a very small fraction of the total expenses (less than 3 percent). Conversely, the largest nonprofits ($10 million or more in expenses) comprise only 4 percent of nonprofits in the United States, but account for over 80 percent of total expenses. The structure of the nonprofit sector is also skewed by subsector (Boris, 2006, figure 4). Health accounts for only 14 percent of nonprofits but these organizations incur 59 percent of the total expenses of the sector, while human service nonprofits account for 35 percent of nonprofits but only 14 percent of the total expenses. Educational nonprofits account for 17 percent of both the number of nonprofits and total expenses. Religious nonprofits account for only 5 percent of nonprofits filing an IRS Form 990 (many churches do not) and only 1 percent of the expenses. All this suggests that most nonprofits will have very small fund-raising programs and that only a few nonprofits, concentrated in certain parts of the sector, will have well developed fund-raising programs.

Indeed, in a census of all nonprofits in Indiana, Grønbjerg and Clerkin (2004) found that only 52 percent have any paid staff, while most of those with any employees are quite small, the median nonprofit having three full-time and three part-time employees. To the extent that these smaller nonprofits raise funds, it must be done through volunteers and/or other supporting organizations. Based on survey research, Hager, Pollak, and Rooney (2002) found that 74 percent of nonprofits rely on volunteers for some fund-raising, but only 11 percent rely on volunteers for *all* of their fund-raising dollars, and another 12 percent rely on volunteers for most of their fund-raising dollars. Furthermore, 63 percent of all nonprofits do not have *any* paid staff member whose full-time job is to raise money. It is no surprise then that Hager, Pollak, and Rooney (2001) found that of all nonprofits filing IRS 990s, only 34 percent (66,500) reported earning $50,000 or more in direct contributions, and of these, only about half (35,244) reported any fund-raising expenses. Rooney, Hager, and Pollak (2003) also found considerable differences in the return on investment (ROI) for various fund-raising tactics. In general, "entry level" tactics which are largely available to any nonprofit (e.g., direct mail, telephone, special events, Internet, and e-mail) have a lower ROI than do more "advanced level" tactics (e.g., foundation and government grants, capital and federated campaigns, major and planned gifts) which typically require that the organization be in business for a number of years and project an image of long-term stability.

In theory, nonprofits could "optimize" their investments in fund-raising by spending on fund-raising (by each tactic) up to the point where an additional dollar raised would be just offset by the last dollar spent (see Steinberg, 1991). This efficient approach, analogous to profit maximizing in the business world, faces some practical problems in the nonprofit sector, but it serves as a useful benchmark in managerial and board decision-making about investments in fund-raising. Practical problems include the difficulty of measuring and monitoring fund-raising costs and returns at the margin. More importantly, fund-raising takes place in a public forum. With the digitization of IRS Form 990 data and the requirement to make them readily available to all who request them, nonprofits are increasingly viewing their IRS Form 990 as a "marketing tool." Hence, they may be reluctant to report high (if any) fund-raising costs. In fact, Wing, Pollak, Hager, and Rooney (2005b, 2005c) confirm that some nonprofits feel pressure from donors and funders to report low overhead and/or fund-raising costs and that the majority of nonprofits with fund-raising revenues in excess of $50,000 report *no* fund-raising or special events-related costs. Incredibly, 18 percent of nonprofits raising $5 million or more in donations report *no* fund-raising or special events costs.

While nonprofits may have always felt pressure to report low fund-raising or overhead costs, the existence of rating agencies like the Better Business Bureau–Wise Giving Alliance and Charity Navigator, as well as a plethora of magazines that devote an issue annually to rating the "best nonprofits" based primarily on "input" ratios from IRS Form 990, has put even more intense pressures on nonprofits to operate within "standards" promulgated by these rating groups. Nonprofits may fear that individual donors (as well as institutional funders) may react adversely to these ratings, especially when some of the rating agencies regularly publicize that some NPOs are doing well and others are doing poorly—even on a city-by-city basis (e.g., Charity Navigator). Unfortunately, such ratings have little to do with the attainment of fund-raising efficiency (see Wing, Pollak, Hager, and Rooney, 2005d) and nothing to do with the outputs, outcomes, or impact of the NPOs—or even whether or not the NPO does what it says it was going to do. As a result, many nonprofits are probably underinvesting in fund-raising and therefore raising less money than they might were they to utilize more efficient strategies or invest more in their fund-raising operations.

The Center on Philanthropy conducts a semiannual survey of senior development professionals across the country, reported in the Philanthropic Giving Index (PGI). One set of questions asks about the success of various fund-raising techniques. A recent PGI (December 2004) reports that most of the "entry level" fund-raising tactics, which are primarily directed toward individual donors, are rated as "successful techniques" by relatively few development experts (Internet = 26 percent, e-mail = 23 percent, special events = 56 percent, and telephone = 41 percent). However, direct mail at 68 percent did better than some of the more "advanced techniques" (foundation grants = 64 percent, corporate gifts = 44 percent, and planned giving = 59 percent). (It should be noted that planned giving is down substantially in this PGI, from historical trends in the mid-70 percentiles.) Major gifts continue to be viewed as the most successful fund-raising technique by the PGI respondents (85 percent). In all, the results reflect the advantages of larger scale in mounting a productive program of fund-raising.

Theory

To establish a conceptual basis for understanding why people voluntarily contribute to nonprofit organizations, we begin with economists' ideas of "public goods" and "externalities." Pure public goods are goods or services characterized by two properties: nonrivalry and nonexcludability. Nonrivalry means that one person's consumption of the good does not diminish another person's consumption of it. This is different from a pure private good such as a slice of pizza or pair of shoes that two people cannot both (simultaneously) consume. Nonexcludability refers to the supplier's inability to exclude somebody from consuming the good—once it has been provided for anyone, it is provided for all. By contrast, someone can be excluded from consuming a good such as a slice of pizza or a pair of shoes if one does not pay for it. Goods that exhibit nonrivalry and nonexcludability cannot be sold profitably in the marketplace: hence they enter the realm of government and nonprofit provision.

Public radio is a good example of a pure public good provided by the nonprofit sector. Once it is provided for anyone, we cannot exclude anyone from consuming it (nonexcludable), and we understand that our individual consumption of it does not diminish the simultaneous consumption of it by other individuals (nonrival). There are very few pure public goods, but there are many more goods that have public good aspects, and there are many more other goods that have some positive or negative "externality" associated with their production or consumption (see Young and Steinberg, 1995). Externalities are positive or negative effects that impact disinterested third parties (i.e., others besides the buyer and seller). Cars, for example, produce negative externalities in the form of pollution and congestion. Alternatively, an outdoor concert (which some can hear for free) produces positive externalities, as does K through 12 education in the form of societal benefits deriving from a more productive or socialized citizenry.

Pure public goods and goods with large, positive externalities will be supplied in inefficiently small quantities, if at all, in a free market economy, while if left to the market alone, goods with negative externalities will be oversupplied. One approach to addressing these problems is for the government to supply public goods and to regulate, tax, or subsidize goods with large positive or negative externalities. However, even where government provision might be efficient it may not be politically feasible. Hence, private provision via philanthropy and the nonprofit sector may provide a "second best" option. This suggests that nonprofits may seek funding both from individuals and the government by referencing the "public goods" nature of their work and emphasizing that the public's taxes are lower than they might be otherwise if the government were providing this good or service.

The chief limitation of relying on private philanthropy to fund public goods is that many who benefit can be "free riders" in the sense that once the good is provided, they can enjoy the benefits without paying their fair share of the costs. Of course, the free riding problem is overcome when government provides public goods and imposes involuntary taxes to support them. However, the political process may fail to provide adequate quantities of these goods through the public sector, because citizens may differ in their preferences for these goods (Weisbrod, 1988). Allowing for choice and mobility among local government jurisdictions with different packages of taxes and benefits is one way of addressing different tastes and preferences for public goods and goods with large positive externalities when the costs and benefits are confined to the local level (Tiebout, 1956). Clubs and associations are yet another approach to solving the public goods and free riding problems in a local context. But all of these solutions are imperfect, leaving an important role for philanthropically funded nonprofits at the local as well as national and international scale.

Most democratic societies, including the United States, rely extensively, if not exclusively, on some form of representative democracy with simple majorities to determine both who the representatives are and how the elected officials allocate tax burdens and budget dollars. This system has significant implications for decisions about whether or not to provide public goods. In particular, the majority group will follow its own preferences for what services to provide, how much of those services to provide, and how much to tax. Clearly, then, one role of private philanthropy and the nonprofit sector is to serve as a means for providing the public goods preferred by various minority groups whose preferences differ from those accommodated by the majority of voters in the political tax-spend process.

Further insights on the public goods rationale for giving may be gleaned by examining giving patterns in different nonprofit subsectors. If we review table 2.1 above, it is clear that in almost all fields the government plays some role in funding nonprofits. However, if we sort that table in ascending order by the share funded by the government, we find the following: foundations (0 percent); religion (1 percent); education (10 percent); arts/culture (10 percent); public benefit (15 percent); international (20 percent); health (45 percent); human services (60 percent). While there is undoubtedly some variation of preferences for public goods by different groups, among different subsectors, other factors are also at work. For example, it makes sense that the government would not fund religion in the United States, given both the constitutional separation of church and state and the very private nature of religious activities.

Although there are huge positive externalities to arts and culture, it is also a good or service that can be readily excluded, so the market can play an important role. Nonetheless, our society is concerned about access to and involvement in the arts and cultural events, and private philanthropy can help ameliorate these concerns. The two subsectors with the largest shares of government funding are health (45 percent) and human services (60 percent). While there are clear private benefits for both health and human services, there are also huge public goods aspects and large positive externalities associated with various parts of each of these subsectors. For example, inoculation programs work better when the entire targeted segment of the population is vaccinated. This will only occur when those who cannot pay the market price are nonetheless accommodated. Similarly, many human service agencies serve those who cannot participate in the market for wages and salaries (because of significant physical, mental, or emotional disabilities) or who have had their market earnings disrupted through no fault of their own (e.g., plant closings and layoffs).

Despite the balance of public and private funding in various nonprofit subsectors, one cannot argue that these combinations have produced an optimal level of overall funding. It remains likely that our society is underproviding public goods and goods with large positive externalities, because of free-riding problems and limitations of the political process. In addition, government funding of nonprofits can displace private funding, or slow its rate of growth. While some have argued that government funding may actually stimulate additional private philanthropy (i.e., "crowding-in;" see, for example, Rose-Ackerman, 1986), the bigger concern and the more common empirical finding is "crowding out" of private contributions by government revenues (Steinberg, 1993). This phenomenon has been widely studied (Brooks, 2003b), with only a few scholars finding evidence of crowding in (Schiff, 1985, 1990; Hughes and Luksetich, 1999). According to Steinberg (1993, 105): "In most studies, we can reject the hypothesis that crowd out is zero for at least some specifications, and estimated crowd out ranges from $\frac{1}{2}$ percent to 35 percent per unit of government spending." In fact, the majority of the research summarized by Steinberg suggests a relatively small share of crowd out (10 percent or less).

Brooks (2004a) reports that public radio's reliance on matching grants may create the necessary incentives for crowding in. Payne (2001) found that government funding of research grants might crowd in philanthropy for education, but Andreoni and

Payne (2003) found that successes in attracting government funding for the arts as well as social services might lead nonprofits to reduce their fund-raising efforts significantly and, therefore, may lead to a crowd out result, in effect, by lowering fund-raising productivity.

As seen in table 2.1, the top three subsectors in terms of private philanthropy receipts (religion, education, and foundations) are also the lowest three in terms of government funding shares (foundations, religion, and education). By comparison, while health and human services are big subsectors and capture a relatively large percentage of total philanthropic dollars, they are two of the three slowest growing subsectors with respect to philanthropic funding (religion being the other). Health and human services currently receive the largest shares of government funding overall (45 percent and 60 percent) and government has played an increasingly important role in funding these sectors in the last forty years. For example, the federal health and human services (HHS) budget increased from $68.3 billion in 1980 to $459.4 billion in 2000—a 460 percent increase (*Statistical Abstract of the United States: 2002*) (see table 2.2 below). HHS has increased much more rapidly than total government expenses over the same time (203 percent), but while philanthropic giving to health and human services nonprofits has grown at quite a respectable rate during this same period (261 percent), it has grown much more

Table 2.2. Federal Outlays by Agency: 1980–2002

		(in billions of dollars)				
				Percent Change	*Percent Change*	*Percent Change*
Department	1980	1990	2000	1980–1990	1990–2000	1980–2000
Total	590.9	1,253.2	1,788.8	112.1	42.7	202.7
Education	14.6	23.0	33.9	57.5	47.4	132.2
Health and Human Serv.	68.3	175.5	382.6	157.0	118.0	460.2
EPA	5.6	5.1	7.2	−8.9	41.2	28.6
International	7.7	10.1	12.1	31.2	19.8	57.1

Source: *Statistical Abstract of the United States: 2002* (Table 452).

Table 2.3.   Private Philanthropy

	(in billions of dollars)			Percent Change 1980–1990	Percent Change 1990–2000	Percent Change 1980–2000
Subsector	1980	1990	2000			
Total	48.6	100.5	229.7	106.8	128.6	372.6
Education	5	12.4	31.7	148.0	155.6	534.0
Health and Human Serv.*	10.2	21.7	36.8	112.7	69.6	260.8
Environment	N/A	2.5	6.2		148.0	
International	N/A	1.3	3.7		184.6	

Source: Giving USA 2005.
* Note: Health and Human Services are combined just to facilitate comparisons with federal expenditures in Table 2.2.

slowly than philanthropy in general (373 percent, see table 2.3). This "dynamic" crowding out suggests that donors and funders do indeed react to shifts in government funding over time.

Further evidence of this dynamic crowding out is provided by comparing the rates of growth of funding for education: government funding grew 132 percent (vs. 203 percent overall) and philanthropic funding grew 534 percent (vs. 373 percent overall) (see tables 2.2 and 2.3). While we cannot make similar comparisons for the environment and for international programs much before 1990 (Giving USA began disaggregating these two subsectors in 1987), we see very similar trends for both of these subsectors in the 1990s. For example, government funding for both of these areas grew more slowly than average (environment grew 41 percent and international grew 20 percent vs. 43 percent overall from 1990 to 2000; see table 2.2), but philanthropic giving to these two subsectors grew more rapidly than average than philanthropy overall in the 1990s (environment grew 148 percent and international grew 185 percent vs. 129 percent overall from 1990 to 2000; see table 2.3). Moreover, international, the subsector with relatively slower growth in government spending, has experienced much more rapid growth in philanthropic giving than environment, a subsector with relatively faster growth in government spending. While these are only simple comparisons of growth rates, they are highly suggestive that significant crowding out has occurred over the last ten to twenty years.

Explanations for individual giving behavior go beyond economic motives associated with public goods and government spending. Hence, other factors must be taken into account in addressing the free rider problem and encouraging private giving. Vesterlund (2006) summarizes much of the economic theory and empirical literature on individual giving, especially game theory developments. She stresses the dichotomies between the "public benefits" of the sector (namely the output of nonprofits) and the "private benefits" for giving (Arrow, 1974; Andreoni, 1989; Cornes and Sandler, 1984; Steinberg, 1987; Schiff, 1990). Private benefits that can be associated with donations have been found to include material rewards and membership benefits (consistent with Olson's (1965) "selective incentives"; also see chapters 5 and 6 of this volume); reputation (Tullock, 1966) and social acclaim (Becker, 1974); signaling of wealth (Glazer and Konrad, 1996) and prestige (Harbaugh, 1998a, 1998b); warm glow (Andreoni, 1989, 1990); assuaging guilt; commitment (Sen, 1977); and fair-share motivations (Rose-Ackerman, 1982b).

While personal reasons for giving are not easily studied, there have been many attempts to measure and/or categorize them. Panas (1984), in interviews of 20 donors who had donated $1 million or more in a single year, found some significant differences between what large donors thought were important factors and what the NPOs thought were important to the donors. Schervish (1988, 1991) examined how 130 millionaires elected or preferred to relate to various NPOs. Boris (1987) delineated several archetype motivations for establishing a foundation among 435 respondents, including 16 percent who were donors themselves: altruism, beliefs, instrumental motives, memorial, community, and peer pressure. Based on responses from 140 wealthy donors, Odendahl (1990) created a list that included various philanthropic stereotypes: dynasty, lady bountiful, first generation man, and elite Jewish giver. She also found that religious motivations and gender makes a difference for some donors. Similarly, Prince, File, and Gillespie (1993) surveyed several hundred wealthy donors and identified other stereotypes based on philanthropic "style":

communitarians, the devout, investors, socialites, repayers, altruists, and dynasts.

Finally, individuals give to nonprofit organizations not only because of their public benefits, their level of government support, or the personal benefits they derive, but also because they are asked (Independent Sector, 1996). Frequently, who asks and how they ask (donor cultivation and fund-raising tactics) can affect whether somebody gives at all and at what level.

Extending the Knowledge Base

There is much that is known about some of the key correlates of giving such as income, wealth, educational attainment, religiosity, gender, and marital status (Schervish and Havens, 2001; Wilhelm et al., 2004; Rooney et al., 2005, 2004; Vesterlund, 2006), as well as the importance of methodology in the measurement of philanthropy (Wilhelm, 2003; Rooney, Steinberg, and Schervish, 2001, 2004). The Center on Philanthropy Panel Study (COPPS), which is being fielded as part of the University of Michigan's Panel Study of Income Dynamics (PSID), is tracking the same (approximately) 8,000 households over time and across generations on their philanthropic behaviors. There is great eagerness for the results of this work, as it will enable us to more accurately measure changes in giving over the life span (marriage, children, divorce, remarriage, college expenses, unemployment, disability, retirement, changes in tax policies, etc.). COPPS will also allow scholars to examine the transmission of philanthropic values from one generation to the next (Wilhelm, Brown, Rooney, and Steinberg, 2004). These and other studies will substantially enrich our understanding of who is giving how much to which organizations.

Unfortunately, from the perspective of fund-raisers and nonprofits, little of the research really gets at *how* to be a better fund-raiser, that is, which fund-raising techniques work better for which nonprofits or for particular types of donors and potential donors. How does (or should) one convince a potential donor to make a major or planned gift? How long does it really take for a new development person (or program) to generate positive net revenues? What is the expected return on investment (ROI) for hiring development staff—at various levels of sophistication, within different fields of service, and for different sizes of organization? What is the "optimal" number of cultivation calls before asking for a major gift?

None of the research addresses the questions of *why* some low-income households give much more money to charities than some high-income households or why some high-income households give much more than others. None of the extant research addresses how or why philanthropic values are shaped and either enhanced or diminished. Why do some households only give to religious nonprofits, while others only give to secular ones? Why do many donors give to both religious and secular causes, and why do some households give relatively more or less to health, education, human services, or the arts?

Improving Practice

For many nonprofits, government agencies may be a new or expanded funding source. However, our discussion of crowding out suggests that donors may reduce their gifts following expanded government funding, especially over the long run. To confront this challenge, nonprofits providing public goods or addressing externalities may want to incorporate into their fund-raising literature and websites text to the effect that their provision of goods and services helps to address the limitations of government provision and effectively lowers tax rates relative to what they would be if the government were supplying the goods and services directly. NPOs may also want to consider the range of "selective incentives" (Olson, 1965) that might make a donation or membership more attractive to current and potential donors and/or members.

With a better understanding of both market and government failures and their implications for the nonprofit sector, nonprofit CEOs, boards, and fund-raisers should be able to shape a more sophisticated and sharpened message to funders, donors, and potential donors about the role of the nonprofit sector in our society, and the roles of their particular nonprofits in address-ing relevant market and government shortcomings. This sharper, more sophisticated message could enhance the ability to raise funds.

In any case, a nonprofit organization that is considering im-plementation or expansion of its capacity for raising funds from individual contributions should ask itself a number of critical (di-agnostic) questions, such as the following:

1. What kind of good or service does my organization pro-vide? Does it have a public good aspect? If so, is that fea-tured in the fund-raising and donor education literature and websites?
2. Does my organization have a fund-raising strategy that specifically targets individuals, who give over 80 percent of all gifts? Does my organization have a strategy that gives special attention to local donors and high income and/or high net worth households, who give a disproportionate amount of total giving?
3. Is my organization aware of the possibilities of crowding out of private philanthropy if it gains government funding? Does it have a plan for addressing crowding out over time?
4. Does my organization have a comprehensive development program? Does it include multiple strategies or are we putting all of our eggs in one basket?
5. What private incentives (e.g., gifts to donors and "member benefits") can be offered to potential donors to make giving more attractive to them?

Conclusion

Findings reported here suggest that nearly all giving is local. To the extent that nonprofit-provided public goods and those goods/services with large positive externalities are primarily lo-cal in nature, private philanthropy is allocated properly. How-ever, given that many of these goods and services are national or international in nature, a "propinquity effect" seems likely as well, that is, that donors may give disproportionately to (local) nonprofits from which they feel a large proportion of the benefit themselves.

While there are donors and nondonors at all income and wealth levels, big donors are generally those with high incomes and/or assets. Fund-raisers used to talk about the 80-20 rule (the top 20 percent of donors give 80 percent of the total gifts in a campaign), but many now subscribe to a 90-10 rule. This concentration of giving and fund-raising and cultivation strategy may make perfect sense pragmatically, but it may also yield problems for nonprofits and society. While high income/net worth donors generate a disproportionate share of total giving, they may also expect a disproportionate share of influence on the boards of non-profits and even in their daily operations. This outcome is not inherently bad; however, the nonprofit sector must also be cognizant of its public nature and the public welfare entrusted to it. While nonprofits may seek advice and target their solicitation of funds from donors at particular levels of income and wealth, they must also remain focused on serving all of their constituencies and fulfilling their respective missions. Control of nonprofits cannot simply be abdicated to the wealthiest among us.

Given the recurring energies required for philanthropic fund-raising and the uncertain returns to various fund-raising efforts, it should come as no surprise that some nonprofits would prefer the presumed stability of government funding. However, as we have seen, donors and funders seem to react to increases in the growth of government funding with slowdowns in the rate of growth of private philanthropy. While this is unproven as a causal relationship, it seems to be a consistent pattern: nonprofit subsectors that have experienced the most rapid growth rates in government funding over the last ten to twenty years have also experienced the slowest growth in funding from private philanthropy and vice versa. Hence, managers and boards of nonprofit organizations ought to be careful in what they wish for when seeking government funding, and remain attentive to the challenges associated with raising contributions from individuals.

Note

1. The author would like to thank Arthur Brooks, Heidi Frederick, and Dennis Young for very helpful and detailed comments on the penultimate draft. In addition, this chapter benefited from comments from the other chapter authors at the NCNE authors' conference, especially from Rich Steinberg, as well as at the discussions at ARNOVA. Finally, Heidi Newman provided excellent editorial comments. Of course, any remaining errors or omissions remain solely my responsibility.

3

Institutional Philanthropy

Joseph Cordes and Richard Sansing

Introduction

In 2003, there were just over sixty-three thousand grant-making 501(c)(3) organizations that held over $476 billion in assets and made over $30 billion in grants. These organizations include family foundations, corporate foundations, community foundations, and supporting organizations, which we refer to collectively as philanthropic institutions. A private foundation is a 501(c)(3) organization whose financial support is provided by a small group of donors, usually members of the same family (a family foundation) or a corporation (a corporate foundation) (§509(a)).[1] The principal charitable activity of most private foundations is the making of grants to public charities. A community foundation operates like a private foundation in that its primary charitable activity is the making of grants. Unlike a private foundation, however, the financial support for a community foundation comes from the general public. Supporting organizations are typically grant-making organizations that would be treated as private foundations because much of their financial support comes from investment income. However, a supporting organization is controlled by, and operates exclusively for the benefit of, a public charity, and so is not considered a private foundation (§509(a)(3)). A private foundation pays a tax on its investment income of 1 or 2 percent and must spend at least 5 percent of its assets on charitable activities each year; a public charity does not pay tax on its investment income and does not face an annual distribution constraint.

These philanthropic institutions control endowments whose assets are held for the benefit of current and future public charities. They act as conduits that transfer private wealth today to charitable beneficiaries in the future in a way that generates current tax deductions to donors. Moreover, they produce virtually tax-exempt future investment returns between the time the assets are transferred to the foundation and the time the assets are transferred from the foundation to a public charity. The assets of these philanthropic institutions are unusual in that public charities *in the aggregate* have a claim on their returns and because the tax laws governing nonprofit organizations forbid those assets from being diverted to private interests (known as the nondistribution constraint; see Hansmann, 1980). However, no particular charity has any claim on the returns of these assets.

The purpose of this chapter is to provide managers of grant-seeking public charities with an understanding of the philanthropic institutions that make $30 billion in grants, and which account for about a fifth of contributions received by operating public charities. The chapter examines several facets of institutional philanthropy that bear on the finances of nonprofit organizations. First, we broadly summarize recent patterns and trends in grant-making behavior by philanthropic institutions and discuss some broad implications of these patterns and trends for the place of institutional philanthropy as a source of finance for nonprofit organizations. Next we examine data on how these institutions operate and what differences exist in grant-making practice. Then we review both economic and organizational theories of how philanthropic institutions behave. The economic theories show how certain government policies affect the propensity of philanthropic institutions to spend from their endowments, which ultimately determines the flow of resources from institutional philanthropies to operating charities. The organizational theories characterize the behavior of foundations in terms of their institutional identities and operating styles. We then discuss which further research questions should be explored to better understand how philanthropic institutions behave. We conclude with guidance to managers of nonprofit organizations based on what we have learned about philanthropic institutions.

Patterns and Trends

According to data compiled by the Foundation Center, in 2003 a total of $30 billion in gifts were made to nonprofit organizations by independent, corporate, community, and grant-making operating foundations. This amount represented a drop from the previous year of just under $100 million in current dollars, and $170 million in constant dollars, following a period of fairly robust growth in value of grants between 1997 and 2000.

Compared to revenue garnered from sources such as fees and charges and donations from private individuals, private foundations provide a modest, though not inconsequential, source of financing for nonprofit organizations. For example, in 2000, private foundations made just over $27 billion in grants to nonprofit organizations. By comparison, in the same year, 501(c)(3) organizations that filed IRS 990 returns reported almost $119 billion in private contributions, which include foundation grants. Data compiled by the Foundation Center on all grants of $10,000 or more made between 1998 and 2003 provide information on several trends and patterns.[2]

Table 3.1 presents summary data on the value and number of grants of $10,000 or more made between 1998 and 2003. During this period, foundations as a group appeared to increase both the number and value of these grants. The dollar value and average grant increased but the effects of a declining stock market were beginning to be felt in 2002, when the number of grants continued to rise but the amount per grant fell from $134,000 to $125,000. Over the period from 1998 to 2003, the average overall grant amount increased by 19 percent, compared with a comparable increase in the consumer price index of 10 percent. As a consequence, the amount of the average grant more than kept pace with rising costs.

Table 3.2 reveals that when one compares the distribution of foundation grants and grant dollars with the distribution of

Table 3.1. Amount and Numbers of Grants over $10,000, 1998–2003

	1998	1999	2000	2001	2002	2003
Grant Dollars	$9,711,395	$11,574,183	$15,015,467	$16,763,304	$15,924,895	$14,323,389
Number of Grants	97,220	108,169	119,778	124,844	127,728	120,721
Average Grant	$100,000	$107,000	$125,000	$134,000	$125,000	$119,000

Source: Foundation Center: Statistical Information Service (www.fdncenter.org/fc_stats).

Table 3.2. Distribution of Foundation Grants and Foundation Dollars by Subject Area, 2002

Subject	% of Foundation Grants	% of Nonprofits	% of Foundation Grant Dollars	% of Spending by All Nonprofits	Average Grant
Education	26.4	17.4	20.7	16.3	$149,000
Medical	18.3	13.7	11.9	58.2	$187,000
Human Services	14.8	35.1	26.0	13.4	$71,000
Arts and Culture	12.2	10.5	14.6	2.6	$103,000
Public/Society Benefit	11.4	11.6	12.1	5.1	$110,000
Environment & Animals	5.9	3.7	6.1	0.9	$121,000
Science and Technology	3.6	0.6	1.7	1.1	$184,000
Religion	2.7	5.5	3.1	1.2	$88,000
International	2.6	0.9	2.4	0.9	$125,000
Social Science	1.9	0.3	1.2	0.2	$172,000
Other	0.1	0.7	0.1	0.1	$115,000

Source: The Foundation Center (Foundation Grant Data): Statistical Information Service, and National Center on Charitable Statistics, Digitized Data (data on numbers of nonprofits by NTEE classification).

nonprofit organizations and total spending by broad subject area, the distribution of grants and grant dollars does not simply mirror that of nonprofits and nonprofit spending. For example, although human services organizations accounted for just over 13 percent of total spending by nonprofits, these organizations received over one-fourth of foundation grants. Similarly, nonprofits involved in arts and culture, which accounted for less than 3 percent of total nonprofit spending, received almost 15 percent of foundation grant dollars. Conversely, health nonprofits, which accounted for almost three-fifths of total nonprofit spending, received less than 14 percent of foundation grant dollars. The size of the average grant also varied substantially by subject area, from a low of $71,000 for human services to a high of $187,000 for medical research.

Table 3.3 shows the distribution of grant dollars by type of support provided. During the period from 1998 to 2003, just under seventy cents of every grant dollar was allocated to program support (activities such as program, curriculum, and staff development), general support (including general operations, annual campaigns, and income development), and capital support (including capital campaigns, building and renovation, equipment, and endowments). Within this set of categories, however, there was a shift in the relative sizes of grants for capital support, general support, and program support. Specifically, over this time period the average grant for general support increased more than 20 percent, from just over $83,000 to just over $102,000, while the average grant for capital support remained essentially flat, rising

Table 3.3. Percentage of Total Grant Dollars by Type of Support

Type of Support	1998	1999	2000	2001	2002	2003
Program Support	33.8	32.3	34.2	35.1	36.9	33.7
Not Specified	30.3	31.7	27.4	27.2	22.9	30.1
General Support	15.1	14.8	17.7	17.8	21.4	15.1
Capital Support	10.9	11.3	10.8	10.0	9.4	10.9
Research	5.9	5.7	4.9	5.0	4.6	5.8
Student Aid Funds	3.6	3.3	3.8	3.7	3.6	3.6
Other	0.4	0.9	1.2	1.2	1.2	0.9

Source: The Foundation Center (Foundation Grant Data): Statistical Information Service.

from a little over $204,000 to just over $211,000, while program support grants increased by roughly the rate of inflation, from just under $120,000 to just under $135,000.

Current Practice

The foregoing trends and patterns of grant funding reflect practices that determine both *how much* support foundations are apt to provide from their financial resources as well as *how* such funds are disbursed through grants made to nonprofit organizations. For example, how much an individual foundation chooses to pay out in any given year affects both the number of grants it makes and the amounts of such grants. The pattern shown in table 3.1 of growth in foundation giving between 1998 and 2002 followed by declining giving in 2003 mirrors the pattern of change in the value of assets held by foundations, which increased from $385 billion in 1998 to $486 billion in 2000, and then declined to $467 billion in 2001 and to $435 billion in 2002.

In the 1960s, Congress became concerned that some foundations were making investment and operating decisions in a way that benefited the private interests of foundation donors instead of the interests of public charities. These concerns led to the enactment of several tax provisions in 1969 designed to ensure that private foundations fulfill a charitable purpose (Troyer 2000). One concern was that foundations would excessively accumulate funds instead of making distributions to charities. To address this concern, Congress enacted the minimum distribution requirement, which imposes a lower bound on the level of charitable expenditures that a foundation is permitted to make. Later, Congress made the tax rate on endowment income a function of the level of the foundation's charitable expenditures, in an effort to further encourage charitable expenditures.

The minimum distribution requirement is designed to prevent excessive retention of assets within foundations. The "distributable amount" is equal to 5 percent of the fair market value of the foundation's investment assets, less the taxes imposed on the foundation (§4942(d)).[3] This amount, which is calculated in the private foundation's annual tax return (Form 990-PF), must be paid out during the next year. Failure to do so triggers a 15 percent tax on the undistributed amount (§4942(a)). Failure to correct the error within the succeeding year triggers an additional tax equal to 100 percent of the remaining undistributed amount (§4942(b)). Distributions in excess of the distributable amount decrease the distributable amount in future years (§4942(g)(2)(D)).

The minimum distribution requirement can be satisfied via either grants to 501(c)(3) organizations or foundation administrative expenditures (§4942(g)), which include amounts paid for assets used by the foundation (§4942(g)(1)(B)). Richard Sansing and Robert Yetman (2006; hereafter, SY) examined foundation distribution behavior from 1994 to 2000. They documented substantial variation among foundations in the percentage of assets spent on charitable purposes, with a mean distribution percentage of 8.7 percent. About four-sevenths of their sample appear to adhere closely to the 5 percent minimum distribution requirement, spending less than 5.5 percent of investment assets on grants and administrative expenditures. The remaining three-sevenths of foundations in the sample distribute substantially more than the law requires.

SY also found that foundations that distribute substantially more than the legal minimum are more likely to receive new donations and are growing more quickly than do foundations that adhere closely to the legal minimum. They also tend to be smaller than the average foundation, where the measure of size is foundation assets. The minimum distribution requirement appears to act as a binding constraint for foundations that are large and "cold" in the sense of having no source of new donations and a relatively low rate of asset growth.

Finally, SY find that 7 to 10 percent of qualifying distributions are in the form of administrative expenditures and 90 to 93 percent are in the form of grants paid to public charities. They also find statistically significant relations between a foundation's overall payout style and what it spends on administration per dollar of investment assets. Foundations that adhere strictly to the minimum distribution requirement tend to spend less than average on administration; those that spend substantially more than required tend to spend more on administration.

Private foundations are subject to a tax on their net investment income (§4940). In general, a private foundation faces a 2 percent tax rate (§4940(a)). However, this tax rate is halved to 1 percent for a foundation that makes a sufficiently large qualifying distribution (§4940(e)). To qualify for the reduced tax rate, the ratio of a foundation's qualifying distributions to investment assets must be at least as large as the sum of the average ratio of "adjusted qualifying distributions" to investment assets over the preceding five years, plus 1 percent of the foundation's net investment income. For example, suppose over the preceding five years a foundation had, on average, 6 percent of its investment assets in adjusted qualifying distributions. Suppose this year the foundation has investment assets of $100 million and net investment income of $8 million. If this year's qualifying distributions are less than $6,080,000, then its tax is $160,000; if qualifying distributions are $6,080,000 or more, then its tax is $80,000.

Adjusted qualifying distributions are defined as qualifying distributions minus the reduction in tax in a year in which a foundation qualifies for the 1 percent tax rate. This adjustment prevents the foundation from having to make a steady increase in its level of qualifying distributions to continue qualifying for the 1 percent tax rate. Continuing the above example, if the private foundation made qualifying distributions of exactly $6,080,000 in the current year, its adjusted qualifying distributions would be $6,000,000—the qualifying distributions less the $80,000 tax reduction. So next year's base period ratio of qualifying distributions to investment assets would remain at 6 percent.

SY found that slightly fewer than half of the foundations in their sample qualified for the lower tax rate. Foundations qualifying for the lower tax rate tended to be larger, suggesting some economies of scale in tax planning. They also had higher expenditures on employee compensation, trustee fees, and professional fees (as a percentage of assets). Low tax rate foundations were more likely to receive new donations, suggesting that foundations that had new donations coming in were more likely to raise charitable expenditures to the level needed to qualify for the lower tax rate. Finally, fast-growing foundations were less likely to qualify for the lower tax rate, suggesting that expenditure levels did not keep up with asset growth.

SY also found that the "cliff effect" in the tax rule appears to induce foundation distributions just large enough to qualify for the lower tax rate. About 30 percent of their sample made distributions between 90 percent and 110 percent of the point at which the tax rate changes. Of these foundations, nearly two-thirds qualified for the lower tax rate. Foundations qualifying for the 1 percent tax rate distribute a higher percentage of investment assets than the 2 percent tax rate foundations (8.7 percent versus 6.7 percent) but also had a lower base period percentage (6.7 percent versus 11.1 percent).

Aside from how much to disburse in any year, foundations must also decide how such funds are to be disbursed. These policies have important ramifications for the type of financial support that nonprofit organizations can reasonably expect to receive from foundation grants. A recent survey[4] conducted by the Urban Institute of practices at 1,192 community, corporate, and independent foundations provides important new insight into how these foundations go about making grants to nonprofits (Ostrower, 2004).

One important factor affecting patterns of grant making are the broad goals that foundations seek to achieve. In this vein, respondents to the Urban Institute survey were asked to indicate the relative importance of five broad objectives: (1) strengthening particular organizations; (2) strengthening particular fields of activity; (3) strengthening particular groups; (4) strengthening the foundation's local community or region; and (5) strengthening social change and/or strategies for change.

The response to the questions, which are presented in table 3.4, indicate that each of these goals is valued at least to some degree by many foundations, but there are differences in the relative importance attached to the various goals. If, for example, the percentage of respondents who rated a goal as "very important" is taken as a rough indicator of priority, the responses suggest that community foundations are more likely to give priority to grants that are seen to strengthen the foundation's local community or region, followed by grants that strengthen particular fields of activity, particular organizations, social change, or particular groups. Corporate foundations are also more likely to favor grants that strengthen the foundation's local community or region,

Table 3.4. Foundation Goals in Grant Making

	Community Foundation		Corporate Foundation		Independent Foundation	
	N	%	N	%	N	%
Strengthen particular organization(s)						
Not at all	17	7.17	5	5.62	66	8.04
Not very	27	11.39	8	8.99	75	9.14
Somewhat	112	47.26	37	41.57	328	39.95
Very	81	34.18	39	43.82	352	42.87
Strengthen particular field(s) of activity						
Not at all	5	2.11	2	2.22	40	4.80
Not very	34	14.35	7	7.78	80	9.60
Somewhat	103	43.46	30	33.33	266	31.93
Very	95	40.08	51	56.67	447	53.66
Strengthen particular group(s)						
Not at all	5	2.13	5	5.68	78	9.54
Not very	40	17.02	10	11.36	144	17.60
Somewhat	122	51.91	34	38.64	299	36.55
Very	68	28.94	39	44.32	297	36.31
Strength the foundation's local community or region						
Not at all	0	0.00	7	7.69	92	11.18
Not very	1	0.42	7	7.69	141	17.13
Somewhat	25	10.55	18	19.78	240	29.16
Very	211	89.03	59	64.84	350	42.53
Strengthen social change and/or strategies for change						
Not at all	9	3.86	11	12.36	125	15.28
Not very	45	19.31	18	20.22	194	23.72
Somewhat	108	46.35	37	41.57	267	32.64
Very	71	30.47	23	25.84	232	28.36

Source: Francie Ostrower, Attitudes and Practices Concerning Effective Philanthropy, 2004, p. 60, table 1.

followed by grants that strengthen particular fields of activity, particular groups, particular organizations, and social change. In contrast to both community and corporate foundations, independent foundations would seem to favor grants that strengthen particular fields of activity, followed by grants that strengthen particular organizations or the foundation's local community or region, particular groups, and social change and/or strategies for change. Interestingly, strengthening social change and strategies for change rank at or near the bottom for each type of foundation.

Respondents were also asked more specific questions about the types of grants that they typically make. One important issue is the degree to which foundations are receptive to funding unsolicited proposals, rather than proposals that address specific foundation initiatives. As one might expect, more than 60 percent of community foundations and corporate foundations, and almost half of independent foundations, indicated that they made grants for foundation-designed initiatives either often or sometimes. However, 55 percent of community foundations, 52 percent of corporate foundations, and 57 percent of independent foundations also indicated that grants were often or sometimes made in response to unsolicited proposals. Corporate and community foundations, however, were more likely than independent foundations to respond that they "often" made grants for foundation-designed initiatives.

The survey also asked respondents to indicate how often they made grants to support general operations, organizational and/or management development, research, and advocacy. Seventy percent of corporate and independent foundations responded that grants were often or sometimes made for general operations, while the corresponding figure for community foundations was 49 percent. More than two-thirds of community foundations responded that they made grants often or sometimes for organizational/management development, compared with 42 percent of corporate foundations, and 47 percent of independent foundations. By comparison, just under 20 percent of community foundations, 35 percent of corporate foundations, and 37 percent of independent foundations responded that they often or sometimes made grants for research; and 33 percent of community foundations, 22 percent of corporate foundations, and 38 percent of independent foundations responded that they made grants for advocacy. In addition, a majority of community foundations, but not corporate or independent foundations, responded that they provided in-kind support in the areas of board development, strategy and planning, and fund-raising assistance.

Respondents were also asked about the duration of grants. A majority in each foundation category indicated that grants were either never or rarely made for three years or longer. The tendency to make grants of less than three years was particularly strong among community foundations. There was, however, variation in grant duration by foundation size, with the proportion of foundations that indicated that they "sometimes, often, or always" made grants of three years or more rising from 37 percent among foundations with assets of $10 million or less, to 72 percent among foundations with assets of more than $400 million.

Approximately four-fifths or more of all foundations responding to the survey indicated that the following factors were either very or somewhat important in the decision to make grants: strength of proposal, donors' interest in the cause, staff input, and measurable outcomes. In addition, board members' interest in the cause was also important in making grant-making decisions among corporate and independent foundations (76 percent and 81 percent, respectively), and somewhat less important among community foundations (50 percent).

The attitude of foundations to so-called "innovative" proposals was mixed. On one hand, innovativeness was regarded as somewhat or very important by about four-fifths of community and corporate foundations, and by seven out of ten independent foundations. On the other hand, about half of community and independent foundations, and seven out of ten corporate foundations indicated that low risk of failure was somewhat or very important.

The most common way that foundations of all types monitor whether grant funds are used appropriately is by requiring a final report, but this method was more common among community foundations. Final reports were often or always required by 92 percent of community foundations, 80 percent of independent foundations, and 69 percent of corporate foundations. Just as important, three-fourths or more of all foundations indicated that learning about the implementation and the outcomes of funded work was a very important part of the monitoring process.

Theory

Just as economic and sociological theories are useful for understanding the behavior of individual donors, and how this behavior can be shaped by changes in the economy and public policy, so too it is useful to draw on the insights of economic theory and organization theory to put the behavior of foundations into broader perspective.

All foundations face a choice between current and future distributions to charitable beneficiaries. This choice reflects a trade-off between the foundation leadership's preferences between current and future charitable beneficiaries and the financial rate of return on the foundation's endowment. This trade-off can be thought of as a comparison between a nonfinancial and a financial discount rate. If the nonfinancial discount rate is higher, the foundation's assets will be depleted over time; if the financial discount rate is higher, whether the foundation's assets grow or shrink over time depends on a comparison between the rate of return on the foundation's assets and the minimum distribution requirement. Different stakeholders can have different preferences regarding the normatively appropriate nonfinancial discount. One interpretation of the minimum distribution requirement is that Congress is concerned that the nonfinancial discount rate used by foundation managers is too low.

In the appendix we develop and analyze a mathematical model that determines the present value of a foundation's current and future charitable distributions for a foundation that makes the minimum level of distributions required by the tax law. Two important insights emerge from our analysis of the model. First, if the nonfinancial discount rate is equal to the foundation's rate of return on its investments, the rate at which the foundation makes its charitable distributions has no effect on the present value of the foundation's current and future charitable distributions. That is because the nonfinancial discount associated with future distributions (relative to current distributions) is exactly offset by the fact that a dollar invested today will yield more dollars available to charitable beneficiaries in the future.

Second, the present value of the foundation's current and future charitable distributions increases (decreases) with an increase in the minimum distribution percentage if the nonfinancial discount rate is greater than (less than) the financial rate of return on the foundation's assets. A policy argument regarding the minimum distribution requirement at least implicitly reflects a belief that the nonfinancial discount rate used by foundation managers is too low.

Unlike the minimum distribution requirement, the dual tax rate system provides two countervailing incentives for foundations to modify their distribution decisions so as to qualify for the 1 percent tax rate. First, foundations have an incentive to make current-year distributions at least as high as in prior years (as a percentage of investment assets) so as to qualify for the lower tax rate. On the other hand, any current-year distribution increases the base period percentage that will determine whether the foundation will continue to qualify for the lower tax rate in future years. This effect will deter current-year distributions in excess of what is needed to qualify for the 1 percent tax rate. Finally, the dual tax rate system features a severe "cliff effect" in that a $1 shortfall in qualifying distributions doubles the tax on investment income. So although the tax rates are low relative to those faced by other taxpayers, the marginal effect of distributions around the threshold for the 1 percent tax rate is extremely large.

Several writers have offered organizational frameworks for distinguishing among foundations in terms of their grant-making practices. Nielsen (1985) uses the Mellon and Ford foundations as examples of different approaches to grant making. These differences manifest themselves in the type of institution that receives grants, the type of project that they fund, and the degree of involvement the foundation has with the grant recipients. The Mellon approach to grant making tends to support established institutions in the areas of education, health, and the arts. These grants support elite scholars and scientists who compete for Mellon grants on a competitive basis. Support for the disadvantaged comes in the form of scholarships and fellowships to provide educational opportunities. Mellon's administrative costs are low and Mellon tends not to expend significant amounts on grantee oversight. The Ford approach differs from Mellon's in several respects. Ford is more likely to support new, inexperienced organizations that are trying to develop new ways to address social problems. Ford often funds economic development projects and neighborhood organizations, advocacy projects, and minority leadership development programs. Ford spends more on administrative costs per dollar of grants as it takes an active role in overseeing the projects it funds.

Young (2001) classifies foundation grant-making styles into four groups that reflect the foundation's organizational identity, which Albert and Whetten (1985) define as an organization's central, distinctive, and enduring characteristics. The four groups differ primarily in terms of the degree and nature of the foundation's involvement with the projects it funds. The "Genial Altruist" foundation sees itself as having a broad mission of providing charitable support for a community or area of interest. Its role is to evaluate competing proposals, often relying on the advice of external experts or the reputation of the applicant in choosing which projects to fund. The "Mission-Driven" foundation focuses its grants much more narrowly than does the genial altruist, funding grants that advance a particular mission. It tends to rely more on its professional staff than outside experts to evaluate grant proposals. It is more likely to pursue a grant strategy that preserves the value of the foundation's endowment than is the genial altruist. The "Problem-Solving Catalyst" foundation sees itself as a leader and innovator in its field of interest. In addition to funding grants, it strives to set the agenda for its field of interest and coordinate activities between grantees and other charitable institutions in its field. It not only makes grants, but also invests in professional staff that maintains its position as a leader in the field. It chooses a grant-making policy that preserves or increases the value of the endowment to ensure that the foundation is a permanent actor in its field. The "Venture Capitalist" foundation aggressively seeks promising projects to fund and provides substantial financial and intellectual support to the project until it can sustain itself without additional support from the foundation. It engages outside consultants to provide in-kind support to the new project and focuses its attention on only a handful of projects. It does not strive to maintain the foundation's endowment over time.

Basic microeconomic models of grants also provide some insight into the consequences of different foundation grant structures for the behavior of recipients. Ideally a nonprofit organization would like to receive grants from foundations that have little or no restrictions on their use, leaving the nonprofit organization free to allocate the additional dollars as it sees fit. While the evidence from both Foundation Center data and the Urban Institute survey shows that foundations are willing to make seemingly unrestricted grants to support general operations, in practice, foundations are at least as likely to designate that particular grants be used either for specific operational purposes (e.g., capital development) or programmatic purposes.

The fact that many foundation grants are restricted in some form raises the issue of whether dependence on foundation funding has the potential to tilt the activities of recipients in favor of those activities designated by the donors. Economic theory suggests that this outcome is possible, though not necessarily a given. Two key variables are: (1) whether the grant is structured as a nonmatching or matching grant; and (2) how much of the organization's budget is already devoted to the "restricted" activity prior to receipt of the grant.

When a grant is restricted, but is nonmatching, the recipient simply receives a specified sum that is to be spent on the restricted or targeted activity. Unless the grantor attempts to require the recipient to maintain the same level of spending on the targeted activity as before the grant was received, there is nothing to prevent a recipient from simply substituting grant funds for what it would have spent on the targeted activity, thereby freeing up these resources for other uses. The result is that so long as a recipient was already spending at least as much of its own resources on the designated activity as the amount of the grant, it can effectively convert what appears to be a restricted grant into an unrestricted cash equivalent. For example, if a nonprofit that was already spending $500,000 per year of its own funds on capital development received a capital development grant of $300,000 from a foundation, it could simply reduce what it would have spent on capital development by $300,000 and thereby free up these funds for other uses.

There are two circumstances under which an individual non-profit organization would face difficulties in converting a restricted but nonmatching grant into an equivalent amount of unrestricted funds. One is a case in which the grantor seeks to limit the ability of grantees to act in this manner by including "maintenance of effort" requirements, which constrain recipients to maintain spending on the designated activity at "pre-grant" levels. Such requirements are often difficult to monitor in practice, however, and may leave the nonprofit organization some leeway in converting at least a part of the restricted grant into the equivalent of unrestricted funds.

The other circumstance arises if the nonprofit was spending less than the amount of the grant. For example, in the above example, if the recipient of a $300,000 grant for capital development was spending only $100,000 on this activity, then although it could reduce its own spending on the activity by $100,000, effectively converting $100,000 of the grant into an unrestricted gift, the remaining $200,000 would have to be spent on capital development. In this case, receipt of the grant would require the organization to increase its overall spending on the designated activity.

As an alternative to making nonmatching grants, foundations may instead require a recipient to match a portion of foundation grant dollars with other resources. These matches can be of two broad types. A foundation may offer to provide $1 of funding for every X dollars of additional contributions raised by a recipient. Or, a foundation may offer to match, with additional foundation funds, each dollar spent by a recipient on a specific purpose or activity.

The two types of matching grants have different implications for the recipient. In the case of what might be termed a matching fund-raising grant, the effect of the match is to encourage a potential recipient to devote more resources to fund-raising activities because each dollar of contributions raised from other sources leverages additional contributions from the foundation that proposes to make the matching grant. In the case of a grant requiring an internal match of resources, the grant creates a clear financial incentive for the recipient to shift more resources than it otherwise would to the activity or activities that qualify for matching funds.

Improving Practice

The analysis in the preceding sections suggests that funding from grant-making philanthropic institutions as part of the revenue portfolio of operating nonprofit organizations features significant possible benefits, but also potential costs. The decision to pursue grants involves considering both benefits and costs of seeking and receiving grants.

Support from philanthropic institutions provides three types of benefits. First, the financial grant itself provides additional dollars for the operating charity to fund its programs and capital investments, and build its own endowment; these funds can be part of a diversified portfolio of revenue streams for a nonprofit organization. Second, some institutions provide additional support in the form of consulting services to help the grant recipient implement the new program. Third, because foundation grants tend to be relatively visible and prestigious sources of funds, receipt of such funding can create a bandwagon effect, making it easier to raise funds from other sources.

Seeking and receiving grants also involves costs. First, applying for grants requires either staff time that could be used on other activities or the use of outside consultants. Second, most philanthropic institutions have requirements for reporting and monitoring of grants, so that administering the grant also takes up scarce organizational resources. Although these requirements may have been modest in the past (Grønbjerg, 1993), they have increased in recent years. Third, the organization making the grant may be striving to achieve certain objectives based on the foundation's mission, which may not be the same as the mission of the operating charity seeking the grant. Therefore, accepting the grant may alter the mission of the charity. Fourth, grants may be unreliable sources of funding from one year to the next. A charity should avoid being dependent on grants unless it is also prepared to terminate the program that the grant funds or to fund it in some other manner.

As Grønbjerg (1993) has documented in her case studies of revenue management and funding among social service and community organizations, some nonprofits have (at least implicitly) weighed these benefits and costs and made a conscious choice to systematically pursue foundation support as a source of financing. These organizations make use of available information from diverse sources such as local councils on foundations, annual reports filed by foundations, and previously made foundation awards to identify corporations whose funding priorities and operating styles match their own. What Grønbjerg describes as "self-screening" by potential recipients not only helps increase the likelihood that they will receive funding, but also helps economize on scarce organizational resources spent on seeking and managing foundation support. She also conjectures that some organizations may find foundation grants support attractive because they lack natural constituencies to target for fund-raising efforts.

At the same time, Grønbjerg also notes, some organizations have chosen either not to seek foundation funding at all or to do so on a more ad hoc basis, because they have access to stable funding from other sources, or do not believe that their activities are a good match for foundation priorities. Similarly, as illustrated by the case of the Pittsburgh Human Services Center (HSC) Corporation discussed in chapter 13, foundation funding may be seen to be a sufficiently uncertain revenue stream so as to prompt an organization to consciously seek to replace foundation funding with other sources of funding.

Thinking through the following diagnostic questions should help nonprofit leaders decide when and whether to pursue institutional (foundation) grants:

1. Is there a close fit between the mission of the operating charity and the grant-making institution? Seeking a grant when the fit is not close is unlikely to be successful, is costly to attempt, and can divert resources and attention away from the operating charity's mission.

2. Does the grant-making institution offer nonfinancial services that are of value to the operating charity? The value provided by a philanthropic institution can go well beyond the grant itself.
3. How likely is it that the grant can be leveraged into a sustainable revenue stream, either from the institution making the grant or from other funding sources? Leverage can greatly magnify the value of the grant.
4. If the grant is not leveraged into a sustainable revenue stream, is the operating charity willing to either terminate the program the grant funds or fund it in some other manner? Be wary of activities that cannot be sustained in the future.

Conclusion

Philanthropic institutions in the United States control financial assets worth about $500 billion, from which they make about $30 billion of grants annually. This $500 billion can be thought of as an endowment held for the benefit of operating charities. However, no particular charity has a claim to any part of the return to this endowment.

Philanthropic institutions exhibit considerable variety in their behavior. Private foundations must spend at least 5 percent of their assets on charitable activities each year to avoid violating the minimum distribution requirement. Many foundations spend substantially more than this. Foundations that distribute more than the minimum tend to be smaller and growing more rapidly than the average foundation. Foundations also vary in terms of differences that manifest themselves in the type of institutions to which they make grants, the type of projects that they fund, and the degree of involvement the foundations have with the recipients of their grants.

While funding from philanthropic institutions can be an important element of revenue diversification for some nonprofits, there is no "one-size-fits-all" approach. A rational approach to determining what role, if any, foundation funding should play in the overall revenue portfolio of an organization is to weigh the benefits and costs both of investing scarce organizational resources in seeking such funding, and of relying on this particular source of finance.

Although the costs and benefits of relying on foundations for support are difficult to quantify, it is possible for nonprofit organizations to make such assessments in deciding on the role of foundation grants in their revenue portfolios. Overall, the "benefit-cost" balance associated with pursuing foundation funding as a revenue stream is more likely to be positive when (1) the mission and strategy of the operating charity are aligned with the mission and strategy of the grant maker and (2) when an operating charity is in a position to leverage a grant into a sustainable revenue stream.

Appendix

We use the following stylized model to illustrate the minimum distribution requirement and show how it affects the present value of charitable distributions. The foundation invests its assets in a portfolio that generates investment income (dividends, interest, and capital gains) at a rate $R \geq 0$. This income is taxed at a rate τ.[5] The foundation begins the year with assets with a value of V_0 and ends the year with assets with a value $V_1 = V_0[1 + R(1 - \tau)] - d_1$, where d_1 is the minimum level of charitable distributions that the foundation is permitted to make. Satisfying the minimum distribution requirement involves making a distribution that is equal to the beginning-of-year assets multiplied by a statutory percentage $m > 0$, less the tax paid on the foundation's investment income. This implies:

$$d_1 = mV_0 - \tau R V_0. \tag{1}$$

This in turn implies that the foundation assets grow at a rate of $1 + R - m$ and the fraction of assets distributed to charity each year is a constant $m - \tau R$. Therefore, the present value distributed to charity in year t is $\frac{(m - \tau R)V_0[1 + R - m]^{t-1}}{(1+r)^t}$. Using the fact that $\sum_{k=1}^{k=\infty} x^k = \frac{x}{1-x}$ implies that the present value of future charitable distributions from a foundation following a minimum distribution strategy is:

$$\frac{V_0(m - R\tau)}{m + r - R}. \tag{2}$$

The discount rate r reflects one's personal valuation of current versus future charitable distributions, whereas R is the market return on invested capital. Different interested parties, such as foundation managers, public charities, and government policymakers, may each have different opinions regarding the appropriate discount rate r. If $r > R(1 - \tau)$, then the present value of future charitable distributions is less than V_0, in which case the foundation should terminate itself immediately and distribute all of its assets to public charities. A foundation that does not choose this course of action, by revealed preference, uses a discount rate $r < R(1 - \tau)$.

Differentiating the expression in (2) with respect to m shows how the present value of future charitable distributions changes as the minimum distribution requirement changes. This value is increasing as m increases if $r > R(1 - \tau)$ and decreasing if $r < R(1 - \tau)$. One interpretation of m is a judgment by Congress that the discount rate r preferred by foundation managers is too low, so an increase in m increases the present value of future charitable distributions from the point of view of Congress while at the same time decreasing it from the point of view of foundation managers.

One interesting implication of the expression in (2) is that if the discount rate r is equal to the aftertax return $R(1 - \tau)$, the distribution percentage m has no effect on the present value of charitable distributions. In that case, lower distributions today are exactly offset by higher distributions in the future.

Notes

1. This figure does not include grants made by foundations that are classified as private operating foundations or public foundations. Using data from the National Center for Charitable Statistics, we tabulate

that in 2003 there were 145 private operating foundations making grants that totaled approximately $27 million, and 992 public foundations that made grants totaling $273 million. Adding the grants made by these foundations to the total grants tabulated by the Foundation Center would increase the total volume of grants in 2003 from $30 billion to approximately $30.3 billion.

2. The Foundation Center grants database includes all grants of $10,000 or more awarded by about 1,000 of the largest private and community foundations. The foundations sampled represent less than 3 percent of all foundations in terms of numbers but account for about half of all grant dollars awarded. For further information on the Foundation large-grants sample see fdncenter.org/fc_stats/grantsampling. html.

3. Assets used in carrying out the foundation's exempt purpose (e.g., an office building in which the foundation conducts its operations) are not included in the calculation of the distributable amount (§4942(e)(1)(A)).

4. The distribution of foundations surveyed consisted of 853 (72 percent) independent foundations, 238 (20 percent) community foundations, and 92 (8 percent) corporate foundations. The overall response rate was 35 percent, ranging from 25 percent among foundations with less than $10 million in assets to 58 percent for foundations with assets greater than $400 million. For more description of the sample see www.urban.org/UploadedPDF/411067_attitudes_practices_ FR.pdf.

5. For the sake of tractability, we ignore the effects of deferring the taxation of capital gains until realization.

4

Government Funding of Nonprofit Organizations

Michael Rushton and Arthur C. Brooks

Introduction

Nonprofit leaders are generally aware that government can be a source of funds to address their missions. Of course, industry leaders in the for-profit sector also look to government when they think the political opportunities are favorable for targeted subsidies and protection from competition. But nonprofits and government have what is mostly a more benign relationship, with the state willing to provide support for general operations, specific projects, or contracts to deliver public services to citizens on behalf of government. There are also income tax exemptions for donors, and corporate income and property tax exemptions for the organizations themselves, which also represent a form of government support for nonprofit organizations.

The questions we pose in this chapter are not so much about how organizations can most easily access government funding. Rather, we ask whether it is sometimes in the nonprofit's better interest *not* to pursue every dollar of government funding that might be available. Government funds rarely come without strings, and so the nonprofit leader must ask whether the strings are either loose enough, or closely enough aligned with the nonprofit's guiding mission, to make the funding worth pursuing.

We begin the analysis with a brief survey of the landscape for government funding and nonprofits, and then move to considering in more detail the trade-offs nonprofit decision makers must assess.

Patterns and Trends

The most obvious sources of government funding to nonprofits are direct subsidies and grants. Indeed, these sources of revenues are usually used to summarize government funding in general. Direct government subsidies to American nonprofits came to $208 billion in 1997 (Independent Sector, 2002). At 31 percent of total nonprofit revenues, direct subsidies were higher than private donations, but lower than earned revenues.

Government subsidies have grown enormously since the mid-1970s, with no period of stagnant or falling government spending. This source of revenues has almost always exceeded or kept pace with the overall growth of the nonprofit sector. These past trends are especially interesting because they have transcended major political shifts over the period that might otherwise be assumed to affect government funding of the sector. That being said, it is not at all certain that the growth in government subsidies will continue. At the time of writing, the U.S. federal government's fiscal obligations for Medicare and Social Security represent a liability that dwarfs current annual budget deficits, and there are few economists who would deny that a major reckoning is forthcoming on how to raise taxes and/or cut discretionary government spending to meet the government's budget constraint.

Individual nonprofit subsectors receive different levels of support from governments. While health-related nonprofits clearly receive the lion's share of all government subsidies to nonprofits (66 percent), this funding amounted to only 42 percent of total nonprofit revenues in health care. Social welfare organizations, which in terms of revenues are a smaller subsector, relied on government subsidies for 52 percent of their revenues. Religious nonprofits are an interesting case: While they received only 3 percent of all direct government subsidies, they captured 55 percent of all private giving. This largely reflects the inability of governments to fund sacramental activities. We deal with the thorny issue of religious nonprofits and government funds in more detail later in this chapter.

How does the American nonprofit sector compare with that of other countries, with respect to the percent of its revenues that come from direct government subsidies? The U.S. figure of 31 percent is slightly below average by world standards. In general, Western European governments cover far larger parts of their nonprofit sectors' budgets than does the United States. For example, direct subsidies come to 77 percent in Ireland and Belgium, 64 percent in Germany, 59 percent in Holland, and 58 percent in France. Not coincidentally, these figures are accompanied by very low percentages of total revenues from donations (Brooks, 2003a).

While direct subsidies are fairly easy to comprehend, they do not comprise all of the government funding to nonprofits. In many areas of the nonprofit sector, indirect subsidies make up a substantial portion of total revenues, yet are frequently not attributed to the government. As a matter of public policy and financial management, however, we must understand them.

Indirect subsidies come in three basic varieties: tax payments forgone on corporate activity and tax-deductible contributions, tax credits, and funding through nonprofit partnerships with government. Consider each type in turn:

At the federal level in the United States and many other countries, as well as in many state and municipal jurisdictions, qualified nonprofit organizations are exempt from paying corporate taxes (Weisbrod, 1991). Indeed, this is the effective quid pro quo that nonprofits enjoy for agreeing not to distribute profits to corporate owners. The nonprofit form of organization solves different sorts of market failure by removing profit motives, and the favorable tax policies are the means by which government can enhance the attractiveness of adopting the nonprofit form (Brown and Slivinski, 2006).

The implicit subsidy in this system is the tax forgone on either net or gross revenues (depending on the tax system); that is, the money that would have been paid to the government if the firm had been organized as a for-profit organization. While this may seem like a considerable sum, given the scale of the nonprofit sector (approximately $665 billion in gross revenue in the United

States in 1997), two caveats are in order. First, a sector that has low net revenues because of its inability to distribute profits may be forgoing relatively little corporate tax. Second, were it not for tax exemption, some (perhaps much) nonprofit activity might be infeasible in the first place, so there is actually little opportunity cost to government from exempting the activity (Simon, 1987). Indeed, a recent study by the Congressional Budget Office (2005) suggests that if the general tax exemption on nonprofit income were removed, nonprofit organizations would have increased incentives to simply decrease net revenues, either by rewarding employees more favorably, overinvesting in capital, or lowering fees for clients. We return to the general tax exemption for nonprofit net revenues below.

An arguably more important source of indirect subsidy comes in the form of government revenues forgone on tax-deductible contributions (Brooks, 2004a). Many governments, including the U.S. federal and many state governments, allow donors to qualified charities and causes to deduct their contributions (generally up to some level of total income) from taxable income. That is, if the marginal income tax rate—which is the tax rate that applies to one's last dollar of earnings—is, say, 30 percent, then each dollar donated to charity consists of a net cost to the donor of only 70 cents, and an indirect subsidy from the government to the nonprofit of 30 cents.

The size of indirect subsidies from tax-deducted donations is considerable. The U.S. Internal Revenue Service, for example, estimates that in 2002, individuals donated and deducted $142.4 billion in money and in-kind gifts. (Obviously, this does not represent total private giving, much of which is not deducted for tax purposes.) Breaking this figure down by income class and applying 2002 marginal tax rates for these classes, we can estimate that this represents forgone income tax revenues—and hence a government subsidy—of about $37.2 billion, which is nearly a fifth as important as direct subsidies to nonprofits.

As financially important as these subsidies are, the preceding figure aggregates across all nonprofit activity, underestimating their importance for certain subsectors. For example, research examining this indirect source of funding to the arts has found that it outstrips direct subsidies to American arts nonprofits by about $14 to $1 at the federal level (Brooks, 2004b), and $5 to $1 for all levels of government (Schuster, 1987).

Theory

In this section we consider how economists have analyzed the incentives and implications for nonprofit organizations of various indirect (tax-related) and direct (programmatic) government policies—including tax exemptions for charitable contributions, the unrelated business income tax, property tax exemptions, tradable tax credits, and partnerships with government.

How do donations tend to respond to changes in marginal income tax rates? An increase in tax rates lowers the effective cost to the donor for giving. The "tax price of giving" is the cost, after taxes, of donating a dollar to charity. If the marginal tax rate is 30 percent, the tax price of giving is 70 cents, and if the marginal tax rate is 40 percent, the tax price of giving is 60 cents. It has been found that a 10 percent increase in the tax price of giving will lower giving by 12 percent, all else being constant (Steinberg, 1990). It stands to reason that the sensitivity of giving to tax price changes might depend on the type of giving involved, although researchers have rarely investigated this possibility, and it remains a question for future research.

Nonprofits themselves also receive favorable tax treatment, and clearly this is a source of net revenue. What makes the detailed examination of tax policies worthwhile from a practical perspective is that understanding of the differential tax treatment of nonprofit and for-profit organizations can identify possible means of tax avoidance by nonprofits. Note that here we follow Stiglitz's (1985) distinction between *tax avoidance*, which is legal and involves making transactions in light of the provisions of the tax system that provide incentives for certain economic decisions, and *tax evasion*, which is illegal and generally involves misrepresentation of relevant facts to the tax authorities.

From the introduction of the Corporate Income Tax in the United States in 1913, charitable nonprofit organizations have been able to claim exemption of their earnings under section 501(c)(3) of the Internal Revenue Code. In 1950 the Unrelated Business Income Tax (UBIT) was introduced, with the stated goal of preventing "unfair" competition by nonprofit organizations with for-profit firms. As the name implies, it is applied to earnings from activities not related to the core mission of the nonprofit. The prototypical example of an unrelated activity is the ownership by New York University Law School of the Mueller Macaroni Company, which provided the spark that led to the introduction of the UBIT (Rose-Ackerman, 1982a).

Economists have examined the question of whether the general corporate tax exemption combined with the UBIT encourages or discourages nonprofits' commercial activities. This economic analysis is interesting because it tells the nonprofit manager whether the tax system is structured so that an investment in a venture that, on its face, is not worth pursuing might in fact be valuable as a result of the structure of the UBIT (and conversely, whether a venture that does look promising is in fact discouraged by the provisions of the tax). For this part of the analysis we put to one side a question dealt with in other chapters in this volume: how much does it matter to a nonprofit organization that some of its revenue-raising tools take the organization into providing services that are not directly related to the mission of the organization, and that perhaps represent an activity whose returns would have to be above a high threshold for the nonprofit to be willing to consider such an investment? Here we assume for simplicity that the nonprofit organization simply wants to raise revenue, but that unrelated activities are subject to the UBIT.

Suppose that nonprofits and for-profits each invest in commercial activities up to the point where the profit on the marginal dollar invested is just equal to the return on the next best way to invest funds. If we suppose that the "next best way" is to invest in bonds, which pay a rate of interest of, say, 6 percent, and if we suppose that for-profit firms pay corporate income tax on earnings from all sources (and are able to fully deduct interest expenses), then *both* for-profits and nonprofits will invest to where the marginal return on investment equals 6 percent, regardless of the corporate tax rate. For each type of organization, for-profit or nonprofit, we would expect managers to invest in all the projects with the highest rate of return first—ones yielding returns on investment of 20 percent, 15 percent, 10 percent, and so on. When managers have worked their way through all the possible high return projects, and are now looking at projects paying a return of 6 percent, they are just indifferent to carrying out the project or investing in bonds instead. And no manager will opt for a project yielding a return of less than 6 percent. But the rate of corporate tax does not affect whether to invest in a project.

As long as the corporate tax is *neutral*, that is, its structure does not favor certain types of investments or ways of financing them, the rates that apply to for-profit and nonprofit earnings will not affect the levels of investment in each sector, even if the nonprofit gets to keep more of its earnings (Cordes and Weisbrod, 1998). But this suggests that for efficiency we should *abolish* the UBIT, since it will introduce a distortion in how nonprofits choose their investments. According to one scholar:

> Nonprofit organizations have incentives to concentrate their investments in bonds and other assets the returns of which are highly taxed—and that the market prices accordingly. Subjecting the unrelated business income of nonprofit organizations to the UBIT then serves to discourage unrelated business activity to an inefficient degree. In the absence of UBIT, nonprofit organizations face the same incentives that taxable investors face between investments in bonds and investments in unrelated business. (Hines, 1999, p. 66)

Ironically, if the UBIT forces nonprofits to invest only within the few sectors that are mission related, it would be more likely to have an effect on the rates of return to investment for for-profit firms in those sectors. However, if nonprofits could invest in any sector on a tax-exempt basis, they would be unlikely to have a large enough effect to influence the for-profits' rates of return. Thus the UBIT is likely to create the very "unfairness" to for-profits that it was meant to eliminate (Rose-Ackerman, 1982a).

When are nonprofits most likely to invest in "unrelated" revenue-generating activities? Such activities will be more favored when there are complementarities in the production of the mission-related service and the unrelated activity, for example, when physical plants can be used to support both types of activities, or where staff expertise can be applied to both types of goods (Sansing, 1998). Presence of these factors enhances the returns to investing in unrelated commercial activities for two reasons. First, the lower costs of production associated with the complementarities can provide an advantage to the nonprofit in competing with other suppliers. Yetman (2003) finds that such opportunities are especially prevalent in medical and educational nonprofits. Second, where the nonprofit's costs are shared between the different sorts of activities, a tax advantage arises from declaring as much of total costs as the law will allow as being attributable to the "unrelated" commercial activity, and thus lowering the tax liabilities under the UBIT. Indeed, a substantial recent literature has arisen suggesting that cost shifting is common, so much so that the government revenues from UBIT are relatively small. Yetman (2001) reports that in the United States, tax-exempt nonprofits reported over $50 billion profit on tax-exempt activities, but for taxable activities report annual *losses* of $1 billion on about $4 billion of revenues. For 1994, Hines (1999) reports that under $200 million was collected under the UBIT; "tax experts widely agree that for many nonprofits, most, if not all, income earned from commercial undertakings is effectively tax exempt" (Cordes and Weisbrod, 1998, p. 85).

As for the decision to engage in commercial undertakings rather than "passive" investments (investments in mutual funds, bonds, etc.), the payoff from active commercial activities needs not only to be at least as high as the return from passive investment, but must also be high enough to compensate for the costs of any distraction of the organization from its core mission.

How do nonprofits shift costs from mission-driven to unrelated income? Costs that apply to both related and unrelated activities—say a building that is used for both types of activities—must be allocated between the two types of activities on a "reasonable basis," by Treasury Regulation §1.512(a)-1(c):

> Because the Treasury Regulations require only that the allocation be reasonable, and the exempt organization controls the information system that supports the cost allocation method,

exempt organizations, in practice, will be able to use allocation methods that reduce or even eliminate UBIT. The more heterogeneous the activities are with respect to the use of activity measures, the easier it is for the [tax] exempt [nonprofit] organization to find an allocation base that enables it to eliminate its tax liability. (Sansing, 1998, pp. 297–98)

It is not completely clear what the tax authorities will consider a "reasonable basis." For example, Yetman (2001) reports that it has not been determined unambiguously whether a facility that is used for unrelated business income purposes ten days in a year, when the facility is put to use for mission-related activities thirty days in the year, should have 10/40 (the proportion of days the facility was used that were for unrelated business income) or 10/365 (the proportion of days in the year the facility was used for unrelated business) of the facility's costs assigned to unrelated business; of course the nonprofit would prefer to claim 10/40 of the costs as being attributable to unrelated business earnings.

Yetman (2001) generates estimates of cost shifting by nonprofits by comparing costs claimed for tax purposes between related and unrelated activities, and what we would expect the division of costs to be if they were proportional to revenues earned in related and unrelated activities. He finds evidence that medical nonprofits have the highest degree of cost shifting, but also that there are significant, although lower, amounts of cost shifting in educational nonprofits.

Nonprofits with annual gross unrelated business revenues over $1,000 are required to submit IRS FORM 990-T, in addition to the Form 990 that declares tax-exempt earnings; the proportion of nonprofits filing 990-Ts has increased from less than 5 percent in 1975 to over 12 percent in 1995 (Yetman, 2001, p. 299). While Forms 990-T are confidential, researchers are able to use publicly available Forms 990 to identify whether the nonprofit at least filed a Form 990-T. Hines (1999), using data from Forms 990, finds that nonprofits are more likely to have unrelated business income to declare when the organization is large in terms of size of assets, and when it has higher service-related expenses, and nonprofits are less likely to have unrelated business income when government grants are a significant source of revenue. Hines finds that the evidence confirms the hypothesis that unrelated business income is indeed a less-preferred means of earning income, and so nonprofits will only do so where there is a pressing need.

As a general rule real property owned by nonprofits is exempt from the property tax. (For an extensive discussion of this subject see Brody, 2002.) The rules governing the application of the property tax are set by the individual states (although it will in general be the local governments who bear the burden of the tax exemption), and while there is some variance, particularly in whether the property tax exemption holds for property primarily used for unrelated business activity (Brody and Cordes, 1999), the exemption is general. There are two ways to think about the property tax exemption from a policy perspective: that it is a subsidy by the state to charitable activity based on the public good from nonprofit organizations; or that the exemption reflects the "sovereignty" of nonprofits, and an effort to limit state entanglement with the activities of nonprofits, especially churches. From this latter perspective we would be hesitant to view the property tax exemption as a "tax expenditure."

Estimating the value of the property tax exemption for nonprofits is a difficult exercise, first because much of the property owned by nonprofits does not have its value properly assessed (local governments, sensibly, will not devote great effort to assessing the values of properties that are not subject to tax in any case [Netzer, 2002]), and second because the general incidence of the property tax is not straightforward and remains an area of debate among economists (see for example: Fischel, 2001; Henderson, 1985; Mieszkowski and Zodrow, 1989; Zodrow, 2001). As a first observation, note that the majority of nonprofit organizations do not own real property; Cordes, Gantz, and Pollak (2002, pp. 85–88) report that only 42 percent of nonprofits own real property valued at $100,000 or more, and only 27 percent own real property valued at $500,000 or more. Nonprofits providing accommodation (retirement homes, shelters, and so on), higher education, health services, and the arts are the most likely to own real property. In aggregate, they estimate (for 1997) that U.S. nonprofits owned about $900 billion in real property, and that if we exclude houses of worship that figure drops to around $500 billion. The value of the property tax exemption has been estimated at about $6 billion (Brody and Cordes, 1999), with over $5 billion of that amount attributable to hospitals and education. The tax savings as a proportion of total revenue for all nonprofits is, by this figure, about 1.1 percent of total revenue, but Cordes, Gantz, and Pollak (2002) remind us that the value of the exemption to those nonprofits that actually own property is between 2 and 3 percent of their total revenue.

Nonprofit managers should keep in mind that the property tax exemption alone is not a reason to own property rather than rent, any more than the income tax deduction for mortgage payments is alone a reason for a household to own rather than rent. Even with an exemption from property tax, renting has its advantages, including flexibility when needs change in terms of size, design, and location of space, and the inherent risk that comes from owning property that might decrease in value (especially when the financial pages warn of a property price "bubble" in major cities).

Local governments, hard pressed for revenues, are increasingly asking property tax–exempt nonprofits for payments in lieu of taxes, or PILOTs. This source of revenue is particularly attractive when there are local nonprofits with substantial revenues whose source is from outside the jurisdiction. Brody and Cordes (1999) explain that nonprofits will prefer to make such "voluntary" payments when the goodwill generated is likely to be favorable to the nonprofit in the long term—imagine a situation where a nonprofit requests a zoning change from local government. It surely helps the case if there is a history of the organization having made PILOTs and there is a likelihood that in the absence of any payment the property tax exemption would be challenged by the local government and result in a much more damaging bill to the nonprofit.

It is debatable whether the general tax exemption for mission-related income of nonprofits, or the property tax exemption, are "tax expenditures," since that term is reserved for departures from an ideal tax system to achieve some social objective, and people will disagree on whether nonprofits would be taxed in the ideal system. But the Low-Income Housing Tax Credit (LIHTC) surely counts as a tax expenditure, as it does not generally apply to low-income housing, but is awarded by a competitive grants process, and in addition is available to for-profit organizations as well as to nonprofits.

The LIHTC was introduced in the federal tax reform of 1986, and represented recognition that while government might be helpful in providing funding for housing projects, such projects are best developed and run through the private sector. The federal government provides funds to state-level housing authorities, which are responsible for the allocation of the credits and for providing matching funds. The funds are directed at providing rental accommodation to families below 60 percent of the median income of the relevant geographic area as defined by HUD, or to households with special needs. Credits are paid over a ten-year period. The 2004 allocation by the federal government to the states is $1.80 per capita.

Each state must set aside at least 10 percent of its funding for nonprofits. The nonprofit must be a 501(c)(3) or 501(c)(4), not affiliated with or controlled by a for-profit firm, and have the fostering of low-income housing as one of its tax-exempt purposes. In their detailed evaluation of the LIHTC, Cummings and DiPasquale (1999) write, "states often give priority to nonprofit developers because they usually bring important community support and commitment to a project. In addition, nonprofits can be important players in community development strategies and this broader mission often leads them to tackle more difficult projects."

States award credits through an elaborate points system used in evaluation, reflecting the goals of state policy; Smith (1999) notes that the allocation process can become quite political, as there is much more demand for tax credit funding than there are dollars available, the applicant agency's reputation will play a role in the evaluation, and applicants will game the points system. When a nonprofit's proposal is funded, it sells the tax credits to investors who hold tax liabilities. It is difficult to obtain hard data on the value of the tax credits in the investor market, but Smith suggests that nonprofits "can expect to receive 80 cents or more on the dollar" (1999). As private investors purchase the credits, they come to own up to 99 percent of the project, although the nonprofit agency remains the controlling partner. Controversies can arise not only for the usual reasons that come from a nonprofit receiving public funds to deliver a service (examined in more depth below), but also because of the role of private investors. Nonprofits, to retain their tax-exempt status, must be directed to their mission and not to furthering the interests of for-profit investors. Yet "shelter investors approach the matter of tax credit purchase as a business deal. They want guarantees. They want security. They don't have to care if those provisions affect the tax exemption of the nonprofit organization, or preclude material participation on its part" (Sheppard, 1997).

A significant factor for nonprofits applying for the LIHTC is that it allows for up to 15 percent of the funds to be considered a "developer's fee," which can underwrite program administration, unexpected costs, and mission-related activities (Smith, 1999). However, it has been noted that while some nonprofits are truly committed to developing their projects, "others are courted by developers, are required to participate minimally, and happily accept their fees and go away" (Sheppard, 1997).

There are two interesting areas of debate around the LIHTC. The first is why it is that nonprofits' projects are more expensive than those developed by for-profits. A report by the U.S. General Accounting Office (1999) found that higher nonprofit costs were attributable to four factors: they were located more in high-poverty areas; they were eligible for additional credits because they were located in areas where development costs were high relative to incomes; they built larger units; and they were more concentrated in the high-cost Northeast or Pacific regions. However, Cummings and DiPasquale (1999) find that when various cost factors are accounted for it remains the case that nonprofits bring higher costs (but also see Roberts and Harvey, 1999, and Stegman, 1999).

The second controversy is whether the LIHTC is good policy at all. The alternative to government subsidy of the supply of housing is the subsidy of its demand, and a number of economists have argued that subsidy of the demand-side of the market—essentially by the granting of rental vouchers to low-income individuals and families—is significantly more cost effective at improving housing conditions than subsidy of housing supply (Olson, 2003; Shroder and Reiger, 2000; Sinai and Waldfogel, 2002). There is evidence that LIHTC housing "crowds out" at least some of the housing that would have existed in the absence of the policy (Sinai and Waldfogel, 2002; Malpezzi and Vandell, 2002), and vouchers have the benefits of allowing more choice by consumers and of generating more competition in the setting of rents at the low end of the market. Although there are nonprofits whose very existence is predicated on the notion that the provision of housing is important for the public good, these critiques raise the question of whether housing provision is an effective outlet for our charitable impulses, as opposed to other services (also see, for a general analysis of U.S. housing markets, Quigley and Raphael, 2004).

Another important source of revenue for many nonprofits arises from contracts with different levels of government to deliver services. For many human services, a decision by government to fund the service does not necessarily entail having a government agency deliver the service, and a choice can be made to contract with a private organization. Governments have the ability, through their power to tax, to raise significant revenues for services, especially important when the social norms for private funding of human services are not strong enough to overcome the problems of free-riding. But that does not mean governments are necessarily the best organizations for the *delivery* of the services (Young, 1999).

When do we expect the contracts to be with a nonprofit? One, perhaps surprising, result of the modern theory of contracts is that in a world where the government manager could perfectly monitor the performance of the individuals tasked with delivering a service, and in addition could perfectly specify in the contract exactly what was to be done in the service delivery under every possible contingency, it would not matter whether the government supplied the service "in-house" or contracted out to a private (for-profit or nonprofit) agency, since in any case the service delivery would be of the same quality and cost (Shleifer, 1998). The decision on whether to contract out is interesting because we do not live in such a perfect world, but instead live with imperfect monitoring and incomplete contracts.

As a general rule, we expect public sector employees to have "low-powered" incentives for discovering innovations in the quality of service delivery or ways to control costs. Also, we know that many cost-reduction strategies might come with decreases in the quality of service. For those activities where the quality of product is easily monitored, and there are high probabilities for useful innovation, we expect that governments will choose to contract with for-profit firms, with their "high-powered" incentives (Hart, Shleifer, and Vishny, 1997). This explains why for many physical goods used by government the provision is by for-profits: there is a trend of ongoing innovation in the production of manufactured goods, and quality is relatively easily verified by government inspectors. For services where there is some possibility for innovation, but where quality is somewhat more difficult to verify, the government would prefer to contract with nonprofits. Nonprofits have an advantage over government in-house service delivery in that, with the competition between nonprofits, there are more incentives for innovation. Moreover, nonprofits have the advantage over for-profit service delivery in that non-profit managers have less incentive to surreptitiously reduce the quality of provision while cutting costs, since they are restrained (to a degree) from being able to personally benefit from the increase in net revenues. Ben-Ner (2002) argues that the trend in improving the flows, analysis, and storage of information, combined with the discipline that derives from increased competition in the for-profit sector, might reduce the advantage nonprofits have over for-profits in contracting in the future. However, a countervailing force might be the improvements in nonprofit governance that arise from those same information-management innovations.

Salamon (1999b) provides a useful reminder to U.S. readers that the assumption that European nations have large government bureaucracies for delivery of human services is incorrect, and that there is a significant amount of service delivery by nonprofits, under contract with government. He notes that the collaboration between sectors in northern Europe is long-standing, and in part was a way of dealing with religious differences. Specifically, using government funds to finance services delivered by private organizations allowed the continuation of

Protestant hospitals and schools, Catholic hospitals and schools, organizations with ties to labor unions, and so on.

In the United States, the expansion of government contracting began in the 1960s with federal government spending on new programs such as community action agencies, mental health centers, neighborhood health centers, and child protection agencies. Contracting expanded further in the 1970s with government-funded support of a network of drug and alcohol treatment programs, in the 1980s with funding of nonprofits dealing with homelessness and AIDS, and in the 1980s and 1990s with a devolution of many other services previously delivered by government, especially in connection with the 1996 welfare reforms (Smith, 1999). Smith sees as one of the most important developments in government-nonprofit relations the increase in managed care in state and local government, beginning in the late 1980s. Under managed care, a third-party agency is contracted on a capitated basis (i.e., based on the size of the population in the catchment area) to manage a service, which in turn subcontracts with nonprofit service providers. This was seen as a way to increase efficiency in the delivery of services, with lower costs and more opportunity for outcome-based performance evaluation, although Smith (1999) warns that the system can leave the locus of accountability for performance somewhat uncertain.

A current challenge for nonprofit managers is the increased appeal for government financing of services through consumer vouchers (Grønbjerg and Salamon, 2002). While nonprofits have always competed for government contracts, vouchers change where the competition takes place, and also open the door to increased competition from for-profit organizations and faith-based organizations.

Extending the Knowledge Base

The challenges and outcomes arising from the increased scale of government contracting with faith-based providers of services in the United States since the Charitable Choice provisions of the 1996 reform of the American public assistance system have generated significant questions in the following areas:

- the interpretation of constitutional provisions protecting free expression and nonestablishment of religion;
- whether allowing faith-based providers to be exempt from some of the usual government regulations on contractors enhances or lessens equality of opportunity among potential contractors;
- whether faith-based organizations are efficient or cost-effective relative to secular providers or government agencies; and
- the administrative challenges for the parties to these new forms of contracting.

During the period of expansion of contracting with nonprofits that began in the 1960s there was certainly substantial contracting with faith-related organizations (Smith and Sosen, 2001, who distinguish between *faith-related* organizations, with an affiliation to a denomination, but which operate much the same as a secular nonprofit human services agency, and those institutions whose operations are more explicitly influenced by their faith, or *faith-based* organizations).

According to John DiIulio, former head of the White House Office of Community and Faith-Based Initiatives, faith-based organizations "have literally received tens of billions of dollars in public support." However, he notes that, "The only nonprofit organizations that have consistently been left out are grassroots religious groups" (DiIulio, 2004). Charitable Choice, introduced in 1996, and expanded under President G. W. Bush, is intended to make eligible for government contracting these grassroots groups. The large charities mentioned above are treated as "essentially secular organizations with a religious link or inspiration" (Carlson-Thies, 2004, p. 59), but there have been claims that smaller faith-based organizations have faced discrimination in contracting, even when their programming was purely secular. These faith-based organizations should be distinguished from congregations, which for the most part do not operate their own human services programs, but instead contribute to service provision through coordinating the efforts of volunteers to work with other nonprofit organizations, which might in some cases be secular. Chaves (2002) points out that, in 1998, only 3 percent of U.S. congregations received any funding from government.

The rules comprising Charitable Choice are as follows (Carlson-Thies, 2004):

1. No organization can be excluded from federal funding because it is religious.
2. The government must respect the religious character of faith-based providers, which includes allowing the institutions to maintain their religious character and can take this into account in hiring staff.
3. Respect for the religious liberty of clients must be maintained, which means ensuring that alternatives are available for clients who do not wish to deal with faith-based providers.
4. Public funds must be used for the public purpose for which they were intended, and cannot be used to fund inherently religious activities.

Are the services provided by faith-based organizations different as a result of the religious beliefs of the employees (and perhaps also the clients)? This may well be the case. However, there is no tangible evidence at this point that faith-based nonprofit service providers deliver services markedly differently, or more "holistically," than secular organizations (Monsma and Mounts, 2001). However, there is reason to believe that a large expansion of government funds to faith-based providers could ultimately provoke a change in these organizations. James Q. Wilson (2000) writes that, "Government aid tends to turn recipients into the organizational equivalent of the bureaucracy that supplies the aid. The essence of the religious experience is . . . not one that could be supplied under the aegis of the Federal Register and the United States Code." There is a vast amount of evidence on how contracting with government changes the nature of secular nonprofits, from the mission of the organization to the role of the boards of trustees, and it is hard to imagine that any church entering into a contract agreement with government would be immune to change.

When it comes to the way societies organize institutions for the financing, production, and distribution of goods and services, economists tend to be optimists, holding that as technologies and societal wants change, institutional structures will also change, in ways that enhance efficiency. Entrepreneurs, in the public, nonprofit, and for-profit sectors, will suggest innovative changes in institutional arrangements when it becomes apparent that existing arrangements are not optimal.

For that reason, we predict that government-nonprofit relations will continue to adjust, in terms of direct support, contracting, and taxation, so that the particular relations we find at this date might be very different twenty years hence. The activities that nonprofits perform now, and the degree to which they receive government support, are not set in stone.

Some particular developments might provoke the following research questions:

1. Can we expect greater use of government-funded consumer vouchers in the future? How would this affect the level of government funding going to nonprofits, if for-profit firms were able to compete for voucher-funded activities?

2. How will the entry of more faith-related agencies into the field of contracting with government affect the position of current nonprofits receiving government contracts, especially if there is no overall increase in the level of government funding?

3. At time of writing there are signals from the federal government that major tax reform is a possibility during the next few years. How will any changes to individual and corporation taxes change the financial decisions of nonprofit organizations and their donors? Will the property tax continue to be the key source of local government revenue? If not, what taxes will replace it, and will they confer on nonprofits the same tax advantages as the property-tax exemption? Would nonprofits be tax exempt under a new (to the United States) national value-added tax?

Improving Practice

While the benefits of direct and indirect government funding to nonprofits are easy to see, there are potential costs to these funds as well which go beyond the impact on taxpayers. Authors have identified two types of unintended consequences of government subsidies, which may harm nonprofits and thus must be considered in financial decision-making. These consequences are *crowding out* and *resource dependency*.

The "public goods crowding out hypothesis" asserts that the public's willingness to support a nonprofit might be diminished if the government increases responsibility for the organization's funding. In other words, government subsidies—either direct or indirect—might displace private gifts. There are several reasons why this might be the case (Brooks, 2000). First, a nonprofit may begin to look like a quasi-public agency when it receives a large portion of its revenues from government sources. Second, it may also look less economically viable, discouraging donors who seek long-term organizational health. Third, increases in government subsidies may lower the financial control over nonprofits of some individual donors, leading them to decrease their donations.

The crowding-out hypothesis does not state that positive government social spending should always vary inversely with private charitable giving, just that the *relationship* between public and private funding—in isolation from other variables—should be negative. In fact, Salamon et al. (1999) show that countries with the most generous government social spending per capita also tend to have the highest levels of private giving: In general, rich countries fund charitable activities both publicly and privately more liberally than do poorer countries. However, the crowding out hypothesis suggests that private giving would be even *higher* in developed countries if government funding were lower.

Many tests of the crowding out hypothesis have appeared in the economics literature, as well as a comprehensive survey (Steinberg, 1993). The results are mixed, but the majority of studies suggest that a dollar in government subsidies crowds out private donations at a rate that is less than dollar-for-dollar—usually less than 35 cents. In the few articles that have looked at it, this pattern of crowding out has also sometimes held for volunteering time to nonprofit organizations (e.g., Menchik and Weisbrod, 1987). For example, Day and Devlin (1996) found that an extra $10,000 in public education spending per capita in Canada in the mid-1990s was associated with a decrease in total average volunteering of about 5.6 hours per year.

"Resource dependency" refers to the case in which nonprofits become overly reliant on government as a source of funds. The dangers from this are twofold. First, nonprofits that are excessively reliant on government funds are exposed to the vagaries of public budgeting processes, which can change their funding dramatically from year to year (Froelich, 1999). Second, they may succumb to "vendorism," effectively ceding control of the organizational mission to funding agencies when financial survival depends on providing what the government requests (Smith and Lipsky, 1993; Grønbjerg, 1993). O'Regan and Oster (2002), for example, in a study of New York nonprofits, found that increased government contracting will result in a greater demand for monitoring activities by the nonprofit's board, which will "crowd out" the board's operational role, and also lead to less time spent on fund-raising from alternative sources by board members. The clear implication of these dangers is that *nonprofits are wise to diversify funding sources to the extent that they can, not relying excessively on government funding.*

As Smith (1999) notes, many nonprofits arise out of a community with the desire to provide a service to those in need within the community, for whom volunteers and donors feel a special connection. Governments, on the other hand, approach the delivery of services with a special attention to fairness, where service deliverers will be held accountable if it is suspected that one group is being treated differently from another. Out of these different perspectives, tensions are bound to arise within the nonprofit relying on government contracts. For example, a nonprofit social services organization which relies on government contracts to fund its operations may find it has lost the ability to choose its clients, as eligibility for services will be determined by state policy and referrals and not set at the discretion of the nonprofit. If the nonprofit and state goals on serving clients co-incide, this might not be so much of a problem. But what of those cases where the nonprofit wants to serve some individu-als it believes are deserving, but who do not meet state eligibility requirements?

We do not wish to stress only the negative: even with our caveats regarding crowding out and vendorism, the government is an important source of funds that can provide key support to the nonprofit and its mission. But nonprofit leaders should also have a sense of the indirect consequences of accepting government funds.

The research surveyed in this chapter also stimulates a number of questions that nonprofit managers might ask as they continue to cultivate and monitor their relationships with government:

1. Is our organization making the most of the indirect sub-sidies we receive? For example, given that these subsidies are effectively a "matching grant" from the government, can we possibly use this as a kind of leverage with donors?
2. As our organization expands, what are the prospects for commercial revenues? If there are any, will they constitute unrelated business income, subject to tax?
3. While nonprofits are exempt from corporate income taxes everywhere in the United States, other sorts of taxes are imposed asymmetrically across jurisdictions. For example, some states and localities impose PILOTs, others impose (or are contemplating) property taxes. Should our organi-zation take tax treatment into account as we select a locality for operations? Is our current tax environment congenial to nonprofit activity?
4. If the government contracts with us for services, are these contracts ultimately in our interest? Are government funds crowding out private philanthropy? Are we resource de-pendent? As a result, if and when government funding streams are altered, will we be dangerously financially ex-posed?

Conclusion

Nonprofit organizations are always mindful of their relationship with government, in terms of tax treatment, potential for grants (either directly to the organization or indirectly through the subsidy of clients), and contracts for the provision of services. In all these respects there are parallels in the for-profit sector, but a key difference is that the goals of a nonprofit organization are complex, and will typically extend beyond the maximization of net revenues. Indeed, discretion over the activities and mission of the organization matters in an important way. While we have tried to remind nonprofit leaders of some of the pitfalls of increasing revenues from government, we have tried not to present too bleak a picture; it is not as if the goals of government social service, health, education, and cultural departments are completely at odds with the missions of the nonprofit organizations who could work with government in the supply of those services. However, the nonprofit leader will want to keep a watchful eye on trends in government funding and in government thinking about what sorts of programs justify taxpayer support, since the dynamic nature of government-nonprofit relations poses the greatest danger of becoming resource dependent.

5

Fee Income and Commercial Ventures

Estelle James and Dennis R. Young

Introduction

Operating income from fees for service has long been an important component of the financial support of nonprofit organizations in the United States, and it is more important now than ever. Such income comes in various forms. In some cases, nonprofits charge fees for mainline services that contribute directly to their social missions, to partially or fully offset the costs of providing those services. In other cases, nonprofits charge fees for ancillary services, in order to generate financial profits to support other activities or contribute to the accumulation of capital assets.

Both of these practices have deep historical roots. For instance, when Catholic Sister Elizabeth Seton established a school for area residents in Emmitsburg, Maryland, in 1809, tuition covered some of the costs, but the education of impoverished children was financed by commercial activities, including the sale of cloth and clothes (McCarthy, 2003). Bible sales by the American Bible Society and Massachusetts General Hospital's ownership of the Massachusetts Hospital Life Insurance Company offer prominent nineteenth-century examples of substantial commercially generated income for nonprofits, while Girl Scout cookies and New York University's ownership of the Mueller Macaroni Company are among the more famous nonprofit commercial ventures of the twentieth century.

Fees, of course, have long been common in nonprofit venues such as the arts, education, and health care. The most recent available figures (circa 1997) indicate that private fee income (broadly defined to include investment income) constitutes almost half of the revenues of the U.S. nonprofit sector, compared to a third from government and a fifth from philanthropy (Salamon, 2002a). Similarly, private fee income accounted for approximately half of the sector's revenue growth in the period from 1977 to 1997. Not all fields within the nonprofit sector are equally reliant on fee revenue, of course. Education is most reliant at approximately 65 percent, followed by health care (54 percent), arts and culture (45 percent), social and legal services (43 percent), and civic organizations (27 percent) (Salamon, 1999a). (Note that government reimbursement or insurance payments such as those from Medicare and Medicaid are not counted as fee revenue in these figures.)

While reliance on private fee income is holding steady as a proportion of overall sector finances, this source has been growing especially rapidly in fields that have not traditionally been fee-dependent. For example, between 1977 and 1997, fee income increased 587 percent in social services, 272 percent in arts and culture, and 220 percent in civic organizations, compared to 77 percent in education (Salamon, 2002a). Thus, the adoption of fee-based practices is becoming more pervasive. In addition, commercial practices such as undertaking venture activity explicitly to generate profits are also increasing. Thus, gross unrelated business income increased steadily, in current dollars, from $3.4 billion in 1991 to $7.8 billion in 1997, while taxes paid by nonprofits on unrelated business increased from $116.6 million to $418.4 million (Riley, 2002a, 2002b).

If one takes a naïve view of nonprofits as pure "charities," the heavy reliance of these organizations on fees and commercial income may come as a revelation. However, this dependence is actually quite consistent with several streams of theory addressed to understanding the role and behavior of nonprofit organizations in a market economy. On the "supply side," scholars including Hansmann (1980), James (1983), and Young (1983) have pointed to the important role of (social) entrepreneurs as catalysts in establishing nonprofit organizations, new programs, and other initiatives. Entrepreneurs are opportunistic agents who operate in the marketplace. So it should be no surprise that they would exploit fee income or profitable venture activity as part of the resource packages that secure their social ventures.

On the "demand side," one of the key streams of nonprofit theory is "contract failure" associated with the problem of asymmetric information between producers and consumers of certain goods and services, sometimes called "trust goods"—such as day care for young children or nursing home care for the elderly. This theory suggests an important role for nonprofit organizations in the provision of private marketable goods and services, hence the likelihood that a substantial portion of the economic support for nonprofits would be derived from fees. Government funding is also an important source of nonprofit finance. But most of that funding comes in the form of fees and consumer subsidies or tax credits, which require the same entrepreneurial behavior as private fee revenues (Weisbrod, 1998).

Finally, an important behavioral theory of nonprofit organizations, originally formulated by James (1983) and expanded by Weisbrod (1998) and others, argues that nonprofits are really multiproduct firms run by managers who generate profits in some service areas so that they can support the provision of other less marketable but important mission-related services. Here again, fees and commercial activity are seen as intrinsic elements in the economic infrastructure of nonprofit operations. Still, fee income has never been a completely comfortable fit with nonprofit organizations, for various reasons related both to ideology and behavioral risks such as "mission drift."

Our intent in this chapter is to develop a firm theoretical foundation for the appropriate place of fee income in nonprofit finance. We focus on two broad components of such revenue— fees derived from private payments associated with the delivery of mission-related goods and services, and revenues developed from profitable commercial ventures that may or may not have a close connection with the mission.

In the next section we review, in greater detail, the present patterns and trends in nonprofit fees and commercial revenues.

After that we examine variations of current fee practices in different parts of the sector. The conceptual foundation for nonprofit fee and commercial income is analyzed next. Subsequently, we step back to identify further research needed to verify the hypothesized relationships and connect the conceptual framework to management practices. Finally, we offer a series of diagnostic questions for nonprofit managers seeking to enhance their fees and commercial revenues in pursuit of an expanded financial base for their mission-related activities.

Patterns and Trends

Nonprofit dependence on fee and commercial income varies by field of service, has changed over time, and is influenced by various other factors. As noted above, we observe substantial differences among broad fields of service such as education, health care, social services, and the arts, both in the degree of reliance on fees and in the relative growth of fee income. Further insights may be derived from examining narrower slices within these fields. For example, private higher education receives some 70 percent of its revenues from fees, more than nonprofit educational institutions in general. Symphonies, theaters, and dance companies all depend on earned income for roughly 60 percent of their revenue, substantially more than nonprofit arts and cultural institutions overall (Salamon, 1999a). These figures are not surprising because nonprofits in these fields are traditionally more dependent on tuitions and box office ticket sales, compared to other institutions such as research institutes or museums. The services offered in these fields have much of the character of a "private good," allowing them to be more easily sold in the marketplace. By comparison, civic organizations and foreign aid nonprofits depend on fees for only a quarter of their income, as their services more closely resemble "public goods" not easily transacted in the marketplace (Salamon, 1999a). Nonetheless, it is interesting that revenue growth in the latter fields increasingly emphasizes fee income, suggesting that even nonprofits that produce essentially public goods are finding closely related services that they can sell. This pattern is consistent with data assembled by Segal and Weisbrod (1998) which show that dependence on program service revenue (including government reimbursements) for U.S. 501(c)(3) organizations increased from 63 percent in 1982 to 71.3 percent in 1993.

Similarly, the degree to which nonprofits undertake commercial ventures varies by field of service. Based on a self-reporting sample of nonprofits responding to an on-line survey, Massarsky and Beinhacker (2002) found organizations in the field of arts and culture most likely to operate "earned-income ventures," followed by health services, "public society" organizations, environmental organizations, educational institutions, and religious organizations.

Analyses carried out by Cordes and Weisbrod (1998) demonstrate a statistically significant relationship between field of service and dependence on fee or commercial income, using two measures—program service revenue as a percent of total revenue and likelihood that a nonprofit files an unrelated business (UBIT) tax return. With program service revenue as the dependent variable, health care is calculated to have the largest impact on fee revenue, followed by education, human services, and the arts. (Government reimbursements from Medicare and Medicaid are included in fee income for health care.) Nonprofit health providers are also shown to be most likely to report revenues subject to UBIT, with nonprofits in arts and education next. Human service providers are much less likely to file UBIT returns than other types of nonprofits.

The Cordes and Weisbrod analysis also indicates that dependence on fee and commercial revenue is greater for larger organizations (as measured by assets). Perhaps it is more difficult for small nonprofits to cover the start-up and fixed costs that are necessary to generate fees. Massarsky and Beinhacker (2002) find that older organizations and those with larger numbers of employees and larger budgets are more likely to report an earned income venture. Cordes and Weisbrod (1998) demonstrate that nonprofits located in states with relatively high taxes depend more heavily on commercial revenues—possibly because nonprofits are able to "shift" some of their costs from nontaxable mission activities to taxable business activities, giving them a greater competitive advantage relative to for-profits in higher tax states.

Furthermore, the Cordes and Weisbrod analysis indicates that the more a nonprofit's contributed income derives from public grants, the less it tends to depend on fee and commercial income—implying that public funds crowd out entrepreneurial behavior to a larger extent than private donations. Using data for 2,679 nonprofits observed from 1985 to 1993, Segal and Weisbrod (1998) find that declines in donations yield significant increases in commercial activity for some industry sectors but not for others. In particular, a negative relationship is found in the housing, arts, and culture subsectors, a positive relationship in universities and human service organizations, and no relationship is found in hospitals. This suggests that an untapped potential for commercial activity exists and is used to compensate for declining philanthropy in some cases, but not all.

The pursuit of fees also appears to be strongly influenced by "interdependencies" between mission and prospective commercial initiatives. First, a nonprofit's mission-related activity may involve certain resources that can easily be shared with a commercial initiative, giving the nonprofit a cost advantage for such an activity. For example, a museum already has gallery space that can easily double as an attractive facility in which to hold a private party during off hours. Second, a nonprofit's mission may be complementary, in a demand sense, to certain commercial initiatives. For instance, museum patronage generates demand for an in-house parking garage or a gift shop, which can then serve outside traffic as well. Finally, a nonprofit's mission may be partially addressed through commercial initiatives that are capable of generating fee revenue. For instance, the museum can sponsor occasional "blockbuster" shows that generate substantial revenues while also serving its education mission. A recent study by Young (2006), based on a survey of nonprofits with ventures in the field of community and economic development, showed that most commercial ventures have a close relationship to mission and special competencies associated with mission. The survey by Massarsky and Beinhacker (2002) also produced corroborating evidence. Overall, 87 percent of respondents explicitly tied their ventures to the organization's mission.

Current Practice

Nonprofit "earned income" practices have become increasingly diverse and sophisticated over the last decade. Venture philanthropists and even traditional foundations now require nonprofits to develop business plans to demonstrate how the applicant organizations will sustain themselves, or their proposed new initiatives, after the initial donation is exhausted. This new emphasis on the part of institutional funders, along with the squeezing of government funds and increasing competition for limited charitable donations, has led nonprofits to become more creative and systematic in pursuing fee revenues and commercial income.

Three types of practices generate earned revenues: pricing, new commercial ventures, and corporate partnerships. "Pricing" encompasses various ways in which nonprofits choose to charge for their services. "New commercial ventures" refer to the commercial initiatives nonprofits undertake and the organizational forms used to pursue them. "Corporate partnerships" include alliances that nonprofits are entering into with profit-making businesses, which yield net revenues to the nonprofit.

One way that nonprofits can generate additional fee revenue is to charge for services they previously provided free. As Oster, Gray, and Weinberg (2004) note, however, this is not a trivial decision. First, a nonprofit's core values and mission may be intrinsically tied to free service. For example, the Cleveland Museum of Art, which is well endowed, has always opened its galleries to the community without charge and considers it a basic part of its tradition. Similarly, the Free Clinic in Cleveland ties its very identity to the practice of free health care to indigent and uninsured individuals. It would be considered unethical and destructive to the ethos of the Red Cross if it charged for disaster relief services. More generally, imposing a price rations usage by turning away people who are unwilling or unable to pay the price, creating a tension between service usage and revenue generation.

There are, however, some compensating factors in this tension. In general, prices serve a positive rationing function in a market economy, helping to efficiently allocate scarce goods and services to those consumers who value them most. For example, charging prices for admission to a nonprofit theater of limited capacity helps ensure that those individuals who value theater the most will be able to see the performance. In addition, some nonprofit organizations find that imposing a (perhaps nominal) fee actually enhances mission by associating greater gravity to the service. Customers or clients may take it more seriously if they have to pay, and staff may give their clients more serious attention if they know they are paying customers. This may hold for services such as drug and alcohol counseling, education, and preventive health care. Moreover, charging a nominal fee may help remove a stigma associated with "charity." If poor elderly residents are charged a nominal fee for a bus service that takes them to the community center, or offered lunch at a modest charge, they may be more likely to utilize these services than if they were offered for free. Also, fees can have a signaling effect that consumers use to judge quality. A day care center that charges a price may be viewed by some as better quality than a free day care service, and may be more heavily used.

Finally, a major reason why nonprofits should charge fees for some of their services is that this garners them the revenue to produce more and reach more clients than they could otherwise. Often, the choice is to charge and expand or not to charge and contract. So the issue generally is not whether pricing should be used, but rather how it should be used.

To reconcile revenue and mission-related goals, many nonprofits tailor their fee schedules in a manner that is sensitive to consumers' willingness and ability to pay. For the nonprofit, price discrimination permits service to clients who are unable to pay, but who are important as mission targets, and raises additional money from those clients who are able to pay relatively more. For example, some orchestra seats may be set aside for students or young people with low incomes, with losses covered by more affluent clients who purchase the remaining tickets at much higher prices. Or charges for health or social services can be differentiated by family income so that needy clients are not excluded. Museums or performing arts institutions can charge different prices on different days of the week, or offer discounts for families with children, with the understanding that these policies address alternative audiences with different levels of willingness and ability to pay.

In order to more fully appreciate the nuances of price discrimination, as well as other pricing approaches, a brief digression on the difference between "marginal cost" and "average cost" of providing a good or service is helpful here. If a nonprofit is serving 100 clients, its marginal cost is the additional cost of serving the 101st client, whereas its average (or per unit) cost is the total cost of serving 100 clients, divided by 100. Thus, for any given level of service a nonprofit can estimate both its average and marginal cost. Note, these two costs are not equal, in general, especially where fixed costs ("set up" costs which must be incurred before the first units of service can be offered) are high. Understanding the difference between marginal and average cost also helps illuminate why engaging in price discrimination is sometimes essential for an organization to break even. An organization with high fixed costs and low marginal costs (additional costs of serving clients once the fixed costs are accommodated) will have high average cost over a wide range of output. In this circumstance there may be no level of service for which all potential clients are willing to pay a price equal to average cost. However, by charging some people more than average cost and others less, the organization may be able to find a way to minimize losses, break even, or perhaps even make a profit.

For-profit firms also engage in price discrimination, but only if this serves to increase net revenues. In particular, businesses would practically never set lower echelon prices below marginal cost, because this would entail lower profits. Nonprofits may do so, however, to reach clients who cannot afford to pay marginal cost.

Also, nonprofits may find it easier to differentiate fees because clients may trust them more and may therefore be more willing to honestly reveal personal information, such as family income. So-called "sliding scale" practices are common to the nonprofit sector. In one variation, certain classes of consumers are asked to pay more than average cost, generating a margin that can be used to cover the fixed cost of the program or to subsidize other groups who pay less. A second variation tailors prices so that most consumers pay less than average cost, but to different degrees. This is a common practice among institutions of higher education, where most graduate students (and some undergraduates) are subsidized through tuition remission and fellowships. The difference between average cost and price for these students is covered by contributions and government grants (James, 1978, 1980, 1986; James and Neuberger, 1981; Oster, Gray, and Weinberg, 2004).

Finally, a third variation is for a nonprofit to vary the levels or quality of service along with the price to different groups of consumers. For example, higher paying opera goers get better seats and also generate more net revenue, while lower paying clients sit in the cheap seats. Similarly, members of a community center who utilize the more exclusive health club services may be paying higher margins that help to subsidize less wealthy clientele. For-profits also engage in similar practices—Broadway plays and airline flights come immediately to mind. The difference between them is subtle but crucial. If the activity is intended primarily as a revenue producer, nonprofit pricing policy is likely to follow a profit maximizing strategy. However, if the activity is substantially mission-driven, pricing policy will depart from that which would produce the greatest net revenue. Indeed, many nonprofit services are appropriately priced to lose money as they contribute in some way to mission—while for-profits will never intentionally do that.

In general, price discrimination can often be a productive strategy for nonprofit organizations, but it requires some work, creativity, and experimentation. It is only with reference to purpose that a nonprofit can choose its appropriate pricing policies. Market research is needed to find the right structure and levels of prices, and evaluation and adjustment over time are required to ensure that prices remain synchronized with mission, market demand, and costs.

The example of membership in a community center highlights another interesting fee strategy for nonprofit organizations—the bundling of different services into packages with a single "membership" fee (Oster, 2004; Oster, Gray, and Weinberg, 2004). This can be a helpful strategy, for several reasons. First, package prices reduce transaction costs compared to collecting fees for use of every individual service. If a YMCA or JCC charged a client separately for using the pool or the gym, administration would be more complex and costly while users would be more burdened making and paying for these choices, perhaps resulting in reduced demand overall. Package pricing may also allow the organization to promote its mission more effectively. For example, concert goers often purchase subscription packages that include a mix of different musical offerings—some well known and popular, and others more experimental or avant-garde. If the orchestra's mission includes exposing people to new music, it can advance this mission by selling packages that include such music. Again, for-profits may follow a similar package strategy, but the objective for them is to maximize their net revenues, rather than shape behavior or tastes.

Nonprofit organizations undertake explicitly commercial ventures for two purposes: to raise net revenues or to contribute in some direct way to the achievement of the nonprofit's social mission (or both). Massarsky and Beinhacker (2002) found in their survey that more than half of respondents operated their ventures at break-even or to generate a surplus, and two-thirds cited financial return as the primary reason for the venture. Nonetheless, the vast majority of respondents tied their ventures to their mission in some way. A large proportion of respondents indicated that their ventures provided employment, training, and therapeutic opportunities for their constituents, generated positive community relations, or helped revitalize their neighborhood and community. Three-quarters of respondents indicated that they considered social benefit in evaluating the "profitability" of their venture, though only 8 percent calculated social returns on their investments.

Clearly the notion that a commercial venture can contribute directly to mission underlies much of the rationale for what is known in contemporary terms as "social enterprise." In Europe, for example, social enterprise is seen as a way to train or employ marginalized groups (the unemployed, physically or mentally challenged, etc.), through direct market participation, so that they become more productive members of society. In a sample of commercial ventures undertaken in the field of community and economic development in the United States, a number of driving social objectives were identified, including employment and training, local business development, helping low income residents, and improving local community infrastructure (Young, 2006).

Commercial enterprises can be undertaken by nonprofits in different formats. One way is to include the venture as a direct program of the organization. Another is to organize it as a separately incorporated venture, owned or controlled by the nonprofit. Some evidence suggests that ventures intended solely for net revenue generating purposes are more often separately incorporated (generally as for-profit corporations) while those more intrinsic to mission favor the internal programming format (Young, 2006). A venture tied closely to mission can be better controlled and coordinated with other mission-related activities within the core organization. In contrast, a venture intended essentially for revenue generating purposes may best be kept separate to avoid cultural conflicts between profit-oriented and mission-oriented staff and to ensure that commercial activity does not threaten the core organization's values or tax-exempt status. Furthermore, the profit-making form may bring with it certain practical advantages, such as greater access to capital, than would be available to the nonprofit for an internally organized venture (Skloot, 1988).

Finally, nonprofits exploit various kinds of competitive advantages in pursuing their commercial ventures. Three very important sources of competitive advantage are their good name, intellectual property rights, and other mission-related expertise. Examples are Arthritis Society aspirins, Cleveland Orchestra CDs, museum of art reproductions, Public Broadcasting System Sesame Street books and toys, botanical garden seeds and garden tools, and university alumni association educational tours to exotic places. These products are attractive because they reflect the high quality associated with the organization's general reputation and institutional integrity. These reputations can give the nonprofit a competitive advantage in the commercial market. It doesn't always work out that way, however. The Arthritis Society's brand of aspirin was a failure, possibly *because* aspirin is a commodity without much quality differentiation to underpin a reputational advantage or higher price. Such examples are also a reminder that nonprofits bear serious risk when they put their names and prestige on the line for a commercial product.

Some nonprofits exploit other, more mundane factors, such as locational convenience, that give them a special cost or demand-related advantage. Museums successfully run in-house gift shops, restaurants, and parking garages because visitors demand these services in the course of touring the exhibits. Universities can successfully run bookstores, fitness facilities, and parking lots for the same reason. Another factor is the availability of mission-related resources whose costs can be easily shared with a commercial venture. A museum with attractive exhibit space or an arboretum with beautiful grounds can rent these facilities during off hours to private parties for weddings, bar mitzvahs, or corporate receptions, at a lower marginal cost than commercial catering halls, since they have a large available capacity stemming from their mission. A museum can open its parking facilities to general use during hours when the museum is not open. A nonprofit that owns its own building can rent out some office space to other organizations. And so on.

Increasingly, nonprofits generate commercial revenue by teaming up with business corporations in mutually beneficial partnership arrangements of various kinds. The simplest form of such collaboration is for the nonprofit to make its asset of trust and reputation available to a corporation—for a price. For example, the nonprofit may attach its name to a corporate product, such as a credit card, a tobacco patch, a health insurance plan, or a nutritional food. MBNA makes a contribution to Stanford University each time its Stanford Alumni Association MasterCard is used to make a purchase. The first such venture was started by American Express in collaboration with the Statue of Liberty–Ellis Island Foundation to help restore the Statue of Liberty in the 1980s, and currently American Express has such arrangements with other charities, such as Share Our Strength, where credit card purchases help fund international hunger relief.

Alternatively, the nonprofit may endorse certain brands in exchange for substantial payments from the corporation, such as the American Cancer Society's and the American Lung Association's agreements with tobacco patch manufacturers, or the American Humane Association's arrangement with pet food manufacturer Ralston Purina. Or, a nonprofit may offer "good housekeeping" seals of approval to providers of worthy products that contribute to its social goal. For example, the American Heart Association puts its seal on food products that meet its standards, in exchange for a set fee. Of course, the very real danger in these arrangements is that the organization sells its name for a price to a corporation that does not deserve it. Due diligence is essential here so that the nonprofit does not lose its reputation as a result of the deal.

Going beyond this nominal type of collaboration, nonprofits can sell or license their expert services or intellectual properties to corporate partnerships, in return for income. For example, IONA Senior Services sold its expertise to the Fannie Mae Corporation, on a contract basis, to help the corporation's employees cope better with problems of caring for their elderly parents. Similarly, it is common for corporations to support educational programs by providing scholarships to executive MBA and other midcareer programs.

One of the biggest and most controversial examples of the sale of intellectual property rights involves partnerships between universities and corporations, the latter offering contracts and grants for research in biochemicals, genetic engineering, and other programs with potential commercial applications. In exchange for these grants, the corporations get priority access to research findings and may patent some applications of the research, which may limit the access of others for many years. Besides getting the grants and contracts, the universities may be joint holders of the patents. This has generated substantial controversy on grounds that it threatens the integrity of the university's mission by limiting the distribution of new knowledge or adversely affecting university priorities. But it does allow the research to move forward, probably more than it could without corporate funding (Kirp, 2003; Powell and Owen-Smith, 1998).

In general, a potential problem with all these commercial practices is that they may change the culture of the nonprofit. Personnel who are hired with the expectation that they will raise revenues may bring with them values that place revenues above mission. If they succeed in bringing in substantial revenues, this potentially enables the organization to carry out more of its social objectives, but it also raises their status within the organization, which may adopt the pursuit of profits as a priority in itself. The head of the nonprofit, who has limited time and capacity, may devote an increasing amount of effort to making money instead of furthering the original mission of the organization. These are some of the dangers that nonprofits must avoid as they embark upon the search for fees and commercial ventures.

Theory

In the paradigm of economics, the fee and commercial income that will be generated by nonprofit organizations depends on demand and supply. First, we need to understand what kinds of goods and services people are likely to buy and second, we need to understand why and how nonprofits are willing to supply them.

Nonprofits can secure fee and commercial income only by selling goods and services that are sufficiently "private" in character. In particular, the organization must be able to "exclude" individuals who are not willing to pay—otherwise everyone would consume but expect others to cover the cost. (While "suggested" voluntary fees are also possible, such payments are considered "donations" for purposes of this discussion.) Nonprofits that produce services such as public art or advocacy for social change are not able to exclude and charge. However, nonprofits do produce many excludable goods and services—ranging from social services like day care or nursing home care to performing arts and educational services.

The distinction between public and private goods may be further qualified by considering a second characteristic—whether

Table 5.1. Taxonomy of Public and Private Goods

	Rival	Nonrival
Excludable	Private Goods	Toll Goods
	Girl Scout Cookies	Museums and Public
	Counseling	Lectures—up to full capacity
Nonexcludable	Common Pool Goods	Pure Public Goods
	Food Banks*	Environmental
	Soup Kitchens*	Advocacy
		Public Radio
	*Technically, these services are excludable but the nonprofit mission or philosophy precludes exclusion in such cases.	

consumption of the good is rival or nonrival. Rivalness refers to the degree to which a unit of the good or service may be simultaneously consumed by more than one consumer. A loaf of bread is fully rival—if consumed by one person, it is no longer available for consumption by another. Enforcement of clean air standards is fully nonrival. Once produced, all citizens in the vicinity enjoy its benefits simultaneously.

Table 5.1 illustrates the various combinations of excludability and rivalry that may characterize any particular good or service. The table also illustrates that nonprofits indeed provide all types of goods, but fees may play a different role in each cell. In particular, goods that are "excludable" can feasibly generate fee revenue, while those that are nonexcludable cannot do so directly. Moreover, the efficiency of charging fees for excludable goods and services depends on their degrees of rivalness. Excludable goods that are fully rival constitute the conventional type of private goods that are sold in the marketplace. In truth, however, there are many intermediary cases that pose tricky pricing issues.

Nonexcludable goods cannot be supported with direct fees because consumers cannot be prevented from using these goods if they choose not to pay. Nevertheless, indirect forms of commercial revenue generation are possible, even for such goods. For example, nonprofits such as public radio can pair free radio time to listeners (a pure public good) with limited forms of advertising (a private good because advertisers can be excluded if they do not pay). For-profits such as Google do the same thing—they open their web services to all consumers on a free nonexcludable basis, but have become highly profitable by selling strategically placed advertising space. Similarly, common pool goods such as soup kitchens can attract and advertise corporate sponsors, who are excludable.

If the good is a "toll good" (excludable but nonrival) such as a museum gallery or a lecture program, a fee can be charged, but choosing the fee poses a dilemma, because the marginal cost of extending the service to an additional person is very low. Thus, if a substantial fee is charged, it may exclude some people whose benefit exceeds the additional cost for that individual to participate. But if no fee is charged, the nonprofit may not have enough revenue to cover its fixed cost and produce the good at all. If the nonprofit is interested in maximizing public benefit, its problem will be to set the fee low enough (or to charge a differentiated fee) to admit most potential consumers, subject to generating enough revenue to cover its full costs. A for-profit firm would look at this situation differently, seeking to set a (higher) fee that maximizes profits.

Examples such as museum galleries or lecture halls remind us that toll goods are not nonrival indefinitely. They do eventually run into capacity constraints, and price can be a good way of rationing limited space. In this case it may be difficult to distinguish between the behavior of a nonprofit and a for-profit. An opera performance is an example of a toll good with space constraints produced by nonprofits, while a Broadway play exemplifies toll goods with space constraints produced by for-profits.

We can identify at least three subclasses of private goods and services that exhibit excludability and rivalness but nevertheless pose pricing dilemmas for nonprofits. First is the case where the good is purely commercial in nature, and its benefit is received entirely by the consumer, on an excludable and rival basis. This would be so where a nonprofit undertakes a commercial venture for financial reasons only, based on some competitive advantage it may enjoy, such as location or expertise. In this instance the nonprofit can essentially follow the same rules as a private profit-making firm by determining the price that will yield the greatest net profit. In the second case, the good involves an asymmetry of information between consumers and producers, and consumers choose to purchase from a nonprofit because of greater trust. Examples include day care for young children and nursing home care for fragile elderly people. In this case, the nonprofit may feel it must limit its ability to raise price or lower quality, in order to fulfill and maintain this trust.

In the third case, consumption of the good by an individual produces a positive "externality" for others, so that the total benefit consists of a private component that accrues to the consumer plus a public (nonrival, nonexcludable) component that accrues to others in society. For example, individuals who are vaccinated against a certain disease receive a private benefit for which they are willing to pay, but a social benefit is also produced each time someone is inoculated, because each inoculation reduces the risk of contagion. Nonprofits that have a redistributional objective (e.g., providing educational or recreational services to low income youth), because other members of society value this targeting of services, are a special case within this category. Here, the organization may limit fees still more, in order to induce consumers to acquire a service that generates external benefits to others, even if consumers don't place a high value on that service themselves. Of course, it can do so only if it is able to generate enough revenue from other sources to cover its costs.

In cases two and three, the generation of fee revenues involves a delicate balance for the nonprofit organization. In case two, it is a matter of setting prices that seem reasonable so that the consumer feels treated honestly and fairly, and extra profits may be forgone in favor of additional service. In case three, nonprofits must charge prices low enough to encourage access but high enough to finance and subsidize benefits to the intended groups, or to develop a sliding scale price schedule that accomplishes both of these objectives.

Finally, pricing may be affected by interactions between demand for one specific good or service and other goods provided by the organization. First, a particular good or service may be a "complement" of, or a "substitute" for, another service. For example, gift shop sales and museum admissions are complements—if the price of one rises, it will probably cause a drop in demand for the other. Second, sales revenues may have an interactive effect with other sources of revenues, in the form of "crowd-in" or "crowd-out." For example, as we have noted previously, increases in sales revenues may have a chilling effect on donations. The implication is that fees associated with a particular activity cannot be set in isolation. If the nonprofit is concerned with overall revenue as well as mission-related consumption of all of its goods and services, it must set its pricing policies in tandem with one another.

So far our discussion of theory has focused on the "demand-side" of the marketplace. The supply side brings in other subtleties for nonprofits seeking fee and commercial income. Supply-side theory of profit-making firms is straightforward. Firms set the prices and quantities of the goods and services they offer so as to maximize net profits, which enterprise owners can then appropriate to themselves. To do so, firms simply sell as much they can until marginal cost rises above market price. While nonprofits can also earn profits, those who control these organizations are precluded, by the so-called nondistribution constraint, from appropriating those profits. Rather, financial surpluses must ultimately be used to further the social purpose of the organization. This leaves the question—what does the nonprofit organization seek to achieve within the limits of that constraint? And, relatedly, how can it influence the magnitude of resources available within that constraint?

Theorists have identified a variety of entrepreneurial objectives that can motivate nonprofit leaders, some of them personal such as power and autonomy, others more closely connected to the social purpose of the organization, such as professional achievement or belief in a cause (Young, 1983), and still others closely tied to a religious or secular ideology (James, 1987; James and Rose-Ackerman, 1986). For purposes of this analysis, a useful and widely accepted framework for understanding the behavior of nonprofit organizations is the theory of nonprofit organizations as multi-product firms (James, 1983; Weisbrod, 1998). This theory posits that nonprofit leaders achieve satisfaction from producing certain goods and services that satisfy their (nonpecuniary) entrepreneurial motivations, but are also willing to provide "non-preferred" but profitable goods and services that will help finance the former. The example given by James involves a university, which subsidizes graduate education and research, but charges more than marginal cost for its undergraduates, especially lower division undergraduates, who are often taught in large classes that have only a small faculty time cost per student (James, 1978; James and Neuberger, 1981).

In one version of this theory, nonprofit leaders direct their energies toward maximal achievement of the organization's social mission. Hence, "preferred goods" translate into goods and services that directly contribute to mission, and "nonpreferred goods" correspond to profitable goods and services that may be peripheral to mission but can help finance its achievement. In another version, nonprofit leaders are concerned with the distribution as well as the production of goods and services. For example, a nonprofit school may wish to ensure access for children from low income families, a university may wish to ensure a diverse student body, an orchestra may wish to expose schoolchildren to classical music, and so on. In these instances, the organization must earn a profit on some of its (nonpreferred) customers, in order to finance a subsidy to its preferred customers.

In still another version, a religious or idealistic leader starts a service such as a school or hospital with the expectation that it will be a breeding ground for new believers (James and Rose-Ackerman, 1986). Such an entrepreneur will try to keep price low on its primary services, while producing commercial goods such as books or wine to finance the proselytizing objective. All these organizations are structured as nonprofits because they wish to undertake certain activities that run counter to profit maximization, or because they wish to benefit from tax exemptions and privileged access to grants that nonprofits often enjoy, but in each case they have an incentive to earn a profit on some set of goods.

In reality, the goods and services produced by nonprofit organizations fall along a continuum, from those that are profitable but contribute nothing directly to mission, to those that contribute directly to mission but generate no revenue, with many services in-between contributing both to mission and revenue in varying proportions. This framework suggests that nonprofit organizations must generate an overall balance of mission impacting and revenue generating services, such that in the end they are able to be financially sustainable while maximizing their mission objectives.

Clearly, the theory of the nonprofit organization as a multi-product firm is only an approximation of actual behavior, given the various possible flavors of leadership motivation. However, it demonstrates that nonprofits may address their social missions more effectively by expanding their resource constraints, through judicious choice of fees and commercial ventures. Indeed, this theory is the basis for the "product portfolio map," popular in nonprofit management circles, which argues that nonprofits should find the appropriate balance of profit-making and mission-impacting activities so as to achieve mission within bounds of economic feasibility (Oster, 1995; Oster, Gray and Weinberg, 2004). A stylized version of that map is illustrated in table 5.2.

This map suggests that a nonprofit should understand both the mission and revenue implications of each of its potential programs and choose to pursue stars, saints, and cash cows, but not dogs. It also implies that any given program might be adjusted so that it moves from one category to another, or improves within its own category. For example, dogs might be improved to become saints or cash cows, and saints might be converted into stars. The profile map reminds nonprofits that they should not become so involved with a cash cow that they forget it is merely a means to an end, not an end in itself. But the most important interpretation of the product profile map is that it needs to be considered as a whole—that it is the combination of stars, saints, and cash cows (and programs that combine their characteristics in various

Table 5.2.   Product Profile Map

	High Mission Impact	Low Mission Impact
Net Revenue Producing	Stars	Cash Cows
Net Loss Making	Saints	Dogs

proportions) that determines the overall impact and success of the organization.

The multiproduct model of the nonprofit firm suggests how nonprofit organizations should react when various sources of revenue change. In essence, the model stipulates that in order to provide certain mission-impacting goods and services, namely saints, some source of subsidy is required. Such subsidy might come in the form of external grants and contributions or in the form of a cross-subsidy from cash cows and stars. Given the constellation of revenue sources and service markets that serve as its economic environment, the nonprofit organization should choose that combination of services, prices, and other supporting revenues that maximizes its mission impact. But if something changes, adjustments will need to be made. For example, if charitable donations or government grants decline, then the nonprofit will have to put more emphasis on cash cows, or increase the net revenues from stars, or cut back on saints.

The lessons from this supply-side theory are essentially threefold: First, the services of a nonprofit organization must be analyzed in tandem and it is a mistake to insist that all its offerings achieve both mission impact and net revenues. Second, setting prices and quantities of services is an exercise in portfolio analysis that must take account of both the mission and revenue impacts of each component as well as the external economic environment that determines feasibility. Third, organizations should be sensitive to the danger that revenue maximization is a tempting goal that could take over once started, unless concrete steps (such as careful choice of personnel and delineation of success indicators that tie revenues to mission results) are taken to avoid this outcome.

Extending the Knowledge Base

A business model specifies how an organization makes its money in order to sustain itself and address its mission. One way of bringing together knowledge of how nonprofit organizations finance their varieties of private and public goods is to document and analyze their business models. This would entail analysis of the nature and combinations of services they produce, the revenue streams sought to finance them, the strategies utilized to accommodate and exploit the interactions among revenue streams, the complementarities (and substitutability) among services, and the potentials for cross-subsidization of some services by others. Probably such a research agenda would best be carried out within fairly narrow fields of service so that apples can be compared to apples. Thus, studies of the alternative business models of nonprofit theaters would yield a number of different approaches, and the same is likely to be found for hospices, food banks, research institutes, and so on.

Studying a variety of such services might begin to reveal a small number of generic models, with the choice depending on the economic environment faced by the organization. For example, some nonprofits (e.g., in the performing arts and education), earn their support in large measure by "filling seats," while others (e.g., in social services or health care), do so through one-to-one servicing of clients. Still others, such as research institutes and advocacy groups, essentially create and disseminate broad knowledge bases that many people can consult or subscribe to. Identifying these generically different ways of "doing business," and the factors that determine the choice, may allow the development of a fairly compact theory of nonprofit fee and commercial revenue reliance with wide application across the sector.

Improving Practice

Diagnostic questions can help nonprofit managers discover the fee revenue potentials within their own particular venues. The main thrust is to identify the particular character of the goods and services they offer, or could offer, and to translate this information into appropriate revenue and pricing strategies. Below, we offer a series of questions that may begin to serve this purpose:

Nature of goods and services. Start by listing all the goods and services that you provide or might provide. For each one, discuss the following questions with your staff and with focus groups composed of current clients or community residents who might become clients of current or potential future services. These questions essentially identify which services are good candidates for fee revenues.

1. Is it feasible to exclude people from consuming the service if they refuse to pay?
2. How will this service be financed if a fee is not charged?
3. Will the payment of a fee enhance the value of the good to clients or the quality of services provided by staff?
4. Is the service intended to finance the mission of the organization or address that mission directly? (This tells you what quadrant of the product portfolio map the service fits into.)
5. Can the benefits of this service be extended to additional individuals at little or no (marginal) cost, once the fixed production costs have been incurred? Would fees exclude potential consumers even though the marginal cost of serving them is low? Who are these people and are they mission targets?
6. Does the service entail an element of trust which provides the organization with a competitive advantage compared to other providers?
7. Can related services be added that will enjoy a cost advantage in the market (because of location, excess capacity, reputation) and have the potential to raise revenue because excludability is feasible (e.g. gift shops, museum cafeterias, advertising opportunities)?
8. What is the extra cost that the organization would have to incur to start up the new service (including hidden costs such as time of the CEO and other key staff), and will the likely new revenues exceed that cost?

Subsidy, differentiation, and sponsorship. The following questions assess the degree to which it is important to subsidize prices, introduce tailored price schedules to take account of public, mission-related benefits, or exploit those benefits by eliciting commercial sponsorships or donations. These questions should be discussed by the organization's board and managers:

1. Does the service produce benefits to people other than those who consume it directly? If so, it might be efficient to subsidize consumers to induce greater usage, if you can find a way to finance this subsidy. How can fees or donations be captured from the indirect beneficiaries for this purpose?
2. To what extent is it important to serve individuals with limited abilities to pay for the service? Is such redistribution an important part of the organization's mission?
3. Is it feasible to charge differentiated prices for different groups of consumers? Would you differentiate by individual characteristics (age, income) or by quality of service (location of seats, choice of dates)? If age and income, how would you get accurate information about these characteristics?
4. Can corporate sponsors be obtained, to substitute for fee income for those who are unable to pay? Can the nonprofit gain revenues by allowing private companies to utilize its good name? Which corporations would stand to gain by being associated with this organization and its mission?

Mission and revenue combinations. The final set of questions helps nonprofit managers think about rebalancing and expanding the organization's services and revenue streams, emphasizing the interrelationships among the organization's multiple services and revenue sources. In some cases, managers might wish to engage a business consultant to help them brainstorm about the answers or design surveys to provide information about potential consumer demand and cross-product effects.

1. What other services offered by the organization might experience an increase in demand if fees were increased on this service (substitutes)?

2. What other services offered by the organization might experience a decrease in demand if fees were increased on this service (complements)?
3. How would donations and/or government support be affected if fee revenues were increased or decreased for this service?
4. Where does this service fit into the overall portfolio of goods and services of the organization? Is it primarily a net revenue generator or a direct contributor to mission (and possibly a loss maker)?
5. How much of the CEO's time and effort will be consumed by new revenue-enhancing activities that might be undertaken by the organization? Will this detract from important mission-related activities that require his or her time and effort? How can this trade-off be reduced?
6. What are the potential pitfalls in terms of conflicts between mission and revenue-enhancing activities? What are the dangers that revenue-generation can "take over the organization" and how can these dangers be avoided? What success indicators can we establish to identify the primary mission-related services and ensure that they maintain a dominant position relative to the revenue-generating activities that have a secondary or enabling role?

Conclusion

Fees and commercial revenue constitute a basic staple of nonprofit organization finance. Nonprofits themselves generate such revenue in many different ways, through a variety of pricing strategies, commercial ventures, and institutional collaborations. There are no explicit formulas to guide nonprofit managers in determining the degree to which they should rely on this form of revenue, or the pricing, subsidy, and coordination policies that work best in particular situations. Identifying successful policies is an art, the essence of nonprofit entrepreneurship.

However, nonprofit economic theory can help to develop a set of guiding principles. This theory identifies the types of nonprofit goods and services amenable to fee revenue support, their interaction effects with other services and revenue streams, the multiple forms these commercial ventures may take, the complex considerations to bear in mind as fees are set, and the appropriate strategic balances between services that generate profits versus others that cannot or should not, but may be central to the organization's mission.

6

Membership Income

Richard Steinberg

Introduction

Many kinds of membership organizations serve many kinds of members. Some exist to provide services to members (*member-serving organizations*), others to provide benefits to the public as well as members (*public-serving organizations with members*). Some members are intimately involved in the activities and governance of their organizations; others write a check once a year and might read a newsletter. Some organizations derive all of their income from members; others rely also on donations, grants, contracts, and fees. Members may be individuals or organizations. With this diversity, it is not surprising that there does not seem to be a single theory encompassing the proper way to obtain revenues from members. What *is* surprising is the near absence of authoritative guidance on how to secure revenues from members.

This chapter aims to set out the key questions, offer some guidance, and inspire practitioners and researchers to move the discussion forward. I first discuss the blurred lines between member dues, fee income, and donations and then summarize available evidence on the importance of membership income. Next, I outline the set of choices organizations face, from ongoing decisions about rate increases to occasional decisions about dues structures. Then I discuss key factors to consider when reforming dues rates and structures. First and foremost of these is organizational mission. Dues provide resources for accomplishing that mission, but also affect missions directly. Organizations will want rates and structures that are defensible and regarded as fair, and will also want to consider member motivations, the difference between member recruitment and retention, and how dues affect member tax obligations. Organizations should also consider any effects of dues on other sources of revenue and the nature and strategies of competing organizations. Next I expand on financial considerations and show how to project the impact of rate and policy changes, using an illustrative case study. Finally, a set of diagnostic questions is provided that managers, board members, and consultants can ask themselves as they formulate member-ship policy.

Patterns and Trends

Members provide income in three ways: dues, purchases, and donations. Dues are only a portion of income derived from members, but they are the only portion regularly and widely reported to the public. Although we know how much income comes from sales and donations, we don't know how much of each comes from members. Before turning to reported data, we need to define "dues" more carefully.

Sometimes it is not even clear to the member what constitutes dues. For example, members of the American Economics Association (AEA) receive three free journals, but they can choose not to receive one of them and deduct $9 from their 2005 annual dues. Is that last $9 part of "the fee for membership or use of a college, club, etc." (Oxford English Dictionary's 1989 definition of dues) or is it the purchase price for a journal? Another example is provided by the Association for Research on Nonprofit Organizations and Voluntary Action (ARNOVA), which lists 2005 dues of $110 for "individual members" and $500 for "supporting members." Although both are labeled as dues, the organization honestly admits, "$390 of the Supporting Member amount can be claimed as a donation to ARNOVA" (www.arnova.org).

In these two examples, the blurriness of revenue categories is due to the nature of organizational services. Chapter 5 by James and Young in this volume gives us some helpful categories here. They point out that some goods and services matter only to the seller and buyer. These are *private goods,* sold by for-profit firms or by nonprofits seeking unrelated business income to subsidize their mission-related activities. Other goods are *collective* in that a class of individuals benefits from their provision. Collective goods are either *excludable* (meaning that restricting consumption of the collective group to a smaller group is possible—usually those that pay an admission fee) or *nonexcludable collective goods.* Nonexcludables cannot be sold because nonpaying customers get the same services as the paying ones. Any payments are voluntary, taking on the character of a donation. Member-serving organizations provide excludable collective goods whereas public-serving organizations provide nonexcludable collective goods. These ideas help us formulate a functional definition of "dues" that is useful across the varied kinds of membership organizations. In particular, consider how "dues" can function as donations, purchases, dues, or some mixture of these pure categories:

"Dues" function as donations when an organization provides nonexcludable collective goods and members do not govern. For example, WFYI provides Indianapolis with both a public radio and television station. Anyone who contributes during their pledge drive is called a member, but members have no voting rights over the decisions of the stations. Public broadcasting is a nonexcludable collective good because anyone can watch or listen, whether they pay "basic member dues" or not. Thus, "dues" are just like donations. Listeners who joined WFYI at the $65 level in its recent pledge drive received a monthly programming guide and a member card redeemable for discounts at selected restaurants. These members are, in effect, combining a donation with a purchase of an excludable private good.

Member-serving organizations, such as local Better Business Bureaus (BBBs), provide excludable collective goods. The oversight provided by the BBB is a collective good (a bureau with a good reputation helps the sales of all of its members), but an excludable one (only members in good standing are entitled to include the BBB seal in their advertising). Organizations that provide excludable collective goods are known in economics as *clubs,* a category that clearly overlaps the use of the word in common

English (e.g., country clubs, social clubs) but is broader in meaning, also including international treaty organizations and BBBs. Member payments to clubs provide our functional definition of pure dues. Members benefit and nonmembers do not from payments of "dues" (so they do not function like pure donations, which, at least to qualify for tax deductibility, must benefit an indefinite class of individuals). However, "dues" improve services for all members, and so differ in function from a member purchase.

The World Medical Association (WMA) has, as constituent members, the various national medical associations whose members, in turn, are doctors and related health professionals. Its mission is "to constitute a free, open forum for the frank discussion...of matters related to medical ethics, medical education, sociomedical affairs and medical topics generally." By serving as an authoritative international voice WMA provides nonexcludable collective services. However, member "dues" are more than donations because member associations participate in policymaking general assemblies and elect the officers of the WMA. In sum, to the extent organizations provide nonexcludable collective goods, "dues" function as donations unless those organizations offer governance rights. Then member payments function more like pure dues.

The National Center for Charitable Statistics (NCCS) provides data on "member dues and assessments" as defined by the federal tax code, which is very different from our definition above. Specifically, organizations report only that portion of dues and assessments that "compares reasonably with available benefits.... Whether or not membership benefits are used, dues received by an organization, to the extent they are more than the monetary value of the membership benefits available to the dues payer, are a contribution that should be reported [elsewhere].... If a member pays dues mainly to support the organization's activities and not to obtain benefits of more than nominal monetary value, those dues are a contribution to the organization" (IRS 990 Instructions 2004, pp. 55–56). Not every organization is obligated to report this information (the main organizations that do not report are religious congregations and those whose gross annual receipts are less than $25,000), and some inaccuracies creep into the data despite extensive efforts by the NCCS (NCCS Data Guide, 2005). However, much can still be learned from this data.

Table 6.1 reports dues as a share of total revenue for various kinds of 501(c)(3) organizations (the tax code classification for nonprofit organizations engaged in educational, religious, scientific, or other forms of charitable behavior) and for other nonprofit organizations exempt from taxation under various sections of 501(c). Dues are less than 1 percent of total revenues for the average 501(c)(3) organization. If we were to include everything the organization labels as "dues" the figure would be higher, but for the average organization, dues are simply not an important source of revenue. Dues are most important for recreation, sports, leisure, and athletics organizations, providing about 11 percent of revenues; animal-related is next at 5.05 percent, and no other category received more than 5 percent of its revenues as dues.

Dues are more important for other tax code categories. Social and recreational clubs (501(c)(7)) receive about 60 percent of their revenues as dues. Organizations that educate or instruct labor, agricultural, or horticultural groups (501(c)(5)) receive a larger share of revenues from dues (66 percent) than any other 501(c) group. Business leagues (501(c)(6)) receive about 40 percent of revenues from dues and an additional 6 percent in donations that presumably are mostly from members. Of the other categories, only domestic fraternal organizations and possibly war veterans associations receive more than 25 percent of revenues from dues plus likely member donations. About 11.5 percent of non-501(c)(3)s report no income from dues.

Earlier, we distinguished member-serving organizations from public-serving organizations that have members. One expects the former to rely more on dues than the latter, and this is what the data show. 501(c)(3) organizations mostly serve the public, and average reliance on dues is less than 1 percent. Other 501(c) organizations mostly serve members, and sure enough they rely more heavily on dues. Variations in the percent of revenues coming

Table 6.1. Dues as a Percent of Total Revenue, 2003

Arts, Culture, and Humanities	3.49%
Education	0.66%
Environmental Quality, Protection, and Beautification	3.19%
Animal-Related	5.05%
Health	0.31%
Mental Health, Crisis Intervention	0.20%
Diseases, Disorders, Medical Disciplines	1.71%
Medical Research	0.54%
Crime, Legal Related	1.32%
Employment, Job Related	1.51%
Food, Agriculture, and Nutrition	0.40%
Housing Shelter	0.30%
Public Safety	4.84%
Recreation, Sports, Leisure, Athletics	10.78%
Youth Development	4.20%
Human Services—Multipurpose and Other	2.43%
International, Foreign Affairs, and National Security	0.40%
Civil Rights, Social Action, Advocacy	1.22%
Community Improvement, Capacity Building	1.94%
Philanthropy, Voluntarism, and Grantmaking Foundations	0.59%
Science and Technology Research Institutes, Services	2.21%
Social Science Research Institutes, Services	3.81%
Public, Society Benefit—Multipurpose and Other	4.89%
Religion Related, Spiritual Development	1.41%
Mutual/Membership Benefit Organizations, Other	1.09%
Unknown	1.87%
Total, 501(c)(3)	0.90%

Other 501(c) Organizations	Dues, % of Total Revenue	Contributions Plus Gov. Grants, %
2 – Title Holding Corporation for a Tax-Exempt	2.54%	3.06%
4 – Civil Leagues, Social Welfare Organizations, etc.	4.86%	7.80%
5 – Labor, Agriculture	66.02%	3.50%
6 – Business Leagues	40.27%	6.45%
7 – Social and Recreational Clubs	59.61%	0.95%
8 – Fraternal Beneficial Societies	2.18%	1.20%
9 – Voluntary Employees Beneficiary Societies	2.93%	0.96%
10 – Domestic Fraternal Societies	25.13%	11.04%
12 – Benevolent Life Insurance Associations	1.07%	2.20%
13 – Cemetery Companies, Providing Burials for Members	0.66%	2.72%
19 – War Veterans' Associations	12.48%	17.24%

Sources: NCCS Data Web, National Center for Charitable Statistics, Core 2003 PC File, Core 2002 501(c) others file.

from dues within the member-serving category may reflect differences in which services are provided as membership benefits and which services are sold to members for a fee, but better data are needed to resolve this.

Additional information is available from the periodic American Society of Association Executives (ASAE) surveys (ASAE, 1996). Although carefully done, the most recent survey (2003) is based on 628 responses from the approximately 7,000 organizations at which ASAE members were employed. It is not known how representative this group is of the more than 100,000 membership organizations ASAE regards as the relevant universe of associations, nor how representative it is of the nonprofit community overall. Most respondents (63 percent) are tax-exempt under section 501(c)(6), 32 percent are 501(c)(3), 4 percent are exempt under other sections of 501(c), and 1 percent are taxable. The average (c)(6) respondent reports a somewhat higher percentage of revenues from membership dues and assessments than revealed in table 6.2 (46.3 percent vs. 40.27 percent), and the average (c)(3) respondent reports a dramatically higher percentage (25.7 percent vs. 0.9 percent), so it is clear these ASAE members do not represent nonprofits generally. Still, they represent an interesting and coherent group, and survey results are of interest.

Two items stand out in table 6.2. First, (c)(3)s rely less on dues than (c)(6)s and organizations whose members are mostly individuals rely less on dues than organizations whose members are mostly other organizations. Second, dues from regular or primary members predominate; dues from associate or supplier members are never more than one-tenth as large. The trend is toward less reliance on dues, which provided more than half of all revenues in 1974 and less than 40 percent today. The report concludes (vol. 2, p. xvi): "This decline in dues as a proportion of total association revenue is generally true for associations, regardless of revenue size, tax status, membership type, or geographic scope." Finally, the 1996 survey of ASAE associations reports the basis on which dues are calculated (table 6.3). Associations whose members are mostly individuals usually levied a flat or fixed rate, whereas trade associations more commonly used various alternatives.

Table 6.2.   Member Revenues for ASAE Associations (Percent of Total Revenues from Form 990)

	All	Members Are Mainly Organizations	Members Are Mainly Individuals	501(c)(6)	501(c)(3)
Contributions, Gifts, Grants	9.8%	7.2%	10.5%	4.2%	19.4%
Program Service Revenue	43.7%	38.8%	48.0%	41.0%	57.3%
Membership Dues and Assessments	38.8%	46.7%	33.4%	46.3%	25.7%

From Survey, Mainly Company/Institutional Members

	Business (N = 102)	Education (N = 11)	Healthcare (N = 18)	Social/ Cultural/ Recreational (N = 7)
Dues, Regular and Primary Members	38.20%	31.10%	44.60%	62.90%
Dues, Associate and Supplier Members	3.80%	0.30%	2.50%	0.90%
Dues, Other	2.20%	0.00%	3.90%	0.00%
Meetings – Registration Fees	8.60%	4.50%	8.90%	8.10%

From Survey, Mainly Individual Members

	Business (N = 63)	Education (N = 29)	Healthcare (N = 49)	Social/ Cultural/ Recreational (N = 17)
Dues, Regular and Primary Members	33.40%	19.20%	32.10%	26.50%
Dues, Associate and Supplier Members	0.60%	1.10%	0.30%	0.00%
Dues, Other	0.90%	0.10%	2.00%	0.30%
Meetings – Registration Fees	11.40%	19.00%	8.90%	4.90%

Source: American Society of Association Executives, *Operating Ratio Report*, 12th Ed., 2003.

Current Practice

Each year, organizations should examine the rates charged to different categories of members. Less frequently, organizations should examine their entire structure of dues as part of their

Table 6.3. Basis of Member Dues

Basis on Which Membership Dues Are Calculated	Members Are Mostly Individuals	Members Are Mostly Organizations
Assets	2%	4%
Flat or Fixed Rate	70%	26%
Total Income	9%	14%
Units of Equipment	0%	3%
Units of Production	1%	7%
Number of Employees	3%	12%
Number of Plants	0%	1%
Payroll	1%	1%
Percentage of Sales	1%	17%
Salary	2%	0%
Other	12%	14%

Source: ASAE Policies and Procedures in Association Management.

strategic planning process. For conciseness, I will refer to these as choices about rates and structures, respectively. Dues decisions tend to be made in times of crisis, but crises can often be prevented by regular reexamination of rates and structures. In this section, I list the elements of dues structures.

Dues are one source of revenue, and should be thought of as part of the organizational portfolio (see chapter 13). Many tools of modern investment theory can be adapted to the nonprofit setting to answer the question "what is the proper mix of dues and other sources of revenue?" Briefly, portfolio theory shows that overall riskiness is reduced if assets covary negatively with each other—that is, if one asset tends to go up in value when others go down. This result applies to dues, but more research is needed to determine the size of fluctuations in each source of nonprofit revenue and the patterns of covariance between them.

Next, the organization should reexamine the basis for membership types. Some organizations (such as ARNOVA) have a category for students and retirees, who pay lower rates. Others (such as AEA) divide their membership types by member income (less than $43,000, between $43,000 and $58,000, more than $58,000 in 2005). Independent Sector, whose members are organizations (charities, foundations, and corporations that make donations), divides membership classes by type of organization and by income: "For charities organizations, dues are 1/4 of 1 percent of the organization's salaries and benefits. For grant makers, dues are 1/8 of 1 percent of the organization's grants. Maximum annual dues are $12,500, and minimum annual dues are $300" (www.independentsector.org in 2005). The U.S. Chamber of Commerce also has membership based on type of organization (small business, local chamber, associations) and gradations within each (for example, dues for small business depend upon the number of employees). The Sierra Club has four types of membership available to anyone (regular, supporting, contributing, life) and types for those who qualify (students, retirees, limited income). Organizations can and do shift their basis for membership classes. For example, several academic societies have shifted from job title (student, assistant professor, associate professor, professor) to income as their basis. Having chosen a basis, organizations can use coarse or fine-grained distinctions to pick the number of types. As mentioned, AEA has three income-based membership categories. In contrast, the American Sociological Association has six income-based types.

Next, the organization should review the member benefits attached to each type of membership. Benefits can be added or dropped, and if dropped can be entirely eliminated or offered for a fee to those members who wish to buy them. Organizations that provide different benefits to different classes should consider whether these differences should be increased or diminished. Benefit differentiation spans the gamut from complete uniformity to complex clusters. For example, ARNOVA provides the same services for all types except institutional members. The Greater Seattle Business Association offers regular membership (with voting rights) and associate membership (without voting rights). The American Heart Association provides a set of basic benefits to all types, with additional benefits specific to "premium professional," "early career," and "student/trainee" types. Finally, the American Society of Association Executives (ASAE) has the most complex structure summarized here, with a different set of services for each type of member: association CEO, association professional staff, industry partner/supplier, full-time student, paying lifetime member, and nonpaying lifetime member.

A related question concerns discounts and surcharges. Organizations commonly add a surcharge for foreign postage, and increasingly offer discounts for multiyear renewal or e-membership (e-members receive their journals online instead of in hard copy). A survey of benchmark associations found that more than half either formally or informally discounted dues and fees, and the average discount was about 7.5 percent per year (Carey, 2005). Some surveyed organizations offered a 15 percent discount for a two-year renewal, registration for one free program or publication, forgiveness of dues for those with demonstrated financial hardship, a 10 percent discount for early renewal, waived application fees for nonmembers who buy a product, receipt of fifteen months for the price of twelve for new members, and bonus discounts for organizations that bring in their entire managerial staffs. The survey also found a variety of incentives and awards, including an "airline style" program providing points for member recruitment, volunteering, and product purchases, where points can be redeemed for a variety of "awards." Other incentives include a small gift for renewal, a special book for first-time members, free event coupons, and free workshops.

Lastly, the organization should consider arrangements for selling selected member benefits to nonmembers. Restricting benefits to members may persuade more to join the organization, but it may be wise to sell to nonmembers as well. (And for services provided to members for a fee, nonmembers can be charged a higher fee.) For example, ARNOVA's flagship journal, the *Nonprofit and Voluntary Sector Quarterly*, is free to members, but nonmembers can subscribe to this journal at rates selected by the for-profit publisher. Many organizations charge higher rates to nonmembers who attend their conferences, training sessions, and workshops.

Sometimes, organizations are required by law to offer their services to nonmembers (Jacobs, 2005). Organizations may have that obligation under antitrust laws when the prospective buyer cannot meet the membership qualifications or other conditions of access to services and would suffer grave competitive harm if the services were denied. Offering services to nonmembers at too high a price could also risk antitrust prosecution. In addition, it is possible that the IRS would find that an organization that charged nonmembers excessive fees was not "organized and operated exclusively for religious, charitable, scientific, testing for public safety, literary or educational purposes" as required by the tax code for 501(c)(3) organizations (and similarly for other tax-exempt organizations). Jacobs notes that there are few precedents and remarkably little discussion of these issues by the courts, antitrust enforcement agencies, and IRS, but cautions organizations against forcing the issue through egregious behavior.

Theory

The literature has not yet developed rigorous guidelines for optimizing rates and structures, but certain factors must clearly be involved. Organizations should tailor their plans to their own particular mission, maintain solvency, embody shared notions of fairness, adjust for member characteristics, and consider the competition.

Every organization has, as its reason for being, its mission. It may not always be clear what that mission is, because missions are contested by competing groups of stakeholders. Further, missions often evolve (through drift or transformation) when the funding and regulatory environments change or when the voting procedures change (Minkoff and Powell, 2006; Steinberg, 2006). Nonetheless, decisions about dues start with consideration of the mission.

Dues structures are tools for furthering mission and for shaping the evolution of mission. Dues raise part of the revenues necessary to provide services to members and outsiders, but they also affect the size and composition of the organization's membership and provide signals to other stakeholders. In this way, dues are like other nonprofit pricing decisions (Steinberg and Weisbrod, 1998).

To make sense of the incredible diversity of missions, we need a set of categories. Mason (1996), for example, classifies missions (in whole or in part) as instrumental, expressive, or affiliative. Instrumental missions are those that seek tangible results (e.g., poor people are fed, member quality is certified, members receive appropriate training, and baseball games are played). Expressive missions do not require results, merely that some sentiment is expressed in some way desired by members. The poor may always be with us, but some satisfaction is gained by publicly stating that something is wrong when poverty remains amidst abundance. Expressive groups may thank the troops, memorialize people, places and things, or express pride in some religion, sexual preference, or ethnicity. Affiliative missions concern the size and composition of membership. Organizations with affiliative missions stress the value of belonging, emphasizing shared sacrifice or the social pleasures of meeting and working with like-minded people. Large groups, seeking to foster the broadest possible social networks, have affiliative missions. So do small groups, seeking to bring together the elite of the elite. Affiliative missions can bring diverse communities together (as in the National Council of Churches) or divide them into separate spaces (as in the Ku Klux Klan).

Public-serving organizations with instrumental missions will generally want a dues structure that maximizes net revenues (that is, money left over after providing member services). This way they have maximal resources available to serve the public. There are some exceptions; for example, an organization that serves the public by testing the quality of consumer products will have an easier time of it if there are many members, whatever the financial surplus these members generate. This is because manufacturers offer higher quality products when they are watched by a large group of consumers. Things are more complicated for member-serving organizations, which provide both private and excludable-collective goods and services. If the collective services are paramount in the organizational mission, the dues structure should maximize net revenues from private services and devote that surplus to provision of collective services. If both matter, little can be said without knowing the exact trade-offs the organization is willing to make between serving individual members and the membership as a whole.

Expressive missions are furthered by including visible and portable tokens of membership. Thus, ACLU members are proud to be "card-carrying." Sometimes, an affiliative element enters expressive missions—the value of expression may be enhanced when one expresses with others in protest marches or poetry readings.

Different strategies are appropriate for the different kinds of affiliative missions. Dues structures obviously affect the number who join (making this number small or large as appropriate to the affiliative mission). Many organizations wish to remain affordable for everyone who "ought" to join (for example, all members of a particular profession, all organizations providing a similar service, all for-profit firms in a particular community, or all believers in a particular creed). Some emphasize special efforts to recruit particular types of members (students, retirees, small organizations, children of alumni, minorities, coreligionists, and the like). When members participate in the organization's decision making through voting for board members or referenda, the organization may wish to exclude those with views contrary to the current mission of the organization (Tschirhart and Johnson, 1998).

Some organizational missions fall outside this trichotomy. For example, the mission of the American Diabetes Association "is to prevent and cure diabetes and to improve the lives of all people affected by diabetes" (www.diabetes.org). Members receive the monthly publication *Diabetes Forecast* that gently encourages them to pay more attention to their diet and test their blood sugar more frequently. This mission contains a large paternalistic element, to change the habits of members for their own good, whether they want to or not. Paternalistic member organizations must decide how hard to push. If members quit, the organization can no longer help them. To be able to push harder, the organization will set its dues as low as possible and provide other benefits sufficient to keeping its members in the fold.

It is relatively easy to specify organizational objectives. The hard but necessary part is to figure out how to trade one part of the mission against another. Is it more important to engage students and retirees who cannot afford the cost of member services or to improve the quality of services for existing members? At what point does the required subsidy grow too large to be worth it? Should all "cash cows" (those willing to pay far more than the cost of delivering member benefits) be encouraged to join in the elite, high-dues categories of membership or does the risk that they would take control from long-term dedicated members outweigh the cash they would provide?

No sacred rule requires that member benefits be paid for by member payments. When having more members enhances the organizational mission, dues should be set lower than costs, *cross-subsidizing* member benefits with revenues from other sources. In contrast, public-serving nonprofits should set dues above the cost of member benefits to cross-subsidize the public mission. Some organizations value certain kinds of members (for example, students or practitioners more highly than other academic researchers), and they will want to set dues for the less-favored categories higher than costs to cross-subsidize dues for the favored categories.

If there are economies of scale, so that per-member costs decline when the number of members increases, then budgeting is more complicated. For example, ARNOVA's contract with Sage Publications specified one cost for providing *NVSQ* to each member when there are 500 or less members, a lower cost for 501–1,500, and a still lower cost when membership exceeds 1,500. The 501st member provides a net cross-subsidy to other members if dues exceed the marginal cost—the increase in cost when membership increases by 1.

When setting dues exactly equal to costs is desirable, overhead needs to be allocated. Even here, the process is not mechanical, for there are many ways to divide overhead costs: equally to each member, proportional to use of services, or proportional to ability to pay. Accounting conventions provide answers, but these answers are without economic meaning. Dues can be set higher for some members and lower for others as long as direct costs and overhead are covered. Division of overhead costs is a strategic decision, based on organizational objectives and shared notions of fairness, rather than a constraint imposed by accountants.

Any change in dues will change the number of members. Dues are the price of membership, and higher prices reduce purchases. Thus, you cannot simply set dues equal to total costs divided by the number of current members and expect to balance the budget. Economists summarize buying behavior by constructing a *demand curve*, which illustrates the number of people or organizations that would like to join at each possible rate of dues during a specified period. Membership demand is downward sloping, showing that higher dues result in fewer members. However, it can still pay to raise rates if the number of members does not change too much. Economists measure price sensitivity in percentage terms, defining the *price elasticity of demand* as the percentage decrease in the number wishing to join that would result from a 1 percent increase in dues. When price elasticity is less than one, we say demand is *inelastic* and when it is greater than one, demand is *elastic*. Rate increases produce more total revenue if demand is inelastic, but are counterproductive when demand is elastic (because so many members, current and prospective, leave). Conversely, rate decreases increase total revenues when demand is elastic. The smaller is price elasticity, the more positive is the effect of rate increases on total revenues.

The size of price elasticity for any given organization is a subject for empirical study, but some patterns hold true across organizations and services. Elasticity is smaller for goods or services that are important, consume a small portion of consumer income, and have few good substitutes. The first point is quite intuitive—members are not likely to quit when faced with rate increases if membership is vitally important to them. However, no matter how valuable, dues can be set so high that members are forced to quit rather than spend everything they have on paying for membership. Finally, if similar organizations do not raise their dues at the same time, members may switch allegiance, so your organization's price elasticity will be large.

Elasticity is not a number set in stone, but a summary of how real people respond to the organizations they join. The way in which dues increases are decided, publicly justified, and explained to members matters a lot, and good marketing can reduce the price elasticity. Elasticity will be low (and hence dues increases will bring in substantial additional revenue) if the process for deciding dues is seen as fair, the case for an increase is clearly explained, and the perceived value received remains attractive after the increase. Perceived value, discussed by Bowman (2004) equals perceived member benefits divided by perceived sacrifice. Bowman recommends segmenting messages by specialties, length of membership, and other factors in order to send messages that best increase perceptions of benefits and decrease perceptions of sacrifice.

If it is too simplistic to raise dues by the amount of any shortfall, it is equally simplistic to cut expenditures on member benefits by the amount of the shortfall. The number of members responds to changes in member benefits. Sometimes, an increase in benefits will cause a more than proportionate increase in the number of members, so that cuts in services are counterproductive. Mechanical rules are too simple. The organization should think strategically.

Members and prospective newcomers must believe dues structures are fair or they will not join. But fairness is a slippery concept, and little has been written on fair dues structures. More has been said about fairness in other arenas, including jurisprudence, tax policy, and cooperative game theory. From jurisprudence comes the concept of procedural justice: outcomes are fair if they result from a fair process. From this perspective, dues structures are seen as fair if the membership is properly consulted and access to decision makers is evenhanded, whatever specific reforms are adopted. An interesting, perhaps extreme, example is provided by the Kansas Pharmacists Association (KPhA) (Levin, 1992). Needing its first major dues increase in ten years and facing a potentially hostile membership, a long-range plan was developed and approved by two committees, the Treasurer, and the board. Along with the dues increase, the board recommended changes in the membership categories, and everything was submitted for approval by the membership. Robert Williams, executive director of KPhA, publicized the proposal in the newsletter and journal of the association, and then asked board members to talk to members at the annual meeting: "We used a little gimmick to get board members feeling more comfortable about starting a cold conversation. We asked them to put a sticker on the badge of everyone they talked to about the increase. Our goal was to have every attendee with a sticker." The new plan was approved by 86 percent of members.

Other approaches to fairness are borrowed from tax policy (Merrill, 1993). Taxes, like dues, are used to pay for collective goods, so it is not surprising that the fairness issues are similar. Tax analysts talk of *vertical equity*—taxpayers in different situations should pay different amounts—and *horizontal equity*—taxpayers in the same situation should pay the same amount. The idea that vertical equity requires affluent taxpayers to pay a larger proportion of their income or wealth in taxes is commonly accepted and enshrined in our progressive personal income tax. However, the proper degree of progressivity and the concept itself are contested (Blum and Kalven, 1953). Defenders of progressivity rely on one or all of the following arguments: that the wealthy have greater ability to pay; that everyone should make an equal sacrifice, which requires the rich to pay a larger share of their income; or that the wealthy obtain more value from, or consume more of, the publicly provided services.

How do these notions apply to dues? Progressive dues structures based on income are common in professional and trade associations. Where privacy, practical, or political concerns mitigate against using income-based categories, eligibility is often determined by things correlated with income, such as student/retiree status for ARNOVA or sales, number of plants, or number of employees for some trade associations (Merrill, 1993). Some organizations encourage dues progressivity on a voluntary basis, offering categories like "supporting member." Progressivity principles are violated, to some extent, if everyone is compelled to pay a minimum dues level or if dues for wealthy members are capped.

Progressive dues structures are justified under the equal sacrifice or ability to pay arguments. However, the third argument, consumption of services, does not always lead to the same pattern of dues as the first two. Merrill recommends that we sidestep this argument by charging user fees whenever services lead to easy-to-measure benefits to identifiable members. However, there are often good reasons to bundle services together, all covered by dues. In addition, the same vertical-equity concerns apply to user fees, so the issue is not entirely sidestepped. Consider a trade association that maintains a professional library for member use. Larger firms have their own libraries and do not value this benefit very highly. Smaller firms use the professional library extensively, and so, on the consumption-of-services theory of fairness, should either pay higher dues or purchase services separately (based on visits, books checked out, or another usage measure). However, smaller firms have less ability to pay and their sacrifice would be great if they paid fees or higher dues.

Horizontal equity, as a theoretical value, is rarely controversial when applied to dues. In practice, however, it is hard to know whether two types of members are in equivalent situations and so should pay the same dues. Is equivalence defined by the costs of providing member services? If so, horizontal equity requires a postal surcharge for foreign members. Is equivalence defined by equal value to the organization? If so, some otherwise inequitable dues structures would pass muster—special introductory rates, lower rates for underrepresented constituencies, honorary life membership for the stars of the field, and the like. Another horizontal equity argument asserts that member dues should be the same as those charged by competing organizations. Levin (1992) warns against pursuing this argument, at least publicly. He argues that by making comparisons you suggest to members that they choose one organization or the other, whichever is cheaper. Prospective members may indeed choose whichever is cheaper, but management may not wish to encourage this line of thinking.

Other perspectives on fairness come from cooperative game theory. One branch of this field looks at cost-sharing arrangements for collective facilities. For example, nuclear power plants have huge fixed costs (costs unrelated to usage) that need to be allocated fairly across customer classes (residential, industrial, and commercial). Another looks at fairness in bargaining situations and the closely related "pie-cutting problem." This approach has been applied to union negotiations, division of marital assets upon divorce, and international treaty design (Brams and Taylor, 1996). One notion of fairness is that an arrangement should be *envy free*, meaning that members in one category, receiving one set of benefits and paying one set of prices, should not envy the treatment of those in other categories. Dues are envy free if no class of members would rather switch into another class. Another notion is given by *partial responsibility theory*, developed by

Moulin and Sprumont (2002). Under this approach, those who demand more services pay higher dues unless they are not responsible for their higher demands. Moulin and Sprumont offer the example of those bound to wheelchairs. Public transit systems incur much higher costs to serve these travelers, but because they are not responsible for their condition, they often pay the same price as everyone else. Applied to dues structures, organizations might not want to charge higher rates for international members, particularly those from poorer parts of the world.

Organizations should take account of the characteristics of their current members and mindfully decide what kinds of members they wish to attract, retain, and repel. Three important characteristics are member motivations, eligibility for tax deductions, and the likelihood of substituting member dues for donations. Member motivations matter in at least three ways. First, not all members want dues set as low as possible. Some members prefer an exclusive club, where if you have to ask what the dues are, you do not belong. This only applies to certain affiliative organizations; more commonly members want to part with as little money as possible and receive the greatest quantity and quality of services in return for their dues payments. Second, member motivations determine the value placed on various membership benefits and therefore whether these benefits should be enhanced or trimmed. Third, there is a fair amount of literature on why people join, remain a member of, and leave organizations, summarized in Tschirhart (2006). She finds that joiners have very different motivations than stayers. This suggests not only that new members should be offered trial periods or reduced rates but that the advantages of membership need to be marketed very differently for prospective and continuing members.

Members differ in their eligibility for tax deductions and reimbursement by employers. Payments of dues may or may not be deductible (from the member's personal or corporate income subject to tax) as a charitable contribution. Dues paid to civic or public service organizations, professional associations, and trade associations are generally deductible; dues paid to organizations whose principal purpose is providing food or entertainment or to social clubs are not. When dues are not deductible as a charitable contribution, they may be deductible as a cost of doing business or as an unreimbursed employee expense. Only that portion of dues in excess of the costs of member services is deductible. 501(c)(4), (5), and (6) organizations and a few others must provide members with the percentage of dues used for nondeductible lobbying costs, and members must reduce their deductions accordingly (Baruffi, 2005). To the extent that dues, but not user fees, are deductible or reimbursable, the organization should shift some services from a fee basis to a dues-supported member benefit.

When donations of time and money are important to the organization, and particularly when members are also donors, the organization needs to consider whether increases in dues come at the expense of decreased donations. This is an empirical question, much analyzed in other contexts (e.g., Steinberg, 1993; Kingma, 1995; Brooks, 2003b). Economic theory provides some hints, suggesting that the degree of crowding out depends very much on donor motivations (Vesterlund, 2006), and the motivations for joining and staying probably matter as well. In the worst case, members/donors wish to provide a fixed level of total support to the organization. Then, increases in dues would be exactly cancelled out by decreases in donations.

Sometimes, increased dues can result in increased donations (crowding in). This seems likely if nonmember major donors (foundation grant makers) condition their support on evidence that the recipient organization is working to reduce its long-term dependency on grants. A dues increase provides this evidence, allowing the organization to continue to receive grants. Alternatively, a wealthy member who is also a donor may feel exploited, threatening to reduce his donation unless others pay their "fair share." Again, increased dues would reassure the donor.

Organizations compete with other organizations for members. Some organizations also compete with themselves, as rate and structure changes for one membership category can cause members in other categories to switch. For example, competition between two umbrella groups (American Cancer Society and United Cancer Council) for local affiliates severely restricted the latter's ability to raise dues, leading to its eventual dissolution. ARNOVA competes with a similar interdisciplinary organization (the International Society for Third-Sector Research) but more importantly competes with the many discipline-specific academic societies (AEA, ASA, etc.) that are often the first choice of those who prefer to join only one organization.

Organizations that offer several categories of membership have several demand curves to consider. For example, a three-category organization would have a demand curve for regular members, another for associate members, and a third for supporting members. Each demand curve shows the relation between a category's rate and number of members, holding constant the dues rate at which one can join other categories. These curves interact, so the number seeking, say, regular membership at a price of $80 depends upon the price of associate and supporting membership. Thus, we have to distinguish two kinds of elasticity—the *own-price elasticity*, which shows how category membership changes with rates in the same category, and the *cross-price elasticity*, which shows how category membership changes with rates in each other category. In this example, there are six cross-price elasticities—between regular and associate there are two, one for the effect of an increase in associate dues on regular membership, and another for the effect of an increase in regular dues on associate membership. Two more cross-price elasticities emerge between associate and supporting, and a final two between regular and supporting membership.

If prospective members have their choice of categories, an increase in the rate for associate or supporting members would cause more people to seek regular membership. Then the cross-price elasticities are positive numbers showing the percentage change in the number of regular members from a 1 percent increase in associate or supporting rates. If, instead, prospective members have no choice of categories (because of restrictive eligibility requirements), rate changes in other categories would have no effect on regular membership and the cross-price elasticity would be zero. For example, working members are unlikely to retire simply because the regular rate has been raised relative to the retiree rate.

Category switches are most worrisome in two cases. First, if supporting members pay higher dues than regular members but eligibility and member benefits are the same, supporting members are functioning as donors. Raising supporting member rates too much would be counterproductive—rather than make a small donation, supporting members might switch to regular membership and forgo their donation entirely. Alternatively, former supporting members might switch and then make a small explicit donation, causing no harm. To the extent that the title itself is an important motivator (say, because it conveys prestige to the donor), care must be taken not to raise supporting dues too high, or to create new categories beyond supporting. The situation is akin to "giving clubs" (Harbaugh, 1998a, 1998b), where donations of sufficient size entitle the donor to an honorific designation like "Patron" or "Golden Donor."

The second worrisome case is where eligibility depends upon self-reported information that is difficult, inappropriate, or impossible for the organization to verify. In particular, if dues are based on reported income, some of those with higher income would lie to reduce their dues. Not even economists are so uniformly selfish that they always lie this way according to the study of Beil and Laband (1996). They find that the share of members joining the American Economic Association in the highest-cost membership category (defined by member annual income) is about two-thirds of what it should be. This is surprising to some scholars (such as Frank, Gilovich, and Regan, 1993) who argue that studying economics makes one more likely to pursue self-interest and in any case, selfish people are attracted to economics. Moreover, the AEA has never sanctioned a member for misreporting income. Some "cheating" at the low end occurred—only 3 percent of respondents reported income that would qualify them for the lowest category of dues, whereas 25 percent actually paid the lowest rate. A follow-up study (Laband and Beil, 1999) compares AEA members with members of the ASA (American Sociological Association) and APSA (American Political Science Association). Actual dues collections are 93 percent of what they should be for AEA members, 91 percent for APSA members, and 78 percent for ASA members.

Laband and Beil cite Hansmann's (1981) argument that customers are willing to donate on top of required fees when they buy from a trusted nonprofit that provides collective goods. Undoubtedly, the trust members place in their organizations matters a lot for category switching. Laband and Beil also argue that the incentives to cheat are greatest for sociologists, who can save 81 percent on their dues by reporting lower than actual income, whereas economists can only save 29 percent and political scientists 48 percent. This confirms what common sense suggests—that category switching occurs to a greater extent when the benefits of doing so are large, and cautions large and impersonal organizations against overly progressive dues structures.

When switching is important (that is, cross-price elasticities are large), raising rates in one category (say, regular membership) while leaving the others unchanged will not bring in much additional revenue. Revenues from regular members may fall, for with good substitutes own-price elasticities are more likely to exceed one, while revenues from other categories (and combined revenues from all categories) will rise. Increasing rates by the same percentage in each category is much more effective when no switching occurs and in effect, the own-price elasticities are smaller. Alternatively, the organization can increase the difference in member benefits and perceived value between the various categories of membership. This reduces both the own and cross-price elasticity, so that a rate increase in one category will have a large effect on total revenues.

If competition is strong, an organization that raises its dues will lose prospective and continuing members to competitors. Its own-price elasticity will be large, possibly so large that rate increases are counterproductive. Rate increases have a much smaller positive effect, or larger negative effect, on revenues because, unlike the previous case, the dues paid by switchers are totally lost to the organization.

If an organization has a budget gap and faces competition for members, what can it do? One strategy is to create differences in member benefits and market those differences in a way that leads prospective members to perceive a higher value in joining the organization that raises its dues. This product differentiation approach is familiar to those knowledgeable in business strategy, and can work well for membership organizations. However, thinking strategically about the reaction of other organizations is important. Will the competitor simply match the enhanced benefits, in which case the organization will continue to lose members and have higher costs to boot? Or will the competitor, facing the same climate that led to a dues increase in the first organization, also raise dues in which case no enhancement in benefits is necessary?

A second strategy is to create and/or market complementarities between membership in the two organizations, by pointing out reasons why members of one organization would also benefit from joining the other. This strategy is win-win, so there is no need to worry about how the other organization will counter the move.

Extending the Knowledge Base

The most critical need is to obtain better estimates of the price and cross-price elasticities of membership, that is, to determine how many members will quit or convert to a different category of membership when rates and structures are reformed. Each organization is unique, and the way that members are served by and react to structures of dues and fees at one organization will differ from reactions at other organizations. Nonetheless, something useful can be learned from good statistical analyses of the experiences of many similar organizations. To conduct these studies, new surveys are necessary. Care should be taken that the same definitions of dues and accounting conventions are used, else the comparison across organizations is meaningless. It is important to track certain details, such as whether member benefits were adjusted at the same time rates changed, whether new competing organizations emerged or old ones departed, and whether the economy was good or bad at the time of the changes.

A second need is to gather data that enable one to study the effects of membership income policies on long-term loyalty and other aspects of the membership mix. Just knowing the number of members following a rate increase is not enough for an organization that cares about retaining particular members or maintaining ethnic, economic, gender, and other forms of diversity.

Finally, more attention needs to be devoted to the strategic aspects of membership income policies. Organizations compete for members. Even if there are no other organizations meeting a particular need, an organization should not be too greedy with its captive audience or dissatisfied members will create the competition. When there is effective competition, the number and composition of members depends on the policies of both organizations, and those policies are set in strategic reaction to the policies of the other organization. Economists have considered similar issues (such as the competition of local governments for residents, using taxes to finance services) but need to pay attention to the particulars of dues-financed services.

Improving Practice

Whatever the reason for change, organizations need to break even in the end. In this section, I show how spreadsheets can be used to project the budgetary impacts of reforms. Consider as an instructive hypothetical example, an ecotourism club directed by Jerry G. (affectionately known as "the Captain") called Long Strange Trips (LST). LST has operated at a deficit the last two years, so the board ("Heads") directed the Captain to explore an increase in dues. In response, Jerry produced table 6.4. First, Jerry gathered historical data (the first three rows in table 6.4), so that he could uncover the trends that led to the current deficit. The number of regular members had been growing at a steady 10 percent per year (column A), but dues were constant (B) and the cost of private-good member benefits like the newsletter had gone up (C). In column D, Jerry calculated the net revenues from regular members by multiplying columns A and B, then subtracting C. He noted that the regular members are still, on balance, paying more than they cost but the surplus has been shrinking. Repeating the same calculation for student members (columns E through H), he found that student members cost more to serve than they bring in, but this is okay provided the net cost does not grow too large. LST also bought and maintains a really good sound system for the collective benefit of its members, and the cost of

Table 6.4. Projecting the Financial Impact of a Dues Increase at Long Strange Trips

	A	B	C	D	E	F	G	H	I	J	K	L	M	N
Year	#Reg Mbrs	Reg Mbr Dues ($/mbr)	Cost, Reg Benfts ($/mbr)	Reg Mbr Net Rev[1] ($)	#Stud Mbrs	Stud Mbr Dues ($/mbr)	Cost Stud Mbr ($/mbr)	Stud Mbr Net Rev ($)	Cost, Collec Ben[2] ($)	Mbr Net Rev[3] ($)	Other Rev ($)	Other Cost ($)	Other Net Rev ($)	Net Surplus (Deficit)[4] ($)
Historic														
2003	100	50	30	2000	50	30	30	0	3000	-1000	5000	4000	1000	0
2004	110	50	45	550	60	30	45	-900	3000	-3350	6000	5000	1000	(-2350)
2005	121	50	45	605	80	30	45	-1200	3100	-3695	7000	5500	1500	(-2195)
Baseline														
2006	133	50	45	665	100	30	45	-1500	3100	-3935	8000	6000	2000	(-1935)
2007	146	50	45	730	110	30	45	-1650	3200	-4120	9000	6500	2500	(-1620)
2008	162	50	46	648	115	30	46	-1840	3300	-4492	10000	7000	3000	(-1492)
Raised														
2006	126	75	45	3780	90	40	45	-450	3100	230	8000	6000	2000	2230
2007	139	75	45	4170	99	40	45	-495	3200	475	9000	6500	2500	2975
2008	154	75	46	4466	104	40	46	-624	3300	542	10000	7000	3000	3542

Notes:

[1] Regular member net revenues are calculated as the number of regular members x (regular member dues – costs). Similarly for student members.

[2] Cost, collective benefits are costs associated with member benefits provided collectively, rather than to any individual member.

[3] Member net revenue is the sum of regular and student member net revenues minus cost of collective benefits.

[4] This is the "best guess" estimate assuming a price elasticity of 0.1 for regular members and 0.3 for student members.

this is reported in column I. Adding together net revenues from each member category (D plus H) and subtracting the costs of collective benefits (I) results in net revenues from members (J).

LST also receives grant, royalty, and investment income, reported in column K, and incurs overhead costs reported in L. Column M summarizes the net revenue that does not come from members, calculated as K minus L, and column N provides the grand total (J plus M). In 2003, the surplus from regular members and from nonmember sources exactly covered losses resulting from student members, but that turned into a deficit of $2,350 in 2004 and $2,195 in 2005.

Membership is growing, so perhaps the deficit will cure itself. To see whether this will occur, Jerry calculated the three rows labeled "baseline" in table 6.4. Jerry projected the number of members forward using the forecasting tools provided by his spreadsheet. He tried several trend lines and moving average approaches contained in Excel. Each of the forecasts looked similar for regular membership and these results looked reasonable, but the forecasts for student membership looked implausible. Jerry knew that the jump in the number of student members in 2005 was a fluke due to the closing of a factory in town. Some of the newly unemployed went back to school and joined LST to participate in those spring break tours of Costa Rica. He thinks rapid growth in student membership will continue for another year, then taper off. Quite properly, he replaces the computer projections with his own best judgment.

In general, membership projections should be adjusted based on experience and knowledge of the factors that determine who will join, renew, and rejoin your organization. Growth due to special outreach efforts cannot be sustained indefinitely. Trends projected forward from times when other rate and structure changes occurred are inappropriate for baseline projections. Multiyear membership and cycles of renewal add their own complications. Excel provides a starting point, but expert judgment should prevail.

Jerry doesn't have to project the cost of member services for 2006 and 2007, as these are contractually fixed. Most costs are fixed for 2008 as well, but a projected postage increase is built into his calculations. In general, costs per member can be projected forward based on expected inflation rates, but any quantity discounts available as the organization grows should be taken into account. The Captain projects that the costs of collective goods (like the sound system) will go up at less than the inflation rate because of technical progress in the electronics industry. He considers a variety of factors affecting other revenues and costs, including an increase in rent when the current lease expires, the raises the Heads tell him to expect, the escalating costs of utilities and health insurance for employees, and the phase-in of revenues from some charitable bequests currently in probate court. In sum, LST expects to enjoy 10 percent growth each year in regular members, have large then smaller increases in the number of student members, and a steady increase in net nonmember revenues. Despite this growth, the budget prognosis is poor if dues are not increased, with projected deficits of $1,935, $1,620, and $1,492 for the years 2006, 2007, and 2008 respectively.

With completion of the historic baseline columns and forward projection of the baseline over five years (only three are illustrated in table 6.4 to conserve space), the effect of a rate increase can be calculated. This is simplest for changes in rates when the dues structure remains constant. Putting the new rates in the appropriate columns and rows is easy ($75 in column B and $40 in F). Projecting the effect on membership in each category is harder. First, Jerry calculates the size of the increase in percentage terms (50 percent for regular members and 33.3 percent for students). He doesn't expect any category switching, so he multiples this increase times the best guess price elasticity (0.1 for regular and 0.3 for student members) to determine the percentage decrease in members that would result from higher rates (5 percent regular and 10 percent student). Here Jerry remembers that these percentage changes should be applied to the forecast baseline number of members, not the current number of members. He places the correct numbers in columns A and E for the final three rows of table 6.4. The net effect is that membership will continue to grow, but the growth will shrink during the first year of the rate increase.

Now, member net revenue is forecast to be slightly positive in each year, which, when combined with the surplus from other sources, provides a good cushion for the organization in case the elasticity estimates prove optimistic.

Most of this process can be automated in a spreadsheet, but Jerry has to figure out what value for price elasticity to use for LST. He forms his best guess estimate after reading several staff studies. The first study calculated percentage changes in membership following previous rate increases at LST and at several comparable organizations. The trouble is that part of the change was a trend unrelated to the rate increase, so these numbers have to be de-trended. There are several ways to do so, but the easiest way is to calculate the percentage growth rate following the change minus the average percentage growth rate over several years before the dues increase.

Staff also conducted surveys of LST members. Special efforts were made to get responses from lapsed and first-time members, who may have different reactions to rate increases. Focus groups were also held with current and lapsed members and a special session was held with people who had never joined LST but were part of its target population. In general, surveys and focus group protocols should be designed by experienced professionals; amateurs will make mistakes that make it more difficult to interpret survey results. In addition, at least three points of caution should be noted. First, questions should mimic the way that dues increases are explained and marketed in practice. An initial negative reaction to a rate increase can be overcome if the justification for the increase is persuasively explained, so explanations should be included in the survey before respondents answer questions about their reaction to a rate increase. Second, survey responders will probably not form a random sample of members. The most likely responders are those who are most committed and knowledgeable about the organization, and this group will presumably respond more positively to the prospect of a rate increase than others would. Third, survey respondents may answer strategically or impulsively, claiming they would quit when they really would not, in the hopes that their response will kill the proposal to increase dues.

Table 6.4 provides best guess estimates of the effect of dues increases for the Heads to consider. Jerry also repeats these calculations with parallel tables (not exhibited here) showing a pessimistic estimate (with higher price elasticity) and an optimistic estimate (with lower elasticity). While no one at LST believes there will be category switching following a dues increase, other organizations in this situation might have to conduct additional calculations to see the effects of optimistic, pessimistic, and best guess cross-price elasticities on financial health. Other organizations might also provide additional projections based on more optimistic and pessimistic projections of the effect of changes in member benefits on membership.

By way of summary, the following diagnostic questions can be used to determine policies toward membership income:

1) Adequacy of Dues

a) What percentage of organizational revenues comes from dues? Are you more reliant on dues than similar organizations (suggesting you can increase nonmember income) or less reliant (suggesting that you can enhance membership and raise dues)?

b) How do dues compare with the cost of member services, both overall and for each category of membership? Note that there is nothing necessarily wrong in disparities here, based on availability of other resources, organizational missions, fairness, and willingness to pay extra to support collective benefits to members and the public. There is a problem if disparities represent miscalculation or historical accident. The difference between dues and cost of member services for various types of members is a key element of organizational strategy and should be decided strategically.

c) Can you continue to rely on net revenues from grant makers, donors, return on investment, sales of goods and services, royalties, and other sources of nonmember income to cover the difference between member income and the costs of providing member services?

d) Do you expect changes in the costs of providing member benefits? General inflation, postal rate increases, staff expansion, and provision of new services commonly necessitate a rate increase.

e) Is the number of members stable, growing, or shrinking? Growth can necessitate a rate increase (if it occurs for categories of members that cost more than they bring in) or allow a rate decrease (if it occurs for categories where dues exceed the costs of member services). Is the trend in membership likely to be sustained, or will emergence of competing organizations, the state of the economy, or other factors change that trend?

2) Increases in Rates

a) Have you projected baseline financial variables, showing the number of likely members, costs, and revenues for the next five years assuming no change is made in rates?

b) Have you projected the same financial variables following an increase in rates? Did your projection take account of changes in the baseline number of members in each category to reflect (i) reductions in recruitment and retention due to the increase (price elasticity), (ii) category switching (cross-price elasticity), (iii) the impact of responses by competing organizations, (iv) the impact of changes in member benefits that would accompany the increase, and (v) effects of the dues increase on other sources of revenue (donations, challenge grants, etc.)?

c) Have you gathered information (through surveys and focus groups) on (i) the response of members to previous changes in rates, (ii) the experiences of similar organizations with rate changes, (iii) members' willingness to pay higher rates? Does this information suffice to refine your judgment of the likely price elasticities?

d) Have you conducted sensitivity analysis to uncover the risks if your judgments regarding price elasticities, cost changes, and membership numbers prove to be

inaccurate? At a minimum, you should calculate financial impacts using a pessimistic, best-guess, and optimistic
assessment of the price elasticity.

e) Have you minimized member concern over rate increases
through meaningful consultation, transparent and accountable decision making, and clearly-explained rationales?

3) Structural Reform

a) In what ways does your current dues structure enhance or
detract from mission? Are you a member-serving organization or a public-serving organization with members? Is
your mission instrumental, expressive, or affiliative? Does
your dues structure encourage key constituencies to join?

b) Do you wish to convert members or encourage them to
take better care of themselves? If so, you will need to be
sure the net benefits to members (willingness to pay minus
dues) are sufficiently large that members will listen rather
than quit.

c) Can potential members only discover the value of membership through becoming members? If so, you might
want to offer free initial membership or other initial in-
ducements.

d) Would rival groups like to subvert your mission? If so,
consider eligibility requirements or limitations on member
voting power to protect against takeovers from within.

e) Are you offering the right mixture of member benefits?
Should some benefits be sold separately, either at cost or
at a discount, rather than rolled into the package? Should
you offer different categories of membership that package different sets of benefits together to meet the needs
of more potential members? Are elements of the benefits
package collective (hence incapable of being sold) or private to the member?

f) Are there differences in the cost of serving certain
kinds of members (for example, foreign postage)? Absent

considerations of mission and sometimes fairness, these differences should be balanced by surcharges and discounts so that net revenues from each kind of member in a category are equal.

g) Is your dues base widely perceived to be fair? Would it be better to shift to an income base (or something easily measured that correlates with mission)? Have you researched the number of members who would sign up in each category following a shift in base? Can your organization afford the risk that your forecast will prove overly optimistic?

Conclusion

Membership income is an important element of nonprofit finance for many organizations. Conceptually, it is much like the other elements. Part of membership income represents the sales of goods and services, a commercial operation. Part of membership income represents donations to help the general public, an altruistic operation. But membership income is more complicated than either of these two pure sources of revenue as it also includes a distinctive element—donations to help other members. This is what makes the setting of dues and fees so complicated.

Most of what we know about the importance of membership income comes from tax data. Dues are a small source of income for most of the charitable nonprofits—less than 1 percent. Social clubs (60 percent) and business leagues (40 percent) rely more heavily on dues, as do a few charities. However, all of these numbers are underestimates—in some cases substantial underestimates—because of the definitions used by tax authorities.

The structure of dues is complicated. Organizations choose the number of membership categories, the benefits accruing to members in each category, and the types of discounts and surcharges as well as annual rates. Money must be raised from members or the organization will not survive, but members are both the source of revenues and the objects of organizational mission. It matters whether there are the right number and mix of

members, regardless of ability to pay, and member income policies determine this membership. There is scant academic literature on membership policies, but dues and structures are set
every day regardless. Hopefully, this chapter will help inform the
judgments of practitioners and encourages meaningful research
and dialogue.

7

Investment Income

*Woods Bowman, Elizabeth Keating,
and Mark A. Hager*[1]

Introduction

Investment income, which consists of interest, dividends, and capital gains, is very important to a small group of nonprofits. A steady source of income requires an endowment or quasi-endowment[2] and the threshold issue is whether any nonprofit organization should be endowed. Board members and staff members who stress service delivery and other mission objectives are among those likely to oppose the accumulation of capital beyond working cash and operating reserves. The prevailing argument is that most nonprofits operate to serve pressing needs *today*, and that accumulating cash shortchanges today's needs for unknown future needs. Several well-known scholars share these sentiments. Unfortunately there is no consensus on the matter (Fremont-Smith, 2002). All we can do here is to present the reasons for and against.

Hansmann (1990) questions whether the accumulation of endowment in universities is a better use of resources than the purchase of materials and quality experiences for today's students. Since the today-versus-tomorrow's needs assessment is very hard to make, many stakeholders argue that money should be spent on current programs rather than hoarded in endowment. According to Fremont-Smith (2002), "[i]f one considers the tax benefits arising from exemptions and charitable deductions as current subsidies, it is a short step to conclude that taxpayers have an immediate right to a real return on that subsidy." A McKinsey team led by former Senator Bill Bradley alleges that nonprofits "currently hold about $270 billion in excess capital in their endowments," and urges that it be spent down over twenty-five years (Bradley, Jansen, and Silverman, 2003). Payne (1995) has advanced the argument that hand-to-mouth privation breeds frugality and innovation, positive attributes for a responsible and responsive nonprofit organization.

People who are concerned with the financial operations of nonprofits are the ones who most often advocate for building endowment. The argument unfolds along several different lines. First, an endowment is likely to generate investment income, which is a particularly attractive resource. Although building an endowment is neither cheap nor easy, once established the investment income it generates requires less staff effort to manage than income from service delivery or fund-raising. When it comes rolling in, it almost always comes with no strings attached, and managers can allocate it to the organization's needs without restrictions.

A second reason to accumulate an endowment regards its availability as a hedge against economic uncertainty. Most nonprofits work on a budget that does not allow for pronounced or prolonged economic downturns, loss of major donors, unexpected lawsuits, or other terminal drains on their resources. These kinds of shocks can quickly overwhelm working cash funds and operating reserves. Unless an organization has access to loans or other resources to cover its shortfall, accumulating losses may well result in bankruptcy and closure of the organization. This doomsday scenario, all too common to even the most worthy nonprofit organizations, argues persuasively for strategic accumulation of an endowment. It may be the tool that allows a nonprofit to weather hard times.

Third, the wishes of donors can also work in favor of accumulating an endowment. While many donors prefer that their contributions go directly to the mission needs of the organization, other donors like the idea of their contribution existing in perpetuity. They do not want their contribution spent; rather, they want their donation to be a lasting legacy to the long-term viability of the organization. A fourth, closely related reason is intergenerational equity. As James Tobin, the 1981 Nobel Laureate in economics, points out, "[t]he trustees of an endowed institution are the guardians of the future against the claims of the present. Their task is to preserve equity among generations" (Hansmann, 1990). However, while donors may value the ability to transfer equity across generations, most leaders of endowed institutions do not see the issue in these terms.

Finally, chapter 12 of this volume argues that a nonprofit that owns real estate needs an endowment because it has higher fixed costs, which threaten its long-term survival. Investment income generated by endowment is the mirror image of fixed cost, so it seems logical to call it fixed revenue. Theoretically, all costs are variable in the long run, but some organizations own privileged assets, which as a practical matter cannot be sold under any circumstances short of liquidating the entire organization. The Yard, for example, is one of Harvard's privileged assets. Costs that are beyond the control of management limit its ability to respond to a long-term decline in income from fees, charges and contracts, and could force early liquidation. Indeed, long-term organizational survival is the one exception that endowment critic Henry Hansmann (1990) recognizes as legitimate.

The chapter will continue with a review of patterns and trends in nonprofits' reliance on investment income, followed by a discussion of current practice, including the legal framework that guides it, and several tools of nonprofit finance. We then discuss several theoretical questions such as how investment income is related to the characteristics of an organization and the impact it has on how an organization is managed, concluding with suggestions to improve practice. An appendix offers a brief overview of the basic technical concepts, such as total return and risk.

Patterns and Trends

Excluding foundations, half of nonprofits derive less than 1 percent of their total income from investments[3] but one in five receives at least 5 percent of their income from investments. The major subsectors where investment income is more than 5 percent of income are arts/culture, education, health care, disease-related organizations, public safety and disaster relief, youth development, human services, community improvement, research institutes, and mutual benefit societies. It is particularly important to higher education where one in five institutions derives 20 percent of its income from investments, and 10 percent derive over half of their income from investments.

Commonfund (2004) surveyed 657 educational institutions and supporting foundations in 2003 with total investments ranging from under $10 million to over $1 billion.[4] The average return on investment was 3.1 percent, net of fees. Few top performers were also in the top categories in earlier surveys. Top performers in 2003 were more broadly diversified in alternative investments (private equity, real estate, energy and natural resources) than institutions posting lower gains. They were more likely to invest in international and high-yield (junk) bonds. Maintaining the proportions required by an investment policy requires *rebalancing* the portfolio periodically. Investments that gain most in value must be sold and the proceeds used to purchase more investments in the category that lost value.[5] Rebalancing reduces overall risk in the portfolio's returns even while boosting the return on the median investment. Seventy-five percent of educational institutions and 84 percent of health care institutions rebalance their portfolios. Of the educational institutions, 51 percent use a fixed rule that targets specific percentages or ranges for each asset (Commonfund, 2004).

A dollar-weighted portfolio representing the group as a whole consisted of domestic stocks (32 percent), international stocks (14 percent), bonds (19 percent), short-term securities, cash and other (2 percent), plus so-called "alternative investments" (33 percent) that were the largest asset class. Thirty-two percent of institutions surveyed anticipate expanding their alternative investments, and only 3 percent plan to decrease them. The dollar-weighted mix of alternative investments consists of hedge funds (45 percent), real estate including real estate investment trusts (17 percent), private equity (14 percent), venture capital

(10 percent), energy and natural resources (9 percent), and distressed debt (5 percent).[6]

A hedge fund is an investment vehicle that is structured like a mutual fund, but exempt from the rules and regulations that govern traditional mutual funds. Therefore, it can own assets and employ strategies that are generally unavailable to a traditional mutual fund, such as selling short, leverage, program trading, interest rate swaps, arbitrage, and derivatives. Hedge fund fees are higher than fees charged by traditional mutual funds, plus they usually take a share of the profit. According to Commonfund (2004), among the 293 educational institutions and supporting foundations that invest in hedge funds, 66 percent use long/short stock strategies, while 50 percent hold distressed debt.

Due to lack of regulation and transparency, investing in hedge funds requires extra care and attention. No law requires hedge funds to report their returns or to standardize the method of calculating returns, and no regulatory agency has the authority to verify that reported hedge fund returns are accurate, although funds seeking pension fund investors voluntarily register with the Securities and Exchange Commission. Educational institutions surveyed expressed concerns about risk transparency (55 percent), individual manager risk (54 percent), oversight and due diligence (33 percent), and position transparency (30 percent).

Most education nonprofits with significant investments have committees composed of board members as well as investment professionals who may or may not serve on the board. The number of investment committee members in educational institutions increases with the size of portfolio. Educational institutions with endowments exceeding $1 billion have an average of 10.5 members on their investment committees, while institutions with endowments of less than $10 million have an average investment committee membership of 6.5. Eighty percent of the members of investment committees overseeing endowments exceeding $1 billion are investment professionals, compared to only 38 percent of the investment committee members for endowments of less than $10 million (Commonfund, 2004). Institutions that make heavy use of alternative investment strategies are also more likely to have a high proportion of investment professionals on their investment committees, regardless of the size of endowment.

Performance leaders among educational institutions use more managers than other institutions and are more likely to hire external managers to implement alternative investment strategies. They also have larger internal staffs: the average institution has 1.1 full-time equivalent (FTE) persons to manage its investments, while those in the top-performing quartile have 2.8 FTEs on their internal investment management staff; top decile performers employ 6.8 FTEs. However, it is not a simple matter to buy performance: large institutions, with over $1 billion invested, use an average of 81 investment managers, but they are not disproportionately represented among top performers.

As portfolios become more complex and institutions hire more managers, cost control becomes increasingly important. However, only 287 institutions of the 657 institutions in the sample monitor this information. Investment management fees cost them 0.542 percentage points. Consulting fees account for 0.119 percentage points and custodial fees, 0.053 percentage points.[7] These fees total 0.714 percentage points, which may seem modest, but it is enough to reduce earnings by 18 percent over a thirty-year period.

Current Practice

The law governing fiduciaries' investing practices has evolved from heavy restriction to allowing considerable discretion. We begin with a synopsis of the legal framework within which nonprofit investors, acting as fiduciaries, must operate. Nonprofit boards of directors and their investment committees use social responsibility screens, but at the same time are becoming more aggressive and sophisticated. Some, like the Guthrie Theater in Minneapolis, are taking advantage of the unique tax-exempt nature of nonprofit bonds to seize arbitrage opportunities. In this section we explore current practices unique to nonprofit organizations.

Though state laws and gift instruments vary considerably, directors of nonprofit corporations have three fiduciary duties in most states: a *duty of care* to be diligent in their oversight of the organization, including its finances and investments; a *duty of loyalty* to act in the interest of the organization rather than to benefit any personal, business, or private interest; and *a duty of obedience* to keep the organization true to its mission and in compliance with applicable laws (see Fremont-Smith, 2004).

If an organization is harmed by an error in judgment rather than a breach of duty, then the directors and officers are not liable under the *business judgment rule*. If the duty of loyalty, obedience, or care is breached, trustees and officers can be held personally liable for monetary damages. In many states, the three duties translate into laws that impose prohibitions on related party transactions, such as personal loans, use of organizational assets by board members, or sale or lease of land or other key assets to a board member without valuations and/or court approval. Further, the law requires evidence that only disinterested board members approve related party transactions and that the transactions are arms-length or produce a net benefit for the organization. Nonprofits must also disclose related party transactions to the board and/or the public.

Included in the duty of care is the requirement that fiduciaries be "prudent" in their business decisions. A few states still have "legal lists" of permissible types of investments, while thirty-nine states and the District of Columbia have adopted the Uniform Prudent Investor Act (UPIA) in some form (DiRusso and Sablone, 2005).[8] Under UPIA the standard of prudence, known as the Prudent Investor Rule, is applied to the total portfolio rather than to individual investments. UPIA identifies the trade-off between risk and return as the fiduciary's central consideration and diversification as an appropriate tool to manage it. Fiduciaries are given great latitude in determining what kinds of investment instruments are appropriate to achieve their risk/return objectives, and they may delegate investment and management functions, subject to safeguards. A companion law, the Uniform Management of Institutional Funds Act (UMIFA), adopted in some form by forty-five states and the District of Columbia (DiRusso and Sablone, 2005), clarifies that an institution can spend a reasonable portion of capital appreciation, in addition to current income (e.g., interest and dividends). These two models incorporate modern portfolio theory into endowment management.

Whenever a nonprofit organization or trust takes on a new financial advisor or portfolio manager, or allows new investment vehicles, it is the board's (directors or trustees) and investment committee's responsibility to engage in ample *due diligence*. Three golden rules of investing are: (1) never invest money in a vehicle if you do not understand the associated risks; (2) never entrust money to a manager that you have reason to believe is inexperienced, incompetent, or unethical; and (3) make your own independent assessment of the investment and the manager. Many very reputable charities were taken in by the Foundation for New Era Philanthropy because they did not follow these rules.[9]

Unlike a for-profit corporation, a nonprofit organization has a public mission, which might be expected to influence its investment decisions. The Social Investment Forum (SIF, 2003) defines socially responsible investing (SRI) as "an investment process that considers the social and environmental consequences, both positive and negative, within the context of rigorous financial analysis." A complete arsenal of institutional SRI strategies includes screening investments that are purchased for the institution's portfolio, taking advantage of the institution's position as a shareholder to advocate for changes at shareholder meetings, and investing in communities underserved by traditional financial services. The prudent investor rule and the business judgment rule are sufficiently flexible to permit using all of these SRI strategies.

Interest in SRI surged in 1989 when the supertanker *Exxon Valdez* ran aground in Prince William Sound, dumping millions of gallons of crude oil on the pristine Alaskan coast. The Coalition for Environmentally Responsible Economies (CERES) created a ten-point code of corporate environmental conduct and eventually it organized the Global Reporting Initiative to press for an international standard for corporate reporting on a "triple bottom line" of economic, social, and environmental performance. Lately, the Global Reporting Initiative has added global climate change as a significant risk to the long-term value of corporations and the viability of financial assets.[10] According to the Social Investment Forum's 2003 report, assets under management in portfolios assembled according to SRI principles (screened portfolios) rose by 7 percent between 2001 and 2003 and totaled $2.14 trillion in 2003.

SRI screens can be exclusionary, qualitative, or inclusionary. *Exclusionary* screens proscribe "sin stocks" in certain industries (e.g. alcohol, gambling, tobacco), or in companies with bad records on the environment, human and animal rights, or corporate governance. *Qualitative* screens identify companies with socially desirable products or services, or companies with good records on particular issues (e.g. diversity, executive compensation). *Inclusionary* screens, based on such things as CERES's ten-point code, identify companies that pledge themselves to specific conduct.

Fiduciaries are often concerned about a possible adverse effect that an SRI screen might have on a portfolio's return. They reason that, since a social screen restricts investment choices based on factors other than return, it could preclude them from owning securities that could improve a portfolio's performance. But "could" is not the same as "would." A 2003 analysis conducted by Morningstar, the mutual fund research company, provides evidence that SRI screens are not necessarily detrimental to financial performance:

> Moreover, looking at domestic-equity [stock] funds, we see normal distributions of performance and star ratings—average performance, in other words, which would indicate that SRI screens don't have a big impact on returns.... So, a fund with social screens that also has the important fundamentals you want in any fund—a sound strategy, low costs, and good management—ought to do a fine job of helping investors reach their goals. (Zimmerman, 2003)

However, the average domestic stock SRI mutual fund tends to charge fees that are 0.21 percentage points above the average non-SRI domestic stock fund, so socially responsible investors will need to carefully shop around.

Box 7.1. Case Study—Now Playing at the Guthrie Theater: Arbitrage Investing[1]

The forty-two-year-old Guthrie Theater wanted to construct a $125 million three-stage theater on a new site overlooking the Mississippi River in downtown Minneapolis. The financing plan included $85 million in individual and institutional contributions and $25 million in state bond funds. Unfortunately, that left the project short $15 million in June, with ground-breaking required by October 1, 2003.

To finance the shortfall, the City of Minneapolis issued $85 million in tax-exempt 501(c)(3) variable-rate demand revenue bonds. All individual and institutional contributions went into the Guthrie's Endowment Fund, and the bond proceeds financed actual construction. This arrangement creates arbitrage, because if all goes well, the difference in earnings from the endowment (expected return of 6.5 percent) and the costs of the bonds (expected cost of 2.5 percent) will earn enough over the construction period of 60 months to significantly reduce or eliminate the $15 million gap.

The Guthrie Board agreed to the arbitrage financing with the understanding that if the arbitrage yielded little, the Guthrie would have to carry up to $15 million of long-term debt on the new theater facility. To get an "AAA" rating on the bonds, a group of local banks was formed to issue a letter of credit to back the bonds. A complicated negotiation ensued because the banks wanted a three-year letter of credit, a clear schedule of contribution goals by date, and the right to foreclose on the collateral of the facility, even though it was partly owned by the city/state. In the first eighteen months, arbitrage return exceeded $4 million, net of borrowing costs.

[1] Case was written by Jay Kiedrowski, Senior Fellow, Hubert H. Humphrey Institute, University of Minnesota and Treasurer of the Guthrie Theater.

Nonprofits with the capacity to borrow for capital improvements are employing a relatively new investment technique known as arbitrage finance. A pure arbitrage strategy is one that has a 100 percent chance of making money by taking advantage of existing price differentials. In practice prices vary over time, so the chances are not 100 percent, but they remain temptingly high. Nonprofits can employ arbitrage by issuing bonds at tax-exempt rates (currently 2.5 to 3.5 percent) to pay for capital improvements, while simultaneously soliciting capital contributions to construct them. The debt proceeds are used to pay for the construction, while the capital contributions are held in an investment portfolio that earns a higher rate (currently 5 to 8 percent). As the debt matures, the investments are sold to repay the principal. The nonprofits make money on the spread between the rates at which they borrow and invest.

This investment strategy is relatively new, as nonprofit organizations (other than hospitals) have issued relatively little debt in the past.[10] The ability of nonprofits to issue debt has been limited by state statutes and, during the late 1980s and early 1990s, a federal cap that constrained the amount of tax-exempt debt states and municipalities could issue on behalf of nonprofits. This cap was lifted in 1997 (Danzig and Neel, 1998), allowing colleges and universities, and increasingly museums, access to the capital markets to finance facility construction.

Arbitrage transactions are difficult because they generally involve the support of a state or municipal entity that may make costly demands and they entail holding an investment portfolio that is both riskier and imperfectly correlated with borrowings. In addition, the transaction can be put in jeopardy if capital contributions are not raised or paid as soon as expected, if construction costs exceed expectations, if the construction is delayed, or if the investment portfolio does not perform as expected.

Theory

In this section we inquire into the relationship between investment income and organizational behavior. We are concerned with such questions as why and how endowed organizations are different. To begin, we distinguish among endowment, working cash, operating reserves, and plant funds. A working cash fund is an internal revolving loan fund used to smooth an organization's intra-year cash flow. To back up this fund, nonprofits may also maintain a revolving line of credit at a bank. An operating reserve is also an internal revolving loan fund, but it is used to cover unplanned budget deficits that occur from time to time. Money withdrawn from these funds should be repaid as soon as practicable. Plant funds, on the other hand, are accumulated for the purpose of expending them, although they are replenished on a predetermined schedule or as needed. They are generally designated for new construction and major maintenance.

Working cash, operating reserves, and plant funds may simply be an accounting designation that denotes the board's intent to limit a portion of unrestricted net assets for these purposes. In other cases, specific cash or investments may be designated for such purposes, and the funds may be separately invested or may be managed jointly with endowment funds. Of the four types of funds, only endowment is invested with intent to produce a permanent source of income. As used below, the term investment capital includes working cash, operating reserves, and endowment, but excludes money in deferred compensation plans, pension plans, and planned giving accounts because in these cases an organization is either a custodian or acts on behalf of others, not itself.

Capital accumulation reflects a strategic choice, with pools ranging from tens of billions at Harvard University to small nonprofits that invest earmarked capital in a mutual fund at a local bank. The size of the investment capital is the cumulative result of the fates and fortunes of a given nonprofit. However, if a nonprofit has an endowment, its donors or its board of directors have likely earmarked accumulated income for the purpose of long-term investment.

Individual decision making aside, what kinds of organizational characteristics are associated with endowment accumulation? We propose that a nonprofit's relationship to other entities, its structural characteristics, and the degree to which it is integrated in its community dictate the potential of the benefits of accumulating investment capital and managing it to greatest effect. The recent work by Hager and Pollak (2004) informs the remainder of this section.

First, we contend that nonprofits that are embedded in, or share strong interorganizational ties with, other organizations or systems benefit less from endowments. On the other hand, freestanding nonprofits with few ties benefit more. This proposition stands on the observation that reserves benefit nonprofits that might otherwise be devastated by sudden or prolonged environmental shocks. However, nonprofits with other resources to insulate against shocks, such as strong interorganizational ties, have less need for the insulation provided by endowment. For example, we say a nonprofit performing arts center that serves a university is embedded in the university. The embedded nonprofit is insulated from shocks due to its relationships with other organizations. It would benefit less from being endowed than a community performing arts center without strong ties to any other organizations. Small nonprofits with affiliate or other strong ties to large nonprofits, government, or business interests have other places to turn to in the event of economic downturns or other slips of fate.

Second, we argue that larger, more-established nonprofits are better positioned to generate and benefit from endowment. Investment income is certainly attractive to small and young nonprofit organizations. Since the accumulation of assets and the creation of endowments is a trendy management strategy, fledgling nonprofits have fewer barriers to establishing endowment today than in previous eras. However, despite the appeal, few have the wherewithal to generate excess capacity. Fledgling nonprofits contend with the so-called liability of newness: the lack of routines and relationships that an organization needs to operate effectively. While unrestricted investment income would be useful in bridging these liabilities, nonprofits need relationships to generate endowment and routines to manage it.

For these reasons, we should not be surprised to find that older, more-established nonprofits are more likely to generate and benefit from an investment strategy. Endowment accrues over a long period of time. Even if a nonprofit is convinced of the value of building endowment and reaping investment income, it may be unable to do more than fund its working cash and operating reserves. Only over long periods of small incremental advance and occasional capital campaigns do some nonprofit organizations see benefits of an endowment accumulation strategy. By the time a nonprofit establishes a sizable endowment pool, it is more likely to have the internal specialization and expertise to manage its investments for greater returns. A larger investment pool brings with it a secondary benefit: the potential for diversification because investment managers with large amounts of capital have access to a greater range of investment vehicles, with potentially higher rates of return.

Third, we contend that nonprofits with community connections, support, and legitimacy are more likely to generate endowment. As the breadth of topics in this book illustrates, nonprofits generate income from a broad range of sources. Some business models may allow nonprofits to generate endowment through the accumulation of earned income, where program service revenue substantially exceeds the cost of delivering services. However, few nonprofit organizations get rich in this way. More commonly, endowment accrues through contributions, especially major gifts. Contributions flow from connections to the community, especially when donors perceive that a nonprofit delivers essential and outstanding services to the community.

Three different elements condition community connections and generation of endowment. First, nonprofit organizations can benefit directly from the connections to institutional donors: government, foundations, and business. While these connections surely give them greater access to contributions for operating revenues, they also increase the potential for tapping these donors for dollars that can be earmarked as endowment. Second, the size and composition of the board of directors may be indicative of the potential for generating endowment. Board members can be key boundary spanners between nonprofits and resource-rich partners. They can facilitate access to these resources, and possibly lend expertise in investment options and opportunities. Third, a reliance on annual contributions signals a symbiotic relationship between the nonprofit organization and the goodwill of the community, although it also brings uncertainty in resource flows. Fortunately, to the extent that this community connection facilitates accumulation of endowment, the resulting investment income helps to smooth out the uncertainty of donations.

Extending the Knowledge Base

In this section we report on our research into how investment income affects the way an organization is managed (Bowman, Keating, and Hager, 2005). As we noted in the introduction, when an organization earns revenue by selling its services, it must take care to control production costs and to reinvest in the systems that are necessary to keep revenue flowing. An organization with investment income can spend it in a variety of ways without having an adverse effect on generating future income from this source. An independent source of income likely weakens incentives for cost control.

In the language of organization theory, investment income creates slack, which is defined as resources in excess of the minimum necessary to maintain current output (Cyert and March, 1963). The concept of slack has a long history in the academic literature dating back to Simon (1947). It developed in reaction to the rationalistic, profit-maximizing models of for-profit corporations. The word *slack* evokes an image of waste, which is antithetical to profit maximization. Perhaps because they never have been concerned with profit maximization, nonprofit scholars have virtually ignored slack. They are more concerned about organizations having an ability to realize their ambitions in relation to their mission, so they developed the remarkably similar concept of organizational capacity. Whereas the word *slack* carries a negative connotation, *capacity* is enabling. But both concepts describe resources in excess of the minimum necessary to maintain current output.[11]

Whether we call excess resources slack or capacity, they have negative and positive attributes. On the one hand they are associated with waste. On the other hand they facilitate internal cooperation and control (Bourgeois and Singh, 1983) and serve as a financial cushion in bad times (Chang and Tuckman, 1991).

This suggests that there may be an optimal level of slack or capacity where the negative costs and positive benefits balance at the margin. This interesting question is beyond the scope of this chapter. Here, we focus on the threshold issue of whether investment income is, in some sense, a resource in excess of that necessary to maintain current output. The nonprofit literature is newer than the organizational behavior literature, so the concept of capacity has not been as well worked out or as rigorously evaluated as the concept of slack, so we choose to ground our research in the literature of slack and adopt its vocabulary. Taking a cue from Bourgeois and Singh (1983), we define three kinds of slack—available, recoverable, and potential. Each type, it happens, corresponds to a standard measure of financial health—liquidity, profitability, and solvency.

The first type of slack, *available* (also called *unabsorbed*) *slack*, is measurable by liquidity in excess of the amount necessary for day-to-day operations. Liquidity is the difference between current assets and current liabilities. The second type of slack, *recoverable* (also called *absorbed*) *slack*, is measurable by excess overhead expenditures. Nonprofits with significant investment income have weak incentives to control costs. Nonprofits with significant investment income pay their executives more (Frumkin and Keating, 2004). We measure overhead by the ratio of executive salaries to all wages and salaries. An increase in overhead will reduce profitability at all levels of output, unless investment compensates. The third type of slack, *potential slack*, we measure by unused debt capacity, which is directly related to an organization's solvency. An organization with substantial investment income can afford to do things it could not otherwise do. Investment income acts as a lump sum subsidy to an organization. Duizendstraal and Nentjes (1994) proved that a lump-sum subsidy is the most effective way to create organizational slack, so we hypothesize that investment income positively correlates with all three kinds of organizational slack.

We tested our hypotheses using data from IRS Form 990. To focus on the behavior of nonprofits with a critical mass of resources and a potential for substantial investment income, we restrict our analysis to the organizations with positive cash flow and at least

$1,000,000 in total expenses. In addition, we eliminate two kinds of nonprofits: (1) those whose primary activity is fund-raising in support of governmental or other nonprofit entities and (2) membership and mutual benefit organizations, since their main activity is often insurance or pension management. We observed a positive and significant relationship between the ratio of investment income and total income and *available* slack in all subsectors. We also observed that size and a heavy reliance on rented facilities are strongly and negatively associated with available slack, as we expected. Health and human service organizations show the greatest aversion to converting investment income into liquidity.

We then examined how investment income is related to *recoverable* slack. The income stream from investments decouples an organization's costs from the market for its output, with implications for how the entire organization is managed. When an organization earns revenue by selling its services, it must take care to control production costs and to reinvest in the systems that are necessary to keep it flowing, but an organization with investment income can spend it in a variety of ways without having an adverse effect on future investment income. In theory, an independent source of income should weaken incentives for cost control.

We find, as expected, that firms with heavier reliance on investment income devote a significantly higher percentage of their expenses to overhead. This finding is consistent with Frumkin and Keating (2004) who show that well-endowed nonprofits compensate their officers more highly than their less investment-rich peers. There are several potential interpretations: Well-endowed organizations may be rewarding senior managers for successfully raising or overseeing invested funds, or their management team may be larger. Higher salaries no doubt attract and retain more highly qualified managers. Arts organizations expand administrative costs in conjunction with extra investment income at a significantly higher rate than other nonprofit organizations, while educational and health organizations display similar but less substantial overhead cost expansion. The human services subsector is an exception to our general finding; it appears to be reluctant to convert investment income into more or better-paid officers.

Finally, we find a significant positive association between *potential* slack and investment income. In both the human services and health subsectors, investment income is not used as readily to expand organizations' unused borrowing capacity.

Improving Practice

Several ways to improve practice emerge from the foregoing discussion, which we frame as diagnostic questions:

1. Is capacity (slack) put to good use, or is it wasted?

Tuckman and Chang (1992) observe that a nonprofit may seek to accumulate equity without necessarily planning to use it in direct support of its mission. Investment income gives an organization greater capacity. It frees an organization from dependence on resources that are under the control of others. It enables an organization to undertake long-range planning. It also gives nonprofit leaders and managers greater confidence in their plans by reducing the range of uncertainty in income projections. But, it has a dark side. It is likely to silence objections to paying unnecessarily high salaries and extravagant office decorating. Investment income provides opportunities; it is up to an organization to make the most of them.

2. Does your organization have sufficient working cash funds, an operating reserve, and plant funds?

These are the basic tools of financial security. An organization should not consider building an endowment without having these tools in place. The key is to calibrate the size of the funds precisely. If they are too lean, the organization will be living from hand to mouth and be tempted to cannibalize its endowment. If they are too fat, the organization is being wasteful. Funding sources may look askance at excessive amounts of liquid resources, and the organization will need to be able to answer their questions with appropriate supporting documentation. A working cash fund should be sufficient to cover the largest expected gap between monthly cash inflow and outflow. The appropriate size for an operating reserve depends on the nature of a nonprofit's business. Most funding sources would probably approve of an operating reserve provided it does not exceed the common standard of three months of expenses. The size of a plant fund should be based on a capital investment plan that provides for preventive maintenance and replacement of systems at the end of their useful life.

3. Is there a written, board-approved investment policy that distinguishes between a working cash fund, an operating reserve, plant fund, and endowment?

Organizations should have a written investment policy if the organization has surplus funds to invest, even if there is no endowment. If the organization does not have an endowment, such a policy can be very straightforward. It merely needs to maintain each fund's integrity and define the investment vehicles that provide a degree of liquidity appropriate to each fund's objective. If the organization has an endowment, having a written, board-approved investment policy is more critical because the organization will be using professional advisers and money managers and will need to give them clear, unambiguous instructions. An investment policy should spell out duties, responsibilities and range of discretion of the board, the investment committee, investment advisers, and investment managers. It should identify which asset classes are permitted and which are prohibited. If the board approves the use of a social responsibility screen for investments, the investment policy should specify the precise criteria.

4. Do board members facilitate access to resources? Do they have investment expertise?

Board members can play an important role in connecting nonprofits to wealthy donors. They themselves may not have the potential to make major gifts, but they may simply know someone who is wealthy. Ordinarily major gifts are cultivated over an extended period of time and major donors want to be connected to the top: to the board and the chief executive. As the organization accumulates more and more resources, it becomes increasingly important to have board members with investment expertise to guide the investment committee, which may include non-board member experts. People with investment expertise are more likely to know wealthy people.

   5. Are investments diversified? Does the investment policy set guidelines for asset allocation and rebalancing?

Diversification is the main tool for controlling the balance between return and risk. The simplest method is to specify the desired asset allocation. If the organization has very little money to invest, perhaps it can rely on one balanced mutual fund. As endowment increases, other asset classes can be added. An investment policy should also address rebalancing. If the portfolio is not rebalanced, the control exercised over the return/risk trade-off will steadily erode. Besides, it is a proven way of increasing returns over time without exposing the portfolio to additional risk.

   6. Are investment managers vetted? Is their performance evaluated and questioned?

A wise investor never invests with a person or firm without vetting them, and *never* invests in a product or vehicle that she does not understand. Investing is a complex business, so the organization should have investment advisers who are different from and independent of the investment managers as a check and balance. One cannot always tell whether a manager is competent by his or her client list. A better way of evaluating new investment managers without a long track record in bull as well as bear markets is by investing a small amount on a trial basis with an escape clause. Question them about how they achieved their returns.

7. Are investment fees and costs monitored and controlled?

This is the single biggest lapse in otherwise very strong investment programs at major institutions. Recall that only 287 institutions of the 657 institutions in Commonfund's sample of educational institutions collect this information. Fees charged by most mutual funds are widely regarded as too high. The industry has responded sluggishly to incessant pressure from regulators, editorial writers, and investors to lower fees. As we have seen, even small costs significantly erode the value of an investment over a long period of time. And, hedge fund fees are much higher.

Conclusion

Investment income consists of interest, dividends, and capital appreciation arising from endowment and quasi-endowment. There is an active scholarly and public policy debate on the question of whether endowment shortchanges current needs. While this question is not yet settled, there is no debate that it provides financial stability. But endowment should not be confused with working cash, operating reserves, and plant funds, which also provide financial stability of a different sort. Unlike the other pools of invested funds, endowment is managed so that it provides a reliable source of income over the long term. The prudent investor rule and the business judgment rule give nonprofit directors and managers considerable flexibility to manage an organization's finances, provided they are diligent and act in the interests of the organization. The law raises no barrier to socially responsible investing in its various forms. Nonprofit organizations are taking advantage of this flexibility to explore new investing territory: alternative investments and arbitrage investing, to name just two examples.

A nonprofit's relationship to other entities, its structural characteristics, and the degree to which it is integrated into its community dictate the potential of the benefits of accumulating investment capital and managing it to greatest effect. Income from investment provides nonprofit organizations with several kinds of organizational capacity, or slack, corresponding to different measures of financial health: liquidity, profitability, and solvency. Nonprofits with investment income must be extra careful managing their operations because investment income weakens incentives for cost control.

Appendix

Investing Basics

Readers who encounter an unfamiliar investment term may consult an online glossary at www.investorwords.com. Three important dimensions of an investment are total return, risk, and liquidity. Total return (or *return*, for short) is the sum of interest, dividends, and the increase or decrease in the market value of a security, usually expressed as a percent of an initial investment. If a pool of invested funds receives new contributions, or loses capital through withdrawals, the total return calculation requires adjustment. The adjusted formula approximating total return assumes that contributions and withdrawals occur at a uniform rate, and is given by $((EB - x)/(BB + x)) - 1$, where EB is the ending balance in a fund, BB is the beginning balance, and x is new contributions minus withdrawals divided by 2. To express total return in percent, multiply by 100.

Risk refers to the variability in total return. In general, when the chance of making money rises, so too does the chance of losing money. In general, risk is positively correlated with return, so a comparison of historic returns on different securities is meaningless without considering the differences in their risks. The *Sharpe Ratio* is a risk-adjusted measure of return that can be used to compare two investment vehicles. It is defined as the return on that investment above the return on a risk-free security divided by the standard deviation of the difference. Although no investment is perfectly risk-free, the ninety-day U.S. Treasury bill is the usual standard.

Risk can be broken down into two components: *systematic risk* and *unsystematic risk*. Systematic risk is associated with an entire class of assets, like stocks or bonds. It is also known as market risk because it is caused by market trends affecting all members of the asset class. Although the risk is systematic, investors experience it to different degrees depending on the mix of assets they hold. Unsystematic risk is the risk associated with a particular firm or industry. The distinction between these two kinds of risk is important because unsystematic risk can be virtually eliminated by *diversifying* a portfolio—that is, by owning a mixture of different securities with uncorrelated or negatively correlated prices. If they are positively correlated, the value of diversification diminishes with the degree of correlation.

Market risk cannot be avoided or reduced to zero, but it can be managed by investing in several markets simultaneously, a process called *asset allocation*. An *efficient portfolio* of investments is one that maximizes return for a given risk, or alternatively, that minimizes risk for a given return. Most organizations that own significant investment portfolios have written investment policies specifying the proportions of the total value that should be in each asset class, and specifying prohibited categories, if any. The single most important decision an investor can make is how to allocate a portfolio among different asset classes.

With the lowest return and lowest risk, cash (money market funds) is the most conservative investment. Of the plain vanilla investment vehicles, stocks (equities) are the most aggressive investments because they have the highest returns and highest risk. Bonds (fixed income securities) are less aggressive than stocks and more aggressive than cash.

Notes

1. Woods Bowman (DePaul University), Elizabeth Keating (Harvard University), and Mark A. Hager (University of Texas at San Antonio) would like to thank the other authors of this volume and Harriet L. Fader, Executive Director of the Diabetes Association of Greater Cleveland, for reading and commenting on an earlier draft.

2. Strictly speaking, an endowment is restricted as to purpose, whereas a quasi-endowment is unrestricted. For simplicity, this chapter will use the term endowment to refer to both concepts. Endowment

should be distinguished from working capital and operating reserves. We refer to the sum of these three concepts as investment capital. See chapter 12: Managing Endowment and Other Assets.

3. Under accrual accounting, all capital gains are revenue. On Form 990, only the realized portion counts as revenue. We rely on IRS Statistics of Income (SOI) data, which uses the IRS Form 990 definition of revenue. Data here are projected from the IRS Statistics of Income for fiscal year 1999 using the sample weights supplied with the data. Churches and nonprofits with less than $25,000 in revenue are not required to file 990s. The sample contains 14,386 records. Eliminating foundations (NTEE group T) resulted in a sample of 13,408. Weighted averages are based on a universe of 156,551. This is still less than the entire universe of reporting public charities because the SOI database emphasizes larger entities, which are more likely to have investment income. The statements made in this paragraph are likely to overstate the importance of investment income.

4. Commonfund is a nonprofit organization founded in 1971 with a grant from the Ford Foundation to improve investment management at nonprofit educational and heath care organizations. It actively manages $32 billion in assets and engages in institutional research.

5. The purchases merely must be in the same asset category as the investments that lost value, not the specific securities themselves.

6. Distressed debt is the debt of firms near bankruptcy. It is sold at a deep discount, which gives canny investors an opportunity to make money. Upon liquidation, a firm's bondholders have first claim on its assets. Although they are likely to get less than par, there may be enough value left in the firm to pay more than the bonds would fetch in the open market. It is not an investment vehicle for amateurs.

7. A more common metric for expressing fees and other costs is basis points. There are 100 basis points in a percentage point, so 0.542 percentage points is 54.2 basis points.

8. States rarely adopt a uniform act verbatim, so counting states that have adopted a substantially similar law is problematic. We cite DiRusso and Sablone because theirs is the most recent article to attempt to count states adopting both the Prudent Investor Standard and the Uniform Management of Institutional Funds Act.

9. The Foundation for New Era Philanthropy derived its name from offering a new approach to fund-raising, with a heavy emphasis on matching grants from "anonymous benefactors." In the early 1990s, hundreds of individuals, religious, educational, cultural, and charitable organizations invested funds with Foundation for New Era Philanthropy,

believing that these funds would be doubled in six months by guaranteed monies that the founder, Jack Bennett, had secured from several very wealthy benefactors. There were no anonymous benefactors, and Bennett was using new funds to repay principal and matching funds to prior depositors. It was actually a Ponzi, or pyramid, scheme, in which money from later investors is used to pay earlier investors. See Arenson 1995.

10. Line 64a on IRS Form 990 reports tax-exempt bond liabilities, but apparently there is so little activity in this category that it is not picked up in the Statistics of Income file that the National Center for Charitable Statistics makes available.

11. To further confuse casual readers on the topic, economists use "economic rent" to describe a payment to the owner of a resource that exceeds the minimum amount necessary to employ it.

8

Volunteer Resources

Anne E. Preston

Introduction

Volunteer labor provides important benefits to the nonprofit sector. According to the Bureau of Labor Statistics, 29 percent of the U.S. population sixteen years of age or older, or 64 million individuals, volunteered for a formal organization in 2003–2004. Median hours volunteered over the period were fifty-two, making the total number of volunteer hours equivalent to 1.68 million full-time employees. Using the Independent Sector's estimate of the hourly value of volunteer labor ($17.55 for 2004), these hours of work constitute 58.9 billion dollars of resources, or about a quarter of the total charitable donations. In comparison to the 12.5 million paid workers in the nonprofit sector documented by the Independent Sector, hours of volunteer work make up about one-seventh of the hours of paid workers, but volunteer workers swamp paid staff almost six to one. The challenge of the nonprofit sector is to use this valuable but unwieldy resource to its fullest.

An economic understanding of the role of this resource in nonprofit production and the motivations behind volunteer supply will help managers meet this challenge. This chapter begins with an examination of some of the patterns, trends, and current practices in volunteer work, and then offers a textbook description of the supply and demand for volunteer labor. It continues with a more detailed look at the demand for different types of volunteers, the costs they impose on the organization, and restrictions the firm might impose to assure increased productivity. Then a discussion on supply of volunteers considers the relationship between paid and volunteer work. Finally, a short empirical description of the characteristics of volunteers and their motivations leads into a culminating discussion on managing volunteer labor.

Patterns and Trends

Trends in volunteer labor are hard to identify. Data collected by the Independent Sector, the Census Bureau, and the Center for Philanthropy come up with different estimates of volunteering, often through slightly different survey methods and questions conducted at different points in time. The Independent Sector together with the Gallup Poll present estimates from biennial surveys, which have the potential to show changes over time. Estimates over the period since 1989 show that the percent of individuals eighteen or over volunteering in a given year was 54.4 percent in 1989, fell as low as 47.7 percent in 1993, and rebounded to 55.5 percent in 1998. The estimates for 2000 are low at 44 percent but the sample was altered to include only individuals twenty-one years of age and older, and the survey methodology was changed so comparisons with earlier estimates are impossible. The Center on Philanthropy included questions on volunteering on the biennial Panel Study of Income Dynamics Survey beginning in 2001; the answers to these questions will be helpful as we move into the future. The evidence reveals no definitive evidence that volunteering has fallen in response to the increasing labor force participation of women since the 1970s or the increase in real wages over the same time period. Wilson (2000) posits that volunteering has continued to thrive over this time period as the organizations that women volunteer for have changed with their entry into the labor force, as outdated clubs and associations have been replaced with grassroot community organizations, and as a more vibrant elderly population has manned the volunteer lines.

Volunteer services are concentrated in certain subsectors of the nonprofit sector. According to *Volunteering in the United States,*

Independent Sector's study on volunteering in 2004–2005, volunteer hours, similar to charitable contributions, are most likely to be supplied to religious organizations; 34.8 percent of volunteers cite a religious organization as the main organization to which they volunteer. Education and youth organizations come in a relatively close second, with 26 percent of respondents citing these organizations as the focus of their volunteer efforts. Behind these two types of organizations there is more dispersion of volunteer effort, with 13 percent focusing on community service organizations and 7.7 percent on hospitals and health organizations. *Volunteering in the United States* goes on to show that the types of activities most commonly conducted are fund-raising or selling items to make money, with close to one third of volunteering women engaging in this type of activity. The second most common type of activity, undertaken by about one quarter of all volunteers, is collecting, preparing, or distributing food. Third in line is teaching or tutoring, carried out by about one-fifth of all volunteers.

Current Practice

Focusing on primary activities masks the diversity of tasks undertaken by volunteers. A quick perusal of the volunteer wanted ads at www.idealist.org shows the variety of needs that organizations seek to fill through volunteer labor. Organizations are looking for skilled workers to perform legal work, write newsletters, maintain computer laboratories, and photograph special events. They are looking for intelligent and conscientious individuals who can be trained as guides for museum exhibits, mentors to teenagers in life and career skills, and nonprofit managers. And they are seeking compassionate souls to provide transportation for the sick and elderly, to chop vegetables for meals for AIDS patients, and to dole out food (and friendship) in local soup kitchens. These volunteer ads do not include the needs of the larger organizations such as fire departments, hospitals, and international nonprofits such as the Red Cross, which have established volunteer departments with well-developed recruitment programs. With this vast array of activities that nonprofit organizations need performed and volunteers choose to pursue, a simple economic analysis of volunteering seems particularly daunting.

Theory

What are the forces that result in more than 1.5 million full-time equivalent volunteers, the equivalent of 3 billion volunteer hours, working in the nonprofit sector over a given year? These 3 billion hours are the result of the interaction of volunteer demand and volunteer supply in the market for volunteer labor. A textbook analysis of this market identifies two sets of actors: nonprofit organizations and individuals. The organizations are the demanders in the market, and their needs and constraints dictate the demand for volunteer labor. The individuals are the suppliers, and their preferences and constraints dictate the supply of volunteer labor. The demand for volunteer labor is a "derived demand" since it is derived from the nonprofit organizations' goals of producing goods or services. Volunteer labor is one of several inputs into the "production function" of the nonprofit organization, and the nonprofit firms' demand is based on the value of extra output produced by each individual volunteer during an hour of employment. Assuming that volunteers work with a fixed amount of other inputs such as buildings, computers, paid employees, and so on, there will be a point at which the value of the extra output produced by a subsequent hour of volunteer work will start to decline and this demand curve will become downward sloping. The demand curve is displayed in figure 8.1 where the vertical axis measures dollars, or the value of production, and the horizontal axis measures hours of volunteer labor. Any point on the demand curve such as A gives the value in dollars of the hth volunteer hour employed in the sector.

The supply of volunteer labor by individuals, the number of hours that individuals are offering the nonprofit sector, is determined by preferences of the volunteering population. However, displaying supply on the same axis as demand poses problems since labor supply is usually elicited through pay, and volunteer labor receives no regular compensation. My esteemed colleague Richard Steinberg suggested a neat solution: consider the dollar value on the vertical axis as per hour recruitment costs rather than wages. With such a reconceptualization, we can line up potential volunteers in the economy along the horizontal x-axis according to their preferences for volunteering with those with the strongest preferences to volunteer at the origin and those with weaker preferences further along the axis. We further assume that those with the strongest preferences need no convincing to volunteer while those with weaker preferences will have to be asked, cajoled, or may be even bribed to work as a volunteer. Recruitment becomes the means to attract volunteer labor and as recruitment costs per hour increase the volunteer hours supplied increase as well. Therefore the volunteer labor supply curve is the upward sloping curve in figure 8.1.

Economists are always fixated on the intersection of curves, and in this instance the intersection of the demand for volunteer labor and the supply of volunteer labor gives the "equilibrium level" of recruitment costs. On the demand side of the market

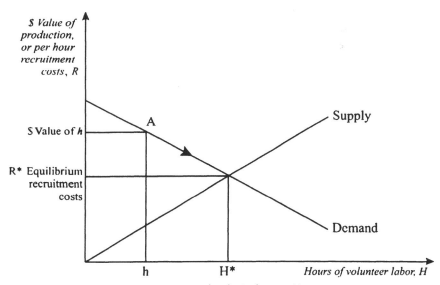

Figure 8.1. Market for Volunteer Hours.

organizations will employ an extra volunteer hour as long as the cost of recruitment is less than or equal to the productivity to the organizations generated by that extra hour. On the supply side individuals will supply their hours to volunteer as long as the recruitment costs spent by the organizations are great enough to overcome any natural inclinations not to volunteer. At the level of recruitment costs associated with the equilibrium, the volunteer hours supplied just equal the volunteer hours demanded. At any higher level of recruitment costs more volunteer hours will be supplied but the value to the firm of these extra hours exceeds the costs of recruitment, so less will be demanded; essentially there will be excess supply of volunteer labor hours. Similarly at lower recruitment costs, more labor hours will be demanded since the value to the firm of extra volunteer hours will exceed the recruitment cost, but these lower recruitment costs will not elicit as many volunteer hours.

This graph is a simple aggregated representation of the American volunteer labor market showing how the equilibrium number of volunteer hours employed (about 3 billion) and hourly recruitment costs are determined. Especially important is that this diagram helps us determine how changes in the supply or demand of volunteer labor will alter equilibrium values. For instance, if newer technology associated with production makes the unskilled volunteer less productive, the demand for volunteer labor will shift down and to the left, making equilibrium hours employed and recruitment costs fall. On the other hand, if recent tragic events such as the Asian tsunami or the destruction of New Orleans by Hurricane Katrina make people more willing to volunteer, the supply of labor will shift to the right and the new equilibrium will be associated with more hours volunteered and lower recruitment costs. Therefore we can use this diagram to explain past changes or predict future changes in volunteer labor.

Decisions concerning input usage are the result of a process where, given input costs and available technologies, the manager chooses the cost minimizing method to produce a predetermined amount of a good or service. In the case of nonprofits that have access to volunteer workers, one might anticipate that managers choose a highly labor intensive production process staffed exclusively with volunteers. Certainly in situations where the nonprofit has an undependable or even nonexistent stream of resources, this method is optimal, and the extent of capital usage depends on donated supplies and equipment. However, there still has to be some comparison of recruitment costs and value to the firm. Each additional volunteer should only be hired if the value to the organization exceeds the recruitment cost necessary to hire the volunteer. These volunteer nonprofits tend to fill a niche that is not met by any for-profit or government counterpart, and are fairly small in their scale of operation. However, for nonprofits with a constant stream of resources, alternative production processes and volunteer usages are preferable for a number of reasons. First, volunteers are not really free. There are costs to recruitment as depicted in the demand curve above, and there are additional selection, training, and monitoring costs, all of which may be higher per hour of work than the same costs for paid workers because volunteers are more likely to be both temporary and part time. Second, volunteer hours are not unlimited and may be difficult to attract for some organizations. Third, the big advantage to volunteer workers can often be a drawback as well. Without a paid wage, the manager has no obvious carrot to motivate (or stick to punish); volunteers are potentially less reliable than their paid peers. Finally, there are types of nonprofits, such as hospitals or public television, that, in order to compete with for-profit counterparts, must use increasingly sophisticated technologies complemented with highly trained professionals. In such scenarios volunteers may add little value and may even create negative value as they distract the professionals from the work at hand.

In order to understand the varying role of volunteers in the nonprofit firm, table 8.1 gives some useful, although still general, classifications. I have separated the organizations into those that are staffed by volunteers exclusively and those that are staffed by both paid and unpaid employees. The differentiation between the two is important because for the latter type, the relationship between the paid and unpaid worker potentially impacts both organizational demand for volunteers and human resource practices towards volunteers. In determining which tasks will be taken on by the paid laborer and which taken on by the volunteer, the organization with a mixed labor force is likely to hire paid workers for the day-to-day running of the organization and the operations which most closely define the mission of the nonprofit. The consistency, reliability, and professionalism of the paid worker are qualities needed in these activities. In the volunteer organization, these activities will be taken on by the most highly committed volunteers, possibly the founders who, while not paid, constitute the core workers. In some instances the choice between paid and volunteer worker can also be a product of institutional restrictions. For example federal and state funding of social service organizations often cannot be used for fund-raising activities. Thus small organizations that rely heavily on governmental funding can only engage in fund-raising through volunteer activity.

Within the organization volunteers are differentiated according to responsibility, with the top layer of volunteer for both types of organizations being the board member. Below the board member is the skilled worker who brings a certain expertise to the organization and uses that know-how in her role as volunteer. Within the organization that hires both paid and unpaid employees, the skilled worker may be a substitute or a complement for a paid worker. A substitute in production is defined in the following way. If increasing wages of the paid employees causes the use of volunteers to increase, volunteers are substitutes for paid workers in production. They are being hired to do the same tasks and thus can replace the paid workers. Alternatively if increasing wages of paid employees causes the use of volunteers to decrease, then volunteers are complements to paid workers. The paid workers and complementary volunteers work together to produce the nonprofit product and the productivity of the paid employee will be positively related to the productivity of the volunteer. Finally, within table 8.1, the volunteer with the lowest level of responsibility is the unskilled worker. This employee can also be either a complement or a substitute to a paid employee. The unskilled worker need not be unskilled, and usually is not, but possesses skills that have no special value to the organization. For example, one would never dare to describe the economist helping in a soup kitchen as skill-less—clueless, maybe.

Table 8.1. Volunteers by Type of Responsibility

Nonprofits with Paid Plus Volunteer Employees		Nonprofits with Volunteer Employees Only
Board Members		Board Members
Skilled, Complements to Paid Workers	Skilled, Substitutes to Paid Workers	Skilled
Unskilled, Complements to Paid Workers	Unskilled, Substitutes to Paid Workers	Unskilled

Any organization with a mix of paid (core) and unpaid workers may employ volunteers as both complements and substitutes to paid (core) workers. For example, a rape crisis center may use paid staff to man the help phone lines during the day but substitute volunteers for this same task at night when night-shift pay would be especially daunting. The same center's educational department might employ volunteers as a traveling performance troupe to help bring the message of rape awareness to local schools. The relationship between volunteers and paid workers generally is an empirical issue that has not been well researched. Rosemarie Emanuele (1996) did explore the responses of managers of nonprofit organizations in four different cities to increasing wages during the 1980s. While she found that a large majority of these managers respond consistently over the period by either continually increasing or continually decreasing reliance on volunteers, she did not explicitly report the extent to which the organizations' actions are signaling substitutability or complementarity of the two inputs. However, close examination of her data reveals that, of the 439 organizations showing consistent behavior, 270 were acting as if paid and volunteer labor were complements while 169 were acting as if the two inputs were substitutes. Some of the 270 organizations which reduced reliance on volunteers may have done so because they see their volunteers as complementary to paid labor or alternatively, on the supply side of the market, because the higher wages are motivating increased paid work effort and less time for volunteering.

The volunteer's skill level, role in the organization, and relationship to paid (core) employees all impact organizational demand and effective human resource practices. At the top of the ladder, the board member, regardless of the mix of paid and unpaid workers, is the volunteer who is supposed to bring vision, passion, a needed skill set, and often funding to the organization. Because of the unique role of the board member and the high payoff for a good fit, the organization will need to develop and implement an appropriate search process and selection criteria, which may involve costs in terms of time and monetary resources. While board members are probably most often sought through word of mouth and informal networks, want ads on a Philadelphia nonprofit website, www.idealist.org, call for a few applications for board members to serve on organizations such as the Girls Action Initiative. But there are also ads highlighting an organization that trains and places individuals willing to sit on boards of arts organizations. The productivity of the board member is likely to increase with time as she becomes familiar with the organization, its processes, and personnel. The costs of search, together with an acknowledgment of increasing productivity with time on the job, calls for well specified rules concerning participation, that is, minimum numbers of meetings per month and minimum years of service, to ensure a positive return on the organizational investment. Because board members work together to implement the mission of the organization, the optimal size of the board is likely to fall within limits; it has to be big enough to provide the necessary skill sets and small enough so that decisions can be negotiated without excessive haggling.

Skilled volunteers in a nonprofit organization who are acting as substitutes for paid (core) workers often bring a skill that is needed only periodically so that hiring an ongoing paid employee for the task is not efficient. According to want ads from www.idealist.org, these volunteers might be asked to design a website, prepare a tax statement, implement a fund-raiser, or teach a short computer class. Selection criteria may emphasize the skills and degrees of the applicant, but because these volunteers often work separately from the paid staff, extensive interviewing may not be necessary. In general, these types of volunteers need no training since they are using the training that they have invested in and they are asked to continue the activity only until the task is completed. While knowledge of certain aspects of the organization might be imperative to complete the task, an ongoing relationship with the organization need not increase the volunteer's productivity. The demand for these types of volunteers is limited by the auxiliary tasks that the organization undertakes, tasks that might be similar to those outsourced in for-profit firms. The decision about outsourcing versus using volunteer labor will depend on the availability of the necessary skills in the volunteer population. Recruiting costs for specific skills are bound to be high and must be compared to outsourcing fees.

Skilled volunteers who act as complements to the paid staff are potentially higher risk since, while a good fit will increase the productivity of the paid staff, a bad fit impacts the paid staff negatively. These employees, while skilled, will need to understand the organization and thus engage in either a formal training session or informal on-the-job training. Both types of training require time commitments of paid staff and ensure that the productivity of the volunteer, along with the paid staff with which she interacts, will be increasing over some specified period before it plateaus. For these types of employees, in order to ensure a good fit, the selection process will be more extensive, complete with multiple candidates, interviewing, and reference checks. In addition, in order to ensure a positive return on the selection and training costs, there should be minimum requirements on frequency and length of service. Such requirements may make this type of volunteer rare, especially in strong labor markets where skilled workers have plentiful paid opportunities. A perusal of www.idealist.org shows no obvious advertisement for this type of position, and a skilled individual willing to make this type of commitment may be more interested in work as a board member with its associated prestige and control.

The unskilled volunteer who complements the activities of the paid (core) worker, like the skilled worker in this category, will need to fit into the organization and engage in informal or formal training. As a result there will be a selection and recruitment process and minimum length of service obligations. Teaching assistants, Little League baseball dads assisting trained coaches, patient care advocates, and mentors for formerly homeless women are all examples of these types of volunteers. The longer and more frequent the obligation, the more limited the types of applicants, biasing away from high-wage individuals toward individuals who are retired or out of the labor force for other reasons or who are looking for marketable job experience. The demand for this type of worker is limited by the size of the organization, in particular its staff, and the type of production process implemented.

The unskilled worker who is a substitute for paid workers can fall into two types. Some may engage in operations that require training, such as the rape crisis volunteer who answers phones at night, the dad who becomes the head Little League baseball coach, or the community member manning the phones at the PBS telethon. The level of training needed will vary by job, but these individuals will need to make a commitment to the organization in order for the organization to recoup its training investment. Therefore there should be both a selection process as well as minimum length of service requirements. The demand for these employees is likely to be heavily dependent on wages of paid employees who are potentially being displaced. Alternatively there are unskilled employees who are substitutes for paid employees and who are generally engaged in labor-intensive operations that require little training. In these positions, organizations need not require an application, an interview process, or a time commitment. The open-arm welcome to all volunteers to a local soup kitchen is the attitude that mistakenly implies an unlimited demand for volunteers. However, for these types of positions, and these positions alone, volunteer labor is close to costless.

Extending the Knowledge Base

Economists' understanding of the relationship between paid labor effort and volunteering is still not complete. A simple model of volunteerism might identify volunteering as a form of leisure. Individuals choose the amount of time spent working in the labor market and the amount of time at leisure in order to maximize their happiness, which is a function of income and leisure. They are constrained by the market wage, limiting potential income, and the fixed number of hours in a day. Of the time allocated to leisure, some portion is allotted to volunteering, given the preferences of the individual. In such a scenario, as labor supply increases for an individual, leisure time falls and volunteering is likely to fall as well.

Given our understanding of the effect that wages have on labor supply, we can also model the effect of wages on volunteering. Individuals have a reservation wage, the wage below which it is not worth entering the labor market. This wage level is determined by preferences and the value one places on leisure. As the wage offered to the individual increases beyond the reservation wage, the individual will increase hours spent working in the labor market. However, there will be some threshold wage above which the individual will start to cut back on hours of paid labor. In this scenario, the income earned through the higher wage compensates for the fewer hours and the individual is happier with more leisure time. In this model of the labor market, the demand for leisure, the number of hours of leisure demanded per week in relation to the wage offered in the marketplace, is a mirror image of the supply of labor. At very low wages, individuals will not bother to work and spend all their time at leisure. With increasing wages the demand for leisure falls as labor is substituted for leisure. At some very high wage, the individual will find that increasing work hours is not necessary. In fact, fewer hours generates enough earned income so that higher wages begin to be associated with more leisure.

Such an analysis predicts that, for the individual who is prone to volunteer, volunteering will be highest during periods of non-work and will tend to fall with increases in the paid wage as labor supply increases. At high wages, as the individual cuts back on paid labor effort, volunteering may then start to increase again. Volunteer work is a substitute for paid work. Empirical studies have not given strong support for this relationship. Freeman (1997), using data from the 1989 Current Population Survey (CPS) and the 1990 Gallup Survey of Charitable Giving and Volunteering, shows that people who work are more likely to volunteer and people with higher wages are also more likely to volunteer. However, he does find that for those who have made the decision to volunteer, those who have a higher paid wage volunteer less than those with a lower paid wage. Thus conditional on the decision to volunteer, there is some substitution between volunteer and paid labor. Cross-section data, however, are not well designed to test these hypotheses since comparing volunteer behavior for different people is always flawed by the inability to control for intrinsic tastes for volunteering. New data collection efforts through the Center on Philanthropy Panel Study, a longitudinal survey tracking both labor market and volunteer behavior of individuals over time, will give more definitive results.

Several different data sets measuring volunteer behavior give a consistent picture of who volunteers, what kinds of people translate leisure time into time volunteering. Below are estimates from the Center on Philanthropy Panel Study (COPPS) conducted in 2001, as an appended module of the Panel Study of Income Dynamics—a biannual longitudinal survey. In 2001, 7,406 families were surveyed, and the family head as well as the spouse of the head were each asked the question, "During 2000, did you do any volunteer work through organizations that totaled ten hours or more?" (See table 8.2.) If the response was yes, the individual was asked to determine hours of volunteer time. In addition there was a question about whether any of the volunteering was to organizations helping people in need of shelter or basic necessities. Below are unweighted percentages of individuals who responded "yes" to the initial question on volunteering. Percentages show that the COPPS estimates of volunteering are lower than the Independent Sector estimates and are more comparable to the 1989 and 2002 CPS estimates. Discrepancies may be the result of differences in focus of the surveys. The Independent Sector surveys are focused on charitable giving and volunteering and, because of the constant attention to these issues, they may remind individuals of past volunteer behavior that otherwise would be forgotten. The CPS and COPPS data are additions to larger surveys that have a more general focus. Alternatively the differences may be a result of differing response rates of the two surveys. The COPPS response rate is quite high while the Independent Sector survey response rates are well below 100 percent for questions on donations. If those who do not donate or volunteer are likely to skip

Table 8.2.   Percentage Who Volunteered for an Organization at Least 10 Hours
in 2000 by Family Head and Wife of Family Head

	Head of Family	Wife of Head
Total	24.2	29.8
Sex of Head		
Male	24.8	N/A
Female	21.1	N/A
Age		
Youngest 25% of age distribution	19.6	21.8
Middle 50% of age distribution	27.5	24.7
Oldest 25% of age distribution	24.4	28.6
Number of Children		
None	22.9	26.3
One	23.6	26.3
Two	26.3	37.9
Three	30.4	36.2
Four	25.6	29.0
Five or more	12.7	24.7
Head Marital Status		
Married	26.4	N/A
Never Married	17.1	N/A
Widowed	22.6	N/A
Divorced	21.9	N/A
Separated	20.6	N/A
Employment Status		
Working	25.5	30.4
Temporarily Laid Off	16.2	37.2
Looking for Work	15.1	23.5
Retired	25.1	31.8
Disabled	9.8	12.8
Keeping House	15.8	29.3
Student	25.9	31.7
Race		
White	28.2	34.1
Black	17.6	21.0
Asian	28.6	28.4
Latino	9.3	12.2
Religion		
Atheist	19.0	25.8
Catholic	24.3	29.3
Jewish	31.9	38.4
Protestant	24.8	30.2
Donations		
Donated last year	32.5	37.5
Did not donate last year	8.7	9.9

Continued

Table 8.2. Percentage Who Volunteered for an Organization at Least 10 Hours in 2000 by Family Head and Wife of Family Head (*Continued*)

	Head of Family	Wife of Head
Years of Education		
8 or less	6.7	6.3
9	12.9	10.3
10	10.8	17.0
11	15.4	11.6
12	18.5	26.3
13	25.5	29.7
14	30.0	31.8
15	32.8	35.9
16	37.0	44.5
17 or more	41.9	51.4
Total Family Income		
Bottom 25%	14.1	13.8
Middle 50%	23.9	26.3
Top 25%	34.4	40.7
Hourly Wages		
Bottom 25%	17.6	24.8
Middle 50%	23.4	28.9
Top 25%	34.5	38.3

questions on volunteering and donating because of concerns about social approval, then the estimates for giving and volunteering may be too high.

According to the results, wives volunteer more than husbands, but comparing female heads to male heads, the female head of family volunteers less than the male head of family. However the difference may be due to marriage. Married heads of family volunteer more than nonmarried heads, and by construction the female heads are never married. Men in the middle of the age distribution are more likely than other men to volunteer while women in the oldest quarter of the age distribution are most likely to volunteer. Having an extra child increases volunteering until three children after which more children reduces volunteering. Interestingly and different from other surveys, for both heads and wives of heads, the probability of volunteering is equal for working individuals, retired individuals, and students. While for heads, these three categories are most likely to volunteer, for women, those most likely to volunteer are the temporarily laid off. As with all surveys, volunteering increases with education, with hourly wage, and with income. Jews and whites were more likely to volunteer than other demographic and religious groups. Finally, those who made donations to charity in 2000 were much more likely to volunteer than those who did not.

Reasons for volunteering are hard to pinpoint. The previous results show that people who are involved—at work, highly educated, having high family demands—are more likely to volunteer, possibly because they are more likely to come in contact with needy organizations. These organizations may also be those that cater to family needs—the local soccer club, the church, or the Girl Scouts—making the motivation not purely altruistic. Cultural factors also make a difference. Adults who have volunteered in their youth, who feel motivated to improve the welfare of others, and who go to church regularly are more likely to volunteer than their peers (Brown, 1999a). Clary, Snyder, and Stukas (1996) use the Independent Sector/Gallup organization 1992 survey on giving to examine motivations behind volunteering. They divide motivations into categories including *values*, helping others or working for an important cause, *career*, gaining valuable career experience or job contacts, *understanding*, becoming aware of and developing strengths, *social*, working for causes that people of importance care about, *enhancement*, working to feel needed, and *protective*, working to help deal with own problems. For the total sample examined as well as for subsamples defined by gender, race, education, income, and age, values is always the most important motivation followed by enhancement. Career is always the least important motivation. These results highlight the altruistic motivations behind volunteering that are sometimes masked by more self-serving behaviors.

Evidence from more recent Independent Sector surveys (2001) shows that being asked to volunteer is also very important, more than doubling the probability of volunteering. Freeman (1997) finds this result replicated with other data sets both within and outside the United States. There is clearly a selection issue: those who are asked are most likely to be individuals who have shown interest in the organization or similar organizations. Also a request from a friend or coworker carries a certain amount of social pressure that may lead to a positive response. The fact that being asked to volunteer is an important determinant of volunteering, together with the fact that those who traditionally volunteer, the white, educated, married, middle-aged women, are those who are asked, may work to keep the volunteer labor force fairly insulated. Asking increases the probability of volunteering beyond what is predicted by demographics; therefore, especially in searching for unskilled volunteers, nonprofit managers should think beyond the traditional volunteer and begin asking the young, the old, minorities, and low-income individuals.

Improving Practice

In managing a paid labor force, even those in the nonprofit sector, the structure of the compensation system is identified as an important tool to attract, motivate, and retain employees. This tool is not available for volunteers. However, in the same way that nonprofits, often strapped for cash, look to nonmonetary rewards to attract, motivate, and retain their paid employees, they can look toward these rewards for long-term volunteers. Because values motivate volunteering, one can assume that volunteers are initially attracted to the organization's mission. Unfortunately, this message is often not well communicated through the community. Posting volunteer openings on websites only communicates needs to the community of individuals acquainted with the nonprofit sector. If the manager is short on volunteers or desires a more diverse workforce, she should design an effort to reach out to nontraditional volunteers. Visits to high schools, senior citizens' centers, and community centers in minority neighborhoods, target individuals who may have leisure time that can be converted to volunteer time. In stressing the mission of the organization, the types of work that would be required, and the potential rewards, the organization is likely to attract volunteers whose values coincide with those articulated in the organization's mission statement.

Retention of volunteers is important since, as noted earlier, there are often sizable investments in training. While it is important that nonprofit managers carefully outline minimum participation requirements, there is no contract and enforcing these requirements may be difficult. Designing nonpecuniary benefits schemes that kick in after certain levels of service or in which benefits increase with service will serve to increase retention. For example, offering tickets to openings of shows for museum volunteers who have completed forty hours of service, or offering a museum shop discount that increases (albeit slowly) with hours of volunteering, will encourage ongoing participation. Volunteers to the local soccer club who help with children's soccer teams might be given subsidized tuition to a training camp held by the organization, after one or two seasons of participation. Volunteers to a local food pantry might be given a gift certificate to a participating restaurant after meeting some service requirement. Organizations should make these nonpecuniary benefits well known to volunteers at the time of hiring and, when possible, as in the case of the museum and the sports organization, design the compensation so that it will be especially valuable to the types of individuals the organization wants to attract. The benefits system then achieves two goals—increased retention and employment of volunteers who further the mission of the organization.

Motivating volunteers requires creative thinking as well. The nonpecuniary benefits discussed above can be handed out according to performance as well as longevity but then staff, whether paid or volunteer, must identify and measure desired performance. Nonprofits, which are not driven by a bottom line, have a notoriously difficult time linking performance to organizational outcomes, and if these types of rewards are given according to subjective criteria, they may foster jealousy and feelings of inequity. Maslow's hierarchy of needs theory and Herzberg's motivation-hygiene theory of job satisfaction both imply that motivation is only elicited through psychological rewards which build self-esteem. Therefore organizations should think about ways to publicly praise volunteer performance. A

202 / Anne E. Preston

volunteer appreciation luncheon with certificates of service and speeches highlighting individuals' contributions, or nominations of special volunteers for community service awards, are likely to make volunteers feel valued. Promises of increased responsibility with longevity and positive contributions to the organization are likely to motivate the committed volunteer. In organizations with a large volunteer staff, successful volunteers might move up a hierarchy into management roles. These types of rewards and praise must be well articulated and public, so that volunteers not only feel valued but also understand the types of goals they can work toward.

The following set of diagnostic questions should help the nonprofit manager assess how best to utilize and manage volunteers in her workforce:

1. How does the manager of an all-volunteer organization decide she has recruited "enough" volunteers?

The manager should try to evaluate for each volunteer the costs as well as the benefits in terms of value of service or product produced. If, for all volunteers, benefits are greater than costs, then the manager should think about hiring more volunteers. Current staff is creating positive "profits" for the organization. If the costs are approaching the benefits for one or more of the volunteers, then no more should be hired. If costs are greater than benefits for any volunteer, that person should be let go.

2. In an organization with a paid labor force, which tasks should be reserved for volunteers?

In general, volunteers should work as substitutes for paid workers so their work does not interrupt the paid staff's productivity. The volunteer should be able to work independently with minimal monitoring. When a volunteer is hired to complement the paid worker, the selection process will entail greater depth to ensure a good match with the existing staff.

3. How much training should be conducted for volunteers?

The training should be sufficient for the task or tasks in the job description. General skills required, such as computing skills or legal knowledge, cannot be taught. Therefore the volunteer with these skills must be recruited. The training should be primarily related to knowledge that is specific to the organization. Examples include acquainting the volunteer with the accounting spreadsheet, explaining proper etiquette when communicating with donors, or explaining organizational rules and regulations.

4. Should volunteers be given hours requirements?

Hiring a volunteer and maintaining a volunteer are not costless. The up-front costs of selection and training must be recouped for each volunteer. Therefore the minimum hours requirement should be determined for each volunteer such that the productivity of the volunteer working those minimum hours exceeds these costs. Often productivity will increase with work at the organization. In this scenario, the organization might want to have even higher minimum hours requirements to ensure that the volunteer reaches her full potential productivity.

5. If common recruitment practices leave me short on volunteer applicants, what practices should I turn to?

Look to nontraditional volunteers: students, elderly, minorities. Go to centers serving these communities, articulate the mission of the organization and the requirements of the volunteer job, and boldly ask individuals to work at your organization.

6. How can I reduce turnover of volunteers?

Design a nonpecuniary benefits program that rewards good performance and longevity. Programs that publicly praise volunteer contributions may satisfy emotional needs of volunteers. Nonpecuniary benefits which are awarded for milestones with the organization reward tenure. Increasing the responsibility of the successful volunteer provides goals to work toward.

Conclusion

The volunteer worker, like the donated computer or free office space, is most likely not made to order. Hidden costs of integration of these "free" resources into existing production processes are exacerbated by storage and repair costs of donated equipment and training and monitoring costs of the volunteer. Hidden costs require nonprofit managers to carefully compare potential costs with the value of potential productivity before agreeing to take on any of these donated resources. Volunteer workers bring another layer of complexity to the decision process since their productivity depends not only on how the organization uses them but also on whether the match between the organization and the volunteer is a good one. Therefore, understanding the demand-side labor needs of the organization and the supply of volunteers to the organization and then developing the selection processes which will best match supply to demand are tools which will enable the organization to employ this "free" labor at its highest potential.

III

SOURCES OF CAPITAL

9

Collaboration and Barter

Renee A. Irvin

> Two men can both make shoes and hats, and one is superior to the other in both employments; but in making hats he can only exceed his competitor by one-fifth ... and in making shoes he can excel him by one-third ... will it not be for the interest of both, that the superior man should employ himself exclusively in making shoes, and the inferior man in making hats?
>
> —David Ricardo (1817, 83)

Introduction

Almost two hundred years have passed since David Ricardo published *On the Principles of Political Economy and Taxation*, yet his text still exhibits a precise and elegant argument. Trade can benefit all trading parties, and by no means should we ignore the potential benefits of trade for nonprofit organizations. When goods being produced are as multifaceted as the complex mission-based outcomes sought by nonprofit organizations, it may not only harm society, but also harm the nonprofit itself to act in isolation.

Nonprofits extend their operating resources by trading what they have with other organizations, in order to obtain new resources that are more valuable to them. In addition, they leverage their resources by entering into partnerships with other organizations for the purpose of exploiting economies of scale, scope, and specialization. This chapter uses several different strands of

economic theory to explore the circumstances and principles under which collaboration and barter can effectively increase the
operating resources available for nonprofits to address their missions, as well as the circumstances where such strategies may be
counterproductive.

We begin with an illustrative report from a survey of 811 nonprofit managers in the United States. This survey, undertaken
by the National Council on Aging (2005), focused on volunteer
management, but its findings echo those found in other nonprofit
management fields:

> The response from small volunteer organizations was particu-
> larly striking: According to local directors and volunteer coordi-
> nators who answered the survey, almost half of the local organi-
> zations with fewer than twenty-five volunteers do not pool their
> resources for any activity. Nor do many organizations appear to
> want to join forces. No more than 29 percent of all the respon-
> dents said that they would be interested in combining efforts
> on transportation, volunteer recognition, background checks,
> best practice information, volunteer coordination, or liability
> insurance. (10)

This sets the stage for the remainder of the chapter: Some
organizations are not collaborating. Why not? To the outsider,
this is often a cause for dismay (see also Knickmeyer, Hopkins,
and Meyer, 2003). The survey report writers go on to exhort:

> Local nonprofit leaders need to be convinced that collaboration
> is to their benefit. Not only does cooperation among local non-
> profits carry financial benefits and potentially improve service,
> it is also increasingly required by supporting bodies. Funders
> are increasingly demanding that local and national groups work
> together and avoid duplicating their efforts. . . . This reality does
> not appear to have influenced the actions of local nonprofit lead-
> ers, *so third-party intervention might be necessary to enlighten people
> at the local level.* (National Council on Aging, 2005, 10)

Italics are added because this is as close as a nonprofit finance
text can get to the sinister tones of a pulp fiction novel. Funders

view the growth in numbers of nonprofit organizations as a mixed blessing. On one hand, a robust nonprofit sector provides a vast array of approaches to produce services with broad public benefit. On the other hand, duplication in nonprofits is not seen as particularly advantageous, because resources may be wasted as each nonprofit struggles to produce its mission-related outputs. If smaller nonprofits could find ways to join forces, the resource requirements of getting a nonprofit up and running might be reduced significantly, and more resources could be devoted directly to mission-related expenses. The same argument applies to the government sector, where duplication is truly despised.

This chapter will borrow from the tenets of trade theory and other fields of economic inquiry to examine arguments for collaboration in the nonprofit sector. We uncover strong reasons for collaboration and even barter among nonprofit organizations, yet also some cautions for the overeager proponent of collaboration. Nonprofit managers and their partners need to understand the decision-making process that precedes successful collaboration. Funders must also understand why some organizations are eager to pursue cooperative projects, while other nonprofits operate in perpetual isolation.

Patterns and Trends

Despite the widespread enthusiasm for collaborative efforts in the nonprofit, government, philanthropic, and business sectors (Arsenault, 1998; Austin, 2000; Bergquist, Betwee, and Meuel, 1995; Berresford, 1989; Renz, 1999; Werther and Berman, 2001; Wondelleck and Yaffe, 2000), it cannot be assumed that the nonprofit sector is the perfect starting point for partnerships and alliances. Foster and Meinhard (2002) summarize the voluminous literature on collaboration and review organizational characteristics that predispose nonprofit organizations to undertaking or avoiding collaborative ventures. They find that larger organizations and those facing negative funding impacts or increases in service needs are more likely to favor collaboration.

Autonomy may work well for some nonprofit organizations, but the nonprofit sector also exhibits an impressive amount of collaborative effort, compared to the government and business sectors. Nonprofit stakeholders have plenty of economic incentives to form collaborations in order to advance the organization and produce more mission-related output. Here we will describe examples of each of the following incentives in detail:

- Reduce fixed costs of operation
- Reduce variable costs of operation
- Use fewer resources via specialization and trade
- Obtain revenue from intangible assets
- Reach more clients
- Reduce mutually destructive competition
- Shape the external environment

Institutional funders such as community foundations know these benefits of collaboration, and it is the rare request for proposals that does not include some encouragement for the grant applicant to collaborate with other organizations in their proposed project. The funder's motivational perspective, however, is somewhat different. Later we will explain why institutional funders have been enthusiastic proponents of collaborative approaches to nonprofit enterprise.

Nonprofit organizations, particularly in health and human services, are key service providers for government-funded initiatives (see Boris and Steuerle, 1999; Smith and Lipsky, 1993). In many situations, this requires working closely with government agencies to explore mutual goals and forge solutions that are clearly collaborative in nature. Governments recognize that nonprofit organizations bring complementary skills to a project, be it an ability to articulate and address the needs of diverse population subgroups, a dedicated volunteer labor pool, or innovative new ways to address problems in the community.

On the noncollaborative end of the spectrum, a nonprofit organization may simply serve as a contractor for the government funder, as the nonprofit performs the required service in exchange for payment. These situations, however, are commonly referred to as "partnerships," even though the nonprofit organizations are often awarded the contracts through competitive bidding. While the labels "collaboration" or "partnership" may seem a bit generous for subcontracting, the vague boundaries of the desired product—better outcomes for the entire community—can require extensive interaction between transaction partners. Government-nonprofit contracting is usually not a simple cash transaction for a tangible product; rather, it is an investment intended to achieve broad social benefits.

Similarly, nonprofits also have increasingly entered into collaborative ventures with businesses. As Austin (2000) describes, this collaboration ranges from a one-time sponsorship or cause-related marketing project for fund-raising, to almost complete (and very rare) integration of the foi-profit's and nonprofit's missions and facilities. It is well to remember that nonprofit and for-profit interaction is not confined to the occasional sponsorship gift. Significant collaboration occurs in all types of nonprofits and businesses as they work together on goals benefiting the broader community. Consider the enthusiasm with which businesses interact with nonprofit organizations. Businesses may provide meeting space for nonprofit groups, encourage and even pay their employees to volunteer for nonprofits, provide goods and services at a discount, and lend legitimacy to a nascent nonprofit by publicly stating their support for the cause. Businesses benefit by providing enjoyable activities for their employees, raising their profiles as community leaders, and perhaps increasing the volume of business due to their actions. Thus, this chapter provides arguments and conceptual tools for nonprofit organizations to approach collaboration with businesses as a trading rather than a gifting proposition.

The existing literature on nonprofit collaboration with other nonprofit organizations, governments, or businesses, is largely laudatory and prescriptive. We are told that collaboration is a very good thing and provides a solution to many nonprofit shortcomings. In this chapter, however, we take a resolute step backward so that we can view the topic of nonprofit collaboration in a broader, more rigorous way. By focusing on the underlying conceptual framework for nonprofit collaboration, we arrive at a more informed understanding about collaborative enterprise and when it is suitable or unsuitable for enhancing nonprofit activities and outcomes.

Current Practice

Despite the plucky go-it-alone character of many community organizations, as nonprofits grow and mature, they begin to recognize the advantages—not just to the community at large, but also for their organization's own internal benefit—of collaborating with other organizations. Below, we examine some of the benefits collaboration promises, as introduced above, by applying relevant theory.

(1) Reduce Fixed Costs of Operation. Fixed costs are costs of operation that do not increase when output—the volume of clients, audience members, and so on—increases. Rent, licensing fees, and even some labor costs can be considered fixed costs, as they are largely independent of the volume of the nonprofit's production. Over a long time horizon, few costs are truly "fixed." For example, the building that the animal shelter just moved into can be enlarged or rebuilt as time goes on. In the short run, however, organizations are faced with expenses that must be paid for, regardless of how many clients are served, how many donations come in, and what their hours of operation are.

Every conscientious nonprofit searches for ways to reduce costs without reducing mission-related output. Because fixed costs usually stay fixed over a large range of output, by definition, it makes perfect economic sense to search for ways to distribute fixed costs over a broader output, thereby reducing the average cost per unit of output. When the individual nonprofit is not in a position to increase output further, it may look externally to partner with another organization seeking similar ways to spread its overhead costs over a wider output range. Reading this very carefully, one might think that nonprofits are inefficient because they have taken on inappropriately large fixed costs and must partner with others to reduce their cost burden. However, arts and human service–related nonprofit organizations, among others, might be saddled with unusually high fixed costs because their production varies by the time of day or season, forcing the organization to have excess capacity to meet times of high demand (Weisbrod and Lee, 1977; Holtman, 1983).

To illustrate the phenomenon of collaboration motivated by fixed cost reduction, one need only think about schools that provide meeting space for nonprofit youth groups after hours, or churches that host preschools on-site during the workweek. Less commonly, nonprofit groups can even share administrators. An excellent illustration of collaboration is provided by the Under One Roof Project (2004), which encourages nonprofit organizations to colocate in one place. Colocation implies savings in shared fixed as well as variable costs per unit of output such as garbage collection, phone service, administration, utilities, and so on. Colocation also may increase revenues from improved access to potential clients, as multiservice clients are referred to other agencies in the building. Colocation efficiencies suggest "economies of scope," where the joint production of two different products in one "firm" results in lower production costs than if the products had been produced independently. Stated another way, economies of scope result when a collaborative effort by two organizations producing various products jointly can produce them more cheaply than if each product is produced by a separate organization (see Panzar and Willig, 1981; Bailey and Friedlander, 1982).

(2) Reduce Variable Costs of Operation. Variable costs, such as materials, supplies, and service-providing labor, may not seem at first glance to be the focus of collaborative efforts among nonprofits. After all, variable costs are directly related to the output level of the individual nonprofit, so no excess capacity exists to exchange with other nonprofits. Note, however, that retailers of supplies such as paper and other office necessities charge lower prices to consumers purchasing in larger quantities. If enough nonprofits band together in purchasing cooperatives, they can reduce their variable costs considerably by purchasing items at wholesale rates. McLaughlin (1998) reports that one strategic alliance by seven nonprofits resulted in savings of $50,000 on dairy products, bread, industrial paper, and plastics.

In addition to supplies, nonprofit organizations also join together with would-be competitors in advertising efforts. We see this phenomenon often in the arts, as regional arts organizations jointly market upcoming concerts or exhibits. Why would they want to pay to be included on an advertisement that lists their competitors? Again, bulk-purchasing efficiencies might apply, with larger advertisements costing less on a square inch (or per-second) basis than smaller advertisements. Smaller nonprofits might want to associate themselves publicly with larger, more prestigious arts organizations. Finally, joint marketing efforts might make enough of an impression to change the habits of a reticent public. After all, first-time visitors to the opera may also become symphony concert goers once they are hooked on classics.

Nonprofits might also purchase group medical and dental insurance more cheaply, because the insurer's risk is spread over a larger group of clients. Admittedly, a nonprofit organization is not likely to form a cooperative venture to purchase inputs that are a small portion of its costs (i.e., we would not expect to see a coalition form to purchase masking tape in bulk). Collaborative group purchases must result in enough savings to justify the transactions costs of the collaboration.

(3) Use Fewer Resources via Specialization and Trade. Aside from reducing the costs of inputs, nonprofits may be able to rearrange their production patterns in a joint effort with other nonprofits to exploit synergies. Synergy can be considered a more general term for the ability to increase production with a given amount of joint resources. Trade theory provides more specific descriptions of synergy arising from "absolute" and "comparative" advantage of two firms.

Absolute advantage, first described by Adam Smith in 1776, is a situation when one country excels in the production of one good, and another excels at a different good, where "excel" means to produce it more cheaply—with fewer inputs or better production technology and thus lower costs. It would be mutually beneficial for these countries to specialize in the good in which they excel, then trade. Total resources used in production will fall, and more of both goods will be produced. To illustrate, for nonprofits

Table 9.1. Gains from Trade under Conditions of Comparative Advantage

	Annual Output Individually		Annual Total Output	
	GreenPower	CATRO	Without Trade	With Trade*
Direct Mail Tons per FTE	20	18	38	36
Lobbying "Hits" per FTE	100	20	120	200

* CATRO produces the direct mail and GreenPower performs the lobbying.

a chamber music group might perform a concert for a special fund-raising event for a children's museum. In exchange, the children's museum designs a week-long summer camp focused on the physics of music, ending with a trip to a chamber music concert for the students and their parents. Clearly, the chamber music group excels in music performance, and the children's museum excels in educating students. By working together, the children's museum makes more money in their special event, and the chamber music group reaches those elusive younger families.

But it is not necessary for each organization to have absolute advantage. Gains to trade can occur even if one organization is better at producing both products. Since this concept of "comparative advantage" may seem counterintuitive, even after reading Ricardo's passage at the beginning of this chapter, an example is provided in table 9.1. Assume that you have two environmental advocacy organizations, both involved in direct mail solicitation as well as lobbying. The larger organization, "GreenPower," is better at mailing than the small organization ("Citizens Against Toxic Run-Off") because they have a fairly sizable mailroom. GreenPower is much better than CATRO at lobbying, because GreenPower employs a very skilled lobbyist. Table 9.1 provides some hypothetical numbers describing this situation, where FTE refers to full-time equivalent units of labor.

Under this admittedly simplistic scenario, GreenPower gives up its mailroom activities, subcontracting to CATRO. Total mailroom production falls a little, but that reduction is more than compensated by the impressive gains in lobbying. Notice that the gains to specialization and trade only accrue if the productivity ratios *differ* between the nonprofit organizations. If GreenPower produced twice as much direct mail per FTE compared to CATRO, as well as exactly twice as many lobbying hits per FTE compared to CATRO, there are no synergies to exploit, and GreenPower should produce both products itself.

It is time to give some voice to the skeptics. What if Green-Power's lobbying does not really benefit CATRO's specialized focus on toxic run-off? What if CATRO is careless and unprofessional in its direct mailing activities? Not only is "lobbying" difficult to quantify, but the trade may require a detailed legal contract specifying desired outcomes from the partnership. When information is incomplete, partnering agencies require either an extremely high level of trust and communication, or a more formal legal structure (see Sanders, 1994).

In the examples above, we concentrated on synergy resulting from labor productivity differences, which is not unrealistic considering the labor-intensive nature of the nonprofit sector. The Heckscher-Ohlin theorem extends this further, however, by describing how a country rich in certain factor endowments (land, for example) will specialize in the production of goods requiring land (agricultural products), and will trade with countries that have abundant amounts of other factor endowments (Ohlin, 1933). This can easily be pictured in a nonprofit context. A city park with a large physical site collaborates with a youth mentoring group. The at-risk teens gain job skills as they perform carpentry and trail maintenance for the Parks Department. In essence, the land-abundant park provides the job-training site for the labor-abundant youth mentoring organization. The Heckscher-Ohlin theorem implies that the most trade will occur between the most dissimilar countries. In our nonprofit context, this means that we expect to see the most collaborative specialization and trade occurring between organizations in differing subsectors.

(4) Obtain Revenue from Intangible Assets. Although businesses and nonprofits interact and cooperate in myriad ways, special attention should be drawn to ways in which nonprofit organizations exchange intangible assets—their community goodwill and good name—for resources from businesses. Chapters 5 and 10 discuss how nonprofit organizations can partner with businesses, but intangible asset trade can occur among nonprofit

organizations as well as government agencies. For example, utilities and government agencies often sponsor activities in the nonprofit sector for some of the same reasons that businesses do: to elevate their profiles as community members. The sponsoring entity "purchases" community goodwill with a gift of money or significant volunteer labor. The etiquette-conscious nonprofit recipient should be careful to gratefully describe the sponsorship as a gift of the sponsor's good name to the nonprofit, however!

(5) Reach More Clients. Marketing your organization via contact with other organizations may seem like a remarkably indirect way to go about increasing revenue. Yet there are certain situations, especially in human services, when collaboration can increase client flow. First, contacts between organizations can result in client spillover from one agency to another, especially if the organizations fill complementary roles for clients. Government agencies may be particularly interested in assisting agencies to colocate because clients may receive superior service and ultimately require fewer government services in the future. Second, in times of heavy demand for services, even direct competitors may refer overflow of clients to other nonprofit agencies. Snavely and Tracy (2000) found that the most common result of collaboration between rural human service nonprofits was trading information about clients. Indeed, the directors involved signed memoranda of understanding about case management relationships, detailing procedures for services provided by the collaborating nonprofits.

Notice that more formal forms of collaboration such as joint production or trade are not necessary to increase client referrals. Increases in client referrals can result from an increased level of familiarity among nonprofit professionals in a community (see Krebs and Holley, 2004). Networking via associations (for nonprofits in specified fields) can have a positive effect on client referrals, but more client volume may occur via networking among agencies not necessarily in the same field of expertise. External funders such as United Way or community foundations often encourage the development of advisory councils and other networking groups of complementary nonprofit agencies, that is, agencies serving the same clients, but in different fields.

Finally, nonprofits interacting and networking with businesses can lead to gains for both parties. A recreational clothing company, for example, can bring employees to an arboretum for a work party. The arboretum garners not only the labor, but also potential new members who become involved in the organization. Meanwhile, the business gains publicity in the arboretum's newsletter or the local newspaper (which might attract arboretum members to become customers), and possibly reduced turnover in their workforce. Probably the most significant and mutually beneficial networking between businesses and nonprofit organizations occurs when employees of firms serve on nonprofit boards of directors. Service on nonprofit boards allows employees to bring their skills to nonprofit organizations and also network with other leading professionals in the community.

(6) Reduce Mutually Destructive Competition. Arsenault (1998, 3) stresses consolidation and merger as a solution for the scenario when "(s)urvival as an autonomous unit is in doubt, and an organization's leadership desires to ensure survival of all or part of its activities." Werther and Berman (2001, 169) also provide the ominous warning, "(c)oordination is an urgent need, especially the need to avoid overlap and duplication of services that causes ruinous competition." Competition is almost a forbidden word among some professionals in the nonprofit sector, but to deny its prevalence would be unwise. Competition occurs among firms in the same subsector, as well as in the context of activities that reach the general public, that is, fund-raising and marketing. If your nonprofit is the only local organization hosting a ten-kilometer road race as a fund-raising event, the goodwill, media exposure, and net revenues may provide a substantial boon to the organization. But if your 10K race is one among many such fund-raising events, the media message will be lost in the crowd and your net revenues may barely justify the organizational effort to host the event. Monopoly power is equally as attractive to a nonprofit as to a for-profit firm!

Competition in marketing requires an organization to convey its message in a consistent, professional, and creative way in order to stand out from the chatter and differentiate its products from those produced by other nonprofits. Competition in fund-raising, however, may require more than individual management savvy. Nonprofits in the same field compete for donation and grants, but even unrelated nonprofits compete for donations from individuals. From the donor's point of view, they are all worthy causes. Thus, the race to reach the individual donor induces multiple mass mailings and employment of large teams (especially at universities) of development professionals.

How can collaboration ameliorate this costly pursuit? Organizations can form a regional quasi-cartel, restricting fund-raising mailings and events during a blackout period and coordinating via one agency to send one main fund-raising appeal to the broader public. This in fact describes some of the activities of United Way and other federated giving organizations. United Way also serves other important functions, such as researching community needs and directing community resources toward those needs. Yet federated giving agencies do have some characteristics of cartels, restricting entry into the federated organization by newcomer agencies (Smith, 2002).

(7) Shape the External Environment. Never shy about coining obscure phrases, economists refer to professional advocacy as "rent seeking." Rent seeking describes expenditures for the purpose of lobbying to support policies that redistribute resources toward special interest groups. Few nonprofit organizations have the resources to take on the federal or state government by themselves to lobby for increased funding in their subsector. But if many organizations cofund a coalition to lobby legislators, favorable legislation could result, with profound effect on the nonprofits' resulting revenues. Salamon (2002b) praises nonprofits for their successful advocacy over the past two decades.

Consider the noncollaborative situation: A handful of smaller nonprofit organizations muster the resources to advocate for favorable funding in the upcoming budget cycle. Each of these organizations represents a constituency of a few thousand voters. Now envision a coalition of twenty nonprofit organizations presenting their persuasive arguments in a united voice and representing a constituency of 100,000 voters. The coalition articulates a much more compelling message for the recipient legislator. In addition, since the coalition's advocacy costs are split among the twenty participating organizations, costs of advocacy to the individual nonprofit are modest.

Despite the many potential benefits, even the most enthusiastic praise of nonprofit alliances can reveal underlying pitfalls. Werther and Berman (2001, 170) write, "Partnerships are not quick fixes but a way of laying a structure for future success. It is because of this strategic importance that they can justify the management time that is necessary to maintain them and work out inevitable conflicts over programs or duties that threaten the win-win relationship." As McLaughlin (1998) points out, the transactions costs of setting up and maintaining a collaborative project are considerable. Decision making is no longer the province of the autonomous nonprofit, and "without a legal entity in place, controlling an alliance is a political and negotiation process . . . it is very hard to identify savings and other direct benefits of the collaboration." Collaborations slow decision making, and also drain energy away from each organization's own mission-related production.

The following illustrations of pitfalls in collaboration originate mainly from problems with transaction costs. There may be benefits in collaborating, but in some cases, the costs of meeting, envisioning collaborative solutions, coordinating on implementation and evaluation, and so on, exceed the benefits:

Pitfall I: Forgetting the Value of Labor. Staff time involved in collaborative efforts is a very real cost, yet since a staff member's salary is "already covered," the additional staff time may not be seen as a financial cost to the organization's bottom line. Snavely and Tracy (2000, 155) report, "collaboration is seen as costing significant staff time . . . but does not result in significant financial costs." But consider the "opportunity costs." Devoting staff time to collaborative efforts means that staff effort is subtracted from other activities benefiting the organization, such as meeting with a major donor, training new employees, or planning a new volunteer program. That lost time is the opportunity cost of participating in a collaborative venture.

Pitfall II: Overvaluing the Process as an End unto Itself. Snavely and Tracy (2000) describe a collaborative project that involved agency representatives discussing "obstacles to their working cooperatively." Their reported devotion of time to building the collaborative should serve as a warning that some collaborative projects may get bogged down in process, leaving little time for actual outcomes (Lubell, 2004; Irvin and Stansbury, 2004). Grant makers who require collaboration as part of a funded project should think long and hard about the costs of the alliance. Will the benefits accruing from the partnership exceed the costs of a process-intensive collaboration? There may not be enough benefit from collaborative behavior (meetings, networking sessions, etc.) alone to justify funding a partnership.

Pitfall III: Failing to Anticipate the Complexity of Human Relationships. This problem is not confined to collaborations but is seen every day, for example, among young couples. And why does it warrant inclusion in a finance text? The literature on collaboration is chock a block with verbiage regarding the importance of maintaining a trusting relationship with open communication, shared visions, and strong friendships. Kanter (1994, 97) states that successful partnerships require a "dense web of interpersonal connections." Lacking these qualities, the partnership's initial intentions can deteriorate into a competitive battle for turf, or it may die a slow and pathetic death from declining effort. Mattessich, Murray-Close, and Monsey (2001) performed a meta-analysis of case study literature on collaboration, defining twenty factors influencing the success of the collaboration. Of those twenty, over half are strongly related to interpersonal skills of the partners, and the most-cited success factor is "mutual respect, understanding, and trust." The economic message is that mutual mistrust among potential partners signals that the collaborative effort is going to involve high costs.

Extending the Knowledge Base

Astute nonprofit managers will seek out collaborative opportunities if the projects are clearly beneficial for both parties involved. In this section, we will first examine the rather odd bartering behavior found in the nonprofit sector. Bartering is a rare phenomenon in the for-profit sector, and also somewhat uncommon in the government sector, due to the requirement of accounting for the destination of all taxpayer revenues. Following a discussion of bartering, we turn our attention to the key role of external funders in stimulating collaboration. Beyond the incentives to the individual organization, there are additional compelling reasons for an external organization to support collaborative ventures.

(1) Bartering for Mutual Gain. Theoretically, we would expect monetized trading to prevail over bartering because bartering requires a "double coincidence of wants." The transactions costs of finding a suitable partner for bartering are just too great for a barter economy to work well. Yet Ben-Ner (1993) and Reisman (1991) provide thoughtful analyses of why bartering often occurs in the nonprofit sector. Barter between organizations could be more attractive if an organization has low cash flow, when a very high degree of trust and mutual interdependency is present, when an organization wishes to avoid sales taxes, and when the nonprofits have excess capacity in facilities or other resources. If bartering resources achieves each organization's goals, "direct trade will be cheaper than selling their respective products on the market and purchasing each other's product with money" (Ben-Ner 1993, 283). Several of the examples of collaboration in the previous section could be cashless transactions, such as the city park partnership with the youth mentoring organization.

Bartering is a more labor-intensive transaction than paying cash, due to the costs of finding the right partner for trading and determining if the transaction is fair and meets the needs of both parties. Nonprofit organizations, with a partially volunteer labor force, have discounted labor costs, compared with for-profit businesses. Volunteer labor, as Anne Preston points out in chapter 8, is not free, but is (usually) cheaper than paid labor. Everything else held equal, we would expect more bartering to occur in the nonprofit sector (compared to the for-profit sector), and we would expect the most bartering to occur among the most volunteer-rich segments of the nonprofit sector.

(2) The Institutional Funder's Collaboration Imperative. Societal problems that the nonprofit sector seeks to alleviate—teen

homicides, for example—are distressingly complex. Because individual nonprofits concentrate on their mission-related strengths, they may not have the incentive to solve a multifaceted problem. Foundations and government funders, on the other hand, view the issues from the perspective of the broader community. Thus, it is no surprise that foundations and government agencies often provide financial incentives for nonprofits to work together by requiring collaboration in grant-funded projects (see Quirk, 1989, for an example of philanthropy's catalytic role in cross-sector collaboration). Resulting community benefits could be manifold, ranging from coordinated service for recipients of human services, to a well planned and executed community-wide strategy to combat a persistent problem.

Grant makers have the biggest challenge when determining whether collaboration should be undertaken. There are collaborations that will occur without philanthropic guidance because the nonprofit leaders are able to recognize a smart, mutually beneficial idea without external assistance. Then there are collaborations that never spontaneously occur because the nonprofit recognizes that collaboration costs exceed the benefits to the individual organization. In the latter case, some of those would-be collaborations are simply not worth pursuing, while other would-be collaborations yield benefits to society (in addition to the benefits to the cooperating organizations) that justify investment in the partnership. It is up to the grant maker to provide incentives in its grant making to bring collaborators "to the table" to coproduce those external benefits. To illustrate, a funder might induce two social service agencies to colocate in the same building. The two agencies might be reluctant to move, yet the benefits to the *clients* to have both agencies in one location may have a transformative effect on the success of their treatments.

External societal benefits, or "positive externalities," therefore, change the decision matrix for the grant maker. These external benefits should provide the tipping point for grant making. Figure 9.1 illustrates this funding decision with a decision tree. Note the implications for sustainability of funding—grant makers should not assume that seed money is all that is needed to sustain a fruitful collaboration.

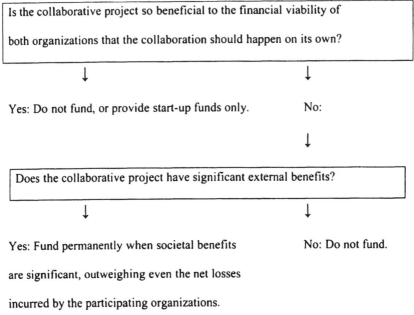

Figure 9.1. *Collaboration and the Grant Maker Decision.*

Improving Practice

This section offers nine diagnostic questions to lead a nonprofit or its funder through the steps of evaluating whether or not to collaborate with other organizations.

Questions for Nonprofit Managers:

1. What problems are common concerns for all organizations? Are the organizations in the same field, or do they produce different (complementary) "products"?
2. What potentially shared inputs are used by each individual organization to carry out their mission? This might include fixed costs such as rent and variable costs such as materials, staff time, volunteer labor, community publicizing, and organizing.

3. If two or more organizations worked together on one project, would it save labor (paid or unpaid), materials, or overhead (fixed) costs?
4. If potential cost savings are insignificant, would collaboration result in a higher quality, more effective, or longer lasting solution for the issue at hand? A grant maker might be particularly interested in collaboration that results in a multisector effort to address a complex problem in the community.
5. Would it be time consuming just to get the organizations to coordinate their efforts on a project? Are the potential collaborators already familiar and comfortable with one another?

Questions for Governments, Foundations, and Individual Donors:

1. Why are the organizations not collaborating with one another? Does it really make sense to collaborate, given the nature of the tasks at hand?
2. What common projects could be addressed collaboratively, yielding significant external benefits?
3. How much funding would induce the organizations to collaborate on a certain project? Funding may allow the organizations to hire a staff member and reapportion the labor burden so that resources can be devoted to the collaborative project. It is probably not enough to fund a "facilitator" for meetings, because the organizations themselves still must reallocate labor toward the new initiative, to allow their staff members to attend meetings and work on the project.
4. For how long a time period should the collaborative project be funded?

Funding should cease under a number of scenarios; the problem is solved (proceed to the next problem), the collaborators see the value of collaborating and are willing to sustain the project on their own (time costs of collaborating are not overwhelming), or the collaboration has failed to produce any external benefits of significance. Funding should continue indefinitely if the external benefits for the community are significant, even though the costs of collaborating to each organization are preventing the participants from collaborating on their own.

Conclusion

For the reluctant nonprofit manager doubtful of the benefits of collaboration, this chapter offers a host of practical reasons why collaboration can yield cost savings as well as improvements in mission-related output quantity and quality. But collaboration is not a universal fix-it tool. Understanding the theory behind collaboration allows us to determine when conditions are right for collaboration to yield the greatest benefit for the participating organizations. Prospective collaborators should look for assets that lie unused, whether that is an empty room, a good reputation as a treasured community institution, clients with energy to expend on a volunteer project, or even a manager who could divide time between two organizations. Once connections are explored with other organizations, be they for-profit, government, or nonprofit agencies, collaborators may find that their relationships have not only reaped cost savings and revenues from unused assets, but also have enhanced their collective ability to advocate for new community-wide initiatives.

Conversely, to the nonprofit manager who is a collaboration enthusiast, this chapter provides a warning to enter an alliance carefully, evaluating the probability of success prior to committing large amounts of organizational resources to the task. Do not forget the hidden costs of coordinating with other organizations in the rush to complete a grant proposal that requires collaboration. Funders will look for and appreciate the perceptive organization that has gone through the diagnostic questions outlined in the last section and precisely pinpointed the collaborations that will yield the greatest returns for the organization and its community.

10

Gifts-in-Kind and Other Illiquid Assets

Charles M. Gray

Introduction

What do personal care and beauty products companies like Avon and Estée Lauder; household products companies like Bed, Bath, and Beyond and Williams-Sonoma; technology companies like Dell and Hewlett-Packard; and clothing retailers like The Gap and Eddie Bauer all have in common—besides trying to sell their products to you and me? They are corporate partners of Gifts in Kind International (GIKI), self-described as "the global leader in product philanthropy," its major rival being the National Association for the Exchange of Industrial Resources (NAEIR). Acting as a go-between, GIKI matches up corporate philanthropy with partner recipient organizations. By offering its services for a modest fee, GIKI saves corporations the time and money of searching out recipient organizations on their own. Economists would say that GIKI and similar organizations reduce the *transactions costs* of philanthropy, and such cost reduction can be a very valuable service. Apparently, there is a growing need for such services.

Gifts-in kind (GIKs) are defined here as any donation that is in a form other than money, or a highly liquid asset such as stocks or bonds that can be easily converted to money, that is, that are "liquid" in the parlance of financial economics. Illiquid assets are GIKs that have been received and that must be managed by the organization. This chapter employs pertinent tools of economics to shed light on the nature of GIKs from both donor and recipient perspectives, including the range of purposes served by GIKs and how GIKs fit into a general approach to understanding and managing organizational financial assets. After all, every GIK becomes, even if only briefly, an asset that must be managed. Accordingly, this chapter will treat both the *flow* concept of gift acquisition and disposal (using the well-known example of Goodwill Industries), and the *stock* concept of gifts as an element of an organization's asset portfolio (illustrated by the choices of art museums). This topic has been largely overlooked in the economics literature pertinent to philanthropy and charitable organizations, and the only book-length treatment of gifts-in-kind (Nelson and Schneiter, 1991) is very applications oriented and is not grounded in economic theory.

Patterns and Trends

Most readers, whether engaged in nonprofits or not, are probably very familiar with the concept of GIK, having donated (or purchased) old clothing, home furnishings, and similar items to the Salvation Army or Goodwill Industries, organizations that resell the donated items at "affordable prices" to low-income purchasers and use the proceeds to finance their program services. Indeed, noncash contributions constitute 46.5 percent of total contributions to Goodwill Industries. The percentage is even greater—60 percent—among food banks and similar organizations.

Noncash (in-kind) contributions constituted nearly 11 percent of total contributions to all nonprofit organizations in 2002 (see table 10.1), and according to a recent report by the Conference Board, the majority of corporate contributions are now gifts-in-kind (Muirhead, 2005).

Table 10.1 portrays the relative proportions of cash and noncash (GIK) contributions among charitable organizations and by major categories of the National Taxonomy of Exempt Entities (NTEE), as reported on IRS Form 990 for the 2002 tax year. This is the only year for which these data are available and maintained

Table 10.1. Cash and Noncash (In-Kind) Contributions Received by NTEE Category, 2002

NTEE Major Category	Mean Contributions Received (dollars)				
	Total	Cash	Percent of Total	Noncash	Percent of Total
Total	826601	739511	89.464	87090	10.536
A Arts, etc.	531860	471413	88.635	60447	11.365
B Education	1158560	1067239	92.118	91321	7.882
C Environmental	723351	587596	81.232	135755	18.768
D Animal Related	581515	543834	93.520	37681	6.480
E Health	1044181	992092	95.011	52089	4.989
F Mental Health	861178	849829	98.682	11349	1.318
G Diseases, Treatment	1270532	1232426	97.001	38106	2.999
H Medical Research	2311436	1692900	73.240	618536	26.760
I Crime, Legal	746331	724494	97.074	21837	2.926
J Employment	1008810	948411	94.013	60399	5.987
K Food	1434349	548462	38.238	885887	61.762
L Housing	304309	285266	93.742	19043	6.258
M Public Safety	161316	154828	95.978	6488	4.022
N Recreation, Sports	138427	126119	91.109	12308	8.891
O Youth Development	416846	399193	95.765	17653	4.235
P Human Services	873433	827243	94.712	46190	5.288
Q International, Security	3157442	2083287	65.980	1074155	34.020
R Civil Rights	708257	688573	97.221	19684	2.779
S Community Improvement	697660	657065	94.181	40595	5.819
T Philanthropy, Voluntarism	1255271	977225	77.850	278046	22.150
U Science Research	1622548	1560960	96.204	61588	3.796
V Social Science Research	2004438	1991932	99.376	12506	0.624
W Public Benefit	1337176	1302107	97.377	35069	2.623
X Religion Related	380183	318877	83.875	61306	16.125
Y Mutual Membership	258311	232276	89.921	26035	10.079
Z Unknown	120904	105954	87.635	14950	12.365

Source: NCCS.

by the National Center for Charitable Statistics of the Urban Institute.

It should be noted at this point that such organizations as Goodwill Industries may underreport GIKs. Since they resell so much of the donated merchandise within a given tax year, inclusion of both the donation and the sale proceeds would constitute double counting. Of course, since resale is such a significant component of Goodwill program income, that income itself may serve as a proxy measure of the value of GIKs.

With that caveat in mind, we note that the first column of table 10.1 is the NTEE category, the second is mean contributions received (cash and noncash) by organizations in the category, the third and fourth columns are mean cash contributions and cash as percent of total, and the last two columns are mean noncash contributions and noncash as percent of total. NTEE category K, food-related organizations, received the greatest amount of GIKs as a proportion of total donations received, while social science research, category V, received the smallest proportion, at less than 1 percent. While food banks and similar food-oriented organizations receive contributions of day-old bread, slightly-past-prime vegetables, and other perishables from grocery stores as well as packaged goods from households, there simply is not much that social science research organizations can do with donated items. For category A, arts organizations, the noncash contributions amounted to about 11 percent of the total contributions, but for art museums (not listed separately in the table), GIKs amounted to more than a third of the total contributions.

Of course, any portrayal of the magnitude of gifts-in-kind must take into account the differing valuations placed on the same item by different parties. A donor may claim a tax deduction of one amount, while the recipient organization may enter a very different value on Form 990. The former may reflect the value imputed by the donor (which may in turn be a strategic overestimate that maximizes the tax benefit), while the latter may reflect the amount the recipient grosses upon resale. The IRS resolves this disagreement by stipulating valuation at "fair market value" (FMV), defined as "the price that property would sell for on the open market" (IRS, Pub. 561). This is not too difficult to determine if the market is well developed, with many sellers and buyers trading products on a frequent basis, such that the prevailing price is well known among market participants. Such would be the case with new food stuffs, cell phones, clothing, and other products with easily ascertained list prices. Used products are a bit more problematic, in part because variable wear and tear creates greater differentiation in resale value. This is especially true with used automobiles. The growing popularity of automobiles as a charitable gift has led the IRS to revise its rules and create a detailed guide to the valuation of a used car (IRS, Pub. 4302).

Some items are so unique that list prices are nonexistent.[1] They may be sold at auction, with the sale price entirely dependent upon who happens to be bidding at a particular time, or sold privately at a negotiated price. The uniqueness of antiques and works of art as donations—typically to art museums—also dictates special treatment by the IRS, as indicated in table 10.2.[2] Gifts of art are discussed further in the section below on art museums.

Current Practice

In general, both individuals (households) and businesses (corporations as well as noncorporate) offer gifts-in-kind. Individuals can contribute personal property, businesses can contribute items from inventory, and both can contribute real estate. Although not an exhaustive list of the possibilities, table 10.3 illustrates some

Table 10.2. IRS Stipulations for Valuing Works of Art

Value Claimed	Requirement
$5,000 or less	Simply claim on tax return
More than $5,000	Attach complete copy of signed appraisal by qualified appraiser to tax return
$20,000 or more	Attach complete copy of signed appraisal by qualified appraiser to tax return; a color photo or slide must be provided upon request
$50,000 or more	Prior to claim, request a statement of value from IRS, such request to include a qualified appraisal, check for $2,500 for up to three separate items, and appropriate IRS forms.

Source: IRS.

Table 10.3.   Examples of Gifts and Uses

Gift	Typical Recipient	Purpose
Household goods—furniture, appliances	Goodwill Industries; resettlement programs	Distribution to the needy; resale
Office furniture and supplies	Goodwill Industries; operating nonprofits	Use in organizational offices; resale
Clothing	Goodwill Industries; services to needy	Distribution to the needy; resale
Books	Libraries; Goodwill industries	Augment collections; resale
Jewelry and gems	Museums; other cultural institutions	Display; auction
Collections—stamps, coins, rare books, etc.	Museums; other cultural institutions	Display; auction
Motor vehicles— automobiles, vans, boats, aircraft	Health-related charities	Use for delivery
Food stuffs—prepared meals, perishable goods, packaged foods	Homeless shelters; Second harvest and other food shelves; Meals on Wheels	Distribution to needy or elderly
Razors, toiletries, other personal items	Homeless shelters	Distribution to the needy
Real estate—land, buildings	Universities; conservation groups	Use for service delivery; place in land banks; resale
Art, antiques	Museums	Display, resale
Stocks, bonds	Organizations with Endowments	Add to endowment; liquidate to support operations
Cell phones	Family violence programs	Distribution to clients

of the types of gifts-in-kind, typical recipient organizations, and potential uses of the gifts. Some gifts, such as prepared meals and other perishables, have a very short shelf life and must be used quickly after receipt. Others may last longer, but require storage space and maintenance or repair capability. Monetary donations require financial management; GIK management can be much more complicated and require a far broader set of skills.

Educational institutions receiving computers on a piecemeal basis from individual contributors must integrate, maintain, and upgrade the hardware, install and support software, and otherwise have access to technical proficiency. Recipients of real estate must have access to property management skills.

By virtue of its "fungibility" and acceptance as a medium of exchange, money is the most efficient gift; it does not require that mutual coincidence of wants whereby the potential recipient needs, say, a computer, and the donor just happens to have a surplus computer that meets the recipient's needs. But the simple fact is that many donors have excess tangible goods that can more easily be converted to cash by the recipient organization than by the donor. This section offers a brief consideration of the managerial complications of selected GIKs, including real estate, art and antiques, and household items, illustrated by specific examples.

The Tubman Family Alliance (TFA), an organization that provides a variety of services to address the issue of family violence, has used gifts of donated property to build or to convert to short-term housing for victims of violence. Since no staff members had property evaluation skills, TFA had to incur the costs of contracting for such services prior to determining the best use of the property.

The University of St. Thomas has received several gifts of real estate. A country estate was converted to a conference center and teaching facility serving a different market area. A manufacturing facility was initially converted to classroom space serving another part of the Twin Cities metro area, then sold with the proceeds being used to purchase a more suitable building nearby that was used for classes, with parts also leased to an assortment of private ventures, including a restaurant. Eventually the demands of property management persuaded the university to sell that building and lease back space for classroom and related uses. Remote property management is not the university's core competency.

Note that as repositories of learning, universities do have the ability to evaluate and manage donations of books and journals. You should not, however, plan to give your collection of old *National Geographic* magazines to the nearest institution of higher education; they already have it.

The collections of all major art museums include—and in some instances are comprised entirely or chiefly of—gifts from museum supporters.[3] The collection is a subset of the assets of the museum. The assets include physical plant and equipment, endowment (which may include a variety of earning assets such as stocks, bonds, and real estate), and the collection. The physical plant and equipment support museum operations, the endowment yields an earnings stream and portions can be liquidated to cover revenue shortfalls, and the collection is largely for display, but it also serves as a potential revenue source. The quality of the collection encourages other donations, memberships, and admissions, and in a crisis, portions of it can be sold in an active market to generate working capital.

Once acquired, of course, a work of art is constantly under at least implicit review regarding its contribution to the mission.[4] It could be that a large gift of several works in a common genre would cause an imbalance in the museum's collection, leading to the desire to "de-access" or sell some portion of the holdings. As many museums have learned, this can be a highly controversial decision, leading to unhappiness among donors and other patrons, as well as unfortunate publicity for the museum.

> In an auction that involved daylong drama and suspense, Chicago's Field Museum sold a collection of 19th Century Western art for $17.4 million . . . to an anonymous bidder and pledged to use the money to expand its holdings of contemporary anthropological artifacts. Included in the sale were 31 paintings of American Indians and bison by artist and adventurer George Catlin, representing the bulk of the Field's Catlin collection, which the museum has owned since shortly after it was founded in 1893. The decision . . . to auction the Catlins, which the artist is thought to have painted during his travels in the American frontier in the 1930s, generated controversy within the museum and on the Field's board of trustees, but museum officials said the sale was part of a strategy to focus its holdings on scientific materials and to expand its collections. (Swanson, Stevenson. *Chicago Tribune Online Edition*, December 16, 2004)

Although in this particular case the Field Museum did not have to deal with a disaffected donor, this recent instance serves to illustrate the challenges of meeting the museum's organizational objectives and simultaneously handling the tender feelings of the public.

According to its website, Goodwill Industries is "one of the world's largest nonprofit providers of education, training, and career services for people with disadvantages, such as welfare dependency, homelessness, and lack of education or work experience, as well as those with physical, mental and emotional disabilities." Donations are resold in more than two thousand retail stores as well as an Internet auction site, and the proceeds of the sales fund job training and other services that prepare clients for employment. Retail sales of $1.37 billion in 2004 constituted 57 percent of total revenue for Goodwill Industries nationwide.

Gifts of clothing, furniture, and other household items typically entail the following steps:

- Households determine that selected items have no further use and drop them off at a Goodwill collection point
- Goodwill receives the items and offers a receipt for the value of the goods
- Goodwill determines donation quality, sorting items into resale or disposal groupings (too many well-intended donations must be trashed because of low quality)
- Goodwill makes minor repairs or otherwise prepares donations for resale, as needed
- Local store staff ascertain product price and stock shelves accordingly
- OR items are listed and made available for online bidding
- Local store staff conduct sales and collect revenues

The steps entailed in this process are a core competency of Goodwill Industries. Other recipients of donated household items are far less likely to be able to handle the donations so adroitly.

Theory

The existence and use of money is of tremendous benefit in an advanced market economy. Money—the currency and coins that you carry, along with the balance in your checking accounts—serve two vital functions that are relevant for our discussion here. The first is as a medium of exchange. In the absence of money, the fundamental economic functions of specialization and exchange would be severely hindered. In an economy without money, individuals seeking to meet their needs through exchange with others would need to seek out individuals, households, or businesses that not only can offer what is needed or desired, but also happen to need a corresponding amount of what the first individual or household has to offer. Such a series of bilateral swaps entails what is known as a "double coincidence of wants" (Ben-Ner, 1993). Time and energy devoted to this search process would be diverted from the more useful economic function of wealth creation.

The second relevant function of money is as a unit of account, providing market participants—buyers and sellers—with a common denominator for measuring the value of goods and services in the economy. In a market economy, the interaction of supply and demand yields a product price that can be thought of as the average value across all market participants. It would not be surprising that some individuals, buyers, will place a higher value on a product than its selling price; otherwise they would not buy it. Sellers, on the other hand, value a product at less than its selling price; otherwise they would not sell it. This differing valuation leads to some interesting implications for the nature of GIKs, and some of these will be addressed below.

Although monetary gifts are usually more efficient than GIKs, in that the "fungibility" of money means that it can be converted by the recipient organization into any of a variety of desired goods and services at little cost, donors may be reluctant to convert surplus assets to monetary form prior to the donation. The schematic in figure 10.1 illustrates the issue. Suppose, in this simple example, a donor contributes to a recipient organization, which then pays a vendor for goods or services received. For the vendor to be paid in cash or its equivalent, either the recipient organization must accept a GIK and convert it to money in a market-type transaction in order to pay the vendor (the sequence illustrated by the top arrows), or the donor must convert the donation to money in a

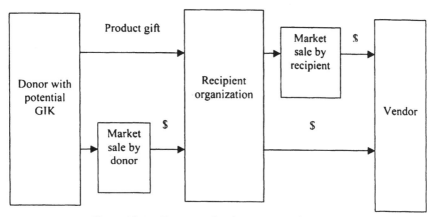

Figure 10.1.   Processes for Converting Gifts-in-Kind.

market transaction prior to donation (the sequence illustrated by the bottom arrows). From an efficiency perspective, the conversion should be carried out by the party—donor or recipient—that can do so at the lowest cost. The cost elements involved in making a transaction happen—product search, evaluation, contracting, monetary exchange, product exchange, etc.—are collectively known as *transactions costs*. Economic efficiency and good stewardship of organizational resources dictate that these transactions costs be minimized.

Extending the Knowledge Base

The academic researcher seeking to acquire, create, and disseminate knowledge on GIKs to the practitioner faces a number of challenges. The most obvious is the dearth of useful data to support academic research. At the present time, only two data sets explore the nature of gifts-in-kind, and both of those pertain to receipt of gifts. The first is the 2002 Form 990 dataset compiled and maintained by the National Center for Charitable Statistics. That is the only comprehensive data on gifts-in-kind (noncash contributions), as reported by organizations. The essential problem is that this tells us nothing about who gives, including demographic descriptors and other donor characteristics.

The second problem is that a single year's worth of data will not support time series analyses, including simple trend statistics, so there is no good way of knowing how gifts-in-kind is progressing over time. A companion piece of research by this author is examining, by NTEE category, the issue of whether and to what extent GIKs and cash donations are complements or substitutes, but the results will not be widely available until a few months after this writing (Gray, 2006).

The second database is that maintained by the Conference Board, based on a survey of business giving. The data are limited to respondents, although results may be generalized to some extent. While this offers the advantage of access to donor information, households are excluded. Understandably, the Conference Board keeps a close eye on its survey data in order to protect the privacy of respondents, so it is not readily available for statistical analysis.

The research community and the nonprofit organizations they serve will eventually be better served as the IRS, National Center for Charitable Statistics, and Conference Board each collect, assemble, and make more widely available data that currently are being reported.

Improving Practice

The nonprofit executive considering whether or not to implement a GIK program may wish to consider the following matters before making a commitment:

- Are GIKs directly relevant to the mission of this organization?
  - Can we use GIKs to serve constituents (e.g., automobiles for delivery, office furniture for functional support, etc.)?
  - Can constituents use GIKs to meet their own needs (cell phones, health-care supplies, etc.)?
  - Can we sell GIKs to raise funds in support of mission attainment (silent auctions, thrift shops, etc.)?

- Do we have core competencies consistent with collecting and managing GIKs?
  - Can we evaluate and market a wide range of GIKs (e.g., automobiles, items for thrift shops)?
  - Can we refurbish GIKs for use or resale (e.g., sheltered workshops)?
  - Do we have access to pick-up and delivery capability?
  - Do we have storage capacity for a variety of gifts, especially automobiles?
- If we do not have competencies directly, can we partner or collaborate with organizations that do (see chapter 9 in this volume for further discussion of collaboration benefits)?

Organizations that can answer in the affirmative to at least one of the questions under each major bullet point above may find GIKs to be a useful means of serving their missions.

Conclusion

This chapter has offered a brief overview of GIKs, including some of the theoretical underpinnings—minimizing of transactions costs and the use of money in efficient exchange—that can enhance understanding of the role of GIKs in the nonprofit sector. In general, GIKs are not as efficient as monetary donations, but intermediaries have arisen to overcome some of the transactions costs that would otherwise hinder both donors and recipients, and some organizations have developed core competencies that enable them to use GIKs efficiently. Organizations that lack these asset management competencies, and for which development of such competencies are not central to the mission, are advised to avoid GIKs.

It is not yet clear how eBay and other online auction services will ultimately affect GIKs to nonprofit organizations. Households that once donated used items to favorite charities both to avoid the disposal costs and to gain a tax benefit may now fairly easily convert many of those items to cash through online auction. Will this reduce donations overall? Or will the conversion of an illiquid asset to money in this fashion lead to more monetary contributions? The net effect has yet to be studied.

In the meantime . . . doesn't your attic need cleaning?

Appendix

Simple Model of Portfolio Structure

This appendix illustrates how a work of art may be considered in the context of the full spectrum of a museum's asset holdings. Although the specific reference is to museums, the principles can be generalized to asset management by any recipient of GIKs.

The following highly simplified example is based on some simplifying assumptions: A work of art is received, held for one year, and then sold; the work generates additional donated, membership, and admissions revenues; the work yields additional utility to viewers in the form of its inherent value; the museum receives the work as a gift but incurs some modest marginal costs in the form of display and maintenance expenses; and the work can be resold in a well-functioning market. Under these conditions, the return to the museum from accepting and holding the art can be expressed as:

$$r_a = \frac{D_a + M_a + A_a + I_a + P_{a,t+1} - C_{a,t}}{C_{a,t}}$$

where, with respect to a given work of art, a, r is the total return over the year, D is the value of additional donations attributable to the work, M is total membership receipts attributable to the work, A is admissions attributable to the work, I is the intrinsic social value of the work (mission relevance), P is the end-of-year sale price, C are costs associated with acquisition and display of the work, t is acquisition time, and $t + 1$ is sale time.

Most of the values in this equation are determined subjectively either because receipts are very difficult to attribute to a specific work or because, as in I_a, there is no explicit and unambiguous monetary value. Yet the subjective valuation of r must exceed 0 or the artwork is not of value to the museum, and furthermore, r must be high enough to warrant allocating scarce resources to the work's installation and maintenance.

Notes

1. Some commentators object to a monetary evaluation of art as a matter of principle. See Hyde, 1983.

2. Please note that this is not intended to serve as a guide either to donors or recipients. See IRS publications, including those cited in the bibliography, for authoritative information.

3. For more detailed treatments of the economics of art and art museums, see Blattberg and Broderick (1991) and other chapters in Feldstein, ed. (1991), and Heilbrun and Gray (2001), chapters 9 and 10.

4. It is unlikely that there exists an art museum anywhere that has not had to contend with donations of dubious artistic merit. Tactful treatment of donors may be one of the most vital qualities among museum administrators.

11

Borrowing and Debt

Robert J. Yetman

A duty dodged is like a debt unpaid; it is only deferred, and we must come back and settle the account at last.

—Joseph Newton, 1515 (Braude, 1962, 193)

Introduction

Nonprofits frequently face the situation where current cash needs exceed cash on hand. Consider a nonprofit that needs to replace outdated equipment, or build a new (or its first) building. Or consider a nonprofit that has been awarded a government grant on a cost reimbursement basis whose proceeds are received only after the costs have been expended. What options does the nonprofit manager have if existing cash balances are insufficient? How will a manager quickly raise the necessary cash to pay for the assets or to pay operating expenses (such as salaries) until the grant funding is received? Even if the organization had sufficient cash reserves, is it always a wise decision to draw down those reserves to pay for these things?

In situations like those described above a nonprofit manager has limited choices of how to quickly raise the needed funds. Fund-raising campaigns take time, and involve several costs themselves. For-profit firms typically solve this problem by issuing stocks or bonds or getting bank loans. Nonprofits do not have access to equity markets, leaving debt as one of the few (and

244 / Robert J. Yetman

in many cases the only) way for a nonprofit to generate the cash necessary to purchase equipment, buildings, or to span the time between expenses and grant receipts.

A couple of important facts motivate this chapter. First, nonprofit use of debt is pervasive. An analysis of the Internal Revenue Service's Statistics of Income files reveals that just over 60 percent of nonprofits have some form of debt outstanding. The average ratio of debt to assets for nonprofits in the IRS sample is approximately 33 percent. The average debt to assets ratio of non-educational and nonmedical nonprofits is 38 percent. To gain a better understanding of the magnitude of nonprofits' use of debt we can compare their debt to assets ratio to that of for-profit manufacturing firms in the United States. Manufacturing firms have an average debt to assets ratio of 36 percent, which is only slightly above that of the average nonprofit organization. Second, nonprofits are sophisticated users of debt instruments. In addition to the traditional and well-known types of debt such as bank loans, municipal bonds, and mortgages, nonprofits also use more exotic debt instruments such as tax-exempt leases.

The goal of this chapter is to provide a means of clearly identifying the issues related to debt financing from both a theoretical and practical perspective. The benefits of borrowing are easy to understand; access to current cash allows one to spend, and in the nonprofit setting spending is typically associated with increased social welfare. What is typically less well understood are the costs and ramifications of borrowing. We develop a theory of nonprofit debt based on the total benefits of investing in a project and the total costs of financing that project. We apply this theory to existing practice as well as discuss ways in which practice can be improved.

Patterns and Trends

A debt is owed because the nonprofit borrowed, regardless of the time frame in which it intends to repay that debt. Existing data group nonprofit debt into three categories: loans from related parties (such as officers or directors), municipal bonds, and other

Table 11.1. Distribution of Debt Load

	Percentage of All Nonprofits Using Debt Type	Dollar Concentration of Long-Term Debt
Loans from Related Parties	1%	Less than 1%
Other Debt	52%	43%
Municipal Bonds	18%	57%
Any Type of Debt	60%	100%

debt (including bank loans). In this section we examine the patterns of these types of debt across types and sizes of nonprofit organizations.

Table 11.1 shows that relatively few nonprofits borrow from related parties. There is little restriction on how much or how frequently a related person can lend money to a nonprofit, although the terms of the loan should be "arm's-length" to avoid the appearance of self-dealing. An arm's-length contract would typically call for a market interest rate and definite and reasonable repayment terms. Approximately 18 percent of nonprofits in the IRS sample have municipal bond debt outstanding, although these bonds account for about 57 percent of the total dollar amount of nonprofit debt. This is not surprising as municipal bond issues tend to be large because of the fixed costs associated with their issuance and the type of nonprofit that qualifies for issuing municipal bonds. The most common source of nonprofit debt is "other," which is a combination of long-term mortgages, bank loans, lines of credit, and leases. These other debt obligations constitute approximately 43 percent of the dollar amount of nonprofit debt.

A common metric used to describe a nonprofit's debt load (how much debt an organization has relative to other firms) is the debt to assets ratio. A second metric used to gauge relative debt load is the ratio of interest expense to total expenses. The debt to assets ratio provides a manager with a relative assessment of how much of the organization's assets are financed with debt, whereas the ratio of interest expense to total expense tells a manager how much of the current cash flow for expenses is being consumed by interest payments.

As previously noted, the average debt to assets ratio for all nonprofits in the IRS sample is 33 percent, but how does this ratio vary by type of nonprofit? Many nonprofits are capital intensive and need large buildings and facilities to produce their charitable output, while others have low capital needs and require little more than an office and some office equipment. Buildings and facilities are frequently financed by using debt. The range of the debt to assets ratio is large, running from a low of 12 percent for international, youth development, and philanthropy organizations to a high of 77 percent for housing nonprofits. Although many people associate hospitals with debt financing, their debt to assets ratio is 35 percent, only slightly above the average.

To what extent is the use of nonprofit debt a function of organization size? At first blush one might presume that larger nonprofits make more use of debt, although the data dispute that presumption. Table 11.2 shows that larger nonprofits have lower debt to assets ratios on average. The ratio of interest expense to total expenses falls somewhat as organization size rises, but less so than does the debt to assets ratio. The results for the use of municipal bonds are striking and suggest that the bulk of municipal bonds are issued by larger organizations. This result is likely driven by two factors. First, larger nonprofits are more likely to

Table 11.2. Distribution of Debt Load Across Size Groupings

Size Grouping	Asset Range (in $millions)	Average Debt to Assets	Average Interest Expense to Total Expense	Average Municipal Debt to Total Debt
Less than 10th percentile	0 to 0.77	37%	5%	1%
10th to 25th percentile	0.77 to 4.46	41%	9%	2%
25th to 50th percentile	4.46 to 7.56	35%	7%	12%
50th to 75th percentile	7.56 to 48.91	31%	6%	26%
75th to 90th percentile	48.91 to 126.31	30%	5%	42%
Greater than 90th percentile	Above 126.31	28%	6%	56%

qualify for municipal bond funding. Second, larger nonprofits are more likely to have large capital needs and municipal bonds issues tend to be large. This raises an important policy issue. Because municipal bonds carry a lower rate of interest they reduce a nonprofit's cost of borrowing relative to other types of debt. However, smaller nonprofits are possibly more likely to be on a less sound financial footing than their larger counterparts and can least afford to pay higher interest costs, but are the very organizations that are less able to access lower-cost municipal debt. Perhaps because of this, several states have programs that attempt to overcome this tendency by making municipal bonds available to smaller nonprofits. Nonetheless, the table below shows an undeniable fact, the larger your organization is, the more likely it is to have access to cheaper money.

Table 11.3 shows the same ratios broken out by revenue mix. This table shows that organizations that rely more on donations as a revenue source (presumably because the goods they provide are more public than private in nature) have less debt. There are several possible reasons for this. First, it is possible that firms that provide more private goods (such as universities, museums, or hospitals) have more need for large capital investments that require debt financing. Second, nonprofits that receive more fee revenue have a more reliable revenue source for obtaining debt financing. Third, nonprofits that provide a more public good may be less inherently inclined to seek debt financing due to the associated costs of debt (discussed below).

Table 11.3. Distribution of Debt Load Across Revenue Mix

Ratio of Donations Revenues to Total Grouping	Ratio Range (in percent)	Average Debt to Assets	Average Interest Expense to Total Expense	Average Municipal Debt to Total Debt
Zero	0	58%	17%	26%
0 to 25th percentile	0 to 1	39%	4%	40%
25th to 50th percentile	1 to 27	34%	4%	35%
50th to 75th percentile	27 to 53	21%	4%	25%
75th to 90th percentile	53 to 89	23%	5%	10%
Greater than 90th percentile	Above 89	23%	3%	6%

The statistics presented here suggest that a significant number of nonprofits have significant amounts of debt. Debt loads vary widely across organizational type, but vary little across time. Larger organizations are more likely to rely on municipal bond financing whereas smaller organizations rely more on bank loans. Few organizations get loan funds from an officer or director. What these statistics do not show is what effect this debt load has on the behavior of nonprofit organizations. Unfortunately, little research is available on this topic. Below, we discuss the possible effects this debt load can have on nonprofit behavior, based on informed speculation.

Current Practice

The goal of this section is twofold—first, to explore the various reasons why a nonprofit might seek debt financing, and second, to discuss the various types of debt financing available. We do not mean to suggest that these are necessarily appropriate reasons to borrow in every case, nor that these are the right ways to borrow. The intent here is to provide managers with information about possible motivations and debt alternatives. With this in mind, consider the following four reasons to seek debt financing:

1. Smoothing short-term working capital needs. Operating revenues and expenses can be smooth or lumpy. A smooth revenue or expense is evenly and reliably spaced out over time. Smooth revenues include interest earned on investments and perhaps fee income, while smooth expenses include wages, rent, insurance, utilities, and so on. In contrast a lumpy revenue or expense is not evenly spaced out over time. Lumpy revenues include government grants and large donations while lumpy expenses include property taxes. If one were to classify all nonprofit revenues and expenses as smooth or lumpy one would quickly find that most revenues are lumpy while most expenses are smooth. This suggests that there will commonly be periods of time when the cash generated from revenues will not exactly match the amount of expenses that must be paid. One way to

smooth out a lumpy revenue stream is to borrow. The borrowed funds are then paid off with lumpy revenues as they arrive.

2. Purchases of property, plant, and equipment. The need for additional spending on property, plant, and equipment arises from growth or obsolescence. Although fund-raising campaigns are frequently used to pay for (or to supplement payment for) fixed assets, nonprofits frequently resort to debt financing for facilities and equipment.

3. Unexpected event or business opportunity. At times, a nonprofit experiences an unanticipated cash need. This can arise from something as mundane as a broken air conditioner to more pressing matters such as a jump in demand for its services (such as a housing shelter after a major hurricane). Similarly, a fee-oriented nonprofit may discover a unique and profitable business opportunity that it does not want to miss out on, but does not have sufficient cash with which to pay for it.

4. Refinance existing debt. If a nonprofit has some fixed-rate debt outstanding and finds that market interest rates have fallen significantly, it might choose to refinance the debt at the lower interest rate in order to reduce its interest payments. Some types of debt, such as bank loans or mortgages, are typically paid off evenly over time. Other types, such as municipal bonds, are paid off all at once at the end of the bond term. If a nonprofit finds itself in the unenviable position that it does not have sufficient cash to pay off a bond issue that is due, it can issue a new set of bonds and use the proceeds to pay off the old bonds. Bond refinancing has little total effect on a nonprofit's financial position, other than to extend (potentially greatly) the time the bonds are outstanding. Municipal bonds may generally be refinanced with another municipal issue only once.

In general all debt instruments can be categorized along four dimensions: funding period, time outstanding, principal repayment, and security. The funding period for some types of debt instruments is immediate whereas others provide their cash as necessary, such as with a line of credit. The time period a debt instrument is outstanding can vary from just a few weeks to as long as thirty years. Principal repayments can be repaid gradually over the life of the debt (such as an amortized mortgage), or can be paid all at once at the end of the time outstanding. Finally, lenders frequently require some form of security for debt. Next, we discuss the various types of debt instruments and highlight which of the above characteristics each debt type has.

1. Lines of Credit. Lines of credit provide a pool of money to the nonprofit from which it can draw funds as necessary. Interest accrues on any borrowed amounts until they are repaid. Typically the repayment terms are flexible, permitting the nonprofit to pay back the line when it can, although the bank might place a time cap on repayment so that the line of credit does not become a de facto loan. The bank will usually require some form of security for the line. If the funds are used to purchase equipment the bank will typically use the equipment as collateral. If the funds will be used for general working capital the bank will likely encumber a nonprofit's general assets and/or future revenues. A bank can usually set up lines of credit in a few days or less. Interest rates tend to be variable and are set at prime plus a spread of several percentage points depending on the type of security obtained. Banks prefer variable rate debt as it protects them against fluctuations in interest rates.

2. Bank Loans. Bank loans differ from lines of credit in that they have more definite repayment terms and the full amount of the loan proceeds (less processing fees) is typically provided all at once in a lump sum to the nonprofit borrower. Loans can have various time periods from one year to five years or more, although bank loans longer than five years are less common. Principal and interest are usually paid gradually over the life of the loan such that the balance is paid off by the end of the loan term, although some loans are set up as "balloons" where the principal (and sometimes even the interest) is not paid until the end of the loan term. The security required is similar to that for a line of credit. Loans can take from a few days to several weeks to process, and typically carry a variable rate equal to prime plus some spread.

3. Mortgages. A mortgage is a loan that is issued specifically to purchase land and/or buildings, and the purchased asset will be used as collateral for the loan. Various types of lenders provide mortgages, and the original funder of the mortgage may well sell the loan to a consolidator who will group many similar

mortgages into pools and sell them as investments. The funding net of fees is provided to the property's seller rather than to the nonprofit itself. Mortgages tend to be longer-term instruments, commonly extending up to twenty or as much as thirty years. Principal and interest payments are typically made over the life of the loan, although balloon or interest-only mortgages are not unheard of. In addition to the property lenders may require additional collateral. To reduce the risk of nonpayment a lender will typically require the nonprofit to pay for some portion of the asset with cash (the "down payment"). Mortgages take from a few days to a few weeks to set up. Interest rates can be fixed or variable. Lenders frequently peg variable rates to the prime lending rate, which fluctuates depending on market conditions. At any particular time fixed rates are almost always higher than variable rates because fixed rate lenders are taking a risk that rates might rise before the debt is repaid.

    4. 501(c)(3) Bonds. There are many types of municipal bonds. Municipal bonds issued on behalf of nonprofits are called "501(c)(3) bonds," after the IRS code section covering nonprofit organizations (Davis, 2001; Internal Revenue Service, 2004). Municipal bonds can only be issued by state and local authorities and not directly by nonprofits. A nonprofit organization can be sponsored by one of these local authorities, which will issue municipal bonds on their behalf. Many states have set up agencies whose specific purpose is to facilitate municipal bond issues for nonprofits. Typically the state or local issuer will sell the bonds to an underwriter (such as an investment bank) who will sell the bonds to investors. The proceeds received by the underwriters are then given (net of fees) to a bond trustee. The trustee then provides the bond proceeds to the nonprofit. The trustee acts as a servicing agent between the nonprofit and the bond holders, collecting interest and any principal payments from the nonprofit and remitting them to bond holders.

    Because the bonds are tax-exempt at the federal level to the holder (and may be tax exempt at the state level as well), the IRS imposes a somewhat complex set of limitations on the amounts and qualified uses of municipal bonds. Nonprofit managers are encouraged to seek professional advice before embarking on a municipal bond issue. Municipal bonds tend to be long term with a minimum period of ten years and a maximum of thirty years. Typically only interest is paid during the bond term with the principal repaid at the end of the term. The security for municipal bonds varies and could include the assets and revenues of the nonprofit. If the nonprofit does not have sufficient assets or reliable revenue sources to act as collateral, the underwriter will require credit enhancement such as an insurance policy purchased from a third party. The insurance company (for a not inconsequential fee) guarantees payment of interest and principal should the nonprofit fail to make payments. An additional benefit of credit enhancement is that it can reduce the interest rate on the bonds. Municipal bonds can take several months to issue. Because bond holders do not pay taxes on the interest income they receive they are willing to accept a lower rate of interest.

Many new types of municipal financing have been created. The largest obstacle to obtaining municipal debt is that the issues tend to be large (typically $15 to $250 million) and expensive due to their complexity. In order to make tax-exempt financing available to smaller nonprofits some underwriters are offering alternative products such as tax-exempt variable rate demand bonds (low floaters), or tax exempt pool bonds (five- to ten-year maturities). Low floaters involve a remarketer which essentially permits the bonds to have a short-term interest rate even though the bonds are long term (short-term interest rates are usually lower than are long-term rates). Pool bonds allow an underwriter to pool together multiple smaller issues from various nonprofits, frequently with shorter maturities (from five to ten years). Pools permit nonprofits to issue smaller denominations of municipal debt while spreading the transaction costs across a group of nonprofits.

5. Tax-Exempt Leases. A recent tax-exempt financing option is the tax-exempt lease. A tax-exempt lease is structured very much as any other lease, except that the lessee must be a tax-exempt organization. The advantage to the lessee is that the lease payments are smaller than they would otherwise be, as these payments are tax-exempt to the lessor. Leases are typically used for equipment

rather than buildings, and provide smaller nonprofits with a convenient way of renting equipment at favorable rates.

Theory

Debt is a financial instrument that breaks the timing link between the consumption of a good and payment for that good. One must of course pay a price for consuming a good prior to actually having the cash with which to pay for it, and that charge is the interest cost. Interest is the miraculous device that lets us disconnect our consumption from our cash flows so the two no longer have to be synchronized. Over time, our cash flows must be large enough to support our consumption, but if we are willing to pay interest, it no longer has to be available when we want to consume. Two distinct cash flow streams leave the nonprofit when it incurs debt: interest payments and principal repayments.

There are two primary theories of debt with respect to for-profit organizations, and these theories will frame this analysis (Harris and Raviv, 1990). The first is called the "pecking order" theory and hypothesizes that an organization will have a preference for certain types of financing (accumulated cash, stock, or debt) over others, depending on the firm's characteristics and knowledge of its own true stock value relative to market prices. The second theory is the static trade-off theory where a firm is hypothesized to trade off the benefits of debt against its costs and arrives at the optimal amount of debt relative to capital stock. The benefits of debt include tax deductions and a reduction of agency costs. Because interest payments on debt are tax-deductible whereas dividend payments to stockholders are not, debt financing effectively lowers a firm's cost of capital relative to stock financing. Unfortunately, neither of these two theories directly applies to the nonprofit setting. Nonprofits cannot issue stock and thus the pecking order theory seems to have no place (although nonprofit managers may prefer one type of financing over another for other reasons or capital campaigns can raise funds which in some ways act like stock). With respect to the trade-off theory nonprofits do not (in general) pay income taxes and thus there appears to be no tax benefit to debt.

Nonetheless some features of existing theory can be applied to the nonprofit setting. Bankruptcy costs are still present. Although a nonprofit organization cannot be forced into a Chapter 7 involuntary bankruptcy, it may choose to undergo a Chapter 11 reorganization. The managerial disciplining effect of interest payments on debt can apply to nonprofits by forcing managers to consider the cost of their investments. With respect to taxes, municipal bonds can generate a positive net cash flow to the extent a nonprofit has sufficient other cash on hand and invests those other proceeds in taxable investments. If the nontaxable interest earned on the investments exceeds the interest expense on the municipal bonds the nonprofit can earn a risk-free arbitrage profit on the bonds, providing an incentive to issue municipal bonds even if the proceeds are not needed. (There is a significant and complex body of tax laws aimed at preventing this sort of arbitrage. See Gentry 2002 for an excellent treatment of effective arbitrage by nonprofit hospitals. See chapter 7 of this volume as well).

There has been some limited examination of nonprofits' use of debt. Some research finds that nonprofit hospitals appear to have target levels of municipal bonds that shrink as the availability of viable capital projects declines and grow as the level of unused debt capacity increases (Wedig, Hassan, and Morrisey, 1996). More recent work controls for the effects of a nonprofit's investments (endowment assets) and finds additional support for the trade-off theory (Bowman, 2002).

Unfortunately, existing theory leaves us with no satisfactory answer to some very simple questions. When should a nonprofit borrow? If an organization borrows, how and how much should it borrow? According to existing theory the only benefit of debt is the potential to engage in tax arbitrage on municipal bonds. But we know from our prior analysis that relatively few nonprofits issue municipal debt and arbitrage is highly regulated, so what of the majority of nonprofits that incur nonmunicipal debt? Given the bankruptcy rules one could also plausibly ask—why don't we see more use of debt? If the benefit of debt in general were that it permitted a nonprofit to supply its charitable outputs sooner rather than later, and increasing social welfare sooner were always deemed better than increasing it later, all nonprofits should have vast amounts of debt, but we do not observe this behavior either. A complete answer must lie elsewhere.

Due to the unsatisfactory nature of existing theory we undertake a modest attempt to develop a new theory of nonprofit debt. The basic economic premise is that a nonprofit firm will invest in a project if the total cost is no greater than the total benefit. For a nonprofit firm the benefit of any project is either financial, social, or a combination thereof, while the cost is the nonprofit's cost of capital plus other nonfinancial costs. In this model the organization is limited to three financing alternatives including free cash, increased fund-raising (including capital campaigns), and debt. Free cash is cash plus investment assets exclusive of the amounts that are not legally available for spending (perhaps due to a donor-imposed restriction) or amounts that constitute an inviolable cash reserve that management wishes to retain for whatever reason.

The decisions of whether or not to invest in a project and how to finance that project are jointly determined. In this setting debt will be issued only if the cost of doing so is not greater than the benefit provided by the new project *and* the nonprofit has exhausted other forms of lower cost financing. A project that is worthwhile if financed out of free cash may become not worthwhile if free cash were insufficient and it were necessary to conduct additional fund-raising or to incur debt to finance the project. This theory adapts elements of both the pecking-order theory and the trade-off theory. Nonprofits have an internal financing pecking order caused by the relative costs of their alternative financing sources. They trade off the total cost of these financing alternatives against the expected benefits of a new project.

The expected financial benefits of investing in a project are the cash flows the project is expected to produce. Expected financial benefits are typically generated by analyzing past data and making rational predictions about future cash flows. The nonfinancial benefits are unsurprisingly more difficult to measure. What is the value of feeding a hungry child, or of displaying a piece of art in a museum? Despite the difficulty of measuring these "softer" outputs, a nonprofit manager must nonetheless attach some form of value to them, so that she can compare that value to the associated financing costs in order to make the proper investment decision. It is neither necessary nor desirable to put value of "softer" outputs in terms of dollars and cents, but their value must be framed in some manner. Only after comparing the total benefits to the total costs of a project can a manager make a rational and informed investment decision.

Earlier chapters of this book contain some important lessons for us here. We have learned that the mix of nonprofit outputs varies by their "public" vs. "private" nature, and that it is easier to charge fees for "private" goods, but that providing "public" goods may lead to higher social welfare. The benefits of private goods projects where a fee will be charged to customers are easier to estimate in financial terms. An aquarium that is considering building a new wing can estimate the additional ticket revenues it will generate from the new wing. (Of course, having a new wing may also provide some nonfinancial benefits that also need to be taken into account.) If the project is a pure public good, such as opening up an additional soup kitchen for the needy, the benefits are much more difficult to measure in financial terms.

The lone cost of using existing free cash to invest in a new project is its opportunity cost. Opportunity cost is the foregone benefit of an alternative use of the cash. In most cases free cash is invested in various types of market investments such as certificates of deposit, stocks and bonds. The opportunity cost of using free cash for a new project is simply equal to the financial returns that the cash would have generated were it not used for the new project. It may seem that an additional opportunity cost that could exist is that an even better project will come along at some later date and using the free cash now prevents it from being used later, but this is always the case with investing decisions and gives rise to a no-investment perpetuity. (If a nonprofit truly felt that a better project was always on the horizon, it would never invest in any project.)

It is well known that the cost of fund-raising per dollar raised increases with the number of dollars raised. (An economist would say that the fund-raising cost function is increasing.) In theory, a nonprofit is financially better off by spending additional money on fund-raising until the last dollar of fund-raising expenses generates exactly one dollar of donations revenues (Rose-Ackerman, 1982b; Steinberg, 1986). At that level, the cost of fund-raising per dollar of donations has risen to the point where further fund-raising is unprofitable. However, prior to that point the nonprofit is strictly better off financially. That analysis leaves out one important factor: donor response to high levels of fund-raising expenses. Research shows us that donors react adversely to high fund-raising expenses (Okten and Weisbrod, 2000). Thus a more complete fund-raising model states that a nonprofit should increase its fund-raising efforts until the amount of additional donations received is equal to the sum of the additional fund-raising costs and the costs of additional donor discontent. We refer to this point as the one at which the nonprofit is spending the "optimal" amount on fund-raising.

The viability of using additional fund-raising to produce additional donations revenues for project financing is entirely dependent on whether the nonprofit is below its fund-raising "optimum" as described above. Only if the nonprofit is below this optimum will additional fund-raising be a viable means of providing new project funding. In some cases grant money may be available for investing in a new project. In this case, the costs include the direct costs of obtaining the grant funding plus the costs of increased managerial oversight (if any) by the granting agency.

There are financial and nonfinancial costs associated with using debt finance to finance an investment. The first financial cost is simply the interest. The interest cost of the debt will vary by the type and characteristics of the debt, with credit-enhanced municipal debt being the least costly and unsecured bank loans being the most costly.

The second financial cost is possible crowding out of future donations. When an organization takes on debt it has promised to allocate a (sometimes significant) proportion of its future cash flows to the lender, and therefore less to charitable beneficiaries. In theory donors should not care about whether their donations are being used to fund future, current, or past charitable projects. To the extent that current and future donations are used to cover interest costs or to repay a loan they simply represent an anticipated payment for the use of someone else's money in order to invest in the project sooner rather than later. Assuming a donor attaches the same value to the benefits and costs of past projects as did the nonprofit's management, the donor should be as willing to cover interest and principal payments as she would be to cover current or future investments in charitable projects. However, if future donors do not value past projects as highly as did management they may be reluctant to finance those past investments with their current donations. Other donors, for whatever reasons, may simply want their donations to fund current or future spending rather than pay for past spending. In either of these two latter cases current debt becomes a substitute for future donations, effectively crowding out the future donations stream. This cost, although financial in nature, is very difficult to measure as it necessarily involves estimating future donor response to current investment choices. In some sense the potential for future donor dissatisfaction and the related potential for crowding out can act as a disciplining mechanism to encourage management to correctly value a current project's costs and benefits.

The nonfinancial cost imposed on the nonprofit when it uses debt financing is caused by inconsistent objectives between borrower and lender. By borrowing, a nonprofit necessarily invites a for-profit party into its managerial decision-making process. This new party, the lender, has but a single objective—to maximize its own profits. The decisions of the lender will almost always be made according to this premise. Given that a nonprofit's objective is not to maximize net profit, problems can arise when trying to reconcile the differing objectives of the nonprofit's management and the lender. In some cases the lender will indirectly affect the manager's behavior while in other cases the lenders will have a more direct effect. For example, a lender may require a nonprofit to charge a particular fee for customers' use of the new project, or it may require an increase in fees at some future time. Management and lender may not agree on a particular fee structure for the new project, but the lender may have the right to enforce particular structures, depending on the loan documents. As another example consider a nonprofit that is unable to make an interest or principal payment, in which case the lender can force the nonprofit to put off other expenses or, in the extreme case force the nonprofit to liquidate some of its assets. The lender expects to be repaid, and this claim to the nonprofit's assets is not in violation of the nondistribution constraint typically associated with claims to assets by for-profit entities. Finally, most debt agreements contain legally binding covenants that restrict a nonprofit's behavior with respect to spending levels, maintenance of cash balances, and financial ratios. These covenants necessarily restrict management's future actions such as selling an asset that is used as security or taking on more debt. Some covenant restrictions act to restrict future cash payments that could be spent on charitable purposes, in an attempt to preserve cash for interest and principal payments. These covenants bind a nonprofit manager's choices. This cost cannot be overstated; a nonprofit must be aware that by accepting debt financing it will implicitly (and sometimes explicitly) have taken on an additional manager who has a pure profit objective function and may cause the nonprofit to make operating choices it otherwise would not have made.

As previously mentioned, the decision of whether or not to invest in a new project must be made in conjunction with deciding on how to finance the investment. The decision starts by estimating the financial and nonfinancial benefits of the proposed project. Next, the viable financing alternatives are rank ordered according to their relative total (financial and nonfinancial) costs. The nonprofit then applies the lowest-cost financing alternative to the project until that financing source is exhausted. Then the next least costly financing source is applied until exhausted, and the process is continued until sufficient funds have been allocated to completely fund the new project. In essence, the nonprofit creates a "pecking order" of its financing options based on their relative costliness.

If the aggregate costs of the financing alternatives are not greater than the benefits provided by the new project, the nonprofit should move forward with the project. The most difficult part of the process will be valuing the nonfinancial benefits and costs. It is not possible to establish a dominant theoretical "pecking order" of alternative financing sources that would apply to all nonprofits. Many of the costs depend on organization-specific and project-specific attributes. The cost of additional fund-raising efforts is entirely organization specific and could be a low or high cost alternative. Free cash is likely to be a lower cost option than is bank debt. Municipal debt is certainly less financially costly than either free cash or bank debt and therefore its relative place in the financing decision is dependent on the magnitude of its nontax costs. As an example, one could easily envision an organization's pecking order as: municipal debt (owing to its low interest cost and potential for arbitrage), free cash, capital campaign, and bank debt. If this nonprofit could raise sufficient municipal debt to cover the proposed project, and the cost of the municipal debt were not greater than the expected benefits of the project, the financing decision would be to undertake the project using only municipal debt.

To be sure, this theory has its weaknesses. We offer it as a modest expansion on existing lines of thought in an attempt to include the unique and specific characteristics of nonprofit organizations.

Extending the Knowledge Base

The costs of using debt financing are many, but there may be times when these costs are more than offset by the benefits provided by the project that the debt will finance. The theoretical model developed above has several practical applications. The model provides a road map for making the new project decision and whether or not debt should be used to finance that project. To operationalize this theory, the manager should keep several things in mind, including nonfinancial costs and lender motivations.

Nonfinancial costs are difficult to quantify and are therefore subject to larger risk of misestimation. It is very possible to underestimate these costs by a wide margin. Indeed, there may be a tendency on the part of management to understate these costs so as to make a new project look more favorable. One way to mitigate this problem is to reduce the magnitude of the nonfinancial costs in real terms, as follows.

With respect to fund-raising, framing the requests for additional donations as a capital project can lower the nonfinancial costs of fund-raising. Not only will donors feel that their gifts will be used for a very specific project, but they will realize that this is not a recurring request. With respect to debt, one way to mitigate the cost of future donors' dislike of paying for past projects is to inform donors of the current benefits past projects are providing. When bargaining the terms of debt with a lender, it is wise to actively work to reduce any effects on future managerial choices. One should avoid pledging future revenue streams if possible. Agreeing to pay a somewhat higher interest rate may well be worthwhile if the nonprofit can avoid additional constraints placed on future managerial decisions. When covenants are written into the debt contract, nonprofits should actively attempt to loosen their terms so that they will be less likely to bind future decisions. One should also be aware of, and clearly understand, all encumbrances. These items are found either in the loan documents, or are recorded in the local county recorder's office. It is imperative that management is aware of exactly how its future behavior will be modified by the debt agreements before agreeing to them.

The motivations of the lender should be kept in mind. A lender will not value as highly the nonfinancial benefits of a new project as will the nonprofit borrower. Nor will a lender be as bothered by the nonfinancial costs imposed on the nonprofit by the use of debt. A lender will therefore tend to undervalue the benefits of nonprofit projects and simultaneously underestimate the costs of using debt financing. In fact, lenders may well view debt financing as the least costly financing source, as they may ignore the nonfinancial costs. This will cause lenders to suggest debt in circumstances where it might not be in the nonprofit's best interest. To a for-profit lender a debt instrument is a money-making product and like all for-profit firms lenders want to sell as much of their products at the highest prices possible, so as to maximize their financial profits.

Box 11.1. Aligning Objective Functions: The Case of Nonprofit Lenders

The Center for Nonprofit Management in Dallas, Texas, a nonprofit organization, provides a variety of services to nonprofit organizations in the state of Texas. One of those services is lending to nonprofits. Because the Center's primary objective is not to maximize its profits, it is willing to offer loans to nonprofits at lower costs and more favorable terms than a for-profit bank would be willing to offer. (www.cnmdallas.com)

A nonprofit manager must be cognizant of the lender's biases. Typically it will be much easier to receive debt financing for a project that will produce cash benefits. These projects will typically involve "private" goods because user fees can be charged. In order for a nonprofit to use debt to finance a "public goods" project for which little or no fee will be charged it must have other assets (such as buildings or a dependable and sufficient donations base) that the lender can use as security for the loan. These tendencies could easily cause a nonprofit to expand its fee producing activities and contract its more intangible outputs, although this behavior may be inconsistent with its mission or with maximizing social value.

Improving Practice

When cash needs do not coincide with cash availability, the choice of whether to issue debt will arise. The best practice is to develop a debt strategy before any debt is actually needed. The types of circumstances under which a nonprofit will seek debt financing should already be in writing as a formal policy statement. The policy should be flexible enough to meet unforeseen circumstances, but nonetheless should provide a framework for thinking about how debt will affect the nonprofit's mission. The time to reasonably think about the costs and benefits of debt is when there is no pressing cash need. By waiting until there is no alternative but to borrow, a nonprofit will naturally discount the costs of debt.

In addition to having a policy in place with respect to debt, nonprofits should consider having some debt outstanding during every year whether they need it or not. We refer to these loans as "reputation loans." Of course, a lender will frequently require a purpose for the loans, and general working capital is typical. There are three good reasons to maintain reputation loans. First, one of the most important qualities that a potential lender will look for is past loan history. If the organization has a history of taking even very small loans and responsibly paying them back, it will be able to access significantly larger loans at lower costs in the future, should the need arise. Second, by getting a series of loans a nonprofit will necessarily develop a relationship with a bank and perhaps even some particular bankers. These personal relationships are crucial. The final decision of whether or not to give a nonprofit a loan is made by a person, not a machine. Should the nonprofit borrow significant amounts at some future time and subsequently have some difficulty making repayments, a strong relationship with the lender can make things much easier on the nonprofit. Finally, by having loans outstanding during the year, the nonprofit learns how to deal with debt. The accounting system will be in place to track debt and the necessary interest payments. Employees will become familiar with the necessary paperwork and deadlines. Many nonprofits find that their first adventure into borrowing is traumatic, as it necessarily involves new technicalities, paperwork, and deadlines that cannot be missed. Reputation loans should be short term, generally not more than one year, and the proceeds of the loan should be quickly invested into a very safe investment such as a bank certificate of deposit. The nonprofit will generate some interest income on the investment that can be used to offset a portion of the interest expense it pays on the loan. The amount of the loan need not be large. The net interest cost of a $1,000 loan will be approximately $50 per year or less, a small price to pay for the potential benefits received.

Below we provide a list of diagnostic questions and guidelines that can be used to help frame the debt decision. Prior to taking on any debt, the organization should be able to clearly answer all of the applicable questions and follow the suggested rules of thumb.

1. What situation has given rise to the cash need?
   a. Facilities expansion: do you really need a new facility?
   b. Refunding prior debt: will you be able to repay at the end of the next term? Is it a municipal refunding that may be limited?
   c. Working capital
      i. Is there a structural cash flow deficiency?
      ii. Will the cash needs frequently recur?
2. Measure the expected benefits of the project.
   a. Will the project produce user fees, and if so, how much?
   b. Will the project provide nonfinancial benefits?
3. Measure the expected costs of financing the project.
   a. Rank order the possible financing sources by relative cost.
   b. Apply the lower cost sources to the project until it is funded.
   c. Is it worth investing in this new project?
      The following questions only apply if the project will be at least partially financed with debt.
4. Which structure of the debt is best?
   a. Match the time of the loan to the underlying project, particularly if the project will generate user fees.
   b. Is a balloon loan preferred to one based on an amortized principal, or not?
   c. Avoid the temptation to meet short-term cash needs with long-term debt.
5. What will provide security (collateral) for the debt?
   a. Will a purchased asset provide all the necessary collateral?
   b. Will the nonprofit's future gross revenues be pledged as collateral?
6. Choose your lender carefully.
   a. Are nonprofit lenders available?
   b. Use the bank that you have your reputation loans with.

    c. If you do not have reputation loans outstanding use a local lender that you have a relationship with.

    d. Keep your lender informed of any changes in your financial position that might compromise your ability to make interest or principal payments.

7. Seek the advice of the board, your workers, and outside professionals.

    a. The board should be an integral part of the debt financing process. Seek their expertise.

    b. Workers know the details of daily cash expenditures and revenues. Ask them what the exact needs are and where the revenues will come from.

    c. Legal and technical advice is crucial so that the organization is treated fairly in the process. A nonprofit may issue debt only once every twenty years, so it is quite likely that the necessary expertise is not on hand within the nonprofit. Hire experts who do this for a living. Remember, you get what you contract for.

The Asian Art Museum of San Francisco offers an instructive case study of the principles considered in this chapter:

Box 11.2. The Asian Art Museum of San Francisco

The Asian Art Museum of San Francisco recently underwent a major expansion of its facilities. The previous location in Golden Gate Park was constraining and did not permit the museum to display much of its collection. The new facility is located in the old San Francisco Main Library and more than doubled the size of the previous building. The cost was approximately $160 million and the new facility opened in March 2003. Funding for the project came from three sources: a $107 million 501(c)(3) bond issue sponsored by the Commerce and Economic Development Program of California, approximately $50 million in city grant funding, and the rest from a capital campaign. The 501(c)(3) bonds were issued on June 1, 2000, and pay a variable interest of 4.25 to 5.5 percent with the principal due in installments starting in 2007. The final

principal payment is due on June 1, 2030. In addition to a first
security lien on the new building the lender required that the
museum also pledge its gross revenues as collateral. The museum's management hopes to earn sufficient revenues from
admission fees and gift and food shops to pay the interest and
principal on the bonds. The museum's debt to assets ratio increased from zero (it had no debt) prior to the issue to 67 percent
after the issue. The ratio of interest expense to total expense
increased from 0 to 9 percent. Approximately $4.5 million in
additional annual ticket and shop revenues are needed to pay
the interest on the loans and another $5 million annually to pay
the principal when it becomes due, beginning in 2007. Annual
ticket and shop receipts at the old location averaged $700,000.
Therefore ticket and shop revenues will have to increase from
$700k to about $9.5 million, fourteenfold, to cover the debt
payments. Because the assets as well as the gross revenues of
the Asian were pledged as collateral for the loan, if program
revenues are not sufficient to cover the debt payments, then
donations will be used to make up the shortfall. The Asian receives public donations of approximately $20 million per year.
("A Home of Its Own: Asian Art Museum Opens Its Doors This
Week," *San Francisco Chronicle*, March 16, 2003.)

It is clear that the Asian Art Museum municipal bond issue
caused a dramatic change in the museum's capital structure. The
debt to assets ratio increased from 0 to nearly 70 percent. Although
the ratio will fall slowly as the museum pays off its debts over
time, it will not again be debt free until the year 2030 at the earliest. Management will certainly face new challenges in operating
what was a debt free but is now a debt rich organization. The
museum smartly matched the repayment terms of the debt to the
expected future cash flows from fees the expansion is expected to
generate. The first debt repayment is not due until 2007, giving
the museum four years to establish the new facility's cash flow.
In addition to this debt, the museum also undertook a capital
campaign, ostensibly because the net cost of raising donations in
this way was cheaper than incurring even more debt. It is also

possible that the bond financing was contingent on the museum raising a certain amount of donations.

By utilizing a state agency to sponsor the bond issue the museum was able to issue municipal bonds, reducing the interest rate significantly below what a taxable debt issue would have required. Without the tax exemption the bonds would have to have paid an interest of approximately 7 percent, increasing the annual interest expense from $4.5 million to $7 million per year. It is quite possible that at this rate of interest the museum would not have been able to carry the debt load and would not have issued the bonds, thereby forgoing its new facility. The museum plans on paying the interest and principal from additional fee revenues, a clearly identified revenue source. However, if fee revenues do not rise sharply then a significant portion of future donations will necessarily be redirected toward interest and principal payments, with a possible effect on future donors, willingness to give.

Although the bond trustee no doubt wishes the museum the best of success and sincerely hopes the museum generates sufficient fee revenues to make its debt payments, the trustee is not depending on those new fee revenues to repay the loan. The bond trustee took a first claim to the museum's gross revenues, which includes donations revenues. The ability of the trustee to have first claim to the museum's donations in the event of nonpayment could influence the museum's managerial decisions in the long run if fee revenues do not sufficiently grow to cover future interest and debt payments.

Conclusion

Debt financing is a large and important part of nonprofit organizations' capital structures. By breaking the link between current cash availability and current spending, debt permits a nonprofit to supply a good or purchase an asset sooner than it otherwise would. Along with this benefit come many associated costs. Carefully considering all the costs associated with debt finance involves not only estimating the financial cost, but more importantly measuring the nonfinancial costs that will be placed on the organization. These costs will vary depending on the project being financed and the terms of the debt contract. There is no clear and definite science that will identify instances where debt financing is appropriate, although there is a general theory that provides some best practice guidelines that can be used to arrive at a decision.

As nonprofits continue to expand to meet the needs of society debt will no doubt continue to play an important role in meeting future capital needs. The most important distinguishing characteristic of debt relative to all other revenue sources is that it must be repaid. From a public policy perspective the issue of nonprofit debt is important. The matters associated with transferring costs and benefits across time are complex and many important issues need to be examined. Is society better off when a nonprofit borrows? What costs have we imposed on the future of nonprofits? Are existing tax laws and lending principles coincident with the objectives of nonprofit managers? In the end, a nonprofit manager is left with a seemingly much less complex decision: should we borrow and buy today, or wait until tomorrow? However, each manager's decision is necessarily a part of the nonprofit system, and the effects of debt on that system are largely unknown.

In sum, debt is an important part of nonprofit finance. It allows nonprofits to provide critical services to those in need during times when cash flow would otherwise not permit that. In many cases the many benefits of debt far outweigh the costs, and no doubt debt will continue to have an important role in helping nonprofits deliver their missions.

IV

INCOME AND ASSET PORTFOLIOS, AND FINANCIAL HEALTH

12

Managing Endowment and Other Assets

Woods Bowman[1]

Introduction

This chapter deals with assets, emphasizing those found only among nonprofits, especially restricted assets and endowment. For a thing to be an asset it must have an owner[2] and either exchange (cash) value or commercial (income) value (Downes and Goodman, 1995). A donated asset with restrictions—permanent or temporary—on its use imposed by the donor is a restricted asset. Endowment, broadly defined, consists of restricted and unrestricted assets managed with the intent of providing a steady source of income over the long term. More precisely, the American Institute of Certified Public Accountants (AICPA) defines *endowment* as "an established fund of cash, securities, or other assets to provide income for the maintenance of a not-for-profit organization . . . generally established by donor-restricted gifts and bequests" (AICPA, §366). Whenever this chapter introduces a financial concept it will identify the corresponding line on IRS Form 990—the principal source of financial information about the nonprofit sector. Unfortunately, 990 forms do not report on endowment.

Patterns and Trends[3]

Seventy-eight percent of secular nonprofits have assets of less than $1 million, representing 1.4 percent of the assets of the nonprofit sector, while the other 22 percent have assets of $1 million or more, or 98.6 percent of all nonprofit assets (see chapter 14). The biggest nonprofits, by asset size, are research universities, hospitals, megacharities, and some cultural institutions.[4] Financial assets of secular nonprofit organizations grew from $777 billion in 1988 to $1.77 trillion in 1998, an annual increase of 7.8 percent, adjusted for inflation (Fremont-Smith, 2002). This growth, which includes new contributions as well as investment earnings, is much larger than the 4.8 percent annual growth in households' financial wealth and the 3.5 percent annual growth in business holdings.

An organization's accounts receivable (IRS Form 990, line 47) represent credit it has extended to entities with which it does business. Pledges (line 48) are receivables in the form of promised donations, and grants receivable (line 49) are promises of future funding. Accounts receivable and pledges are adjusted on Form 990 for doubtful accounts (lines 47c and 48c respectively). The median nonprofit has no receivables, while 10 percent have more than 34 percent of their assets in this category. Functionally, accounts receivable are short-term loans and nonprofits with huge accounts receivable are, metaphorically speaking, operating a bank. This is poor stewardship. Large pledge and grant receivables may be unavoidable but they should be carefully monitored and promptly collected when due or written off.

Receivables from officers, directors, trustees, and key employees (line 50) are loans to insiders. If such loans are made on favorable terms or forgiven, they become an indirect form of compensation and could be subject to intermediate sanctions by the IRS. In some states any loan to an insider is illegal. There are very few situations in which such a loan is appropriate, unless it is explicitly part of a compensation package. Over 90 percent of nonprofits report zero receivables in this category.

There are two investment items on IRS Form 990: investments in securities (line 54) and investments in fixed assets (line 55c). The median nonprofit has total investments equal to 4.6 percent of total assets and less than 1 percent of expenses, but the top quartile has total investments exceeding 24.3 percent of assets and 10 percent of expenses. The top decile has investments exceeding 81.1 percent of assets and 2.7 times expenses. Investment holdings are concentrated in a few subsectors: higher education, hospitals, grant making, membership organizations, and social science research institutes.

Total investments is not equivalent to endowment—on the one hand, the former excludes cash, but on the other hand, it includes working capital, operating funds, and plant funds.[5] As chapter 7 points out, a working cash fund is an internal revolving loan fund used to smooth an organization's monthly cash flow. An operating reserve is an internal revolving loan fund used to cover unplanned budget deficits. Money withdrawn from these funds should be repaid as soon as practicable. Plant funds, on the other hand, are accumulated for the purpose of expending them on new construction and major maintenance, and replenished on a predetermined schedule or as needed.

A common standard for working cash and operating reserves combined, endorsed by Konrad and Novak (2000), is that an organization should have liquid funds sufficient for at least three months of expenses. Barely half of nonprofits meet this standard, but one in five has enough to cover at least one year of expenses.[6] The median organization in public safety, disaster preparedness, and relief has seventeen months of expenses covered. The median mutual benefit and membership organization has one year of expenses covered, and the median philanthropy, voluntarism, and grant-making organization has nine months of expenses covered. Disaster preparedness and relief undoubtedly requires a large amount of ready cash. Mutual organizations in this category largely conduct pension and insurance activities, which require large amounts of cash. Grant-making organizations probably maintain large cash balances waiting to be drawn down by grantees. But, these three categories account for only 30 percent of the 40,000 nonprofits that have over nine months of expenses covered by current assets. In general, large cash holdings are suspect. They may represent lost opportunities to put an organization's money to work in investments.

Current Practice

GAAP requires reporting securities at fair market value, although Form 990 (line 54) gives the option to report their value at cost. Investments in land, building, and equipment, minus accumulated depreciation (line 55c), are always reported at cost, although it might be possible to sell them for more. Form 990 makes a distinction between land, building, and equipment held for investment (line 55c) and land, building, and equipment used in mission fulfillment (line 57). Museum collections are neither included on line 57 nor reported on financial statements because they are unique and it is very hard to assess their value. Besides, under normal circumstances, museum collections cannot be sold to pay general operating expenses. When a museum sells from its collection (deaccession), the guidelines of the American Association of Museums call for using the proceeds to acquire other artifacts, such that the net effect enhances its collection.

Total assets (line 59) minus total liabilities (line 66) equal net assets (line 73)—also called equity—is the amount an organization owns free and clear of any obligation. In the business sector it is known as net worth, and it would be the amount a firm's owners would be able to divide among themselves if they voluntarily liquidated the firm while it was a going concern. In the nonprofit sector, these net assets are a public resource, which a nonprofit must transfer to another tax-exempt entity when it liquidates—subject to the approval of the appropriate state attorney(s) general. There have been cases of an attorney general disapproving of a transfer, or even liquidation, namely, Wilson College (Zehner v. Alexander et al, No. 56-1979, PA Ct. Common Pleas Franklin Co., Orphan's Ct. Div., decree entered May 25, 1979).

In the business sector, equity can be acquired through selling stock or by accumulating retained earnings, that is, profit. Nonprofits cannot sell stock, so their only option is to generate revenue in excess of expenses, that is, surplus, which is called "excess for the year" on Form 990 (line 18). Most 501(c)(3) public charities receive donations as part of their regular annual income, and aggressive ones periodically conduct capital campaigns. Income from this source is not used for annual expenses but to build an endowment or to acquire physical assets. In terms of its impact on a public charity's balance sheet, a capital campaign resembles a public offering of stock.

The equity of a nonprofit organization (line 73) is divided into three categories—unrestricted (line 67), temporarily restricted (line 68), and permanently restricted (line 69). These categories correspond to the three types of endowment: true endowment, term endowment, and quasi-endowment. *True*, or *permanent, endowment* is restricted in a written agreement *by the donor* or is in response to a solicitation that promised to use the gift as an endowment and may not be used up, expended, or otherwise exhausted. The focus on donor restrictions corresponds to the accountants' concept of permanently restricted net assets. *Term endowment* is created for a set number of years or until a future event such as the death of the donor occurs or until certain stipulated conditions have been satisfied. It appears on a balance sheet as temporarily restricted net assets. *Quasi-endowments*, or funds functioning as endowment, are accumulated gifts or revenues that the board elects to put into endowment. In accounting terms, quasi-endowment is part of unrestricted net assets.[7]

State law and common law govern deviations from the express stipulations of a gift agreement (Helms, Henkin, and Murray, 2005), so restricted assets cannot be reprogrammed easily to suit an organization's changing needs. Forty-six states have adopted a variant of the Uniform Management of Institutional Funds Act (UMIFA), which is more flexible than the common law doctrines of cy pres and equitable deviation. In general, organizations seeking to reprogram restricted assets must seek court approval. UMIFA provides that a change is possible if the court finds that a restriction is "obsolete, inappropriate or impracticable." Wise organizations negotiate with donors and write flexibility into their gift agreements.

According to Pollak and Dunford (2005), one in ten public charities manage assets through 509(a)(3) supporting organizations, of which there are three types—Type I are supervised or controlled by the supported organization, Type II are supervised or controlled in connection with the supported organization, and Type III are operated in connection with a supported organization. This wide range of possibilities makes supporting organizations a flexible tool for a variety of financial tasks, although the IRS has expressed concern that they (particularly Type III) may also serve as a tool for tax evasion. The most common legitimate functions of supporting organizations are fund-raising/grant making, endowment management, and real estate management. The most common supporting organizations are linked to educational institutions (26 percent), health care organizations (19 percent), and human services institutions (17 percent), which are endowed organizations owning substantial real estate and/or doing substantial fund-raising. Although supporting organizations numerically constitute 10 percent of public charities, they control 17 percent of charitable assets.

Theory

Endowment holdings by nonprofits are, on average, substantially larger than cash holdings by for-profit firms (Core, Guay, and Verdi, 2005). Endowment does double duty as part of a nonprofit's capital structure (i.e., mix of assets and liabilities) and as an income generator. Furthermore, it is a financing tool that distinguishes nonprofits from for-profit firms.[8] No publicly traded profit-seeking corporation is endowed except as required by law (e.g., cemeteries), not even profit-seeking universities, hospitals, and theaters that coexist and compete with endowed nonprofit universities, hospitals, and theaters. There are likely two reasons for this disparity: (1) capital campaigns are usually used to grow endowments and there are no tax advantages for giving to a for-profit; and (2) if a publicly traded for-profit had an endowment, it would be a tempting target for a hostile takeover or leveraged buyout by investors seeking control of those assets.

Endowment improves financial stability, but "stability" is subject to various interpretations. The following statement is a fund-raising professional's description of how endowment helps an organization achieve financial stability:

> The nonprofit funding environment is volatile and creates a sense of unease and inconsistency. Income from endowment can effectively smooth out the rough spots in a fiscal year. Endowment can be used to underwrite programs that have not been funded, support budgets where there are shortfalls, enable management to move an institution forward and provide a safety net when an unexpected financial crisis occurs. (Schumacher 2003, 3)[9]

The first two sentences are a better description of working capital than endowment. Working capital is an internal revolving loan fund used to finance intrayear cash imbalances, but an endowment should not be an organization's private line of credit. Endowment stabilizes an income stream, but only because its payout is steady from month to month and hence reduces the need for cash flow financing. The third sentence is a better description of an operating reserve, which is also an internal revolving loan fund that finances unplanned operating deficits and unexpected repairs and replacement of fixed assets. Endowment can fund projects that do not pay their own way, but the funding should be permanent, as when a university underwrites graduate programs with its endowment income, or when a hospital underwrites a research program. Good endowment management requires distinguishing between working capital, operating reserves, and endowment, because each requires a different management style.

An endowment is not a source of cash to keep programs going undiminished when other funding dries up. To maintain programs when revenue shrinks would in most cases require increasing spending from endowment above a payout rate consistent with protecting the inflation-adjusted value of the corpus over the long term.[10] This is self-defeating because a smaller endowment will produce less income in subsequent years. When revenues dry up, spending must be cut or new sources of income found. Investment income from an endowment merely puts a floor under spending so basic services can be maintained, thus assuring the organization's survival and protection of its core mission. Unrestricted resources of an endowment can be spent, but they only buy time for an organization to carefully study how to cut back services outside its core mission, and to tap new sources of funding.

Box 12.1. The Brooklyn Academy of Music Builds an Endowment[1]

The 143-year old Brooklyn Academy of Music (BAM), after years of struggling to survive, has been reborn as a result of a $6.8 million facelift and major gifts that increased its endowment from $18 million to $50 million. However, it has no plans to cut back on fund-raising. President Karen Brooks Hopkins argues that the suddenly larger endowment "buys some breathing space for long-range planning amid the hectic pace of fund-raising."

In the 1960s the future looked bleak for BAM, and there was talk of closing it and converting the property into tennis courts. The situation worsened in the 1980s when crack cocaine made inroads into the surrounding community. BAM's response was to stimulate interest by creating something new. It launched the Next Wave Festival, which it has produced every year since. After the festival proved it had staying power, BAM inaugurated an endowment in 1992.

This was wise sequencing. Donors are wary of a dying institution. A life-saving gift creates what insurance companies call moral hazard, meaning the gift reduces an institution's incentive to change its ways. If a large gift does not rescue it, the money is wasted. Donors prefer to give to viable and relevant institutions, and their gifts make it even more viable and keep it relevant.

[1] The information for the case came from Felicia Lee, "Endowment Doubles for Brooklyn Academy," *New York Times*, October 5, 2004, pp. B1, B7.

Chapter 7 addresses the question of whether endowment is justified and examines endowment investment strategies. Here we explore three additional issues: the cost of building an endowment, how much an organization should spend from its endowment, and whether an endowment's corpus should be inviolate.

Cornell University's experience is illustrative of the cost of building an endowment. In a five-year $1.5 billion capital campaign it spent 8 cents per dollar raised. However, "many academic units felt poorer, rather than richer, in the short run [because] university development at Cornell is funded through a "tax" on the units. While the units were paying 8 cents for each dollar raised, those dollars that went into the endowment yielded them only 4 cents of income per dollar raised in the initial year" (Ehrenberg, 2002, 47). The "tax" to pay the cost of Cornell's campaign came from each unit's general operating budget, but the money raised funded new initiatives. In the meantime, existing activities were squeezed. Many of the dollars the university properly reported as raised by the campaign were actually pledges that did not put cash into the university's endowment right away, further reducing the return to fund-raising in the short run. Some of the projects turned out to be inadequately funded, e.g., an endowed chair may not have had adequate funds for associated space and staff support. In these cases, the affected academic unit had to make up the difference out of its general operating budget (Ehrenberg, 2002).

Payout or *payout rate* refers to the proportion of an endowment that can be spent without eroding the value of the endowment in inflation-adjusted terms, while *spending* refers to the amount in dollars withdrawn from an endowment annually in support of operations. According to the Commonfund benchmark survey of educational institutions and their supporting foundations for the year 2003 (Commonfund, 2004),[11] organizations with endowments below $10 million have a lower average payout rate, which suggests that they are trying to build their endowments through internal growth. While 80 percent of endowed organizations made no change in spending policy in the prior year, organizations with endowments below $10 million are the most likely to change from year to year, which suggests that they are more likely to adjust payout in response to budget pressures. This is not a good idea (Guthrie, 1996).

To maintain an endowment's principal in perpetuity, an organization should adopt a payout formula that caps spending from endowment at a level below the anticipated long-term rate of total return minus the anticipated rate of inflation. According to the Commonfund benchmark survey report cited above, the average payout rate for educational institutions has been 4.9 percent. This is nearly identical to the 5 percent payout rate established for foundations by the 1969 Tax Reform Act. Given the long-term growth rate for domestic large company equities of approximately 11 percent, a 4.9 percent payout would allow an endowment fully invested in those securities to grow at 6.1 percent. Because the long-term inflation rate is 3.1 percent, a hypothetical scenario such as this provides 3 percent to cover endowment management expenses and growth above the rate of inflation.

Unfortunately, Commonfund does not provide data on expenses, but expenses can be considerable and should not be neglected. Money management expenses consume 0.7 percent of Cornell's endowment value annually (Ehrenberg, 2002). This may not sound like much, but it cuts the difference between Cornell's endowment's growth and the rate of inflation by nearly one-quarter—and its expenses are much lower than the average commercially available domestic stock mutual fund, which charges 1.43 percent for expenses.[12]

An endowment spending formula should protect its purchasing power over time, which requires taking inflation into account. The simplest formula starts with a moving average of the market value of the endowment over several years and multiplies it by a constant payout rate that permits the endowment to grow by at least the rate of inflation over the long term. A moving average smoothes the ups and downs in an endowment's value, but the formula developed at Yale University does a better job of taking inflation into account. It has two components that are sensitive to inflation in opposing ways. Equity prices perform poorly in periods of high inflation, but well in periods of low inflation. One component of the Yale formula increases payout rates in periods of high inflation, but retards payout rates in periods of low inflation, while the other component behaves oppositely. The allowable Yale spending from endowment is a weighted average: 70 percent of the allowable spending in the prior fiscal year, increased by the rate of inflation, *plus* 30 percent of the long-term payout rate *multiplied* by the most recent four-quarter market average of the endowment's value.[13] In the short term, considerable weight is given to last year's payout rate, which depends on the payout rate the year before, and so on, but in the long run, market return dominates.

When a budget is under severe pressure and the market is performing extremely well, it may be tempting to abandon a formula and spend as much as needed (or possible) as long as spending is below the increase in the endowment's value. The New-York Historical Society is a cautionary tale. In 1975, when its endowment was over $10 million and the stock market was doing well, it began to ignore its payout formula and used endowment to balance its budget. Although it rarely spent more than earnings, in 18 years its endowment shrank to $5 million, and, after adjusting for inflation, it was considerably lower. Guthrie (1996) estimated that had it stuck to its payout formula, its endowment would have been $85 million. "Without an enforced spending limit [payout rate], the total return concept is not an endowment management philosophy; it becomes an improper justification for liquidating endowment principal" (Guthrie, 1996, 170).

It is understandable that a financially threatened organization would borrow from the corpus of its endowment when working capital and operating reserves are inadequate to deal with financial exigencies—it may have no choice if it wants to survive. However, if an organization had been breaking even (counting payout as revenue) before a crisis, it is unlikely to do better later with less income from a smaller endowment. With its cash flow compromised, an organization will have difficulty accumulating working capital, rebuilding operating reserves, and repaying the amount "borrowed" from endowment after the crisis is over. Restoring working capital and operating reserves should be the first priority, but of course, this delays repaying the "loan." Spending endowment in response to emergencies is like throwing cargo overboard to lighten a storm-tossed ship—the captain also has no choice, but retrieving it after the storm is all but impossible. Spending the corpus of an endowment to address a budget problem does not solve it. It only buys time for finding a solution. The New-York Historical Society decision makers did not take advantage of time dearly bought.

There may be circumstances when it is desirable to deliberately spend down the corpus of an endowment. If an organization wants to spend down its endowment as a matter of policy, there are three rules it should follow. First, never spend restricted assets for anything other than their intended purpose without a court order or donor consent. Second, the board should adopt an endowment policy specifying a target level of endowment expressed as a proportion of total assets or spending *before* embarking on a policy to spend down endowment. Third, the amount taken from the endowment should be used to finance nonrecurring projects. Why the last rule? In the event that money taken from the corpus of the endowment is used to finance day-to-day operations, annual income will be less than annual expenses, the difference being financed by endowment spending. But, when the target endowment size is reached, annual income will be inadequate to cover annual expenses, thereby creating a financial crisis. Therefore, the amount taken from the endowment should be used to finance nonrecurring projects. Even if an organization plans its own demise by choosing to spend all of its assets in a cause, the first two rules still apply.

Borrowing from endowment is appropriate only when repayment is swift and certain and it is more costly to borrow externally. For example, when DePaul University in Chicago had an opportunity to buy a piece of property near campus at the same time it was trying to sell another, more valuable, parcel of real estate some distance away, it borrowed unrestricted endowment assets, which it repaid upon consummation of the sale. Borrowing from endowment is tantamount to exceeding a payout formula. Frequent borrowing or protracted repayment schedules compromise the formula. In these cases, payout should be reduced to compensate.

Extending the Knowledge Base

Kevin Guthrie (1996), in his study of the New-York Historical Society, argues that not all of an organization's assets add to its resource base. Some assets actually cost more to own than they contribute in terms of generating income. He refers to this phenomenon metaphorically as the "liability of assets." For example, he explains that the Society's collections are "actually a net drain on its resources. Incumbent with ownership of those collections is an unremitting obligation to catalogue, conserve, protect, and make accessible millions of items" (Guthrie, 1996, 152).

His metaphor is applicable to other types of organizations and other fixed assets. Buildings, particularly monumental churches, ornate halls, cavernous museums, and historic university structures, are expensive to maintain and operate. They are symbolic and may be useful, but if they generate an insufficient amount of income to cover the cost of maintenance and operation, they are a net drain on organization resources. I call assets that, for practical reasons, cannot be sold "privileged assets."[14] The oldest and least productive real estate assets are often the most privileged. Everyone knows a college with an original building that is extraordinarily expensive to maintain but is protected by institutional sentiment. A profit-maximizing investor would get rid of any asset with a negative expected return, but a nonprofit manager is constrained to keep it and to find a way to pay for it. Having costly real estate in an asset portfolio, and not being able to get rid of it, reduces return for every possible level of organizational risk and increases risk for every possible level of return.

An individual investor chooses an acceptable level of risk and invests her portfolio with the goal of maximizing her total return subject to her risk constraint and the particular size of her portfolio. A nonprofit manager solves the mirror-image problem and minimizes risk for a chosen return. To pay the bills, a nonprofit manager has to earn surpluses, but without stockholders to please, she need not maximize surplus, as a for-profit manager should. The organization's mission and various stakeholder interests will depress the target level of surplus. Given that risk and return are positively correlated among the set of all possible efficient portfolios (called the efficiency frontier), this will also lower risk, which will be attractive to risk-averse managers. Holding return constant, a manager can reduce risk through diversification, which involves selecting assets with uncorrelated returns, that is, returns that do not tend to change in tandem with one another. Diversification eliminates unsystematic risk, leaving only an irreducible systematic portion.

Real estate ownership increases fixed cost, threatening an organization's survival over the long run by saddling it with claims on its cash flow that persist independently of its level of output (the definition of fixed cost) and income. If an organization were to cease operations, it would continue to incur the same fixed cost—at least until it could dispose of the assets responsible for generating the cost. This restricts managerial discretion to manage the cost side of the budget. Because factors independent of output affect income from invested endowment funds we call it "fixed revenue" (see chapter 7).

Organizations with their equity tied up in real estate should be endowed for the sake of long-term survival. Unfortunately, in practice the relationship between endowment and occupancy costs appears to be random. Out of 155,000 operating nonprofits, only 14 percent with high occupancy costs (over 25 percent of total expenses) have substantial investment.[15] Hager and Pollak (2004) found that performing arts organizations that owned real estate were not more likely than renters to be endowed. Wise organizations include endowment funding in the financing package for a new building. It is much easier to raise money for a structure than for its future upkeep, but there are ways to tie these goals together through a gift "pricing" policy. Say that naming privileges require a gift of $X for the main auditorium, $Y for a rehearsal room, and $Z for a small plaque on a seat. Each of these prices should include a pro rata share of an endowment for upkeep. In effect, contributions to building endowment can be structured as self-imposed taxes on gifts for construction.

Perhaps planners are afraid the prices will be too high for their donor pool. If so, perhaps the project is too ambitious. It would be an unfortunate irony if they succeeded in building a beautiful, functional structure and the organization foundered because it could not pay for its upkeep. Nonprofits complain that foundations fund programs without including money for overhead, yet when they ask donors for a new building they neglect to ask for enough to cover the increase in overhead cost that accompanies a new building.

Improving Practice

Organizations with endowments should regularly review their management practices to keep them up-to-date. Chapter 7 raised some issues to think about regarding endowment and investment management. Here are other diagnostic questions:

1. *Are your fixed assets a drain on your resources? Do you have an endowment?*

Owning an asset gives an organization more control, but it is costly. You may be surprised how much your real estate costs to own after you account for cleaning, routine maintenance, utilities, insurance, and security. If you have a mortgage, add interest. These are fixed costs; they are constant no matter how many people you serve or how much money you receive in grants and donations, and your real estate tax exemption may not be enough to offset these costs. In such case, you should have an endowment.

2. *Do you negotiate reprogramming flexibility into your gift agreements with your donors before accepting a restricted asset as a gift?*

Of course your donors will not give you total flexibility to do anything you like, but you can negotiate for more flexible terms than offered by the law in your state. In addition, if a donor wants to give you money for a program that takes you in a direction you would rather not go, or that imposes additional costs not covered by the gift, do not be timid about discussing these issues with the donor and trying to find common ground on a different project.

3. *Do you have a written, board-adopted endowment management policy? Does it address payout? Does it address borrowing from endowment or spending the corpus?*

If yours is a small organization, it may be more efficient to include your endowment policy within a comprehensive financial policy. Larger organizations, particularly those that hire professional fund managers, would do better to adopt a separate policy. It should address payout and include a provision specifying the conditions under which borrowing from endowment and spending the corpus is allowable. These should be very narrowly drawn; an absolute prohibition on either would not be unreasonable. The endowment policy should address what happens when the endowment is under water, that is, when its value is less than the initial contribution of restricted assets. Care should be taken to make sure your endowment policy is consistent with state law.

Conclusion

Endowment does double duty as part of a nonprofit's capital structure and as an income generator. It is a financing tool unavailable to for-profit firms. It is a mixture of restricted and unrestricted assets that are managed with the intent of providing a steady source of income over the long term. It should not be confused with working cash, operating reserve, or plant funds, which are not sources of long-term income. A working cash fund and an operating reserve are essential to the smooth functioning of any organization and should be established before initiating an endowment. Plant funds are necessary only for organizations that own real estate.

All organizations should take a hard look at their asset structure, but particularly those that own real estate. Real estate ownership adds a component to an organization's cost structure that is independent of its output, which threatens its long-term viability. Certain kinds of real estate constitute what I call "privileged assets." In a prolonged economic downturn, an organization may be unable to sell off its privileged assets to bring its long-term revenue in line with long-term cost without changing its character to such a degree that it becomes a qualitatively different organization. An endowment adds a component to an organization's income structure that is independent of output (fixed revenue), and the fixed revenue helps offset fixed costs. Wise endowment management involves negotiating with donors over the use of their funds, so the organization is not saddled with unworkable long-term commitments, and maintaining discipline over payout.

Notes

1. The author wishes to thank the other authors of this volume, as well as Robert Rensel, Wes Lindahl, and Francie Ostrower for reading earlier drafts of this chapter and offering useful comments.

2. Ownership implies three distinct and separable rights: the right to control how the thing is used, the exclusive right to benefit from it, and the right to sell or lease the other two rights.

3. Unless otherwise specified, the 1999 data set used here contains organizations with fiscal years ending in 2000, which was a peak in the stock market. Churches and nonprofits with less than $25,000 in revenue are not required to file 990s. Data are projected from the IRS Statistics of Income data set for the calendar year 1999 using the sample weights supplied with the data. The sample contains 14,386 records. Eliminating nonprofits with zero assets or zero expenses resulted in a sample of 14,318. Weighted averages are based on a universe of 164,374. Organizational categories correspond to the one-letter National Taxonomy of Exempt Entities categories.

4. Since churches are not required to report, one can only guess, but those denominations that hold property in the name of a regional group, like a diocese, would likely be big businesses, too.

5. To illustrate the relationships between these concepts in practice, consider the notes to Northwestern University's 2003 financial statements, which provide detail that many other nonprofits do not disclose. Northwestern reports $3.44 billion in investments, not including cash and cash equivalents ($0.27 billion), which are reported separately. This corresponds to the number on its Form 990. Operations and Plant Funds account for $0.71 billion. Total invested endowment is $2.63 billion, broken down as follows: quasi-endowment, $0.99 billion, and restricted endowment, $1.64 billion. Of total investments, not including cash, $0.11 billion is invested short-term, $0.33 billion is invested intermediate-term, $2.90 billion is invested long-term, and the balance ($0.10 billion) separately invested in various planned giving accounts.

6. Working cash and operating reserves are not identified on 990 forms. To empirically explore this issue, I used working capital, which is the difference between current assets (cash, cash equivalents, all receivables, inventories, and prepaid expenses) and current liabilities (all payables). Working capital is liquid and it closely approximates the sum of working cash and operating reserves. Liquid funds are financial resources that are quickly and easily convertible into cash.

7. Black's Law Dictionary and Restatement (Third) of Trusts define endowment in terms of donor restrictions only. The omission of quasi-endowment reflects the legal profession's concern for protecting the interests of donors.

8. An oft-overlooked fact is that some governments have endowments: Alaska's $28 billion Permanent Fund is a prominent example. The Chicago Park District is actively fund-raising for an endowment to maintain its new Pritzker Music Pavilion. This fact does not change the essential point: unless required by law, for-profit firms are not endowed.

9. I omit two of his reasons: (1) "use of risk capital," because it repeats the idea under financial stability that endowment can be used "to underwrite programs that have not been funded"; and (2) "financial control," because I disagree that endowment income is under the control of the organization. Once a payout formula is adopted, control is no longer an issue.

10. Inflation is measured by the Consumer Price Index for the twelve months prior to the start of the fiscal year. Long term is defined as the seventy-two-year period from 1926 to 1997. Both the growth in large-company stocks and the inflation rate are measured over the same interval. *Stocks, Bonds, Bills, and Inflation: 1998 Yearbook* (Chicago: Ibbotson Associates, 1998), pp. 30–31.

11. Commonfund is a nonprofit organization founded in 1971 with a grant from the Ford Foundation to improve investment management at nonprofit educational and health care organizations. It actively manages $32 billion in assets, engages in institutional research, and for several years it has published benchmark studies. The 2003 survey results were published in its 2004 report. A total of 657 educational institutions and supporting foundations participated in the 2003 survey, with total investments ranging from under $10 million to over $1 billion, although 80 percent invested between $10 million and $500 million.

12. Attributed to Morningstar analyst Peter DiTeresa by Elizabeth Frengel, "Demystifying the Mutual Fund, Part 2," Kiplinger.com. See www.kiplinger.com/basics/archives/2002/05/demystify2. html, updated May 30, 2002, accessed May 7, 2005.

13. Commonfund has an analysis of the Yale formula by Dick Ramsden on its website: www.commonfund.org/Commonfund/Archive/News/Yale_formula.htmm (November 25, 2005). To illustrate, assume the average market value of an endowment for the most recent four quarters was $20,000,000, and last year allowable spending was $900,000. Assume inflation, as measured by the Consumer Price Index (CPI) for the most recent twelve months was 3 percent. Yale's long-term payout rate (historical allowable spending expressed as a percent of endowment) is 4.5 percent. An organization just getting started with a new payout discipline should use the average total return on its endowment, or a pro forma endowment invested according to its current asset allocation minus the rate of inflation and investment management expenses during the same period. Then, allowable spending this year is $0.7 \times \$900,000 \times 1.03 + 0.3 \times 0.045 \times \$20,000,000 = \$648,900 + \$270,000 = \$918,900$.

14. An exception to this rule is the sale-leaseback transaction. Both businesses and nonprofit organizations depreciate their buildings and equipment (land does not depreciate), but only businesses receive tax benefits because only they pay income taxes. Therefore, a nonprofit might sell its physical assets to a for-profit business with the understanding that it will redeem them on or before a specified future date and, in the meantime, it will lease them from the buyer. This is functionally equivalent to the nonprofit taking out a loan with a balloon payment at maturity. It is an "off-balance sheet" transaction because technically it does not create a liability. Although it is inconceivable that the nonprofit seller would not redeem buildings that support its mission, it is not legally obligated to do so. The buyer receives tax benefits, which it shares with the nonprofit seller through favorable lease payments. Bond-rating agencies treat such transactions as debt.

15. This definition excludes foundations. All analyses are restricted to organizations with positive assets and expenses in FY 2000.

13

Income Portfolios

Kevin Kearns

Introduction

Nonprofit leaders constantly fret over their income needs and shortfalls. They also worry about their organization's *mix* of income—the relative percentage of total income derived from individual gifts, foundation and corporate grants, government contracts, earned income, endowment earnings, the monetary value of voluntary services, and other sources. Some nonprofit executives worry that their organizations rely too much on one or two income sources while others suspect that their income streams are spread too widely.

Several theories have been proposed to explain why nonprofit leaders might gravitate toward a certain mix of income. One theory suggests that nonprofits develop income streams that will allow them to maximize certain objectives such as return on investment while minimizing other factors such as risk or uncertainty (Markowitz, 1952; Weisbrod, 1974, 1977, 1988; Hansmann, 1980, 1987). Another theory proposes that nonprofits try to diversify their income sources as widely as possible in order to enhance community "buy-in" and increase the perceived legitimacy of the organization (Bielefeld, 1992; Galaskiewicz and Bielefeld, 1998; Galaskiewicz, 1990). Yet another theory suggests that nonprofits sometimes develop one or just a few stable and reliable income sources in order to achieve continuity of programs and funding (Grønbjerg, 1992). And, finally, there is empirical evidence suggesting that income portfolios are related to a host of contingencies including the nonprofit's mission and its investment in fund-raising infrastructure (Chang and Tuckman, 1994).

This chapter explores all of these theories, including yet another approach, *multiattribute utility theory*, which is a tool that may help us understand how decision makers in nonprofit organizations evaluate different income sources and portfolio management strategies.

Patterns and Trends

Nonprofit organizations rely on three major sources of income: (1) payments from dues or fees for service; (2) government grants and contracts; and (3) private contributions from individuals, foundations, and corporations. In 1997, according to the *Nonprofit Almanac*, these three sources of income accounted for nearly 89 percent of the income for 501(c)(3) and 501(c)(4) organizations. Endowment income, earned income from ancillary enterprises, religious contributions, and other income sources combined for just over 11 percent of total income. The distribution of nonprofit income has shown some variation over the past two decades, reflecting periodic changes in economic circumstances and, accordingly, changes in nonprofit financial strategies. For example, the percentage of nonprofit income derived from government grants and contracts and from various types of social enterprise has increased slightly while the percentage of total income from private contributions has shrunk (Weitzman et al., 2002). Nonprofit organizations employ a mix of revenue strategies, with significant variation by subsector. Individual nonprofit organizations respond to changing circumstances in ways that reflect their own unique circumstances. Let's look at a few actual organizations in Pittsburgh to see how they are responding.

Current Practice

Presented below are two case studies of nonprofit organizations in Pittsburgh, Pennsylvania. The first case describes a center that houses a variety of human service organizations and helps them coordinate their services. The second case describes a regional historical society.

The Human Services Center Corporation (HSCC) is a twenty-year-old agency whose mission is to "improve the quality of life in the Monongahela Valley through coordination of services." The Monongahela Valley includes thirty-seven communities located southeast of the City of Pittsburgh along the Monongahela River. This area was formerly home to numerous steel mills, the Westinghouse manufacturing plant, and many other industrial enterprises. Today, nearly all of the valley's manufacturers have closed their doors, creating economic distress for the valley's communities.

HSCC is a human services mall—a kind of one-stop shop that houses fifteen agencies with over eighty social service programs. But HSCC is more than merely a landlord. Through the Monongahela Valley Provider's Council, HSCC helps its member organizations identify community needs and deliver services to citizens. The annual budget of the organization is about $785,000.

The 2004 mix of operating income for HSCC is provided in table 13.1.

According to Executive Director David Coplan, this income portfolio looked quite different just a few years ago. The current portfolio is the result of a conscious strategy to reduce reliance on some sources of income while increasing self-sufficiency of the organization. "We knew we could no longer count on foundations for operating support," said Coplan. "So, we conducted a feasibility study for a new income strategy. It was a very purposeful

Table 13.1.   Income Portfolio of the Human Services Center Corporation, 2004

Gifts from Individuals	5%
Gifts from Corporations	8%
Foundation Grants	2%
Fees for Service (Membership Dues and Rent)	59%
Government Grants or Contracts	12%
United Way Allocations	11%
Commercial Enterprise	3%

process on our part." As a result of the feasibility study, HSCC implemented an income strategy that has gradually reduced foundation grants from 15 percent to 2 percent of its operating budget. United Way support also dropped moderately from 16 percent to 11 percent. Conversely, HSCC steadily increased its annual giving from individuals and corporations from 5 percent to about 13 percent. The organization also moderately increased dues revenues and aggressively pursued certain types of government contracts. HSCC completed a successful endowment campaign as well.

Some changes were the result of shifts in the mission of the organization. "We could not pursue government contracts in the 1990s because we did not provide direct services," said Coplan. Now, HSCC receives government funding for an after school program for at-risk children. Still, Coplan has learned to minimize risks associated with government funding. "We don't want to become dependent on government funding. We use our government funding to buy slots in our youth outreach programs; we do not use it for core programming or administrative support. We don't want to become dependent on government funding. We were burned by that strategy in the past, and we learned a painful lesson."

HSCC just completed a successful endowment campaign that generated over $600,000. "We originally planned to use the endowment income for operations, but with our new income mix we have found that we don't need it for operations. Instead, we will use it as a new venture or contingency fund to finance special projects in the future."

With respect to the foreseeable future, Coplan is vigilant about events and trends that may affect his income strategy. "We're projecting flat trends in corporate giving and individual giving. We're contemplating an expansion of our building, so there will likely be an increase in rental income as well as more government support for new programming that we can accommodate in the larger space. It's conceivable that United Way funding will actually increase again after five straight years of decreases. But we won't count on that."

Thus, in HSCC we see an organization that is using at least four distinct income strategies. First, HSCC has consciously employed a strategy of income diversification to enhance its control over its own destiny. Second, HSCC attempted to reduce its risk exposure by reducing its reliance on foundation funding, which was perceived to be increasingly precarious. Third, within one income stream—government contracts—HSCC has adopted a hedging strategy by using the funds to purchase slots in its outreach program rather than building up an extensive administrative or program infrastructure that would be difficult to dismantle if the government funding dries up. Fourth, HSCC has followed a contingency strategy by establishing a reserve fund to allow it to respond to unspecified opportunities and challenges in the future.

The Historical Society of Western Pennsylvania (HSWP) is dedicated to preserving and presenting the rich history of the Pittsburgh region. HSWP has been in existence for over 120 years, providing exhibitions and programs, operating a historical library and archives, and producing publications. HSWP has a budget of over $5 million. Its main facility is the Senator John Heinz Pittsburgh Regional History Center, a state-of-the-art history museum, family entertainment and education complex, and sophisticated research facility. The income portfolio for HSWP is provided in table 13.2.

According to Betty Arenth, senior vice president, a modest change in the past few years has been the drop in government funding from 14 percent to 11 percent of total operating support. "Previously, we had a group of legislators in Harrisburg who supported us year-in and year-out," said Arenth. "Those legislators no longer are in office, so we must plead our case to the legislature

Table 13.2. Income Portfolio for the Historical Society of Western Pennsylvania, 2004

Donations from individuals	13%
Corporate gifts	6.5%
Foundation grants	19%
Fees for service (admission and other fees)	18%
Endowment income	17%
Government grants or contracts	11%
Enterprise	8.5%
Other	7%

every year. It is very labor intensive and unpredictable. We are trying to get a dedicated line item in the state budget. We would like our government funding to be approximately 30 percent, but it must be a reliable line item—something we can count on year after year."

There is an industry-wide database that allows Arenth and her colleagues to benchmark the income portfolio of HSWP against other comparable museums. "In comparison with other historical societies and museums, we benchmark pretty well on most income sources except earned income," said Arenth. "We would like to increase our earned income, but we are cautious about it. We know that growth in earned income is usually slow and often comes with hidden operating costs that sometimes can't be anticipated. For example, we had an earned income venture that relied on trained genealogists to help families research their family history. We found that there were significant operating costs that we did not anticipate. In the foreseeable future we would like to increase earned income by 5 to 10 percent but any such venture will have to be mission-driven. We will always look for a balance in our income sources that we believe are relatively predictable from year to year."

HSWP is a mature organization that has enjoyed good connections with powerful civic leaders. Consequently, its mix of income sources appears to have been more stable over a more significant amount of time than the much smaller and younger Human Services Center Corporation described earlier. From year to year HSWP's income mix changes incrementally. The change over the past few years has been a moderate drop in government funding, and HSWP seems to be mobilizing to correct that deviation soon.

Despite its relative stability, HSWP must continuously monitor and occasionally adapt its income strategy to match changing circumstances.

Theory

In their comprehensive review of the literature on nonprofit income strategies, Chang and Tuckman (1994) offer competing explanations for how nonprofits develop and maintain their income portfolios. First, there are economic theories that view nonprofits as objective-maximizing firms that consistently pursue strategies designed to optimize certain objectives subject to known constraints. These theories of rational economic behavior suggest that nonprofit organizations develop income portfolios that allow them to maximize total outputs or resources that can be converted to outputs. Chang and Tuckman cite Weisbrod (1974, 1977, 1988) and Hansmann (1980, 1987) as the major contributors to this body of thought. A variant of this theory is found in corporate finance where, according to the mean-variance model of portfolio management (Markowitz, 1952), investors pay attention to two attributes of any given income stream: expected return and volatility (or risk). Often, but not always, there is covariance between return and risk. High expected return is often associated with high volatility, which many organizations cannot tolerate. Using mean-variance models, investors are able to design portfolios that contain a wide variety of income sources along an "efficient frontier" of return and risk on which decision makers can maximize their return on investment given their tolerance for risk.

The idea behind portfolio management is to have a mix of income streams that perform reasonably well despite volatility in the market. Corporate finance experts typically talk about two types of risk. *Systematic risk* includes eventualities like wars, recessions, massive market failures, and other events that are not associated with one particular asset and usually are beyond the control of the organization. *Unsystematic risk* is associated with particular income streams and includes factors like declining demand for a given product or a technological advance that renders obsolete a particular program or service. Diversification is a way to minimize unsystematic risk.

Objective-maximization theories assume that reliable information exists to allow decision makers to maximize the organization's objectives subject to known constraints. This assumption is problematic, especially in the nonprofit sector where access to and use of information is limited and where the linkage between objectives and data is tenuous at best. Also, objective-maximization theories assume that stakeholders will use economic rationality to achieve consensus regarding the organizational objectives they wish to maximize and the risks they wish to minimize. However, in the fields of organization theory and political science, scholars make the more plausible argument that goal ambiguity, conflict, and power differentials are prominent features of organizational life (Bolman and Deal, 1997). This is especially true in less bureaucratized environments like those that exist in many small nonprofit organizations, where diverse opinions and conflict are often encouraged, not just tolerated. So, income theories derived from pure economic rationality must be tempered by other contingencies in order to offer meaningful insights on the income strategies of nonprofit organizations.

Another set of theories, drawn from political science as well as other disciplines, suggests that nonprofits try to diversify their revenues in order to maximize their perceived importance, centrality, and legitimacy in the community (Chang and Tuckman, 1994; Bielefeld, 1992; Galaskiewicz and Bielefeld, 1998; Galaskiewicz, 1990). When a nonprofit organization enjoys support from a variety of community resources, it is more likely to be widely perceived by important stakeholders as making positive contributions and, therefore, worthy of even more support. In other words, success breeds success.

When working as president of a Pittsburgh-based foundation, the author observed that the credibility that any given grant-seeking organization enjoyed was due, at least in part, to whether the organization enjoyed broad support from a variety of community resources. Word would spread from one grant-making organization to another that Organization X was "doing a good job" or was "breaking new ground" and suddenly other grant makers would jump on the bandwagon in supporting the efforts of Organization X. Often the evidence of actual performance was tenuous, but stakeholder impressions and opinion are sometimes more important than objective evidence, especially when the agenda of a grant maker becomes entwined with the activities of a particular organization.

Despite some supporting anecdotal evidence, this body of theory also rests on some questionable assumptions. First, this theory assumes that all sources of nonprofit income contribute equally to the perceived "legitimacy" of the organization. Is a routine operating grant from the local United Way perceived in the same way as a highly competitive grant from a national foundation? Probably not, but this theory does not account for varying definitions of legitimacy and the extent to which available income sources contribute to that legitimacy. Second, there is a chicken and egg problem with this theory. The argument is that nonprofit organizations diversify their revenues in order to gain legitimacy and that legitimacy in turn leads to additional investments from the community. But is legitimacy a cause or effect of income diversification?

A third theory suggests that the activities of nonprofit organizations are influenced by their outside funders (Grønbjerg, 1992; Froelich, 1999). This theory suggests that over an extended period of time a symbiotic relationship evolves between grant seekers and grant makers wherein all of the parties conspire (often in good ways) to serve each others' objectives. Grant makers wield the "power of the purse" to gently (or not so gently) guide and direct the programming of their grantees in certain directions that are consistent with the foundation's goals or philosophy. Over time, such a relationship can prove quite beneficial for nonprofit organizations, especially those that desire continuity of programming and funding. Grønbjerg (1992) suggests that high-performing nonprofits tend to rely heavily on one or a few reliable funding sources. The notion is that the nonprofit organization and its funders reach agreement on a set of goals and, in turn, negotiate a stable source of revenues to accomplish those goals. In this theory, continuity of objectives is valued in the income portfolio strategy.

Finally, Chang and Tuckman (1994) put forward a "contingency theory" of income diversification. Using a creative measure of income diversification and data from a large national sample of 990 forms, their primary finding is that the mission of the nonprofit organization affects the concentration of its income sources. Some nonprofit missions lend themselves to diversified income streams while others are able to attract only a limited range of income sources. Second, the Chang and Tuckman study suggests that commercial nonprofits are more likely to display concentrated income portfolios than donative nonprofits. The theory predicts that commercial nonprofits will rely quite heavily on fees for service while donative nonprofits will pursue a wider range of income sources. Third, the Chang and Tuckman study suggests that nonprofits with high fund-raising expenditures display more diverse income sources. Finally, Chang and Tuckman found some evidence that multiple sources of income are positively related to the financial strength of the organization as measured by operating margin.

In a survey of over four hundred nonprofit organizations in Pittsburgh, and using the same measure of financial diversification used by Chang and Tuckman, the author found evidence to support some of their propositions. Income diversification among Pittsburgh nonprofits varies by mission. Like Chang and Tuckman, the author observed that more concentrated income portfolios are found in organizations dealing with education, crime and delinquency prevention, employment and job training, human services, and religiously-related organizations. More diverse portfolios are found in organizations dealing with the arts, environmental quality, and youth development. Preliminary analysis indicates that organizations that serve a larger number of people have moderately more diverse income streams. However, the Pittsburgh data do not suggest a strong relationship between income diversification and financial strength as measured by operating margin.

Clearly, the major theories of nonprofit income do not always agree in their respective propositions and hypotheses. Resource dependence models suggest that nonprofits will try to concentrate on one or a few reliable sources, yet legitimacy theories suggest that nonprofits will seek investments from many community sources. Objective maximization theories suggest that nonprofits will try to optimize certain outcomes, but contingency theories propose that these outcomes may vary by mission and purpose.

Interestingly, both of the case studies described earlier in this chapter seem to illustrate at least one of these theories, to a limited extent. For example, the Western Pennsylvania Historical Society pursued a *resource dependence* strategy by cultivating a long-term relationship with the state legislature. But this case also demonstrates the hazards of that approach when legislative priorities and actors suddenly change. The Human Services Center Corporation seems to be pursuing a *contingency* strategy by adapting its income portfolio to its changing mission and activities, yet it also seems to be trying to enhance its *legitimacy* with wide-based community support.

Of all the theoretical propositions, contingency theory seems to be the most promising and intuitively appealing. The data analyzed by Chang and Tuckman (1994) suggest that a variety of forces may have bearing on the income strategies of any given nonprofit organization. Some of these forces are environmental, some are mission-related, and some may be related to the beliefs and values of nonprofit executives and trustees. It is worthwhile to explore these contingency theories in greater depth, focusing on the attributes and criteria that decision makers use when evaluating the various income sources available to them.

Extending the Knowledge Base

The theories described above provide insight into nonprofit portfolio management but they do not fully account for the complexity of decisions facing nonprofit leaders as they design and evaluate their income portfolios. Income decisions are not made by "organizations" per se but by people who have opinions, values, beliefs, and biases. These stakeholders interpret organizational missions, strategies, goals, constraints, and contingencies in their own ways and they make decisions regarding the most appropriate revenue streams accordingly. We need a research tool to help us uncover the strategic thinking of nonprofit leaders to fully understand their income choices.

Multiattribute utility analysis is a set of methods that can elicit from a nonprofit leader the criteria he or she uses to evaluate various income sources and make judgments about the likelihood of different income mixes achieving their objectives. Multiattribute utility theory is based on the assertion that each of us has a unique "utility function" that we use to make assessments and trade-offs among various perceived attributes of any choice (Arrow, 1951; Keeney and Raiffa, 1976; Olson, 1996). When buying a new car, for example, each of us has certain attributes in mind such as performance, reliability, safety, size, fuel efficiency, style, and so on, but these attributes will be different from person to person. The values or "utilities" that we assign to these attributes help us make judgments and trade-offs in order to narrow our choices from an almost infinite selection of vehicle makes and models to a manageable number. Again, these values will vary from person to person. If we carefully surveyed buyers in a new car showroom, we could uncover their personal utility functions for various vehicle attributes in order to understand how they perceive the different makes and models and, ultimately, how these consumers make their choices from among those vehicles. Market researchers do this all the time. In a similar way, multiattribute models could add greatly to our understanding of the criteria (attributes) that nonprofit decision makers use to evaluate income options as well as the utilities they assign to those attributes.

For illustration, let's consider the case of Cedar Hill Neighborhood Development Corporation. CHNDC is a fictitious organization, but the circumstances of this case actually were confronted by a similar organization in Pittsburgh. Assume that the mission of CHNDC is to promote economic and social development, including housing opportunities, in a low-income neighborhood near the urban core of an aging city. Let's assume further that there are several key decision makers who have some input into the overall design and evaluation of the income portfolio—the chief executive, the finance committee of the board of trustees, the finance director, and the development officer.

Multiattribute utility theory has produced several tools to help researchers uncover the criteria used by each of these decision makers to evaluate various income sources. One such tool is the repertory grid developed by George Kelly (1955) and applied by others (Kearns 1992a, 1995) to a wide range of social choice contexts. As applied in this example, each decision maker would be presented with short descriptions of three randomly chosen income sources, such as private gifts, corporate gifts, and United Way allocations. Each decision maker would be interviewed separately and asked to think of a way in which two of the income sources are alike and different from the third. For example, when presented with brief descriptions of these three income sources one of the decision makers might conceivably say that individual gifts and United Way allocations provide a "safer" source of income from year to year while corporate gifts are more "risky" in that they often yield less than expected. Then, the decision maker would be presented with brief descriptions of another randomly selected set of three income sources and would once again be asked to think of a way in which two of them are alike and different from the third. Assume that the second randomly selected group of income sources includes social enterprise income, a government contract from the Department of Housing and Urban Development, and membership dues. Again, the decision maker is asked to think of a way in which two of the income sources are alike and different from the third. This time the decision maker thinks for a moment and finally says that social enterprise income and government grants carry certain "opportunity costs" while membership dues are "costfree." Thus, "risk" and "opportunity costs" become the first two entries in an attribute dictionary that grows with each successive round of randomly selected triplets until the decision makers can think of no new attributes that are meaningful to them in distinguishing between alternative income sources. The process is repeated with each decision maker to generate a list of attributes all of them collectively are likely to use when they make decisions about the income portfolio of the organization.

The important feature of this particular protocol is that it *generates* attributes that are grounded in the underlying assumptions of the decision makers rather than allowing the researcher to impose the criteria from some theoretical framework or from the researcher's a priori assumptions (Glaser and Strauss, 1967). The decision makers themselves may not even be aware of these assumptions until they are presented with the choices outlined above. Research has shown that some people have a very rich and diverse set of attributes that they use in any given choice situation while others use a relatively small number of attributes (Kearns, 1992a, 1995).

Now let's assume that following the iterative process described above, the decision makers in our hypothetical case collectively identify the following five attributes that they want to use to evaluate possible income sources:

- *Mission appropriateness*: the extent to which the income source is consistent with and supports the mission, values, and philosophy of the organization
- *Significance*: the short-term and long-term potential of the income source to generate significant streams of income for the organization or to fill important gaps in the existing income portfolio
- *Risk*: the likelihood that a given income source will yield significantly less than expected over a given period of time
- *Opportunity costs or trade-offs*: the prospect that pursuing a given income source will preclude efforts to pursue other income sources
- *Autonomy*: the extent to which the income source restricts the independence or autonomy of the organization

Assume further that the decision makers in our hypothetical example believe that some of these attributes are more important than others. We could ask the decision makers to simply rank-order the attributes from one to five. However, a more sophisticated and reliable approach would be to employ a technique like the *Analytic Hierarchy Process* (Saaty, 1980; Saaty and Kearns, 1985), which is derived from multiattribute utility theory and can be used to elicit judgments from decision makers regarding the weights (importance) they attach to each of the attributes. Limitations on space prevent a full description of the Analytic Hierarchy Process. Briefly, it is a method that uses pair-wise comparisons and matrix algebra to elicit from decision makers the priorities they assign to their decision criteria and, ultimately, to help them make choices based on those criteria. For example, when using the Analytic Hierarchy Process, the decision makers would be asked a series of questions that would force them to

Table 13.3.   Perceived Relative Importance of Income Attributes

Income Attribute (elicited from decision makers via repertory grid technique)	Weight (elicited from decision makers via Analytic Hierarchy Process)
Mission appropriateness	.30
Significance	.30
Risk	.20
Opportunity costs or trade-offs	.10
Autonomy	.10
Total	1.00

compare each income attribute with every other attribute using a nine-point scale of relative importance. A value of "1" signifies that two attributes are judged to be equally important whereas a value of "9" indicates that one attribute is judged to be significantly more important than another. Values between 1 and 9 are used to express nuances of importance. The questioning would begin as follows: "When you compare different income streams under consideration by your organization, what is the relative importance of [in order: mission appropriateness, significance, risk, opportunity costs, autonomy] compared with [in order: mission appropriateness, significance, risk, opportunity costs, and finally autonomy]?" The result of this line of questioning would be a five-by-five reciprocal matrix that can be algebraically manipulated to reveal the relative importance of each attribute. A full description of the method and the underlying theory is presented in Saaty (1980). Assume the decision makers in our case have attached the weights displayed in table 13.3 to each income attribute.

With this information, decision makers are ready to evaluate the desirability of each type of income source with respect to each of the weighted attributes. For example, with respect to "mission appropriateness" our hypothetical decision makers would be asked to make pair-wise comparisons of every plausible income source using the same nine-point scale and the same repetitive protocol described above. Let's assume there were ten plausible income sources as listed in table 13.4. This time, the Analytic Hierarchy Process would yield a ten-by-ten reciprocal matrix for

Table 13.4.   Hypothetical Mix of Income Sources in the Portfolio

Plausible Income Sources	Desired Relative Percentage of the Income Portfolio (derived via the Analytic Hierarchy Process)
Fees for service	.15
Individual gifts (including annual campaigns, planned giving, etc.)	.05
United Way allocations	.00
Foundation grants	.10
Government grants/contracts	.40
Corporate gifts or grants	.15
Endowment earnings	.05
Social enterprises	.10
Congregational/Denominational contributions	.00
Special events	.00
Total	1.00

each of the five attributes. For example, we might ask, "With respect to mission appropriateness, what is the relative desirability of (fees for service, individual gifts, United Way funds, foundation, grants, etc.)?" The process of pair-wise comparison is tedious. Fortunately, there is computer software available to help people efficiently use the Analytic Hierarchy Process without sapping their energy or computational capabilities. Using the Analytic Hierarchy Process, decision makers could determine their desired overall mix of income sources in their portfolio and the relative emphasis they want to give to each source, as illustrated in table 13.4. The right-hand column represents the target or "ideal" mix of income sources for this particular organization, based upon the expressed (hypothetical) preferences of its key decision makers.

Use of this conceptual framework as a research tool could help us learn much more about the criteria used by nonprofit decision makers to compare and contrast different income sources. Currently, the knowledge that we have about these criteria is anecdotal and not well documented.

Moreover, it would be interesting to test congruence among various stakeholders. For example, do executive directors have the same appetite for risk as trustees? Do development directors use mission appropriateness to the same extent as executive directors? Finally, this research agenda could be helpful in determining the extent to which the perceptions and preferences of key stakeholders are reflected in the actual income portfolios of their organizations.

Improving Practice

The use of the repertory grid methods in conjunction with the Analytic Hierarchy Process can significantly enhance the quality of deliberations of nonprofit executives as they plan their long-term income strategies. The technique could be particularly helpful in addressing the following issues that nonprofit decision makers face at various stages in the organizational life cycle:

1. At the start-up phase in the organizational life cycle, nonprofit executives must find the venture capital to launch and sustain the enterprise for at least the first several years. Typically, this requires an initial infusion of a relatively large sum of money from one or a few "investors" such as foundations or government agencies. The techniques described above can help decision makers assess the prospects for and desirability of various sources of venture capital such as foundation grants, government contracts, or other relatively large sums of money.

2. At the growth phase of the life cycle, nonprofit executives often look for ways to broaden community buy-in and support for the enterprise, including individual giving and perhaps capital campaigns to support the growth strategy. The techniques described here can help executives and board members identify market segments for these types of gifts, developing priorities among those markets.

3. At the maturity stage of the life cycle, some nonprofits look for ways to diversify their income streams including various types of earned income. Once again, the techniques described above can help decision makers evaluate these options with respect to a wide variety of assessment criteria.

Multiattribute techniques can also be useful in evaluating specific income opportunities that present themselves to an organization. For example, assume that the Cedar Hill Neighborhood Development Corporation has the opportunity to purchase a grocery store. The current owner of the store wants to retire and there are no heirs to the business. CHNDC does not want the store to go out of business. There is a documented shortage of grocery stores in the inner city, forcing residents to travel to outlying areas to shop for food and necessities. If CHNDC purchases the store, it could remain a focal point for local commerce and serve as an employer of local residents, and also serve as a generator of earned income for CHNDC that could be reinvested in the core mission of the organization. The grocery store opportunity could be evaluated with respect to the income attributes that were generated using the repertory grid technique (see table 13.3 above). The various criteria might be collapsed into an overall *attractiveness* index as indicated in table 13.6. Decision makers might use a simple five-point scale to assess the *attractiveness* of this particular income opportunity on each of the constructs (see top portion of table 13.6). Even though this venture has substantial risks, it is viewed as a fairly attractive income source, scoring 4.1 out of 5 possible points.

While the grocery store may be an attractive source of earned income, the leaders of CHNDC may worry that the organization lacks the internal *capacity* to cultivate, generate, and sustain the grocery store over time. Capacity is a subjective construct that will vary according to the perceptions, values, and beliefs of key decision makers. For example, a list of capacity constructs may include the following:

- *Staff and volunteer competence*: demonstrated ability to cultivate, generate, and sustain the income source based on existing skills, talents, and dedication
- *Infrastructure support*: including information, technology, organizational structure, facilities, and other infrastructure components necessary to effectively manage the income source

- *Community reputation and image*: including visibility, credibility, reputation for competent and accountable leadership
- *Culture and tradition*: including risk propensity, tolerance for failure, investment in innovation

For purposes of illustration, assume that the Analytic Hierarchy Process was used with a group of stakeholders to assign the weights shown in table 13.5 to each of the capacity constructs, conveying their perceived contributions to the organization's overall capacity to cultivate, generate, and sustain a particular income source.

Table 13.6 shows a combined score of 4.1 (attractiveness) and 4.40 (capacity) for the grocery store opportunity, which would clearly make this a wise investment for the organization.

Using figure 13.1 to map this income source in comparison with other possible investment opportunities, the leaders of CHNDC would place the grocery store very near the bottom right cell, an extremely viable income source for the organization. Figure 13.1 provides a kind of visualization or "map" of an organization's income portfolio. Obviously, most organizations would want all of their income streams to fall into the bottom right hand portion of figure 13.1 where high attractiveness of the income source is matched with equally high internal capacity to manage the income stream. A matrix like that presented in figure 13.1 is also useful for continuous assessment of the portfolio as circumstances change.

There are other practical benefits of the multiattribute models described in this chapter. First, they help stakeholders discuss

Table 13.5.   Criteria for Evaluating Specific Income Proposals

Capacity Constructs	Weight (Importance)
Staff and volunteer competence	.50
Infrastructure support	.30
Community reputation and image	.10
Culture and tradition	.10
Total	1.00

Table 13.6. Evaluating Attractiveness and Capacity: Neighborhood Grocery Store as a Social Enterprise

	Attractiveness of Income Source		
Factor	Weight	Rating of Grocery Store (1 = unattractive, 5 = attractive)	Score
Mission appropriateness	.30	5	1.50 (.30 × 5)
Significance	.30	5	1.50
Absence of risk	.20	2	.40
Absence of opportunity costs or trade-offs	.10	2	.20
Threat to autonomy	.10	5	.50
Total Score			4.10
	Organizational Capacity		
Factor	Weight	Rating of Grocery Store (1 = low capacity, 5 = high capacity)	Score
Staff and volunteer competence	.50	5	2.50 (.50 × 5)
Infrastructure support	.30	3	.90
Community reputation and image	.10	5	.50
Culture and tradition	.10	5	.50
Total Score			4.40

Source: Adapted from Hedley (1977).

and come to agreement on the parameters of the problem or opportunity in front of them. Problem structuring is perhaps the single most important task in policy analysis, especially when the problem involves multiple perspectives, values, and incomplete information (Dunn, 1981). Also, multiattribute techniques are helpful in surfacing assumptions, values, and beliefs that can otherwise remain buried. Research has shown that group decision making often breaks down because assumptions and values remain implicit rather than explicit (Mitroff and Emshoff, 1979; Fisher and Ury, 1991). Finally, multiattribute techniques are flexible. The Analytic Hierarchy Process allows decision makers

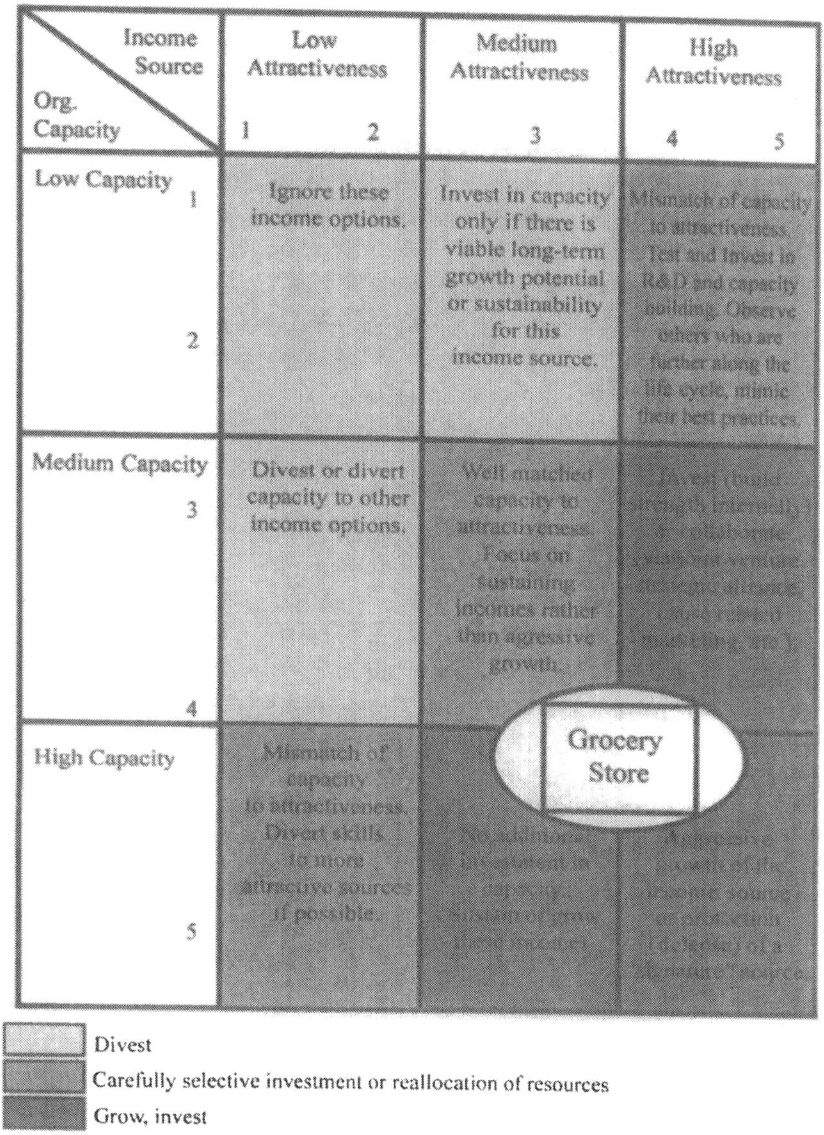

Source: Adapted from Hedley (1977).

Figure 13.1. Mapping Components of the Income Portfolio.

to experiment with and simulate various outcomes, depending on the values that are attached to criteria and optional courses of action.

Clearly, there are substantial limitations to the multiattribute utility approach described here, both as a tool to improve practice and as a research methodology. First, these techniques can be tedious and require a level of effort that is beyond the scope of a typical quarterly meeting of the board or executive staff. Certainly, such techniques would be best used in a format such as an annual management retreat where members of the organization's finance committee or other decision-making body would have the opportunity to focus on the assessment, free of distractions. The use of expert facilitators might be required to ensure that the process is properly designed and implemented.

As a research tool, there are limitations as well. The approaches described above focus on decision makers, not the organization per se, as the unit of analysis. As such, they assume that the current regime of decision makers has total (or at least substantial) power to determine the distribution of the income portfolio. These methods do not account for decisions of prior regimes that may have had path-dependent effects on the existing income portfolios. Historical legacy has an important impact on the design and implementation of any organizational strategy (Mintzberg, 1994).

Second, these methods are far more appropriate for theory development than theory testing. Obviously, one could not generate repertory grids or use the Analytic Hierarchy Process as a data gathering method in large studies. The interview process is simply too cumbersome to be cost effective with large samples. Yet it is highly plausible that interviews with relatively few nonprofit leaders might generate a set of grounded constructs that could then be incorporated into traditional survey instruments with larger populations of nonprofit executives. Prior research has shown that the cumulative distribution of unique constructs usually diminishes significantly after about twenty interviews (Kearns, 1992a, 1995).

In any case, as nonprofit leaders try to design income portfolios appropriate to their purposes, they can begin to ask themselves certain basic questions prerequisite to the use of a formal approach such as multiattribute utility methodology. Such questions include the following:

1. *Are some types of income sources more consistent with the organization's mission than others?* The organization's core purpose and operating philosophy may give priority to certain types of income streams over others. If there is agreement about this among key decision makers, then the mission and philosophy of the organization represents a good starting point for the design of an income portfolio.

2. *Is there evidence that key stakeholders in the organization—board and staff—have subjective and varying perceptions of different types of income sources?* If decision makers bring different assumptions to the task of designing an income portfolio, then the organization could benefit from a facilitated process to help the decision makers surface and discuss those assumptions in an open atmosphere. It could be that such a discussion will uncover significant differences of opinion or, alternatively, it may show that there is substantial convergence of values and beliefs among key decision makers. Either way, the exercise will be useful for an organization that is trying to design an income portfolio.

3. *As opportunities arise to add new income sources to the portfolio, are these opportunities systematically evaluated with respect to stakeholders' perceptions and decision criteria?* Mission creep or mission drift can occur when an organization "chases" certain income opportunities simply because they have surfaced and appear to be obtainable. If these income opportunities have implications for the mission of the organization, or if they are potentially at odds with the values on beliefs of key stakeholders, they should be rigorously evaluated on a case by case basis to ensure that the organization's portfolio does not unconsciously drift from its original objectives.

Conclusion

The income portfolios of nonprofit organizations vary significantly from one organization to another. The variance is likely due to several factors including mission, history and precedent, and the goal-seeking behavior of organizations and their leaders. This chapter suggests that multiattribute utility theory is a promising approach to understanding nonprofit income portfolios. It is a technique that is well matched to the context of nonprofit management, which is often characterized by multiple constituencies who pursue goals that are not always clearly focused or easily measured and optimized. The methods described here can be helpful in developing a fuller theory of nonprofit income management, but they are also useful as guides for more effective decision making.

14

Financial Health

Janet S. Greenlee and Howard Tuckman

Introduction

The need for nonprofits to find effective ways to both survive and grow has never been greater. Rising client demands, increasing numbers of nonprofit organizations, slow progress in the use of new technologies, and governmental cutbacks have increased competition for the limited funds from large donors, government, and the public. Nonprofit administrators find it increasingly necessary to monitor their organization's finances and use modern and effective financial techniques to ensure sound decision making. This chapter presents several tools and methods that can be used by nonprofits to monitor and improve their financial condition at various stages of their development.

Patterns and Trends

At present, a bimodal distribution of resources exists in the sector: twelve percent of nonprofit (501(c)(3)) organizations in the United States own more than 98 percent of total nonprofit assets (Weitzman et al., 2002). The implication of this is clear—a small percentage of nonprofits has access to a substantial asset base while a large majority possesses limited resources to call upon. Although financial management tools exist that can assist administrators to more effectively monitor and deploy their resources, relatively few nonprofits in the latter group do so.

The financial health of a nonprofit is best addressed in a broader context than one that focuses solely on its income and expenditures. At least three additional types of information are important. The first involves assets and liabilities. Assets are the resources an organization has available to use (for example, cash, inventory, buildings) while liabilities are the resources that an organization has incurred to pay to others (for example, accounts payable, mortgages payable, insurance payable). The relationship between the two is important because an organization may be able to use an excess of assets over its liabilities to provide additional funds in time of need. (See chapters 11 and 12.)

The second piece of important information involves the surpluses an organization has accumulated over time. Surpluses can be used during periods when expenses exceed revenues or can be saved in anticipation of growth. Surpluses can be accumulated as working capital, undesignated fund balances, and/or unrestricted current assets.

A third and often-neglected type of information involves measures of organizational efficiency. Such measures have been in the literature for many years but are rarely presented to boards of directors. Examples of these measures include the number of days of cash available at the current spending rate, the number of days the organization takes to pay its bills, how many days it takes for customers to pay the organization, and the ratio of debt to equity.

These measures are usually calculated at a given point in time but successful management involves analysis of time trends. For example, a ratio of current assets to liabilities of "2" suggests that a nonprofit has some room to incur further liabilities, but if this ratio has fallen from "6" in the last three years then a rational decision maker may want to monitor spending much more carefully than if the "2" were viewed in isolation; declines of this type point to serious problems down the road.

Current Practice

Because most nonprofits have inadequate resources to meet their needs, the importance of carefully conserving resources and utilizing them well is clear. Nonprofits can benefit from research that focuses on ways to identify, measure, monitor, and utilize indicators of their financial health. Such monitoring is not only a critical part of sound resource utilization but it is also a critical part of sound governance procedure. Most nonprofit boards examine the financial health of their organizations by comparing budgeted expenditures to actual year-to-date (YTD) data. The board's role typically (and perhaps ritualistically) involves questioning why a difference exists between budgeted and actual expenditures and between projected and YTD deficit or surplus. This process occurs even when the deviations are small and/or when they have little relation to the critical issues facing the organization. Since the discussion normally relates to object codes (such as, labor, copying, utilities), rather than to program categories, considerable effort is devoted to discussing input consumption rather than focusing on longer-term financial stability and growth. This is particularly the case for organizations that make a budget review part of every board meeting. All too often, this process causes the behaviors of both the board and the CEO to be shaped by preparing for this review, absorbing time that could more profitably be spent in creating financial strategies and in monitoring the fiscal health of the nonprofit. In large well-run nonprofits, these larger strategic issues involving financial health are relegated to later strategic planning while in poorly run and/or resource-starved organizations, the measures of fiscal health are neither collected nor discussed. Large, commercially-oriented nonprofits, such as health care and private educational institutions, usually engage in these discussions while smaller nonprofits, such as advocacy and social service entities, are more likely to eschew consideration of their financial health until they are either absolutely necessary or too late. For the latter organizations, a cultural shift is required; discussions of financial health must become an explicit part of the board's agenda.

Theory

The above discussion suggests that dialogues between boards of directors and senior management would be more effective if they involved processes that were focused on identifying and correcting problems earlier rather than later. The key to ensuring a rich and continuing exchange is the process a nonprofit uses to institutionalize the dialogue. One such process is depicted in figure 14.1. An important part of this process is the set of measures that help board members and executives monitor the financial health of the organization. Two basic approaches are commonly used to monitor the financial health of organizations:

> *Ratio analyses.* This method compares relationships between accounting numbers. A set of ratios summarizes the economic characteristics and strategies of an organization. This method is typically used to identify past or current problems. (See, for example, Atkinson, Kaplan, and Young, 2004, chapter 12.)

> *Prediction models.* This approach uses financial ratios to *predict* financial problems. Typically, these models develop equations to see if *past* financial ratios can be used to predict *future* financial health.

While both ratio and prediction methods are used extensively in the business sector, they have only recently been adapted for use in the nonprofit sector. Below, we describe some of these studies.

The business sector looks at financial health in terms of risk of bankruptcy. Several methods have been developed that are widely used to predict the financial health of an organization. All use financial ratios. However, the definition of a healthy organization varies. Almost all of these models (see, for example, Beaver, 1966; Altman, 1968; Ohlson, 1980) claim that an organization is unhealthy, or is "at risk," if it eventually declares bankruptcy. A few models, however, use alternative definitions since not all firms that are at risk declare bankruptcy and many firms declare bankruptcy for nonfinancial reasons. For example, Gilbert et al. (1990) defined a financially vulnerable company as one that reports three consecutive years of net losses. Franks and Tourous (1989) find that companies that do declare bankruptcy are not necessarily financially vulnerable. For instance, a company might declare bankruptcy to put a stop to a labor dispute. Altman (1968) and Ohlson (1980) develop two of the most widely used predictor

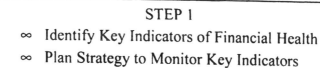

> ## STEP 1
> ∞ Identify Key Indicators of Financial Health
> ∞ Plan Strategy to Monitor Key Indicators
> ∞ Incorporate Indicators into the Governance **Process**

> ## STEP 2
> ∞ Prepare Budget in conjunction with Financial Health Indicators
> ∞ Develop Appropriate Trend Data
> ∞ Relate Indicators to Competitive and Financial Strategy
> ∞ Revisit Short-Term Strategy

> ## STEP 3
> ∞ Revise Budget and Long-Term Strategies based on Assessment of Financial Health
> ∞ Revise Financial Health Indicators Based on Predictive Performance

Figure 14.1. A Process for Effective Financial Management

models in the business sector. Altman uses four accounting ratios and one market ratio in his model while Ohlson uses eight accounting ratios. (Accounting ratios are based on the financial data for an individual organization while market ratios are based on measures in the economy at large.)

The process used by for-profits in monitoring financial health is different from that followed by many nonprofits. First, it involves the identification, collection over time and integration of data that is normally not available to nonprofit boards of directors.

Second, these data are interpreted and incorporated into the decision-making process. The net result is the creation of an "early warning system" capable of indicating when a business is moving toward "ill health" and the specification of a planning mechanism to address identified problems. The process proposed here would establish a means through which board members move from the role of policemen over the budget to that of strategists, sharing their knowledge of competitive environments, interpretation of the data, and development of financial strategies. For some boards, this may require engaging a consultant to educate members, for others selection of new members with different skills, and for still others a refocusing of what is presented at meetings. The net result will be to position a nonprofit so that it can benefit from improved monitoring of its financial position.

Scholars of finance have made much progress in the last few decades. Of particular importance is the finding that for-profits are subject to at least three types of financial risk: market risk, industry risk, and firm risk. (See Brigham and Ehrhardt, 2004.) The first relates to the economic and financial risks that affect all entities. Industry risk deals with threats in a specific industry (e.g., changes in the nature of the competition, technology, consumer tastes, and ways of doing business). Firm risk relates to those features unique to the firm (such as its financial structure or management). Interestingly, these three forms of risk have an analogue in the environment for nonprofits. Unfortunately, the means to measure them can be considerably more difficult, given the absence of organized markets that place an economic value on nonprofit organizations. Nevertheless, a well-informed nonprofit board will find it valuable to educate itself on each form of risk and how it affects its organization. Nonprofits are not valued in the traditional business sense; they are not privately owned and, thus, are typically not sold in a market.[1] They cannot trade in a stock market and cannot be sold by business brokers. Thus, any valuation methods used are not readily validated. (Note that this is not true in all cases. In the 1980s, hundreds of nonprofit hospitals were, in fact, sold [and converted] to for-profit entities).

However, there is an implicit value that rational donors assign to donor-funded organizations. Following traditional economic theory, these entities should be worth the "discounted present value" of the revenue streams that they are projected to produce plus the value of their assets at the time that these streams terminate. (The term "present value" is used in finance to indicate that a dollar today is worth more than a dollar received tomorrow. To make the dollar received tomorrow comparable to that received today, it is discounted, usually by a rate equal to what the dollar today would be worth if it earned interest. See Brigham and Ehrhardt, 2004.) A similar valuation can be obtained for organizations primarily funded by public and private contracts, and by grants. Finally, commercial nonprofits, such as hospitals, can be measured by several methods, including both valuation of their income streams and pairing them with comparable organizations in the for-profit sector. Measures of this type have traditionally not been attempted for a majority of 501(c)(3) corporations, but they are feasible to construct. While there are many thorny issues involved in providing a valuation of nonprofits, the fact remains that a financial value can be identified for these organizations.

Establishment of this point is essential because once the value of a nonprofit can be identified, regardless of whether the value can ever be realized through its sale, it stands to reason that the value will be altered by developments in the larger society, such as recessions, or changes in the stock market or tax laws. Each of these events will affect not only the revenue streams of nonprofits, but the value of their assets. For example, a decline in the national income lowers the income of donors and can potentially lead to a reduction in the overall level of donations received by nonprofits. When a nonprofit's income is reduced, it may be forced to produce fewer services, reduce its surplus (or increase its deficit), and/or reduce the number of employees. Each of these actions reduces the value of a nonprofit, both in a financial sense and in a broader social context. A similar argument can be made when stock market fluctuations lower the value of a nonprofit's dividend income or when cutbacks in government reduce its revenues from contracts and grants. In each case, nonprofit revenues, like stock market prices, can be and are influenced by changes in the marketplace. Thus, there is a "market" risk (or economic risk) that affects each nonprofit.

The second form of risk relates to the industry in which a firm operates. Identification of this type of risk has been facilitated in the nonprofit sector by the identification of National Taxonomy of Exempt Entities (NTEE) codes that provide a classification within which nonprofits can be organized. Although the term "industry" is typically not used in the nonprofit context, NTEE categories provide a rough classification of nonprofits by mission. Risks can arise within categories for a variety of reasons. Industries can differ in both the supply and demand for their services, in the expectation of service users, in the extent of government regulation, in support from private donors, in access to commercial activity, and so on. For example, in the health care industry, Medicare reimbursement regulations have required significant changes in both operations and recordkeeping. Thus industry- or mission-specific risks provide a second source of concern that is part of the financial environment facing nonprofits.

The third form of risk, firm-specific, arises from conditions that are unique to the individual organization, such as the quality of its management, the types of financial controls in place, age of machinery, firm location, the number and quality of a nonprofit's revenue sources, how its assets are financed, its cash flow, the value of its receivables, and its position in its "market." The process of identifying the risks unique to a nonprofit is a valuable one from which a board can learn a great deal. It also begins an important dialogue as to how such risks can be identified, addressed, and planned for.

In recognition that increased risk negatively affects the value of a firm and its ability to survive, many businesses actively practice risk management: they reduce risk by consciously managing their finances. Risk management practices have found their way into some sectors of the nonprofit economy. For example, a number of nonprofit hospitals, health care systems, and educational institutions have adopted risk management practices. However, the vast majority of nonprofits either lack an understanding of the principles of risk management or the ability to put its principles into practice. As a consequence, a majority of nonprofits remain fully exposed to uncertainty and financial harm.

Extending the Knowledge Base

While "risk" in business has focused primarily on bankruptcy, this has not been the case in the nonprofit sector. First, it is difficult to find nonprofits that actually declare bankruptcy. Under the federal bankruptcy code in the U.S., nonprofits cannot be forced into involuntary bankruptcy (11 U.S.C.A. §303(a)), although most states allow nonprofits to dissolve either voluntarily or by judicial order. Second, most nonprofits that may be "at risk" either merge with other nonprofits or simply "disappear" (Hager et al., 1996).

Greenlee and Bukovinsky (1998) adapted ratios from the business sector to the nonprofit sector. They divided these ratios into two groups: those that assess the adequacy of the organization's resources and those that look at how those resources are used in achieving the organization's mission. They computed median ratios for subsectors, but did not relate these measures to "risk." Tuckman and Chang (1991) were the first researchers to apply the concept of risk to the nonprofit sector. They defined risk as an inability to withstand a financial shock, such as a loss of major funding or a general economic turndown, and identified four accounting ratios that can be used to measure this concept: low net assets, little or no slack, a small surplus margin, and few sources of revenue. Using financial data provided by the Internal Revenue Service (IRS), they computed these ratios and then separated the results into quintiles. A nonprofit with at least one ratio in the lowest quintile was determined a priori to be "at risk"; one with all ratios in the lowest quintile was defined as "severely at risk."

Greenlee and Trussel (2000), Hager (2001), Trussel (2003), and Trussel and Greenlee (2004) also used IRS data and Tuckman's and Chang's ratios to develop predictor models. The earliest study (Greenlee and Trussel, 2000) defined "risk" as a decline in program expenses. The next two studies (Trussel, 2003; Trussel and Greenlee, 2004) defined "risk" as a decline in net assets during a three-year period. All three of these studies found significant relationships between "risk" and two or more of Tuckman's and Chang's variables. Hager focused his research on arts organizations, defining "risk" as the actual demise of the organization. He found that the ability of Tuckman's and Chang's ratios to predict "risk" varied within each subsector.

In contrast, Keating et al. (2005) went beyond Tuckman's, and Chang's ratios to develop a new model to measure risk in the nonprofit sector. They added to the ratios developed by Altman (1968), Ohlson (1980), and Tuckman and Chang (1991) two additional ratios and applied all of these ratios to the following four definitions of risk to see if a better model could be developed: negative net assets, a significant decline in net assets, a significant drop in total revenue, and a significant drop in program expenses. Table 14.1 presents the variables they found to be significant in nonprofit financial prediction models.

All of the predictor models have statistically significant power to predict risk on the basis of one or more financial ratios, for the nonprofit sector as a whole and for one subsector. However, none

Table 14.1. Ratios to Predict "Risk" in Nonprofit Organizations

Ratio	Equation	Desired Trend	Source
NA/TR	(assets − liabilities)/total revenues	+	TC
RCI	$\sum_j (\text{Revenue}_i/\text{Total Revenue})^2$	+	TC
NI/TR	Net income/total revenues	+	TC
AE/TR	Administrative expenses/total revenues	+	TC
WC/TA	(current assets − current liabilities)/total assets	+	A
NA/TA	(Total assets − total liabilities)/total assets	+	A
Size	Ln (total assets/GDP price level index)	+	O
TL/TA	Total liabilities/total assets	−	O
CL/CA	Current liabilities/current assets	−	O
NI/TA	Net income/total assets	+	O
FFO/TL	(Net income plus depreciation and amortization)/total liabilities	+	O
CHGNI	Change in net income from negative to positive	+	O
SCHGNI	$(NI_t − NI_{t-1})/(|NI_t| + |NI_{t-1}|)$	+	O
COMREV/TR	Commercial revenues/total revenues	+	K
INV/TA	Investment portfolio/total assets	+	K

TC: Tuckman and Chang, 1991.
A: Altman, 1968.
O: Ohlson, 1980.
K: Keating et al., 2005.

of the research to date has been able to reliably predict *which* individual organization will be at risk. In other words, the prediction models *themselves* cannot be used by boards to predict the future of their organizations. However, the *trends* of these ratios can and should be used as *indicators* of risk.

Improving Practice

The financial health of nonprofit organizations can be improved by looking at the three aspects of risk. *Market risk* can be defined in many ways: as the entire nonprofit sector or as one geographical region of the sector. Specifically, an organization's market risk can be evaluated by comparing an organization's changes in revenues, liabilities, and net worth to the "market," however defined. An organization whose revenues are falling when the "market" (or total revenues for other nonprofits similarly defined) is increasing, is, comparatively speaking, at risk. For example, the board of a nonprofit art museum may choose to benchmark its progress against a subset of similar-sized organizations as measured by revenues and/or assets. Alternatively, it may look at a subset of different nonprofits in the same metropolitan area. Data can be prepared for the board using Form 990s for the benchmark subset and the development of a set of trends can be useful in helping to identify when the nonprofit is experiencing changes in financial health that are departures from those of other like entities in the nonprofit sector.

Sector risk can be defined more specifically using the IRS classifications, which consist of more than four hundred categories and subcategories. An organization can define its sector as one of ten *major* groups, as one of twenty-six subsectors *within* each major group, or as a specific type of organization within each subsector (National Center for Charitable Statistics, 2005). Table 14.2 lists the ten major NTEE groups and twenty-six subsectors. An organization's sector risk can be evaluated by comparing selected financial ratios with the average (or median) ratios of its chosen sector. Of course, the narrower the defined sector, the more useful the comparisons. For example, an organization

Table 14.2.   National Taxonomy of Exempt Entities—Core Codes[1]

I	Arts, Culture, Humanities	Arts, Culture, Humanities (A)[2]
II	Education	Education (B)
III	Environment and Animals	Environment (C)
		Animals (D)
IV	Health	Health Care (E)
		Mental Health and Crisis Intervention (F)
		Diseases, Disorders, and Medical Disciplines (G)
		Medical Research (H)
V	Human Services	Crime and Legal Related (I)
		Employment (J)
		Food, Agriculture, and Nutrition (K)
		Housing and Shelter (L)
		Public Safety Disaster Preparedness and Relief (M)
		Recreation and Sports (N)
		Youth Development (O)
		Human Services (P)
VI	International, Foreign Affairs	International, Foreign Affairs, and National Security (Q)
VII	Public, Societal Benefit	Civil Rights, Social Action, and Advocacy (R)
		Community Improvement and Capacity Building (S)
		Philanthropy, Voluntarism and Grant Making Foundations (T)
		Science and Technology (U)
		Social Science (V)
		Public and Societal Benefit (W)
VIII	Religion Related	Religion Related (X)
IX	Mutual, Membership Benefit	Mutual and Membership Benefit (Y)
X	Unknown/Unclassified	Unknown and/or Unclassified (Z)

[1] Adapted from *National Taxonomy of Exempt Entities – Core Codes (NTEE-CC) Classification System* (rev. May 2005) (accessed November 12, 2005 at http://nccsdataweb.urban.org/kbfiles/324/NTEE%20TWO%20page_2005.doc).
[2] Each subgroup is further categorized into multiple subdivisions. For example, a children's museum would be categorized as IA52.

that provides child day care can define its sector as (1) human services, (2) children and youth services, or (3) child day care services. The number and availability of comparison organizations are greater for the entire human services sector, but the results are more useful when narrowing the field to child day care. Table 14.3

Table 14.3.   Selected Suggested Ratios for Comparisons within Sectors[1, 2]

Ratio	Equation	Desired Relationship to Other Organizations	Explanation
Inventory Turnover	Cost of goods sold/Average inventory[3]	Higher	Efficiency in management of inventory
#Days Inventory	365/Inventory Turnover	Lower	How many days it takes for inventory to sell
Receivables Turnover	Revenues/Average Accounts Receivable	Higher	Efficiency in generating revenues from receivables
# Days Receivables Outstanding	365/Receivables Turnover	Lower	How many days it takes to collect on receivables (a measure of credit policy)
Payables Turnover	Revenues/Average Accounts Payable	Higher	Efficiency in managing short-term debt
#Days Payables Outstanding	365/Payables Turnover	Lower	How many days it takes to pay bills (a measure of credit worthiness)
Total Asset Turnover	Revenues/Average Total Assets	Higher	Efficiency in utilizing assets
Current Ratio	Current Assets/ Current Liabilities	Higher	A liquidity measure (ability to turn assets into cash)
Debt to Fund Balance	Average Total Debt/Average Total Fund Balance	Lower	A long-term risk measure: the proportion of net assets (fund balance) that is provided by debt
Times Interest Earned	Earnings before Interest/Interest Expense	Higher	A measure of the ability to meet interest payments; efficiency of debt utilization

[1] Ratios adapted from White and Fried (2002).
[2] Not all of these ratios will be applicable to all sectors. For example, some sectors might not carry inventory or own substantial fixed assets.
[3] Average can be defined in many ways. Typically it is computed by dividing the sum of beginning and year-end balances by two. (For example: (Inventory 2004 + Inventory 2005)/2.)

suggests some ratios that might be useful when comparing within sectors. For example, it should be noted that comparative data can be developed either using Form 990s from a subset of all cultural organizations, art museums, or specific art museums such as children's art museums, based on careful discussion by the board as to which entities benchmark best against the needs of their organization.

While an evaluation of both market and sector risk concentrates on cross-sectional comparisons, an assessment of *firm risk* focuses on longitudinal analysis. Further, an analysis of market risk focuses on *changes* from year to year, and sector risk focuses on comparative *ratio* analysis, but analysis of firm risk uses several methods. The first consists of preparing common-size financial statements and comparing two or more years.[2] This method allows an organization to quickly see changes in spending or revenues. A second method is similar to sector analysis in using ratio analysis. However, in analyzing an organization's firm risk, the comparisons should be for two or more years. Table 14.4 offers some suggested ratios that should be helpful for examining firm risk.

Since the enactment of the Taxpayer Bill of Rights in 1996, the primary disclosure mechanism of nonprofit organizations has been the Internal Revenue Service (IRS) Form 990.[3] The data is repackaged and sold by the Urban Institute's National Center on Charitable Statistics (NCCS) and by Guidestar (www .guidestar.org). While these datasets are the most comprehensive in the nonprofit sector, they have significant limitations. First, churches are exempt from filing. Second, since only those organizations earning more than $25,000 are required to file with the IRS, the database is biased toward larger entities. Third, many returns are filed late and may be prone to errors (NCCS, 2005). Finally, Guidestar has been increasing its prices, perhaps making it difficult for some nonprofits to purchase these data. However, they are extremely useful for comparative purposes.

In order to use these data to monitor financial health, a nonprofit must consider its stage of development. In particular, what strategy to follow, the appropriate measures of financial health, and the interpretation of these measures all relate to a nonprofit's

Table 14.4. Selected Ratios to Evaluate Individual Firm Risk[1]

Ratio	Equation	Explanation
Defense Interval	(Cash + Marketable Securities + Receivables)/ Average Monthly Cash Expenses	The length of time (in months) that an organization can continue to operate using existing current assets. Low or decreasing may indicate future cash flow problems.
Accounts Payable Aging	Accounts Payable/Average Monthly Payments	High or increasing may indicate payment or future credit problems. Very low may indicate excessive savings.
Savings Indicator	(Revenues − Expenses)/Total Expenses	Evaluate with caution: high or increasing may indicate future variability in revenues.
Contributions and Grants Ratio	Revenue from Contributions and Grants/Total Revenue	This is an indication of an organization's dependence on voluntary support. High or increasing may indicate future variability in revenues.
Endowment Ratio	Endowment/Average Monthly Expenses	High or increasing: implies greater stability.
Debt Ratio	Average Total Debt/Average Total Assets	High or increasing implies possible future liquidity problems or ability to borrow.
Fund-raising Efficiency Ratio[2]	Total Contributions (other than government grants)/Fund-raising Expense	High or increasing: more efficiency in fund-raising.
Fund-raising Expense Ratio[3]	Fund-raising Expense/Total Expense	Evaluate in conjunction with Fund-raising Efficiency Ratio. Small fund-raising expense ratio and high fund-raising efficiency ratio indicate relatively few dollars were spent on fund-raising and that maximized contributions were received.
Management Expense Ratio[3]	Management and General Expense/Total Expense	Low or decreasing may indicate more efficient use of management and general expenses.

(Continued)

Table 14.4.   Selected Ratios to Evaluate Individual Firm Risk[1] (*Continued*)

Ratio	Equation	Explanation
Program Services Expense Ratio[3]	Program Services Expense/Total Expense	High or increasing may indicate efficiency in providing services.
Program Services to Total Assets[3]	Program Services Expense/Average Total Assets	High or increasing may indicate efficient use of assets to provide services.

[1] Adapted from Greenlee and Bukovinsky (1998).
[2] We believe that allocated expenses (such as fund-raising expense, management expense, program expense) can and are often manipulated. Therefore, we believe that all ratios that use any of these expenses must be evaluated with extreme caution and should only be used for internal decision-making purposes.
[3] Not all of these ratios will be applicable to all sectors. For example, some sectors might not carry inventory or own substantial fixed assets.

stage of development. Tuckman (2006) has identified at least five stages that nonprofits potentially go through during their organizational lifetime: birthing, stabilization, growth, diversification, and closedown. For each stage, a set of strategic (diagnostic) questions can help to shape the thinking of the CEO and the board, to formulate a financial strategy suited to realizing organizational needs in that stage and a set of measures to monitor financial health and realization of the selected strategies.

Birthing Stage: Getting the nonprofit on its feet.

- *Questions*: What programs will initially be offered, how will they be financed, and with what revenue mix? How does the organization keep itself alive and focused on its primary mission? How does it ensure that these will be annual revenues and that it is not forced to rely on one-time sources that require continual fund-raising? How will it become known to the public and how will it distinguish itself from other nonprofits?
- *Financial Strategies*: Identification of the appropriate revenue sources, creation of adequate expenditure controls, solicitation of short-term foundation support, and fund-raising by principals.

- *Measures:* cash on hand, burn rate, change in income from previous period(s), comparisons of revenue sources to other similar nonprofits.

Stabilization Stage: Period needed to ensure that the nonprofit has a reasonable chance to survive.

- *Questions:* Are the programs initially selected the ones that will ensure the continued existence of the nonprofit? What actions can be taken to secure the base funding from which services are delivered? What group of revenue sources will ensure stable funding for the next few years? What kinds of reserves should be (and/or can be) established, and should this be done from existing revenues? Is this an appropriate time to start an endowment?
- *Financial Strategies:* Plan for types of assets needed and ways to acquire, explore creation of an endowment, identify vulnerable revenue streams, and identify strategies to counter downturns. Identify of potential large donors.
- *Measures:* Change in revenue over last three periods by source, net income over net revenue, revenue diversification index, current assets minus current liabilities divided by total assets, total assets minus total liabilities divided by total assets, administrative costs divided by total revenues compared to those of similar organizations.

Growth Stage: The period during which the nonprofit grows its existing programs within its existing structure.

- *Questions:* Which of the existing programs are most valuable in pursuit of mission and what is the best way to grow them? Are there some programs that can be eliminated to provide more resources for priority items? Are there ways to take advantage of economies of scale and scope to generate additional income from mission-related programs? Can we do a better job of selling these to donors and governments? What are the goals in growing the program and how will this contribute to building financial strength?

- *Financial Strategies:* Diversify the revenue base as it grows. Consider major capital campaign to grow assets. Consider appropriate role of debt and ability to access it. Continue to identify the most vulnerable revenue streams.
- *Measures:* revenue diversification index, net income divided by total revenue, change in income over time, change in asset ratios and surplus ratios described above, ratio of investment portfolio to total assets, number of days stakeholders take to pay.

Diversification Stage: Expansion to include new programs, some of which may not be mission related. This also may include acquisition of other nonprofits.

- *Questions:* What new programs should be added that increase organizational ability to deliver mission-related services and to build financial strength? Are there commercial activities that can be established to generate revenues to cross-subsidize programs? Does it make sense to acquire other nonprofits with similar missions?
- *Financial Strategies:* Plan ways to grow the financial base of the organization, expand geographically, use Internet and other sales distribution channels, develop sophisticated fund-raising programs, grow partnerships with other nonprofits and for-profits, and access large seed grants from foundations.
- *Measures:* All of the measures shown in table 14.1, as well as market feasibility studies, business plans (as appropriate), and studies of competitors.

Closedown Stage: Managing a nonprofit through the phasing out of its programs and transfer of its assets.

- *Questions:* What is the appropriate time frame for a nonprofit to close its operations? How can this be done with minimum damage to the serviced population? Is there a best way to shift some of the served population to other nonprofits? How can employee morale be maintained during the transition?

- *Financial Strategies:* Identify the best way to dispose of nonendowment assets under IRS rules, explore ways to preserve the nonprofit through merger or acquisition, find an angel donor, and investigate how to dispose of the endowment.
- *Measures:* Change in net income, net income plus depreciation and amortization divided by total liabilities, total liabilities divided by total assets, current liabilities divided by current assets, assets minus liabilities divided by total revenues, number of days to pay bills and to be paid by stakeholders.

Conclusion

Considerable progress has been made in measuring and managing risk in the nonprofit sector and this is improving the transparency (and indirectly accountability) of the sector, as well as slowly leading to more efficient decision making. The fact that several dimensions of risk can be identified and actions can be taken to reduce volatility improves the planning process and increases the odds that an organization will survive and grow. In this chapter we suggest several ways that concepts developed in the for-profit sector can be applied to nonprofits. Specifically, we outline a process through which continuous monitoring of an organization's financial health can be achieved through two alternative approaches, one involving the monitoring of financial ratios and the other the use of more sophisticated predictive models. Our analysis identifies appropriate measures, discusses the relative advantages of each, and explores the question of which financial ratios make sense in the nonprofit context. We also present several ideas as to how these measures can be related to explicit financial strategies that nonprofits might adopt. It is important to note, however, that the choice of methods, measures, and strategies is ultimately a board decision that should be based on the needs, mission, and particular situation of the organization.

It is also important to note that the application of for-profit risk management techniques to the nonprofit sector is in its early stages and that much needs to be done to more fully understand how nonprofits are valued, how market risk affects organizations in the sector, and how best to provide the tools that nonprofit managers need for managing risk. While significant progress has been made by academic researchers in valuation of for-profits, the issues surrounding nonprofits are more intractable and hence progress is necessarily slower. Indeed, the absence of a widely agreed upon bottom line for nonprofits, the absence of market data, the limited instruments for hedging market risk, and other problems, continue to make this area of finance both challenging and important. Given the financial problems currently facing nonprofits, it seems clear that serious effort must be made to adapt for-profit measures of financial health and risk to the nonprofit sector. To accomplish this, a change in the culture involving board review of nonprofit finances is needed. The sector cannot ignore either the volatility introduced by the growing number of nonprofits relative to a slower increase in funding sources or the new pressures for financial stability introduced by Sarbanes-Oxley and the emergent interest in its application to the nonprofit world (see Weitzman, 2002). The techniques and concepts developed in this chapter are an important first step in offering nonprofits useful insights as to how to monitor and respond to the changing world around them.

Notes

1. Several earlier chapters of this book, including 7, 11, and 12, provide interesting insights as to how these items are affected by internal and external events and the items that influence them.

2. A common size income statement is prepared by presenting each account as a percentage of revenues; a common size balance sheet is prepared by presenting each account as a percentage of total assets.

3. This bill required that an organization must permit anyone to inspect its Form 990 if the request is either made in person or in writing. However, this requirement can be waived if the Form 990 is made

"widely available" (§1313(a)(3)), such as posting the document on the Internet, either on its own website or on another's website as "part of a database of similar materials" (Prop. Reg. §301.6104(e) – 2(b)2)).

Interestingly, nonprofit financial statements are *not* public documents. Thus, while models in the business sector are based on audited financial statements (prepared according to Generally Accepted Accounting Principles), nonprofit models have been based on *unaudited* informational tax returns (prepared according to IRS regulations).

V

SYNTHESIS

15

Toward a Normative Theory of Nonprofit Finance

Dennis R. Young

Introduction

Perhaps the appropriate metaphor for nonprofit finance is that of a jigsaw puzzle. As the chapters of this book testify, there are many pieces to this puzzle—many different kinds of nonprofit income, a number of different rationales and factors that help explain why a nonprofit would or should pursue a particular source of income in any given circumstance, and a variety of criteria that bear on the efficacy of particular income portfolios. How then can we put all of these pieces together into a coherent whole—an overarching conceptual framework that will be helpful in guiding the finance decisions of nonprofit managers and leaders? To change metaphors, what are the consistent threads that run throughout the analyses here that, when sewn together, offer a general way of understanding nonprofit finance and improving its practice?

As the major sections of this book reflect, any theory of nonprofit finance must account for three basic issues—financing of current operations, financing of longer term capital needs, and the balance or mix among different sources of income for these purposes. Each of these issues addresses separate challenges for the nonprofit organization. Current operations must be financed in a way that covers current operating costs and contributes maximally to the achievement of the organization's mission in the short term. Capital financing must allow the nonprofit organization to meet its future needs by investing in capacity and covering depreciation, by setting aside funds for emergency purposes and cash flow exigencies, and by establishing capital resources (such as endowments) that will generate needed future operating income. Finally, the balancing of nonprofit income portfolios must address other issues as well, including possible interactions among different sources of income (such as crowd out), risk management, and required adjustments to ensure solvency, mission achievement, and administrative feasibility.

In this chapter we move toward a comprehensive normative theory of nonprofit finance by emphasizing more heavily the first of these dimensions—financing current operations—for two reasons. First, the essential idea behind our theory development—that financing of nonprofit operations must correspond with the nature of benefits conferred on nonprofit beneficiaries—applies as well to issues of capital financing and overall portfolio mixes; so in analyzing operations we also implicitly address capital financing to some degree. Second, many of the issues of capital financing and portfolio diversification can be addressed using conventional ideas from corporate finance, once the nuances emerging from our analysis of operations financing are appreciated. Thus, for example, borrowing or investment practices can follow traditional principles once we acknowledge the fact that social costs and benefits must be accounted for. Moreover, traditional concepts of risk and return can be applied to the design of nonprofit income and asset portfolios, once the special nature of a nonprofit's mission-related social returns and peculiar risk considerations are appreciated. In other words, we are not trying to reinvent the wheel in this book. Rather we are seeking to develop a new vehicle best adapted to the roads that nonprofit organizations travel.

Working Principles

Each chapter in parts 2 and 3 of this book investigates the underlying economic rationale for seeking a particular source of income to support nonprofit operations or capital needs. Each

author probed both the supply and demand sides of this issue—
what resource providers are seeking in return for their particular
form of financing, and how a given source of income serves the
purposes of the recipient nonprofit. The latter consideration is,
of course, of overriding importance. As discussed throughout
the book, nonprofits have diverse stakeholders and supporters,
each with their own agendas. However, it is up to the nonprofit
organization itself to ensure that its resource base is marshaled
effectively to achieve its social mission. In the discussion to follow, we take the latter basically as a given, although we allow
for the possibility of secondary effects wherein nonprofits adjust
their missions to ensure adequate financing. Certainly one cannot
fully separate strategic planning and positioning from questions
of finance. Here, however, we concentrate on how nonprofits can
best finance themselves, given that they have clarified their understanding of mission.

Given their basic mission focus, however, nonprofits must understand how what they are providing is of value to those who
might support them. This is the first step to attracting support and
also the first step in setting an appropriate mind-set for nonprofit
resource development. In particular, given the financial pressures
that nonprofits face, and the importance of their work, nonprofit
leaders must be able to aggressively pursue the resources they
need, without apology. They can do this only if they have confidence that they are providing a good bargain for those who would
support them. Accordingly, our first working principle for theory
construction is the following:

> *Sources of income should correspond with the nature of benefits
> conferred on, or of interest to, the providers of those resources.*

A key implication of this principle is that all nonprofit resource development involves "selling," whether to customers, donors, government or foundation officials, or corporate partners. Another
implication is that nonprofits have value to offer these providers
and should do so as partners or traders, not as supplicants.

A second working principle follows from the fact that nonprofits are so diverse in their missions and hence the kinds of

benefits they confer. As a result they should have in mind to seek support from a variety of sources:

Each source of income has its place—different types of income are appropriate to support different missions and services.

Below, we elaborate on the correspondence between different types of missions and services, the benefits they confer, and the corresponding sources of income appropriate to match those benefits. One of the interesting aspects of this analysis is that various kinds of missions and services confer multiple types of benefits, hence justify mixtures of different sources of income. This is the first cut, therefore, at the question of appropriate income mixes, and the basis of a third working principle:

A nonprofit organization's income portfolio should reflect the mix of benefits its services confer on its potentially diverse set of income providers.

A financing strategy based on these benefit-based principles is likely to be both economically efficient, in the sense of allocating societal resources to their best uses, and financially productive, in the sense that it is likely to be maximally appealing to those who would support the organization. However, it is impractical to assume that such a pure strategy would fully address a nonprofit organization's financial challenges. In particular, there are other organizational concerns that enter income portfolio decisions—concerns focused on the viability of the organization and both its short-term and long-term ability to address its mission. For example, there is nothing to guarantee that a nonprofit organization seeking to cover its expenses with income streams deriving proportionally from its potential beneficiaries will necessarily succeed in breaking even. For example, charitable support is subject to substantial free riding, while government programs often shortchange their contractors or inordinately delay their payments. Moreover, there may be important interactions among different income sources that argue for adjustments in a benefit-determined mix. Crowd out effects or matching programs, for example, may argue for adjustments in one income stream versus another. Finally, there are general considerations of risk management and long-term mission achievement that may call for adjustments in benefit-based income portfolios. For example, the economy may affect alternative sources of income differently over time—arguing for additional diversification to hedge against large peaks and valleys of income flow, while demands for mission-related services may vary asynchronously with ebbs and flows in sources of income—again requiring hedging strategies to avoid future crises. Hence, our final working principle:

> *Nonprofit income portfolios should also reflect basic organizational challenges such as financial solvency, interactions among income sources, the challenges (feasibility) of accessing and administering particular sources of income, risk management, and long-term mission achievement.*

Overall Framework

The foregoing working principles together dictate an overall framework for nonprofit finance that is roughly captured in figure 15.1. The touchstone is mission that in turn determines the kinds of services, goods, and activities in which the nonprofit intends to engage. Those services confer various kinds of benefits that then suggest which groups should be willing to pay for those

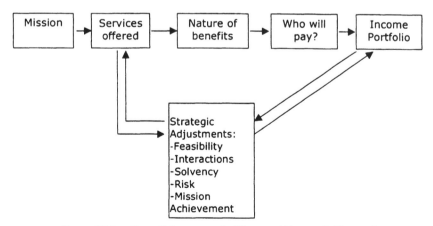

Figure 15.1.   *Overall Structure of a Theory of Nonprofit Finance.*[1]

benefits. Soliciting support from those beneficiaries will then lead
to a portfolio of income support that reflects the distribution of
mission-related benefits. However, such a portfolio may not solve
all of the organization's financial and strategic problems. Hence,
two-way interaction between overall organizational management
and governance on the one hand, and financial portfolio management on the other, is needed to bring about adjustments in the
income mix. This in turn may require changes in the goods and
services offered, which may then set off another round of adjustments in the income mix. For example, for purposes of managing
risk in light of disappointing donations, a nonprofit might decide
to undertake an earned income project, thus altering both the
mix of income and the nature of services offered to various constituencies. As noted earlier, there is also a potential link in this
diagram between the adjustments box and the mission. That is, if
circumstances are such that other adjustments fail to synchronize
an organization's finances with its offerings as dictated by its current mission, a modification of the mission itself may be required.
However, this is a larger question of organizational strategy from
which we abstract in this book. Rather we essentially take mission as the starting point and touchstone for nonprofit financial
decision making.

Given this overall conceptual framework, we must now become more specific about the nature of the benefits conferred by
different types of nonprofit services and their connection to alternative sources of income. This is a matter of putting together the
puzzle pieces laid out in chapters 2 through 12.

Sources of Income and the Nature of Benefits

Part 2 of this volume, which considers the conceptual bases for
nonprofits' reliance on charitable, governmental, fee, and membership income, and volunteering, is founded logically largely
on the theory of markets and market failure. Implicitly at least,
the authors of these chapters argue that unfettered markets are
often inefficient in delivering the kinds of services that nonprofits
provide. Hence fee income must be supplemented, or replaced,

by other forms of income that help account for public or collective benefits, so that efficient levels of provision can be achieved. In this chapter we push this concept one step further—arguing that there are groups and institutions that *will* pay for those collective and public benefits to the extent that the quid pro quo between payments and benefits can be recognized and made explicit.

In this connection, it is helpful to classify the benefits that nonprofits provide into four general categories, as follows:

(1) *Private Benefits* are benefits that accrue specifically to individual consumers or clients, which they recognize and are willing to pay for.

(2) *Group Benefits* are benefits that accrue to an identifiable subgroup of society and are valued by donors interested in helping that group.

(3) *Public Benefits* are benefits that accrue to a sufficiently large segment of the general public such that government financing is politically supported.

(4) *Trade Benefits* accrue to institutions or groups that supply resources to nonprofits; these benefits correspond with the specific missions or interests of those suppliers.

Private and *trade* benefits are straightforward benefits received by individual parties in a market or market-like transaction, while *group* and *public* benefits are benefits that accrue to wider groups and which are unaccounted for in ordinary market transactions. Our theory argues that nonprofits often confer several categories of benefits and hence must design their financing strategies accordingly. Each category is rich in possibilities and nuances.

As suggested in chapter 5, there are many examples of *private benefits* conferred by nonprofit organizations. Individuals who attend performing arts concerts or visit museum exhibits receive such benefits and are willing to pay for them. People who buy souvenirs in a nonprofit's gift shop, eat in its cafeteria, or park in its garage accrue such benefits. Children attending school, a day care center, a recreation program, or a youth group also receive such benefits for which they, or their parents, are willing to pay. Individuals who receive health care in a hospital, clinic, or rehabilitation center receive such benefits as well. Elderly clients who participate in senior centers or live in supported living facilities or nursing homes receive such benefits too. Individuals who belong to churches or social clubs or professional associations do as well.

The strategy of financing private benefits with fees is, of course, not completely straightforward. Individuals who may personally recognize such benefits may not be forthcoming with commensurate payments if they are not required to pay or cannot be excluded without substantial cost to the organization. For example, users of a public library can be charged for their library visits, but this requires a system for collecting these fees and a willingness to deny entry to those who refuse to pay. Moreover, as discussed in chapter 5 and elsewhere, private benefits may be intertwined with public ones, so that the imposition of fees—by reducing consumption—unduly constricts overall benefits. Thus, public libraries seek to expand literacy and encourage reading, objectives that may be compromised by charging a fee. Nonetheless, a good place to start in determining if fees have a role in a nonprofit's financing is to identify the private benefits that it confers.

Group benefits are also a very common output of nonprofit organizations. Environmental organizations that work for the improvement of public parks, the preservation of bird or other wildlife sanctuaries, or the cleanup of a lake or brownfield site, confer group benefits on residents of particular neighborhoods, certain groups of nature lovers, or advocates for environmental conservation. Institutions which seek to help particular ethnic groups, assist those at risk of particular diseases or families of those suffering particular illnesses, improve specific neighborhoods, or work for improved education of children with special needs, confer group benefits on defined clusters of people who, collectively through foundations and other institutions or through individuals whose philanthropic interests correspond to those groups, may be willing to financially support such provision. One important feature that distinguishes nonprofit organizations from government is the fact that they provide collective benefits on a selective and focused basis, with programs that do not necessarily appeal to the wider general public. Hence, the support of those benefits is more logically linked to financing through philanthropy, which, as Patrick Rooney observed in chapter 2, tends to be localized.

Public benefits too are a frequent consequence of nonprofit organizational activity. Nonprofits that carry out research to prevent or treat diseases, reduce crime or other forms of social pathology, improve general social and economic skills that can contribute to greater civility or economic productivity, advocate for social justice, work for preserving biodiversity of the environment, or promote public art that enriches the aesthetic appeal of a large city, all produce widespread benefits that affect many citizens at once. Often such benefits cannot be pinpointed for their impact on particular individuals or groups but they can nonetheless attract political support for government financing or incentives.

The line of demarcation between group and public benefits is necessarily fuzzy. On the one hand, nonprofit outputs that may confer widespread benefits may only be recognized by a small group of those beneficiaries—hence may be more productively classified as group benefits. For example, programs that preserve and protect wetlands provide general environmental benefits, in the form of cleaner air and water; however, such programs may only appeal to a narrower segment of the public that enjoys the recreational benefits of the outdoors or is concerned intellectually with preserving biodiversity. On the other hand, there is often general support through government for nonprofit activities that produce essentially group benefits. This occurs as a result of political deal making which permits representatives of alternative groups to support each others' interests. For example, neighborhood improvement projects or local art shows may be supportable in part by government funding because they are viewed as part of a package supported by coalitions of interest. Also of note, as observed by Michael Rushton and Arthur Brooks in chapter 4, government supports group benefits by creating tax incentives to encourage private giving to nonprofit organizations. These interfaces between group and public benefits do not, however, diminish the general usefulness of the distinction between these categories. Group benefits still point to philanthropic funding for their support, while public benefits point to government. However, it is important to realize that the boundaries are permeable and that significant possibilities exist for government support of group benefits and philanthropic support of public benefits.

Trade benefits are increasingly common and important as nonprofits look to build partnerships and collaborations with other groups and institutions in order to carry out their work more effectively. In such instances, nonprofits must offer something of specific value to their partners in order to engage their support. This is often true even in instances where the partners are essentially philanthropic in nature, as suggested in chapters 3 (institutional giving), 8 (volunteers), and 9 (collaboration), especially. One can divide potential nonprofit partners into several relatively distinct groups: for-profit corporations, nonprofit organizations including grant-making foundations, and individual donors and volunteers. Corporations commonly enter partnerships with nonprofits in the context of their own strategic interests—reflecting the notion of "strategic philanthropy." Thus, food corporations receive marketing benefits from having a heart-healthy seal from the American Heart Association, while Georgia Pacific Corporation enjoys wetlands management expertise and public relations benefits by virtue of its support of the Nature Conservancy. Partnerships among nonprofits are subtler, but here too strategic interests are involved. Foundations usually provide grant support only to those nonprofits that will in some way advance the defined mission of the foundation itself, as specified by its original donors. The nature of these benefits can be quite explicit, such as the Kellogg Foundation's insistence that its grantees advance the welfare of people of color or the Kauffman Foundation's focus on advancing the cause of youth and entrepreneurship. Certainly it is advantageous when the character of the group or public benefits conferred by a nonprofit coincides fully with the interests represented by the foundation. However, adjustments and compromises by grantees are not uncommon, and some of those adjustments can be viewed as accommodating the trade benefits to a foundation in exchange for grant support. For example, a program intended to support economic development in a particular community might be adapted to include a youth entrepreneurship educational component to appeal to a particular foundation.

For nonprofit partners in general, there is an even wider spectrum of trade benefits. Exchanges among nonprofit partners may include various kinds of information, uses of facilities, management services such as accounting, marketing, or box-office ticketing, or components of service to clients such as specialized treatments or evaluations. An interesting insight that Renee Irvin brings to this subject in chapter 9 is that such collaborations work best when nonprofits exploit their *differences* rather than their common interests. The same insight applies to corporations and nonprofits. Essentially, trade benefits are achieved when partners bring different strengths to the table and exchange these capacities in ways that make both parties better off. This is the essence of trade and it clarifies how trade benefits differ from group or public benefits.

Finally, trade benefits apply to individuals who donate their time and money to nonprofits. While the essence of such charitable support is the granting of a gift for the provision of certain collective or group benefits, one cannot ignore the fact that such gifts are given by individuals who have private as well as charitable motivations. As Anne Preston notes in chapter 8, volunteers enjoy various kinds of rewards, including recognition, skill training, and opportunities for socializing which can influence their decisions to offer their time and skills to a nonprofit organization. These essentially private benefits must be considered in the transactions required to attract and retain volunteer support. Similar arguments apply to donors. Major donors often receive recognition in the form of events in their honor, listings in programs and on plaques, or indeed by naming whole facilities and institutions after them.

An important point about trade benefits is that they are distinct from the group or public benefits that resource providers may also be supporting. In many cases, the trade benefit may be a simple quid pro quo without any group or public benefit involved. For example, two nonprofits may trade accounting services for reception space without any implication that they are supporting each other's mission-related benefits. Alternatively, trade benefits can be additional considerations or favors that the nonprofit may need to add to the mix in order to attract or retain corporate, foundation, volunteer, donor, or member support. In fact, the issues surrounding membership discussed by Richard Steinberg in chapter 6 capture much of the essence of such trade benefits. Thus "members" (essentially donors) of a philanthropic institution such as a museum, orchestra, or advocacy organization are solicited for their support of group or public benefits, but the institution may also need to consider what kinds of private benefits, in the form of discounts, special events, or publications would help to bring these supporters into the fold.

Benefits and Resource Providers

As the foregoing discussion suggests, private, group, public, and trade benefits rarely occur in isolation from one another. In particular, the transaction between a nonprofit and a particular resource provider is likely to involve more than one of these kinds of benefits. Table 15.1 sketches how various kinds of benefits apply to different categories of resource providers.

Note that consumers or clients of a nonprofit organization offer the simplest instance where fee revenue is provided in exchange for private benefits. Even this category entails some nuance, however. For example, members of a museum are both consumers and donors; hence they provide both fee and gift support. Moreover, even where formal membership is not involved, nonprofit institutions may often view their consumers as donors as well. For example, alumni of universities and colleges, who have been students, are also prime future donors. Individuals who attend operas or orchestra performances are key target groups for donations to arts institutions. And individuals

Table 15.1. Benefits, Resource Providers, and Income Sources

Type/ Provider	Gifts	Fees	Government Funds	Investment Returns	Barter
Consumers		Private benefits			
Donors/ Volunteers	Group benefits			Group benefits	Trade benefits
Taxpayers			Public benefits		
Organization Partners	Group benefits				Trade benefits

who have benefited from the care received in a nonprofit hospital often become donors as well.

Donors provide support for group benefits through periodic gifts for operations. They also give large gifts such as endowments and capital facilities that indirectly support group benefits by generating streams of investment income. And, as noted, donors may also be seeking trade benefits that take the form of private recognition for their generosity. Similarly, volunteers make gifts of their time primarily to support group benefits, but they may also seek trade benefits in the form of recognition, training, or other perquisites.

Taxpayers constitute another seemingly straightforward instance where benefits coincide with one form of support—government funding. Yet, as noted, government funding can also support group or even private benefits through various forms of political deal making. Finally, organizational partners may primarily seek benefits of trade, although for corporations and foundations this is normally couched in terms of an overall package that supports group and possibly public benefits through donations.

While table 15.1 is useful in highlighting some of the primary connections between particular categories of resource provider and specific types of benefits and forms of nonprofit income, the primary point that this figure makes is that nonprofit finance strategy must be based on a determination of what each resource provider group wants and the arrangements through which it will pay for it.

Combinations of Resource Support

By considering the various combinations of benefits that a non-profit organization may confer on its beneficiaries, one may visualize the prospective mixes of income sources that can effectively and appropriately support it. Figure 15.2 demonstrates that many different combinations are possible.

The four large rectangles represent nonprofit activities or services for which private, group, public, and trade benefits are

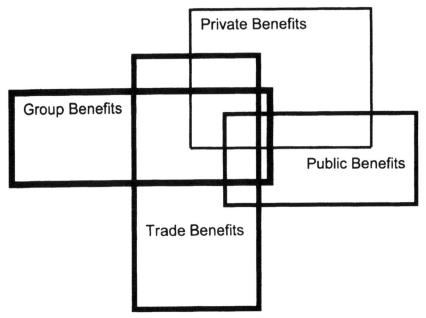

Figure 15.2. Benefit Combinations.

generated. The smaller rectangular or, in some cases, L-shaped areas within the diagram represent intersections between the large rectangles—hence various combinations of these benefits. The diagram suggests that all combinations are possible, and that prospective income combinations depend on which of the particular large rectangles are intersecting. For example, each of the larger rectangles contains an area that intersects with none of the others. These areas represent nonprofits that produce only one kind of benefit and presumably would be supported primarily by one corresponding source of income—for instance, fees in the case of private benefits, or philanthropy in the case of group benefits. A smaller rectangular or L-shaped area contained within only two of the larger rectangles would represent nonprofits that produce two kinds of benefits, for example, group and private benefits, hence might be supported by a combination of fees and philanthropy, and so on, for areas with other combinations of two, three, or four types of benefits.

Table 15.2 illustrates how various combinations of benefits translate into alternative financing mixes for a variety of nonprofit services. Examples may be found for just about every conceivable combination of income sources.

The logic of this table is straightforward. A few examples will serve to illustrate. In the case of preschool care (line 5), children and their families receive private benefits for which they are willing to pay fees, while the general public benefits from the fact that such schooling will help the children become productive citizens, thus arguing for government support. In the case of corporate-sponsored special events (line 8), such as an AIDS walk or an arts festival, particular groups in society benefit from the corporate

Table 15.2. Nonprofit Services with Alternative Income and Benefit Combinations

Income Combination	Example	Why
Fees Only	Gift shop	Consumer benefit only
Gifts Only	Rare disease research	Benefits those at risk or afflicted or their families
Government Funds Only	Offender rehabilitation	Increases public safety
Barter Only	Exchange of museum collections	Participating museums each benefit from trade
Fees and Gifts	Classical orchestras	Private benefits to audience members; collective benefits to art lovers
Fees and Government Funds	Preschool care	Private consumer and general public benefits
Government Funds and Gifts	Environmental quality monitoring program	Benefits to outdoor enthusiasts and general public
Gifts and Barter	Corporate sponsored special events	Group benefits to nonprofit constituency and marketing benefits to corporation
Barter, Gifts, and Fees	Corporate sponsored eye clinic	Group benefits to advocates for the visually challenged, private benefits for those served, and public relations benefit for corporation
Fees, Gifts, and Government Funds	University education	Private student, group alumni, and general public benefits.

gift and the corporation also receives trade benefits in the form of visibility and goodwill that may translate into an edge in marketing. Thus, the corporate support may be considered a combination of a gift and an exchange of benefits with the nonprofit provider that offers its name and cause for identification with the corporation. In this case, both a gift and a quid pro quo are part of the overall package. Finally, in the case of university education, students benefit directly from their education for which they pay tuition, the alumni benefit from enhanced reputation of the school from which they hold their degrees and to which they are willing to donate, and the general public benefits from the increased productivity and social responsibility of college graduates for which tax-based support is justified.

The foregoing logic is the first step toward constructing a rationale for nonprofit income portfolios. So far, we have a very general logic for identifying the role of different categories of income to support particular types of nonprofit activity. Two more steps are required to make this analysis more precise. First, judgments must be made about the proportions of different kinds of benefits emanating from a given nonprofit activity. Second, one must account for the fact that most nonprofits undertake multiple activities in addressing their mission. Hence, the income combinations for each component activity must be overlaid on one another in order to determine an overall income mix for the organization as a whole. Table 15.3 describes in a nominal way how such calculations might be made.

In this table, we consider a research institute whose mission is to advance knowledge through doctoral education and research. These two types of activity generate different mixes of benefits, resulting in alternative potential income mixes supporting each one. Educational programming can be more dependent on

Table 15.3. Composite Income Portfolio of a Research Institute

	% of Budget	Fees	Gifts	Government	Barter
Education	60%	50%	30%	15%	5%
Research	40%	5%	50%	40%	5%
Overall	100%	32%	38%	25%	5%

fees, reflecting private benefits received by students, but it also produces group (alumni) and general public benefits that generate philanthropic and government support. In addition, pro bono support of corporations, in the form of teaching by corporate scientists who receive benefits of faculty status, adds a stream of trade (barter) benefits and in-kind income. The proportions of these various income forms reflect the approximate proportions of these alternative benefit streams. Overall, education reflects approximately 60 percent of the institute's total budget.

Correspondingly, the institute's research program confers a different combination of benefits, reflecting a contrasting income mix. Only 5 percent of income for this program is anticipated to derive from vendor license fees as a result of commercial products deriving from the institute's research program. Mostly the research produces group benefits associated with the institute's research foci, such as treatments and preventive strategies for particular illnesses or new technologies for communication, agriculture, or other fields, for which gifts can be effectively solicited, and public benefits deriving from general productivity gains associated with the production of new knowledge in science and on social issues. Again, a stream of in-kind support from corporations that provide equipment or the time of their scientists, in exchange for advanced knowledge of research findings, also contributes to the mix of support for research activity.

The composite income portfolio for the institute as a whole is a weighted combination of the income streams of the two principal activities of the institute. Underlying this composite is a mix of the kinds of benefits that the organization confers through its two programs. In this example, the overall mix is more balanced among the four general sources of income than either of its components. However, this is idiosyncratic to this application and merely reflects the underlying benefit combinations of the institute's services. The question of balance requires additional considerations, as discussed below. The foregoing analysis of benefits gets us to the first level—the construct of a nominal income portfolio—from which additional issues affecting balance and mix may be considered.

Fine-Tuning the Portfolio

The foregoing benefit-based analysis provides an initial foundation on which to design the income mix of a nonprofit organization because it links the benefits of mission-based services with those individuals, groups, and organizations that value those benefits and hence would be inclined to pay for them through alternative financing mechanisms. However, nothing in this approach assures the nonprofit organization that the resulting income portfolio will sustain the organization. In particular, there are four additional considerations that must be taken into account in order to gain that assurance. First, there is the issue of *feasibility*. Are there mechanisms and conditions in place to enable the proposed transactions between the organization and its beneficiaries in order to ensure that proposed income streams can actually be realized? As discussed below, the answers to this question will vary by type of income stream. Second, a nonprofit organization must consider *interactions* among alternative revenue streams, in particular the possibility that raising some types of income can reduce or magnify the potential to raise other types. If so, a nonprofit may wish to adjust its portfolio to achieve a stronger income mix. Third, the nonprofit must address the fundamental issues of *financial solvency* and *mission achievement*. If adjusted income portfolios cannot cover the cost of the projected services deriving from mission, then adjustments may be required in the mix of programming so that services offering greater potential for income support can be enhanced relative to those that lose money. Alternatively, if the adjusted income portfolio is capable of producing substantial surplus revenues, programming adjustments might be made to expand loss-making services. Fourth, there is the basic consideration of *risk management*. Once a nonprofit organization achieves an income stream that appears able to support its mission, how does it ensure that it can continue to do so into the indefinite future, taking into account the possibilities for changing environmental conditions or other unexpected contingencies over time? This is where the classic paradigm of an investment portfolio contributes to our analysis. In particular, diversification plays a key role in hedging against risk. In addition, certain forms of income, such as returns on endowment, that offer more secure or stable income streams may have a special place. Below, we address each of these considerations in turn.

Feasibility of Income Capture

A variety of factors affect the ability of a nonprofit organization to actually harvest different forms of income. In particular, the nature of the collection problem varies with the form of income. In addition, feasibility may vary with local economic, political, and social conditions.

Fee Income. The key to fee income, as discussed in chapter 5, is to be able to exclude beneficiaries unless they pay. Various factors may inhibit this capacity. Strong traditions of free service may have to be overcome. Or substantial expenditures may be required to put into place the infrastructure and financial controls to actually collect fees and avoid fraud. A nonprofit that has weaknesses in these areas may wish to de-emphasize fees in its portfolio even where it confers substantial private benefits for which recipients are capable of paying.

Charitable Contributions. A major factor in raising charitable contributions, as noted in chapter 2, is the free rider problem—the fact that group benefits come in the form of "public goods" from which exclusion may be impossible. Thus, the challenge to nonprofits seeking to raise donations is to effectively address those who benefit from its services and to convince them that the benefits they receive provide a compelling reason for their support. Essentially this means framing the quid pro quo even though free riding is possible. Nonprofits have various means to do this, including effective messages, social pressure, and enticing incentives that couple modest private benefits to contributions. Public radio offers a good example. During pledge week listeners are reminded explicitly about the value that they receive from the station's programming, they are made to feel guilty if they don't contribute their share, and they are offered discounts and other gifts when they contribute. Nonetheless, traditions of giving vary from place to place, and a nonprofit that operates in a particularly difficult fund-raising milieu may decide, despite the clarity of group benefits that it provides, to de-emphasize charitable giving in its portfolio, relative to other sources of income. A number of factors may enter into this analysis. Certain regions or communities tend to be more oriented to charitable support than others. The beneficiaries of particular types of services that generate group benefits may tend to be more generous or responsive than others. For example, despite clear group benefits of community cleanup projects, raising support for this purpose may be more difficult than for research on Alzheimer's disease.

Government Funding. Securing government funding entails yet a third set of capacities and conditions. Either government funding programs must already be in place or the nonprofit must work to create them, even if the public benefits of its work are obvious. Entering an existing government funding stream, such as reimbursement of a home health care program through Medicaid, requires the time and skill of a manager familiar with how government agencies work, as well as the staff resources to maintain proper reporting and accountability. Creating a new funding stream, for example a legislative earmark, or more ambitiously a new general service program legislated into the regular government budget, requires special political skill, resources for political advocacy, and participation in coalitions or umbrella groups that can garner the requisite broad-based support for such initiatives. A nonprofit that lacks these capacities, or which operates in a field of service where general public support is diminishing, or in a region or community where citizens favor private over public solutions, may wish to de-emphasize government funding as part of its income portfolio, despite the general public benefits that it purports to provide.

Barter. Bartering and collaborative arrangements require yet another set of capacities. For example, the extensive use of volunteers may require specialized staff with expertise in recruitment, reward systems, and other facets of human resource management. Developing productive collaborations with corporations may entail a particular capacity for sophisticated bargaining and the time and resources to explore and refine proposed arrangements in detail before serious commitments are made. Trading with other nonprofits may also necessitate significant time and resources to discuss and bargain over possibilities and arrangements. A nonprofit that lacks these capacities, even if it has unique resources and capabilities that it can offer to other groups or organizations, may wish to minimize the seeking of support through barter and collaboration.

General Concerns. Given that each type of income entails substantially different kinds of costs, capabilities, and challenges, an additional note of caution is in order. A nonprofit organization that is adept at collecting one form of income is not necessarily adept at collecting another form. A nonprofit that excels in charitable fund-raising may do quite well in supporting its group benefits with charitable contributions. However, it may be much less able to capture its private benefits through fees. A museum that has traditionally supported itself through general contributions requires a whole new administrative capacity and infrastructure to begin to collect entry fees or administer a membership program. Thus, there is an understandable and often justified resistance on the part of nonprofits to diversifying their income portfolios beyond sources for which they have demonstrated capacity and familiarity.

Finally, a concern that applies differentially to alternative forms of nonprofit income is "restrictions" on expenditures. Fee revenue is essentially unrestricted, assuming a nonprofit can find the resources to produce what it has promised in exchange. Government income can vary in its restrictions. In the case of contract or reimbursement (insurance) type income, government will normally be quite explicit about what kinds of expenses are legitimate and which are not. In the case of grants, restrictions are likely to be reflected within broad guidelines for a set of general purposes. Contributed income can be restricted or unrestricted, as donors can specify the uses for which they intend their gifts or they can give to a general fund. Similarly, donors of endowment can restrict the use of the investment returns or they can allow those returns to be used for general purposes. Finally, income in the form of barter, or in-kind goods and services, is obviously less fungible than monetary income. The general problem with restrictions on income is that they can distort what might be the most efficient or ideal income portfolio. If income flows do not precisely match expenditure needs then either output must be compromised or more income must be secured. Moreover, the income mix associated with a portfolio containing restricted components is likely to be different from an efficient portfolio whose components are unrestricted.

Income Stream Interactions

The pursuit of a targeted income portfolio mix may be complicated by the fact that different income streams may not be independent of one another. As a result, a nonprofit organization may wish to make adjustments "at the margin" which can potentially enhance its income base. There are two general ways in which these interactions may take place. First, there may be some explicit connections between alternative income streams such that changes in one lead directly to changes in another. One such connection is the phenomenon of "crowd-out" of private donations, identified as an issue in several chapters of this book. Crowd-out reflects the notion that donors may react to a nonprofit's pursuit of government or fee income by reducing their gifts (or possibly that the nonprofit becomes less aggressive in its fund-raising in these circumstances). In fact, empirical research tends to confirm this directionality. However, the possibility of "crowd-in" also exists—for example, where donors are encouraged by the enterprising behavior of a nonprofit and choose to reward it; or where the government establishes a matching program that provides donors with incentives to leverage and enlarge their gifts.

A second level of interaction exists where different income streams support underlying program activities that are substitutes or complements to one another. For example, within the category of fee income, increases in box-office revenues at a nonprofit theater may be accompanied by increases in parking and concession-stand revenues as well, since parking, refreshments, and attendance at the show are economic complements. Alternatively, if the theater decides to offer a new genre of shows, perhaps in an alternative venue, the demand for the new offering might come partially at the expense of demand for the current program. Thus, box-office revenues for the new initiative could diminish those for existing offerings, that is, the new and current offerings are economic substitutes. Such interactions within income categories can easily spill over between categories as well. For example, suppose the new initiative is supported by grants based on the group benefits provided to the local community of theater aficionados. Then the increase in grant funding may indeed lead to a decrease in fee revenues for the nonprofit overall.

How should a nonprofit adjust its nominal income portfolio to account for interaction effects? Essentially, marginal adjustments are called for. The key question for managers is the following:

> How much more overall income can be achieved through income stream A by increasing (decreasing) income stream B by a small amount, say, $10,000?

When the answer to this question is more than $10,000, it suggests that such an adjustment (to income B) should be made. When it is less, a movement in the reverse direction could be productive. When the answer is just $10,000 for each different pair of income streams, the organization can have greater assurance that its income portfolio is properly balanced, at least in the short run.

Solvency and Mission Achievement

Referring back to figure 15.1, note that the array of services and benefits upon which the nominal income portfolio is based is derived directly from a nonprofit's definition of its mission. This is entirely appropriate given the nature and purpose of nonprofit organizations. However, it does not ensure financial feasibility, given the complexities of capturing income from the different forms of benefit. Nor does it ensure that the resource strategy developed through this paradigm necessarily maximizes a nonprofit organization's mission impact. In particular, by carrying out some profitable services not directly relating to mission, a nonprofit organization may ultimately be able to be more effective in addressing its mission.

The well-known product portfolio map captures this thinking. This construction, as discussed in chapter 5 (see table 5.2), applies to nonprofit organizations that offer multiple services that differ in terms of their financial returns and impact on mission. However, it has implications for the income mix of a nonprofit as well as its programmatic portfolio. In particular, the product portfolio map need not be construed simply in terms of potential profits or losses from sales, i.e., fee revenues. If an activity has high potential for attracting donations, government support, or in-kind resources it may be just as financially "profitable" in the way that really matters to nonprofit organizations. Indeed, a service activity that can attract strong donations may be more likely to contribute to a nonprofit's mission impact than another program that generates a profit from fees. For example, a new shelter program for homeless families may generate an extraordinary level of contributions from local citizens (group benefits) such that a financial surplus is realized. Such a program would also have a direct impact on mission. Alternatively, sale of wristbands raising awareness of the homeless problem may generate net profits for the organization but it would contribute little in direct mission impact.

The adjustment of a nonprofit's nominal income portfolio to reflect mission and solvency issues may be pursued, again at the margin, using the product portfolio map as an instrument of analysis. The obvious first question to ask is whether the nominal income portfolio, reflecting the income streams derived from its mission-related service benefits (see figure 15.1), and adjusted for interaction effects and feasibility considerations, permits the organization to maintain fiscal solvency. If it cannot break even, more emphasis on financially lucrative programs and less emphasis on loss-making ones will be required. This again is an analysis at the margin. In particular, the following questions may be asked:

What is the financial impact of increasing expenditure on profitable activity A by a small amount, say, $10,000?

What is the mission-related impact of reducing expenditure on loss-making activity B by a small amount, say, $10,000?

What is the combination of impacts of the above changes together?

In the framework of the product portfolio map, activity A would be a star or cash cow, while activity B would be a saint. (Dogs should be eliminated.) If the answer to the first question is more than $10,000 in income then for financial reasons it appears worthwhile to make this additional expenditure (assuming no loss in mission effectiveness). If the answer to the second question is that a modest loss in mission impact is incurred, this may suggest a marginal retrenchment of the program in order to bring the organization closer to financial solvency. The reason the third question is important is that increasing expenditure on A may require the cutback in B. Thus, it becomes important to ask what is lost in terms of mission impact when resources are shifted from loss making to profitable activity. Overall, the nonprofit should continue to pose this question sequentially and make adjustments until the budget can be balanced.

If, instead, large financial surpluses are projected in the nominal income portfolio, examination may be given to expanding high mission contribution—loss making services (saints) and perhaps even cutting back on profitable activities (stars or cash cows), if such changes increase mission impact. In this case, the appropriate questions at the margin are as follows:

> What is the mission-related impact of increasing expenditure on loss-making activity B by a small amount, say, $10,000?
>
> What is the financial impact of decreasing expenditure on profitable activity A by a small amount, say, $10,000?
>
> What is the combination of impacts of the above changes together?

Here, if the answer to the first question is positive and substantial then part of the surplus may be justifiably spent on activity B. And if the answer to the second question is less than $10,000 then it makes sense to make this reduction, as long as substantial losses in mission impact do not accompany the change. The third question is again important if the increase in spending on A is financed by cutting back on B, though this is not necessarily the case if the organization is running a surplus.

Overall, by examining its array of services under alternative circumstances, ranging from high projected financial surpluses to high deficits, the nonprofit can determine through this analysis whether its income portfolio enables it to achieve maximum mission impact within the constraints of financial integrity.

Two additional ideas can enter this analysis as well. First, it is possible that no adjustments of the kind framed here can bring the nonprofit organization into financial solvency with its current array of programs. Thus, a variety of type A activities might be brought into consideration until a feasible combination is found. Moreover, thought can also be given to excising whole programs that are generating financial losses, especially if they are not contributing strongly to mission either.

Finally, referring back to figure 15.1, there is always the ultimate possibility of revisiting the mission of the organization in order to generate a new combination of services whose benefits can be better supported financially. In some sense this is a last resort because mission is the anchor for a nonprofit, and such an organization cannot bend too far to the financial winds without losing its way. However, social and economic conditions do change periodically, and revisiting mission in the context of strategic management makes sense from time to time. This brings us to the issue of risk management.

Risk Management

The issue of risk management has arisen in several contexts in earlier chapters. In chapter 7 on investment income by Woods Bowman, Elizabeth Keating, and Mark A. Hager and in chapter 12 on endowment by Woods Bowman, it is recognized that certain kinds of funds and their investment returns play a special role in managing risk in nonprofit finance. And certainly the particular investments that nonprofits make for their various short- and long-term funds will be driven in part by their attitudes toward, and assessment of, risks in securities markets. Second, as explained by Robert Yetman in chapter 11, there are certain inherent risks associated with debt financing. For example, debt can crowd out donations because donors may be reluctant to pay for past commitments. Moreover, borrowing is easier for purposes that generate cash, and indeed nonprofits may be pressured by creditors to increase fee income whether or not that best serves their missions.

Third, Kevin Kearns's analysis of nonprofit income portfolios in chapter 13 centers in various ways on the consideration of risk. In particular, Kearns points out several important links between the structure of a nonprofit's income portfolio and its management of risk. For instance, the composition of nonprofit income portfolios can be expected to change over time as conditions in the economy and political and social environment change. Given that many of these changes cannot be fully anticipated, Kearns (as well as Bowman) argues that a sensible risk management strategy must include establishing contingency funds. Moreover, a strategy of diversification among income streams, in addition to balancing risk with performance (return), may serve to enhance a nonprofit organization's legitimacy, as perceived by its various constituencies, rendering it less vulnerable. Adding nuance and perhaps perplexity to the latter, however, certain sources of income may confer more legitimacy than others in some circumstances, suggesting a trade-off between diversification and intensive pursuit of particular income streams. In particular, developing deep relationships with a few key funding sources can be a stabilizing influence. In general, risk plays a key role in Kearns's multiattribute utility methodology through which organizational stakeholders can jointly determine how they wish to design their overall revenue portfolios, taking risk and other considerations into account.

Finally, in chapter 14, Janet Greenlee and Howard Tuckman examine the measurement of nonprofit financial health, which inherently centers on risk. These authors, along with Kearns, point out that nonprofits face economic risks of different kinds, implying different degrees of control. Kearns distinguishes systematic from unsystematic risk, noting that nonprofits can reduce the latter but not the former, through diversification. Similarly, Greenlee and Tuckman distinguish market, industry, and firm level risk, arguing that each of these sources of risk must be managed differently. Market-level risk can be addressed through diversification of revenue streams, while industry-level risk requires diversification of product or service portfolios in order to loosen the link between the organization's fate and that of its particular field of service. Finally, firm-level risk can be addressed

by benchmarking ratio measurements and procedures and policies to ensure that the nonprofit organization is following the best
practices in its particular field.

Given this background, what further steps can be added to
the adjustment process for fine-tuning nonprofit income portfolios? At least four general thrusts are suggested. First, certain
forms of income that do not necessarily fall out from our benefit-
based paradigm can be added to the income portfolio. Second,
the degree of diversification among types of income can be adjusted to address issues of risk. Third, the numbers of income
streams within income categories might also be further diversified. Fourth, developing deeper relationships with (and possible
greater dependence on) key sources of funds may also help a nonprofit to manage risk. Each of these considerations is discussed
in turn:

Income Sources to Reduce Risk. In this chapter, investment income has been included in our theory of nonprofit finance in an
indirect way. We have recognized, for example, that such income
may derive from capital gifts from donors that are invested in the
form of endowments. As such, this income reflects the kinds of
(group) benefits corresponding to donor support. However, endowment as well as other invested funds may derive from other
sources as well, including retained earnings from commercial
ventures or operating revenues set aside for reserve or working
capital accounts.

A particular characteristic of investment income, once the
principal is in place, is that it is accrued independently of the output of a nonprofit organization. That is, it does not require the
nonprofit to produce the private, group, public, or trade benefits
which consumers, donors, government, or collaborating partners
expect in return. Rather, investment income may be considered
"fixed" in the sense that it accrues regardless of the scale of organizational activity. This attribute is helpful in managing risk
for two reasons. First, its volatility depends on factors largely
different from those affecting other types of income. Second, it
is especially helpful in addressing the particularly risky circumstance where nonprofits face high fixed costs that must be paid
for no matter how much they are able to produce or sell.

Consider the latter. Other forms of income may be divorced from output in only a limited way. Fee income obviously requires output in return, as do certain contributions for which some sort of trade benefits is expected. Normally, donors do expect output in return even if the quid pro quo is not explicit, precise, or enforceable. However, some donors may continue to contribute even after a nonprofit reduces its output drastically. In addition, some grants from government or institutional or individual donors may come in the form of general support, not tied to specific output expectations. However, it is unlikely that any of these forms, save investment income, would continue for very long in the absence of substantial activity and output over the long run. Hence the reason that investment income is helpful in managing risk is that other output-dependent forms of income can be quite variable and uncertain, and when a downturn occurs in the context of high fixed costs it can create a major financial liability. Theaters and orchestras incur the same major facility and core staff costs even when audiences decline. Schools have facilities and administrative staff to maintain even if enrollments drop, and so on.

It is not true, however, that investment income is guaranteed. Indeed, it may be argued that a nonprofit organization solely dependent on endowment income is roughly as vulnerable as a nonprofit dependent on any other single form of income. Clearly capital funds, and the investment income they generate, decline with the stock market and with downturns in the economy. Wise investment policies can reduce but not eliminate such risk. What can be said, however, is that the nature of the volatility of investment income is likely to be different from that of other sources. For example, a decline in the stock or bond markets may not coincide precisely with changes in consumer confidence that might affect fee income. And while individual donors whose funds are invested in the market may react quickly to market declines, foundation giving may experience a delayed effect due to the moving average policy that they generally use to calculate the amount of money (e.g., 5 percent of principal) that will be granted in any given year (see chapter 3). Such differentials in the volatility of alternative income sources lead us to the strategy of diversification (below).

In summary, a nonprofit, especially one with high fixed costs, that lacks substantial investment income may wish to adjust its nominal income portfolio to include an investment component. In particular, if reserve funds and working capital funds have already been set aside, the building of an endowment may make good sense (see chapter 12). However, relying solely on investment income is not an assured source of stability in and of itself.

Diversification of Income Sources. Diversification works as a risk management strategy when dissimilar income streams are combined within a portfolio so that favorable deviations in some income streams over time help to compensate or offset unfavorable deviations in other income streams, reducing overall risk. According to classical portfolio theory, *the more components in a portfolio and the less they are correlated with one another, the more effective the portfolio will be in reducing risk.* Since the five basic categories of nonprofit income—fees, donations, government funding, in-kind, and investment income—are unlikely to march in lockstep with each other over time, the more widely a nonprofit's income is spread over these categories, the more stable it is likely to be. Thus, a nonprofit with only one or two distinct sources of income in its nominal portfolio may wish to add another source in order to better manage its risks. Note that even this diversification does not eliminate risk. The *systematic* component of risk that engenders some level of volatility in all forms of nonprofit income as a result of fundamental societal changes cannot be fully eliminated through income source diversification. In addition, a nonprofit that undertakes the development of a new income source with which it is inexperienced faces a risk of failure associated with lack of competence. As observed earlier, the competence to raise charitable funds, for example, is substantially different from the expertise to invest in securities or run a commercial venture.

Diversification within Income Categories. The diversification strategy applies as well within income source categories. Certainly investment income is less vulnerable to risk if funds are invested in the securities of different companies. Indeed, some corporate foundations are particularly vulnerable because they are precluded from diversifying the company stock with which they are endowed. Similarly, risk management can be served through multiple sources of fee income, a broad spectrum of donors, a variety of corporate partnerships, a diverse array of volunteers, multiple government grants and contracts, and so on. Even within categories, particular sources are unlikely to be perfectly correlated with one another over time, yielding further opportunity to eliminate unsystematic risk.

However, as with diversification among categories, there is an important countervailing consideration within categories as well. In particular, given a nonprofit organization's finite management capacity, there may also be risk-related benefits associated with concentrating on fewer sources. Developing deeper relationships with a supporting corporation is likely to build trust, reducing the chance of surprises. Similarly, dealing with fewer government vendors allows closer monitoring of the chosen few and more success in building trustful relationships. Undertaking fewer earned income (fee based) initiatives allows managers to give closer attention to those maintained, hence greater likelihood in anticipating and coping with problems. Cultivating fewer donors on a regular basis may be more effective in maintaining a steady flow of contributions than managing a larger donor pool, and so on. In summary, nonprofits must weigh these countervailing factors in determining how far to diversify within income categories, in order to adjust their nominal income portfolios to account for their risk preferences.

Applying Theory to Practice

Taken together, the elements of the theory depicted in figure 15.1 suggest a twofold strategy for successful nonprofit financing. First, construct a nominal income portfolio based on the nature of benefits that the organization provides as a consequence of offering the services necessary to address its mission. Then make adjustments in the portfolio to account for practical management imperatives including administrative feasibility of capturing each prospective income source, interactions among income sources, financial solvency, and risk management. Following this line of thought, nonprofit finance becomes an exercise in "deal making" between the organization and its prospective resource-providing constituencies, steered by a compass whose "north" is "mission" and modulated by practical considerations to ensure organizational integrity and stability over time, at least for as long as the mission remains relevant and viable. In brief, the foregoing theory reduces to the following operating protocol for the construction and maintenance of an appropriate income mix for a nonprofit organization:

- Start with a service portfolio that addresses mission.
- Analyze the nature of benefits conferred by these services: distinguish private, group, public, and trade benefits.
- Seek income support from alternative sources in proportion with the mix of benefits. Justify resource solicitations as a quid pro quo for benefits provided. Avoid a tin cup mentality.
- Make adjustments to the income portfolio to reflect feasibility factors which may inhibit or enhance the collection of each sought form of income.
- Make adjustments to the income portfolio to reflect opportunities and problems associated with interactions among alternative income streams.
- Make adjustments to the income portfolio to ensure fiscal integrity and maximum mission impact. This may require adjustments in the service mix, particularly the balance between profitable and loss-making activity.
- Make adjustments to the income portfolio to account for risk. This may require adding additional income streams such as investment income from endowments, further diversifying the overall income mix so that it is less concentrated on a few sources, and cultivating more deeply certain income sources which show promise of stabilization through the building of trust.

These guiding principles translate directly into the following set of diagnostic questions, which the management and trustees of a nonprofit organization can use as a guide to design, revise, and adjust the financing of their organization at critical times:

- What is your mission?
- What array of services and activities is essential to effectively addressing this mission?
- Who benefits from the work of your organization? Which consumers, interest groups, segments of the general public, institutional partners, and volunteer groups?
- What are these benefits worth to those who receive them? What can consumers, donors, government agencies, institutional partners, or volunteers be asked to pay or contribute in return for them?
- What overall nominal income mix would result from the combination of these prospective payments and contributions?
- What problems can be anticipated in securing these payments? What adjustments in the income mix should be made to reflect these problems?
- How can the alternative income streams in the nominal mix be expected to interact with one another? Would changes at the margin result in greater overall income support?
- Does the nominal income mix allow the organization to break even? If not, what profitable services or activities can be introduced or expanded to close the gap? What loss-making services can be cut back without major losses of mission impact?
- What financial risks does the organization face over the foreseeable future? Can the introduction or expansion of investment income help with risks associated with large fixed costs? Can the number of diverse income sources be expanded to help reduce risk? Can sources be diversified within income categories? Can certain sources of income be cultivated more deeply to build trust and avoid future instability?

Clearly, at this stage of theory development at least, no specific formulas can be offered to guide a nonprofit in given circumstances to its particular optimal finance strategy. Certainly substantially more research is required to precisely specify and calibrate the various concepts and relationships of the general model. Even if this theory were much more well developed, however, it is clear that it would not suggest any simple "one size fits all" formulation for nonprofit finance. The best income mix for one nonprofit is not necessarily the best for another. There will be no simple ratios of fee, gift, government, investment, and in-kind income to apply for all nonprofits. Nonetheless, future research could be very helpful in developing benchmarks that might provide substantial guidance in particular subfields of activity, for nonprofits of a particular size and life stage, nonprofits located in particular kinds of settings such as large cities, suburbs, or rural areas, and nonprofits operating during different parts of the business cycle. This kind of empirical research could usefully complement theory development by offering concrete markers to nonprofits finding their way in different sorts of terrain. However, benchmark data are no substitute for the hard thinking that nonprofit leaders must do to adapt their finances to their own particular circumstances. For that process we hope the conceptual framework offered here, even in its present rudimentary state, will be helpful.

Note

1. For an earlier framework for nonprofit finance which has some parallels with our approach here, see Herzlinger (1994).

References

Albert, Stuart, and David A. Whetten. "Organizational Identity." In *Research in Organizational Behavior*, Vol. 7, edited by L. L. Cummings and B. M. Staw. Greenwich, CT: JAI Press, 1985.

Altman, Edward. "Ratios Discriminant Analysis, and the Prediction of Corporate Bankruptcy." *Journal of Finance* 23, no. 4 (1968): 589–609.

American Institute of Certified Public Accountants. *AICPA Audit and Accounting Guide: Not-for-Profit Organizations.* New York: AICPA, 1996.

American Law Institute *Restatement of the Law, Third: Trusts.* St. Paul, MN: American Law Institute, 2003.

American Society of Association Executives. *Policies and Procedures in Association Management.* Washington, DC: ASAE, 1996.

——. *Operating Ratio Report.* 12th ed. Washington, DC: ASAE, 2003.

Andreoni, James. "Giving with Impure Altruism: Applications to Charity and Ricardian Equivalence." *Journal of Political Economy* 97 (1989): 1447–58.

——. "Impure Altruism and Donations to Public Goods: A Theory of Warm-Glow Giving." *Economic Journal* 100 (1990): 467–77.

Andreoni, James, and A. Abigail Payne. "Do Government Grants to Private Charities Crowd Out Giving or Fundraising?" *American Economic Review* 93 (2003): 792–812.

Arenson, Karen W. "Bankruptcy Case May Cost Charities Heavily." *New York Times*, May 16, 1995, late edition-final, sec. A, p. 14.

Arrow, Kenneth. *Social Choice and Individual Values.* New York: Wiley, 1951.

——. "Gifts and Exchanges." *Philosophy and Public Affairs* 1 (1974): 343–62.

373

Arsenault, Jane. *Forging Nonprofit Alliances: A Comprehensive Guide to Enhancing Your Mission Through Joint Ventures and Partnerships, Management Service Organizations, Parent Corporations and Mergers.* San Francisco: Jossey Bass, 1998.

Atkinson, Anthony, Robert Kaplan, and S. Mark Young. *Management Accounting,* 4th ed. Upper Saddle River, NJ: Pearson Prentice Hall, 2004.

Austin, James E. *The Collaboration Challenge: How Nonprofits and Businesses Succeed Through Strategic Alliances.* San Francisco: Jossey Bass, 2000.

Bailey, Elizabeth E., and Ann F. Friedlander. "Market Structure and Multiproduct Industries." *Journal of Economic Literature* 20, no. 3 (1982): 1024–48.

Baruffi, Lisa J. "Take Notice: 501(c) 6 Compliance Issues." www.asaenet .org> (20 May 2005).

Bass, Gary, John Irons, and Ellen Taylor. "The Big Squeeze: Impacts of Federal Budget and Tax Policy." *Responsive Philanthropy* (Spring 2004): 6–11.

Beaver, William. "Financial Ratios as Predictors of Failure." *Journal of Accounting Research.* Supplement 4, no. 3 (1966): 71–111.

Becker, Gary. "A Theory of Social Interactions." *Journal of Political Economy* 82 (1974): 1063–93.

Beil, Richard O., and David N. Laband. "The American Economic Association Dues Structure." *Journal of Economic Perspectives* 10 (1996): 179–186.

Ben-Ner, Avner. "Obtaining Resources Using Barter Trade: Benefits and Drawbacks." Pp. 278–98 in *Nonprofit Organizations in a Mixed Economy: Understanding New Roles, Issues and Trends,* edited by David C. Hammack and Dennis R. Young. San Francisco: Jossey Bass (1993).

———. "The Shifting Boundaries of the Mixed Economy and the Future of the Nonprofit Sector." *Annals of Public and Cooperative Economics* 73, no. 1 (2002): 5–40.

Ben-Ner, Avner, and Benedetto Gui, eds. *The Nonprofit Sector in the Mixed Economy.* Ann Arbor: University of Michigan Press, 1993.

Bergman, Jed I. *Managing Change in the Nonprofit Sector.* San Francisco: Jossey Bass, 1996.

Bergquist, William, Julie Betwee, and David Meuel. *Building Strategic Relationships: How to Extend Your Organization's Reach Through Partnerships, Alliances and Joint Ventures.* San Francisco: Jossey Bass, 1995.

Berresford, Susan V. "Collaboration: Models, Benefits, and Tensions." Pp. 137–46 in *An Agile Servant: Community Leadership by Community*

Foundations, edited by Richard Magat. Washington, D.C.: Council on Foundations, 1989.

Bielefeld, Wolfgang. "Nonprofit Funding Environment Relations." *Voluntas* 3, no. 1 (1992): 48–70.

Blattberg, Robert C., and Cynthia J. Broderick. "Marketing of Art Museums." Pp. 327–46 in *The Economics of Art Museums*, edited by Martin Feldstein. Chicago: University of Chicago Press, 1991.

Blum, Walter J., and Harry Kalven Jr. *The Uneasy Case for Progressive Taxation*. Chicago: University of Chicago Press, 1953.

Bolman, Lee, and Terrance Deal. *Reframing Organizations: Artistry, Choice, and Leadership*. San Francisco: Jossey Bass, 1997, 99–262.

Boraas, Stephanie. "Volunteerism in the United States." *Monthly Labor Review* (August 2003).

Boris, Elizabeth T. "The Nonprofit Sector in the 1990s." In *Philanthropy and the Nonprofit Sector in a Changing America*, edited by Charles Clotfelter and Thomas Ehrlich. Bloomington: Indiana University Press, 1987.

———. "Organizations in a Democracy: Varied Roles and Responsibilities." Pp. 1–33 in *Nonprofits and Government: Collaboration and Conflict*, edited by Elizabeth T. Boris and C. Eugene Steuerle. Washington, D.C.: Urban Institute Press, 1999.

———. "Scope and Dimensions of the Nonprofit Sector." Pp. 66–88 in *Nonprofit Sector: A Research Handbook*, 2nd ed., edited by Richard Steinberg and Walter W. Powell. New Haven, CT: Yale University Press, 2006.

Boris, Elizabeth T., and C. Eugene Steuerle, eds. *Nonprofits and Government: Collaboration and Conflict*. Washington, D.C.: Urban Institute Press, 1999.

Bourgeois, L. J., and J. V. Singh. "Organizational Slack and Political Behavior within Top Management Teams." *Academy of Management Proceedings* (1983): 43–47.

Bowen, William G., Thomas I. Nygren, Sarah E. Turner, and Elizabeth Duffy. *The Charitable Nonprofits*. San Francisco: Jossey Bass, 1994.

Bowman, Susanne Connors. "Member Research: An Ingredient to Be Added to the Recipe for a Successful Dues Increase." 2004. www.asaenet.org/asae/cda/generic_pf/1,589,PID21033,00.html> (20 May 2005).

Bowman, Woods. "The Uniqueness of Nonprofit Finance and the Decision to Borrow." *Nonprofit Management and Leadership* (Spring 2002): 293–312.

Bowman, Woods, Elizabeth K. Keating, and Mark A. Hager. "Organizational Slack in Nonprofits" (paper presented to the Academy of Management at Honolulu, Hawaii, August 9, 2005).

Bradley, Bill, Paul Jansen, and Les Silverman. "The Nonprofit Sector's $100 Billion Opportunity." *Harvard Business Review* 81, no. 5 (2003): 94–103.

Brams, Steven J., and Alan D. Taylor. *Fair Division: From Cake-Cutting to Dispute Resolution.* New York: Cambridge University Press, 1996.

Braude, Jacob M. *Lifetime Speaker's Encyclopedia: Vol. 1.* Englewood Cliffs, NJ: Prentice-Hall, 1962.

Brigham, Eugene, and Michael Ehrhardt. *Financial Management.* Austin, TX: Harcourt Publishers, 2004.

Brody, Evelyn, ed. *Property-Tax Exemption for Charities.* Washington, D.C.: Urban Institute Press, 2002.

Brody, Evelyn, and Joseph J. Cordes. "Tax Treatment of Nonprofit Organizations: A Two-Edged Sword?" Pp. 141–75 in *Nonprofits and Government: Collaboration and Conflict*, edited by Elizabeth T. Boris and C. Eugene Steuerle. Washington, D.C.: Urban Institute Press, 1999.

Brooks, Arthur C. "Is There a Dark Side to Government Support for Nonprofits?" *Public Administration Review* 60, no. 3 (2000): pp. 211–18.

———. "Welfare Receipt and Private Charity." *Public Budgeting and Finance* (Fall 2002a): 100–13.

———. "Does Civil Society Stop the Downward Spiral of Bad Government or Speed It Up?" *Nonprofit and Voluntary Sector Quarterly* 31, no. 1 (2002b): 139–43.

———. "Charitable Giving to Humanitarian Organizations in Spain." *Hacienda Pública Española/Revista de Economía Pública (Spanish Journal of Public Economics)* 165, no. 2 (2003a): 9–24.

———. "Do Government Subsidies to Nonprofits Crowd Out Donations or Donors?" *Public Finance Review* 31, no. 2 (2003b): 166–179.

———. "Taxes, Subsidies, and Listeners Like You: Public Policy and Contributions to Public Radio." *Public Administration Review* 63, no. 3 (2003c): 554–561.

———. "The Effects of Public Policy on Private Charity." *Administration and Society* 36, no. 2 (2004a): 166–85.

———. "In Search of True Public Arts Support." *Public Budgeting and Finance* 24, no. 2, (2004b): 88–100.

Brown, Eleanor. "The Scope of Volunteer Activity and Public Service." *Law and Contemporary Problems* 62, no. 4 (Autumn 1999a).

———. "Assessing the Value of Volunteer Activity." *Nonprofit and Voluntary Sector Quarterly* 28, no. 1 (March 1999b): 3–17.

Brown, Eleanor, and Al Slivinski. "Nonprofit Organizations and the Market." Pp. 140–58 in *The Nonprofit Sector: A Research Handbook*, 2nd ed., edited by Walter Powell and Richard Steinberg. New Haven, CT: Yale University Press, 2006.

Brown, Melissa, and Patrick Rooney. "Indexing Giving: Examining State-Level Data about Itemized Charitable Deductions Using Known Determinants of Giving" (paper presented at ARNOVA, Washington, D.C., 2005).

Brudney, Jeffrey L., and William D. Duncombe. "An Economic Evaluation of Paid, Volunteer, and Mixed Staffing Options for Public Services." *Public Administration Review* 5, no. 52 (1992): 474–81.

Cain, Louis, and Dennis Merritt Jr. "Zoos and Aquariums." Pp. 217–32 in *To Profit or Not to Profit*, edited by Burton Weisbrod. New York: Cambridge University Press, 1998.

Carey, Stephen C. "Use of Association Dues Discounts, Incentives and Rewards." *The Canadian Association e-zine.* <*www.axi.ca/tca*> (January 2005).

Carlson-Thies, S. W. "Implementing the Faith-Based Initiative." *The Public Interest*, no. 155 (Spring 2004): 57–74.

Center for Philanthropy at Indiana University. *Philanthropic Giving Index (PGI)*, 2004.

Chang, Cyril, and Howard Tuckman. "Financial Vulnerability and Attrition as Measures of Nonprofit Performance." *Annals of Public and Cooperative Economics* 62, no. 4 (1991): 655–72.

———. "Revenue Diversification Among Nonprofits." *Voluntas* 5, no. 3 (1994): pp. 273–290.

Chaves, Mark. "Religious Congregations." Pp. 275–98 in *The State of Nonprofit America*, edited by Lester M. Salamon. Washington, D.C.: Brookings Institution Press, 2002.

Clary, E. Gil, Mark Snyder, and Arthur A Stukas. "Volunteers' Motivations: Findings from a National Survey." *Nonprofit and Voluntary Sector Quarterly* (1996): 485–505.

Commonfund. *Commonfund Benchmarks Study: Educational Endowment Report*. Wilton, CT: Commonfund, 2004.

Congressional Budget Office. "Taxing the Untaxed Business Sector." Background paper, 2005.

Connor, Joseph A., Stephanie Kadel-Taras, and Diane Vinokur-Kaplan. "The Role of Nonprofit Management Support Organizations in Sustaining Community Collaborations." *Nonprofit Management and Leadership* 10, no. 2 (1999): 127–36.

Cordes, Joseph J., Marie Gantz, and Thomas Pollak. "What Is the Property-Tax Exemption Worth?" Pp. 81–114 in *Property-Tax Exemption for Charities*, edited by Evelyn Brody. Washington, D.C.: Urban Institute, 2002.

Cordes, Joseph J., and Burton A. Weisbrod. "Differential Taxation of Nonprofits and the Commercialization of Nonprofit Revenues." Pp. 81–114 in *To Profit or Not to Profit*, edited by Burton Weisbrod. New York: Cambridge University Press, 1998.

Core, John E., Wayne R. Guay, and Rodrigo S. Verdi. "Agency Problems of Excess Endowment Holdings in Not-For-Profit Firms." Available at SSRN: <ssrn.com/abstract=565241> (2005).

Cornes, Richard, and Todd Sandler. "Easy Riders, Joint Production, and Public Goods." *Economic Journal* 94 (1984): 580–98.

Crimmins, James C., and Mary Keil. *Enterprise in the Nonprofit Sector*. New York: Partners for Livable Places and the Rockefeller Brothers Fund, 1983.

Cummings, Jean L., and Denise DiPasquale. "The Low-Income Housing Tax Credit: An Analysis of the First Ten Years." *Housing Policy Debate* 10, no. 2 (1999): 251–307.

Cyert, R., and J. March. *A Behavioral Theory of the Firm*. Cambridge, MA: Blackwell, 1963.

Danzig, Lisa, and Jennifer Neel. "Debt Issuance Following Repeal of the Tax-Exempt Cap." *Standard & Poor's View on Higher Education* 3 (1998): 4–5.

Davis, Roger. *Borrowing with Tax-Exempt Bonds*. San Francisco: Orrick, Herrington, and Sutcliffe, LLP, 2001.

Day, Kathleen M., and Rose Anne Devlin. "Volunteerism and Crowding Out: Canadian Econometric Evidence." *Canadian Journal of Economics* 29, no. 1 (1996): 37–53.

Deb, Partha, Mark O. Wilhelm, Patrick M. Rooney, and Melissa S. Brown. "Estimating Charitable Deductions in Giving USA." *Nonprofit and Voluntary Sector Quarterly* 32 (2003): 548–67.

Dees, J. Gregory. "Putting Nonprofit Business Ventures in Perspective." Pp. 3–18 in *Generating and Sustaining Earned Income*, edited by Sharon M. Oster, Cynthia W. Massarsky, and Samantha L. Beinhacker. San Francisco: Jossey Bass, 2004.

DiIulio, John C., Jr. "Getting Faith-Based Programs Right." *The Public Interest*, no. 155 (Spring 2004): 75–88.

Dionne Jr., E. J., and Ming Hsu Chen, eds. *Sacred Places, Civic Purposes*. Washington, D.C.: Brookings Institution, 2001.

DiRusso, Alyssa A., and Kathleen M. Sablone. "Statutory Techniques for

Balancing the Financial Interests of Trust Beneficiaries." *University of San Francisco Law Review* 39, no. 2 (2005): 261–318.

Downes, John, and Jordan Elliott Goodman. *Finance and Investment Handbook* (4th ed.). Hauppauge, NY: Barron's, 1995.

Duizendstraal, Anton, and Andries Nentjes. "Organizational Slack in Subsidized Nonprofit Institutions." *Public Choice* 81, no. 3–4 (December 1994): 297–321.

Dunn, William. *Public Policy Analysis*. Englewood Cliffs, NJ: Prentice-Hall, 1981.

Eckel, Catherine C., and Richard Steinberg. "Competition, Performance, and Public Policy Toward Nonprofits." Pp. 57–81 in *Nonprofit Organizations in a Mixed Economy: Understanding New Roles, Issues and Trends*, edited by David C. Hammack and Dennis R. Young. San Francisco: Jossey Bass, 1993.

Ehrenberg, Ronald G. *Tuition Rising: Why College Costs So Much.* Cambridge, MA: Harvard University Press, 2000.

Emanuel, Rosemarie. "Is There a Downward Sloping Demand for Volunteer Labor?" *Annals of Public and Cooperative Economics* 67, no. 2 (1996): 193–208.

Feldstein, Martin, ed. *The Economics of Art Museums*. Chicago: University of Chicago Press, 1991.

Fischel, William A. "Homevoters, Municipal Corporate Governance, and the Benefit View of the Property Tax." *National Tax Journal* 54, no. 1 (March 2001): 157–73.

Fisher, Roger, and William Ury. *Getting to Yes: Negotiating Agreement Without Giving In*. Middlesex, UK: Penguin, 1991.

Foster, Mary K., and Agnes G. Meinhard. "A Regression Model Explaining Predisposition to Collaborate." *Nonprofit and Voluntary Sector Quarterly* 31, no. 4 (2002): 549–64.

Foster, William, and Jeffrey Bradach. "Should Nonprofits Seek Profits?" *Harvard Business Review* (February 2005): 92–100.

Foundation Center. *Researching Philanthropy*. Foundation Center Statistics. 2005. <fdncenter.org/fc_stats/index.html>.

Frank, Frank H., Thomas Gilovich, and Dennis T. Regan. "Does Studying Economics Inhibit Cooperation?" *Journal of Economic Perspectives* 7 (1993): 159–71.

Franks, J., and W. Tourous. "An Empirical Investigation of U.S. Firms in Reorganization." *Journal of Finance* 44, no. 3 (1989): 747–69.

Freeman, Richard B. "Working for Nothing: The Supply of Volunteer Labor." *Journal of Labor Economics* 15, no. 1, part 2 (January 1997): S140–S166.

Fremont-Smith, Marion. *Accumulation of Wealth by Nonprofits*. Emerging Issues in Philanthropy Seminar Series: A joint project of the Urban Institute and the Hauser Center. Washington, D.C.: 2002.

———. *Governing Nonprofit Organizations: Federal and State Law and Regulation*. Cambridge, MA: Belknap Press of Harvard University Press, 2004.

Frengel, Elizabeth (quoting Peter DiTeresa). "Demystifying the Mutual Fund, Part 2." May 7, 2005. <www.kiplinger.com/basics/archives/2002/demystify2.html>.

Froelich, Karen A. "Diversification of Revenue Strategies: Evolving Resource Dependence in Nonprofit Organizations." *Nonprofit and Voluntary Sector Quarterly* 28, no. 3 (September 1999): 246–68.

Frumkin, Peter. *On Being Nonprofit*. Cambridge: Harvard University Press, 2002.

Frumkin, Peter, and Elizabeth Keating. "The Effectiveness of Regulating Governance: The Case of Executive Compensation In Nonprofit Organizations." Working paper, Hauser Center. Cambridge, MA: Harvard University, 2004.

Galaskiewicz, Joseph. "Growth, Decline, and Organizational Strategies: A Panel Study of Nonprofit Organizations, 1980–1988." Washington, D.C.: Independent Sector, 1990.

Galaskiewicz, Joseph, and Wolfgang Bielefeld. *Nonprofit Organizations in an Age of Uncertainty*. New York: Aldine de Gruyter, 1998.

Galper, Harvey, and Eric Toder. "Owning or Leasing: Bennington College and the U.S. Tax System." *National Tax Journal* 36, no. 2 (June 1983): 257–61.

Gentry, William. "Debt, Investment, and Endowment Accumulation: The Case of Not-for-Profit Hospitals." *Journal of Health Economics* (2002): 845–72.

Gifts-in-Kind, International. <www.giftsinkind.org>.

Gilbert, Lisa, Krishnagopal Menon, and Kenneth Schwartz. "Predicting Bankruptcy for Firms in Financial Distress." *Journal of Business Finance and Accounting* 14, no. 1 (1990): 167–71.

Giving USA 2003 (researched and written by the Center on Philanthropy at Indiana University). Indianapolis: AAFRC Trust for Philanthropy, 2003.

Giving USA 2004 (researched and written by the Center on Philanthropy at Indiana University). Glenview, IL: AAFRC Trust for Philanthropy, 2004a.

Giving USA Update Spring 2004 (researched and written by the Center on Philanthropy at Indiana University). Glenview, IL: AAFRC Trust for Philanthropy, 2004b.

Giving USA Update Summer 2004 (researched and written by the Center on Philanthropy at Indiana University). Glenview, IL: AAFRC Trust for Philanthropy, 2004c.

Giving USA 2005 (researched and written by the Center on Philanthropy at Indiana University). Glenville, IL: Giving USA Foundation, 2005.

Glaser, Barney, and Anselm Strauss. *The Discovery of Grounded Theory.* Hawthorne, NY: Aldine, 1967.

Glazer, Amihai, and Kai Konrad. "A Signaling Explanation for Charity." *American Economic Review* 86 (1996): 1019–28.

Goodwill Industries. <www.goodwill.org.>

Gramlich, Edward M. *Benefit-Cost Analysis of Government Programs.* Englewood Cliffs, NJ: Prentice-Hall, 1981.

Gray, Charles M. "Gifts in Kind and Cash Donations: Substitutes? Or Complements?" Working paper, University of St. Thomas, 2006.

Greenlee, Janet, and David Bukovinsky. "Financial Ratios for Use in Analytical Review of Charitable Organizations." *The Ohio CPA Journal* (January–March 1998): 32–38.

Greenlee, Janet, and John Trussel. "Predicting the Financial Vulnerability of Charitable Organizations." *Nonprofit Management and Leadership* 11, no. 2 (2000): 199–210.

Grønbjerg, Kirsten A. "Nonprofit Human Service Organizations Funding Strategies and Patterns of Adaptation." In *Human Services as Complex Organizations*, edited by Yeheskel Hasenfel. Newbury Park, CA: Sage, 1992.

———. *Understanding Nonprofit Funding: Managing Revenues in Social Services and Community Development Organizations.* San Francisco: Jossey Bass, 1993.

Grønbjerg, Kirsten A., and Richard Clerkin. "Indiana Nonprofits: Managing Financial and Human Resources." Working paper, August 2004.

Grønbjerg, Kirsten A., and Lester M. Salamon. "Devolution, Marketization, and the Changing Shape of Government-Nonprofit Relations." In *The State of Nonprofit America*, edited by Lester Salamon. Washington, D.C.: Brookings Institution Press, 2002.

Guthrie, Kevin M. *The New-York Historical Society: Lessons from One Nonprofit's Long Struggle for Survival.* San Francisco: Jossey Bass, 1996.

Hager, Mark A. "Financial Vulnerability among Arts Organizations: A Test of the Tuckman-Chang Measures." *Nonprofit and Voluntary Sector Quarterly* 30, no. 2 (2001): 376–92.

Hager, Mark A., Joseph Galaskiewicz, and Wolfgang Bielefeld. "Tales from the Grave: Organizations' Account of Their Own Demise." *The American Behavioral Scientist* 39, no. 8 (1996): 975–94.

Hager, Mark A., and Thomas Pollak. "Haves and Have-Nots: Investment Capital among Performing Arts Organizations in the United States." *International Journal of Arts Management* 6, no. 2 (2004): 54–65.

Hager, Mark A., Thomas Pollak, and Patrick Rooney. "Variations in the Cost of Fundraising in Nonprofits." Working Paper. 2001. <www.coststudy.org>.

Hager, Mark A., Patrick M. Rooney, and Thomas H. Pollak. "How Fundraising Is Carried Out in U.S. Nonprofit Organisations." *International Journal of Nonprofit and Voluntary Sector Marketing* 7, no. 4 (2002): 311–324.

Hammack, David C., and Dennis R. Young, eds. *Nonprofit Organizations in a Market Economy*. San Francisco: Jossey Bass, 1993.

Hansmann, Henry B. "The Role of Nonprofit Enterprise." *Yale Law Journal* 89 (1980): 835–901.

———. "Nonprofit Enterprises in the Performing Arts." *Bell Journal of Economics* 12 (1981): 341–61.

———. "Economic Theories of Nonprofit Organizations." In *The Nonprofit Sector: A Research Handbook*, edited by Walter W. Powell. New Haven, CT: Yale University Press, 1987.

———. "Unfair Competition and the Unrelated Business Income Tax." *Virginia Law Review* 75, no. 3 (April 1989): 605–35.

———. "Why Do Universities Have Endowments?" *Journal of Legal Studies* 19, no. 1 (1990): 3–42.

Harbaugh, William T. "The Prestige Motive for Making Charitable Transfers." *American Economic Review, Papers and Proceedings* 88, no. 2 (1998a): 277–82.

———. "What Do Donations Buy?" *Journal of Public Economics* 67, no. 2 (1998b): 269–84.

Harris, Milton, and Artur Raviv. "The Theory of Capital Structure." *The Journal of Finance* (1990): 297–355.

Hart, Oliver, Andrei Shleifer, and Robert W. Vishny. "The Proper Scope of Government: Theory and an Application to Prisons." *Quarterly Journal of Economics* 112, no. 4 (November 1997): 1127–61.

Havens, John J., and Paul G. Schervish. "Millionaires and the Millennium: New Estimates of the Forthcoming Wealth Transfer and the Prospects for a Golden Age of Philanthropy." Center on Wealth and Philanthropy, Boston College, 1994. <www.bc.edu/cwp>.

———. "Why the $41 Trillion Wealth Transfer Is Still Valid: A Review of Challenges and Questions." The National Committee on Planned Giving. *The Journal of Gift Planning* 7, no. 1 (1st Quarter 2003): 11–15, 47–50.

Havens, John, Mary O'Herlihy, and Paul Schervish. "Charitable Giving: How Much, by Whom, to What, and How." In *The Nonprofit Sector: A Research Handbook*, 2nd ed., edited by Richard Steinberg and Walter W. Powell. New Haven, CT: Yale University Press, 2006.

Havens, John, and Paul G. Schervish. "Wealth and Commonwealth: New Findings on Wherewithal and Philanthropy." *Nonprofit and Voluntary Sector Quarterly* 30, no. 1 (March 2001): 5–25.

Hedley, Barry. "Strategy and the Business Portfolio." *Long Range Planning* 10, no. 1 (1977): 9–15.

Heilbrun, James, and Charles M. Gray. *The Economics of Art and Culture.* 2nd ed. New York: Cambridge University Press, 2001.

Helms, Lelia, Alan B. Henkin, and Kyle Murray. "Playing by the Rules: Restricted Endowment Assets in Colleges and Universities." *Nonprofit Management and Leadership* 15, no. 3 (2005): 341–56.

Henderson, J. Vernon. "Property Tax Incidence with a Public Sector." *Journal of Political Economy* 93, no. 4 (August 1985): 648–65.

Herzlinger, Regina E. "Effective Oversight: A Guide for Nonprofit Directors." *Harvard Business Review* (July–August 1994): 52–60.

Hines, James Jr. "Non-Profit Business Activity and the Unrelated Business Income Tax." *Tax Policy and the Economy* 13 (1999): 54–84.

Hodgkinson, Virginia A., Kathryn Nelson, and Edward D. Sivak Jr. "Individual Giving and Volunteering." Pp. 387–420 in *The State of Nonprofit America*, edited by Lester Salamon. Washington, D.C.: Brookings Institution Press, 2002.

Holtman, A. G. "A Theory of Non-Profit Firms." *Economica* 50 (1983): 439–49.

Hughes, Patricia, and William Luksetich. "The Relationship among Funding Sources for Arts and History Museums." *Nonprofit Management and Leadership* 10, no. 1 (1999): 21–37.

Hyde, Lewis. *The Gift: Imagination and the Erotic Life of Property.* New York: Vintage Books, 1983.

Independent Sector. *Giving and Volunteering in the U.S.: Findings from a National Survey.* Washington, D.C.: Independent Sector, 1996.

———. *Giving and Volunteering in the United States.* Washington, D.C.: Independent Sector, 2001.

———. *Volunteering in the United States.* Washington, D.C.: Independent Sector, 2005.

Indianapolis Gives 2005. Center on Philanthropy at Indiana University, 2005.

Internal Revenue Service. *Tax-Exempt Bonds for 501(c)(3) Charitable Organizations*, Pub. 4077. Washington D.C., 2004.

———. *IRS 990 Instructions.* 2004. <www.irs.gov/instructions/i990-ez/ar02.html>.

———. *Charitable Donations, Publication 526* (Rev. December 2003).

———. *A Charity's Guide to Car Donations, Publication 4302* (nd).

———. *Determining the Value of Donated Property, Publication 561* (Rev. February 2000).

———. *A Donor's Guide to Car Donations, Publication 4303* (nd).

Irvin, Renee A., and John Stansbury. "Citizen Participation in Decision Making: Is It Worth the Effort?" *Public Administration Review* 64, no. 1 (2004): 55–65.

Jacobs, Jerald A. "Setting Nonmember Fees for Association Services." 2005. <www.asaenet.org/asae/cda/index/1,1584,PID17742,00.html>.

James, Estelle. "Product Mix and Cost Disaggregation: A Reinterpretation of the Economics of Higher Education." *Journal of Human Resources* (Spring 1978): 157–186.

———. "Cost, Benefit and Envy: Alternative Measures of the Redistributive Effects of Higher Education." Pp. 121–41 in *Subsidies to Higher Education,* edited by H. Tuckman and E. Whalen. Westport, CT: Praeger, 1980.

———. "How Nonprofits Grow: A Model." *Journal of Policy Analysis and Management* (Spring 1983): 350–65.

———. "Cross Subsidization in Higher Education: Does It Pervert Private Choice and Public Policy?" In *Private Education: Studies in Choice and Public Policy,* edited by Daniel Levy. New York: Oxford University Press, 1986.

———. "The Nonprofit Sector in Comparative Perspective." Pp. 397–415 in *The Nonprofit Sector: A Research Handbook,* edited by Walter W. Powell. New Haven, CT: Yale University Press, 1987.

———. "Commercialism among Nonprofits: Objectives, Opportunities, and Constraints." Pp. 271–85 in *To Profit or Not to Profit,* edited by Burton A. Weisbrod. New York: Cambridge University Press, 1998.

James, Estelle, and Egon Neuberger. "The Academic Department as a Non-Profit Labor Cooperative." *Public Choice* (1981): 585–612.

James, Estelle, and Susan Rose-Ackerman. "The Nonprofit Enterprise in Market Economies." Monograph. In *Fundamentals of Pure and Applied Economics and Encyclopedia of Economics,* edited by J. Lesourne and H. Sonnenschein. London: Harwood Academic Publishers, 1986.

Kanter, Rosabeth Moss. "Collaborative Advantage: The Art of Alliances." *Harvard Business Review* (July–August 1994): 96–108.

Kearns, Kevin P. "The Analytic Hierarchy Process and Policy Argumentation." In *Policy Analysis: Perspectives, Concepts and Methods*, edited by W. N. Dunn. Greenwich, CT: JAI Press, 1986.

————. "Innovations in Local Government: A Sociocognitive Network Approach," *Knowledge and Policy* 5, no. 2 (1992a): 45–67.

————. "From Comparative Advantage to Damage Control: Clarifying Strategic Issues Using SWOT Analysis." *Nonprofit Management and Leadership* 3, no. 1 (1992b): 3–25.

————. "Attributes of Nonprofit Board Members as Perceived by Chief Executives and Board Chairpersons." *Nonprofit Management and Leadership* 5, no. 4 (1995): 337–58.

————. *Private Sector Strategies for Social Sector Success*. San Francisco: Jossey Bass, 2000.

Keating, Elizabeth, Mary Fischer, Teresa Gordon, and Janet Greenlee. "Assessing Financial Vulnerability in the Nonprofit Sector." Hauser Center for Nonprofit Organizations Paper No. 27, working paper, 2005.

Keeney, Ralph, and Howard Raiffa. *Decisions with Multiple Objectives: Preferences and Value Tradeoffs*. New York: Wiley, 1976.

Kelly, George. *The Psychology of Personal Constructs*, Vol. 1. New York: Norton, 1955.

Kingma, Bruce. "Do Profits 'Crowd Out' Donations or Vice Versa? The Impact of Revenues from Sales on Donations to Local Chapter of the American Red Cross." *Nonprofit Management and Leadership* 6 (1995): 21–38.

Kirp, David L. *Shakespeare, Einstein and the Bottom Line*. Cambridge: Harvard University Press, 2003.

Knickmeyer, Lisa, Karen Hopkins, and Megan Meyer. "Exploring Collaboration among Urban Neighborhood Associations." *Journal of Community Practice* 11, no. 2 (2003): 13–25.

Konrad, Peter, and Alys Novak. *Financial Management for Nonprofits: Keys to Success*. Denver: Regis University School of Professional Studies, 2000.

Krebs, Valdis, and June Holley. "Building Sustainable Communities Through Social Network Development." *Nonprofit Quarterly* 11, no. 1 (2004): 46–53.

Kroll, Mark, and Stephen Caples. "Managing Acquistions of Strategic Business Units with the Aid of the Arbitrage Pricing Model." *Academy of Management Review* (October 1987): 676–85.

Laband, David N., and Richard O. Beil. "Are Economists More Selfish Than Other 'Social' Scientists?" *Public Choice* 100 (1999): 85–101.

Lee, Felicia. "Endowment Doubles for Brooklyn Academy." *New York Times*, October 5, 2004, B1, B7.

Levin, Mark. "Selling a Dues Increase." *Association Management*, 1992. Reprinted in *Association Dues* (Washington, D.C.: American Society of Association Executive, 1999): 91–94.

Light, Paul C. *Sustaining Nonprofit Performance*. Washington, D.C.: Brookings Institution Press, 2004.

Lubell, Mark. "Collaborative Environmental Institutions: All Talk and No Action?" *Journal of Policy Analysis and Management* 23, no. 3 (2004): 549–73.

Malpezzi, Stephen, and Kerry Vandell. "Does the Low-Income Housing Tax Credit Increase the Supply of Housing?" *Journal of Housing Economics* 11 (2002): 360–80.

Mansfield, Edwin. *Microeconomics: Theory and Applications*, 7th ed. New York: W. W. Norton, 1991.

Markowitz, Harry. "Portfolio Selection." *Journal of Finance* 1, no. 77 (1952): 77–91.

Mason, David E. *Leading and Managing the Expressive Dimension: Harnessing the Hidden Power Source of the Nonprofit Sector*. San Francisco: Jossey Bass, 1996.

Massarsky, Cynthia, and Samantha L. Beinhacker. "Enterprising Nonprofits: Revenue Generation in the Nonprofit Sector." New Haven, CT: Yale School of Management—The Goldman Sachs Foundation Partnership on Nonprofit Ventures. Working paper, 2002.

Mattessich, Paul W., Marta Murray-Close, and Barbara R. Monsey. *Collaboration: What Makes It Work?* 2nd ed. Wilder Foundation. St. Paul, MN: Amherst H. Wilder Foundation 2001.

McCarthy, Kathleen D. *American Creed*. Chicago: University of Chicago Press, 2003.

McLaughlin, Thomas A. *Nonprofit Mergers and Alliances: A Strategic Guide*. New York: John Wiley & Sons, 1998.

Memphis Gives 2003. Center on Philanthropy at Indiana University, 2003.

Menchik, Paul, and Burton Weisbrod. "Volunteer Labor Supply." *Journal of Public Economics* 32 (1987): 159–83.

Merrill, G. Lawrence. "Enhance Member Satisfaction through 'Fair' Dues." *A Sharing of Expertise and Experience 11*. Washington, D.C.: ASAE, 1993.

Mieszkowski, Peter, and George R. Zodrow. "Taxation and the Tiebout Model: The Differential Effects of Head Taxes, Taxes on Land Rents, and Property Taxes." *Journal of Economic Literature* 27, no. 3 (September 1989): 1098–1146.

Miller, Clara. "Hidden in Plain Sight: Understanding Nonprofit Capital Structure." *The Nonprofit Quarterly* (Spring 2003): 1–8.

Minkoff, Debra C., and Walter W. Powell. "Nonprofit Mission: Constancy, Responsiveness, or Deflection." *The Nonprofit Sector: A Research Handbook*, 2nd ed., edited by Walter W. Powell and Richard Steinberg. New Haven, CT: Yale University Press, 2006.

Mintzberg, Henry. *The Rise and Fall of Strategic Planning*. New York: Free Press, 1994.

Mitroff, Ian I., and James R. Emshoff. "On Strategic Assumption Making: A Dialectical Approach to Policy and Planning." *Academy of Management Review* 4, no. 1 (1979): 1–12.

Monsma, Stephen, and Carolyn Mounts. "Working Faith: How Religious Organizations Provide Welfare-to-Work Services." Working paper, Center for Research on Religion and Urban Civil Society, 2001.

Moulin, Hervè, and Yves Sprumont. "Responsibility and Cross-Subsidization in Cost Sharing." Houston, TX: Rice University Department of Economics. Working paper, 2002.

Muirhead, Sophia A. *The 2005 Corporate Contributions Report, Report Number R-1381-05-RR*. New York: The Conference Board, December 2005.

National Center for Charitable Statistics. *NCCS Data Guide*. 2005. <nccsdataweb.urban.org/kbfiles/468/NCCSdataguidev3a.pdf>.

National Association for the Exchange of Industrial Resources. <www.naeir.org.>.

National Committee on Planned Giving (NCPG). 2001. "Survey of donors 2000." <www.ncpg.org>.

———. *Guide to Using NCCS Data*. 2005. <nccsdataweb.urban. org/kbfiles/468/NCCS-data-guide-v3a.pdf>.

National Council on Aging. March 2005. "Respect Ability Web Survey Executive Summary." <www.respectability.org/research/survey.pdf.> (6 July 2005).

Nelson, Donald T., and Paul H. Schneiter. *Gifts-in-Kind*. Rockville, MD: Fund Raising Institute, 1991.

Netzer, Dick. "Local Government Finance and the Economics of Property-Tax Exemption." Pp. 47–80 in *Property-Tax Exemption for Charities*, edited by Evelyn Brody. Washington, D.C.: Urban Institute Press, 2002.

New Hampshire Gives 2005. Center on Philanthropy at Indiana University, 2005.

Newman, Diana S. *Endowment Building*. Hoboken, NJ: John Wiley & Sons, 2005.

Niehans, Jurg. "Money and Barter in General Equilibrium with Transactions Costs." *American Economic Review* 61 (1971): 773–83.

Nielsen, Waldemar. *The Golden Donors.* New York: Truman Talley Books, 1985.

Niskanen, William. *Bureaucracy and Representative Government.* Chicago: Aldine Publishing Company, 1971.

Odendahl, Theresa. *Charity Begins at Home: Generosity and Self-Interest among the Philanthropic Elite.* New York: Basic Books, 1990.

OED. *Oxford English Dictionary Online* (2nd ed.). 1989. <http://dictionary.oed.com>.

Ohlin, Bertil. *Interregional and International Trade.* Cambridge, MA: Harvard University Press, 1933.

Ohlson, James. "Financial Ratios and the Probabilistic Prediction of Bankruptcy." *Journal of Accounting Research* 18, no. 1 (1980): 109–31.

Okten, Cagla, and Burton Weisbrod. "Determinants of Donations in Private Nonprofit Markets." *Journal of Public Economics* (February 2000): 255–72.

Olsen, Edgar O. "Fundamental Housing Policy Reform." Working paper, Department of Economics, University of Virginia, November 2003.

Olson, David. *Decision Aids for Selection Problems.* New York: Springer, 1996.

Olson, Mancur. *The Logic of Collective Action: Public Goods and the Theory of Groups.* Cambridge, MA: Harvard University Press, 1965.

O'Neill, Paul. *Nonprofit Nation: A New Look at the Third America.* San Francisco: Jossey Bass, 2002.

O'Regan, Katherine, and Sharon Oster. "Does Government Funding Alter Nonprofit Governance? Evidence from New York City Nonprofit Contractors." *Journal of Policy Analysis and Management* 21, no. 3 (Summer 2002): 359–80.

Oster, Sharon M. *Strategic Management for Nonprofit Organizations.* New York: Oxford University Press, 1995.

———. "Pricing Goods and Services." Pp. 61–76 in *Generating and Sustaining Nonprofit Earned Income,* Sharon Oster, Cynthia Massarsky, and Samantha L. Beinhacker. San Francisco: Jossey Bass, 2004.

Oster, Sharon M., Charles M. Gray, and Charles Weinberg. "Pricing in the Nonprofit Sector." Pp. 27–45 in *Effective Economic Decision-Making by Nonprofit Organizations,* edited by Dennis R. Young. New York: The Foundation Center, 2004.

Oster, Sharon M., Cynthia W. Massarsky, and Samantha L. Beinhacker. *Generating and Sustaining Nonprofit Earned Income.* San Francisco: Jossey Bass, 2004.

Ostrower, Francie. *Attitudes and Practices Concerning Effective Philanthropy: Survey Report.* Washington, D.C.: The Urban Institute, October 2004.

Panas, Jerry. *Megagifts: Who Gives Them, Who Gets Them.* Chicago: Pluribus Press, 1984.

Panzar, John C., and Robert D. Willig. "Economies of Scope." *American Economic Review* 71, no. 2 (1981): 268–72.

Payne, Abigail. "Measuring the Effect of Federal Research Funding on Private Donations at Research Universities: Is Federal Research Funding More Than a Substitute for Private Donations?" *International Tax and Public Finance* 8, no. 5 (2001): 731–51.

Payne, James L. "Should Charities Last Forever?" *Philanthropy* 9, no. 4 (1995): 16–17.

Pollack, Thomas H., and Jonathan D. Dunford. "The Scope and Activities of 501(c)(3) Supporting Organizations." Washington, D.C.: National Center for Charitable Statistics at the Urban Institute. May 31, 2005. <www.urban.org/uploadedpdf/411175_501c3_support_orgs.pdf (accessed 12 June 2006).

Powell, Walter W., ed. *The Nonprofit Sector: A Research Handbook.* New Haven, CT: Yale University Press, 1987.

Powell, Walter W., and Richard Steinberg, eds. *The Nonprofit Sector: A Research Handbook.* 2nd ed. New Haven, CT: Yale University Press, 2006.

Powell, Walter W., and Jason Owen-Smith. "Universities as Creators and Retailers of Intellectual Property." Pp. 169–93 in *To Profit or Not to Profit: The Commercial Transformation of the Nonprofit Sector,* 2nd ed., edited by Burton A. Weisbrod. New York: Cambridge University Press, 1998.

Prince, Russ, and Karen File. *The Seven Faces of Philanthropy: A New Approach to Cultivating Major Donors.* San Francisco: Jossey Bass, 1994.

Prince, Russ, Karen File, and James Gillespie. "Philanthropic Styles." *Nonprofit Management and Leadership* 3, no. 3 (1993): 255–68.

Quigley, John M., ed. *Perspectives on Local Public Finance and Public Policy,* Vol. 1. Greenwich, CT: JAI Press, 1983.

Quigley, John M., and Steven Raphael. "Is Housing Unaffordable? Why Isn't It More Affordable?" *Journal of Economic Perspectives* 18, no. 1 (Winter 2004): 191–214.

Quirk, Bea. "Charlotte: Discovering Poor Neighborhoods." Pp. 313–22 in *An Agile Servant: Community Leadership by Community Foundations,* edited by Richard Magat. Washington, D.C.: Council on Foundations, 1989.

Ramsden, Dick. "Insights into the Yale Formula for Endowment Spending." <www.commonfund.org/commonfund/archive/news/yale_formula.html> (23 November 2005).

Reisman, Arnold. "Enhancing Nonprofit Resources Through Barter." *Nonprofit Management and Leadership* 1 (Spring 1991): 253–65.

Renz, David O. "The Case of Kansas City." Pp. 315–46 in *Philanthropy and the Nonprofit Sector in a Changing America*, edited by Charles T. Clotfelter and Thomas Ehrlich. Bloomington: Indiana University Press, 1999.

Ricardo, David. *On the Principles of Political Economy and Taxation.* London: John Murray, 1817.

Riley, Margaret. "Unrelated Business Income of Nonprofit Organizations: Highlights of 1995 and a Review of 1991–1995." *Compendium of Studies of Tax-Exempt Organizations, 1989–1998*, Vol. 3, Publication 1416 (rev. 5-2002), Catalog Number 15962B (Washington, D.C.: Statistical Information Service, Internal Revenue Service, May 2002a), 577–99.

———. "Unrelated Business Income of Nonprofit Organizations, 1997." *Compendium of Studies of Tax-Exempt Organizations, 1989–1998.* 2002b, 634–65.

Roberts, Benson F., and F. Barton Harvey III. "Comment on Jean L. Cummings and Denise DiPasquale's 'The Low-Income Housing Tax Credit: An Analysis of the First Ten Years.'" *Housing Policy Debate* 10, no. 2 (1999): 309–20.

Rooney, Patrick, Kathy Steinberg, and Paul Schervish. "A Methodological Comparison of Giving Surveys: Indiana as a Test Case." *Nonprofit and Voluntary Sector Quarterly* 30, no. 3 (2001): 551–68.

———. "Methodology Is Destiny: The Effects of Survey Prompts on Reported Levels of Giving and Volunteering." *Nonprofit and Voluntary Sector Quarterly* 31, no. 4 (2004): 628–54.

Rooney, Patrick, Mark A. Hager, and Thomas Pollak. "Differences in Return on Fundraising Investments by Fundraising Methods." Working paper, Center of Philanthropy and the Urban Institute, Indianapolis, IN, 2003.

Rooney, Patrick, Debra Mesch, Kathy Steinberg, and William Chin. "The Effects of Race, Gender, and Survey Methodologies on Giving in the U.S." *Economic Letters* 86, no. 2 (2005): 628–54.

Rose-Ackerman, Susan. "Unfair Competition and Corporate Income Taxation." *Stanford Law Review* 34, no. 5 (May 1982a): 1017–39.

———. "Charitable Giving and 'Excessive' Fundraising." *Quarterly Journal of Economics* 96 (May 1982b): 193–212.

———. "Do Government Grants to Charity Reduce Private Donations?" Pp. 313–29 in *The Economics of Nonprofit Institutions*, edited by Susan Rose-Ackerman. New York: Oxford University Press, 1986.

Rosett, Richard N. "Art Museums in the United States: A Financial Portrait." Pp. 129–77 in *The Economics of Art Museums*, edited by Martin Feldstein. Chicago: University of Chicago Press, 1991.

Saaty, Thomas. *The Analytic Hierarchy Process*. New York: McGraw-Hill, 1980.

Saaty, Thomas, and Kevin Kearns. *Analytic Planning: The Organization of Systems*. London: Pergamon, 1985.

Salamon, Lester M. *Partners in Public Service: Government-Nonprofit Relations in the Modern Welfare State*. Baltimore: Johns Hopkins University Press, 1995.

———. *America's Nonprofit Sector*. 2nd ed. New York: The Foundation Center, 1999a.

———. "Government-Nonprofit Rela ions in International Perspective." In *Nonprofits and Government: Collaboration and Conflict* edited by Elizabeth T. Boris and C. Eugene Steuerle. Washington, D.C.: Urban Institute Press, 1999b.

———, ed. *The State of Nonprofit America*. Washington, D.C.: Brookings Institution Press, 2002a.

———. "The Resilient Sector: The State of Nonprofit America." In *The State of Nonprofit America*, edited by Lester Salamon. Washington, D.C.: Brookings Institution Press, 2002b, 3–61.

Salamon, Lester M., Helmut K. Anheier, Regina List, Stefan Toepler, and S. Wojciech Sokolowski. *Global Civil Society*. Baltimore, MD: The Johns Hopkins Center for Civil Society Studies, 1999.

Salamon, Lester M., and Richard O'Sullivan. "Stressed but Coping: Nonprofit Organizations and the Current Fiscal Crisis." *Communique*, no. 2, Listening Post Project, Johns Hopkins University, January 19, 2004.

Sanders, Michael I. *Partnerships and Joint Ventures Involving Tax-Exempt Organizations*. New York: John Wiley & Sons, 1994.

Sansing, Richard. "The Unrelated Business Income Tax, Cost Allocation, and Productive Efficiency." *National Tax Journal* 51, no. 2 (June 1998): 291–302.

Sansing, Richard, and Robert Yetman. "Governing Private Foundations Using the Tax Law." *Journal of Accounting and Economics* (2006, forthcoming).

Schervish, Paul G. "Philanthropy among the Wealthy: Empowerment, Motivation and Strategy" (paper presented to the Rocky Mountain Philanthropic Institute, Vail, CO, 1991).

Schervish, Paul G., and John J. Havens. "Wealth and the Common-wealth: New Findings in Wealth and Philanthropy." *Nonprofit and Voluntary Sector Quarterly* 30, no. 1 (March 2001): 5–25.

Schervish, Paul G., and A. Herman. *Final Report: The Study on Wealth and Philanthropy.* Boston: Social Welfare Research Institute, Boston College, 1988.

Schervish, Paul G., Mary A. O'Herlihy, and John J. Havens. "Agent-Animated Wealth and Philanthropy: The Dynamics of Accumulation and Allocation among High-Tech Donors." Center on Wealth and Philanthropy, Boston College, 2001. <www.bc.edu/cwp>.

Schiff, Jerald "Does Government Spending Crowd Out Charitable Contributions?" *National Tax Journal* 38 (1985): 535–46.

———. *Charitable Giving and Government Policy: An Economic Analysis.* Westport, CT: Greenwood Press, 1990.

Schumacher, Edward C. *Building Your Endowment.* San Francisco: Jossey Bass, 2003.

Schuster, J. Mark Davidson. "Issues in Supporting the Arts through Tax Incentives." *Journal of Arts Management and Law* 16, no. 4 (1987): 31–50.

Segal, Lewis M., and Burton A. Weisbrod. "Interdependence of Commercial and Donative Revenues." Pp. 105–27 in *To Profit or Not to Profit: The Commercial Transformation of the Nonprofit Sector,* edited by Burton A. Weisbrod. New York: Cambridge University Press, 1998.

Sen, Amartya. "Rational Fools: A Critique of the Behavioral Foundations of Economic Theory." *Journal of Philosophy and Public Affairs* 6 (1977): 317–44.

Sharpe, W. "A Theory for Market Equilibrium under Conditions of Risk." *Journal of Finance* 19, no. 3 (1964): 425–42.

Sheppard, Lee A. "The Road to Hell Is Paved with Good Intentions." *Tax Notes* 77 (November 24, 1997): 888–96.

Shleifer, Andrei. "State versus Private Ownership." *Journal of Economic Perspectives* 12, no. 4 (Fall 1998): 133–50.

Shroder, Mark, and Arthur Reiger. "Vouchers versus Production Revisited." Working Paper, 2000. <papers.ssrn.com/paper.taf?abstract_id=218288>.

Simon, Herbert. *Administrative Behavior.* New York: Macmillan, 1947.

Simon, John G. "The Tax Treatment of Nonprofit Organizations: A Review of Federal and State Policies." Pp. 67–98 in *The Nonprofit Sector: A Research Handbook,* edited by Walter W. Powell. New Haven, CT: Yale University Press, 1987.

Sinai, Todd, and Joel Waldfogel. "Do Low-Income Housing Subsidies Increase Housing Consumption?" NBER, Working paper 8709, January 2002.

Skloot, Edward, ed. *The Nonprofit Entrepreneur*. New York: The Foundation Center, 1988.

Smith, Adam. *An Inquiry into the Nature and Causes of the Wealth of Nations*. London, 1776.

Smith, Steven Rathgeb. "Government Financing of Nonprofit Activity." Pp. 177–210 in *Nonprofits and Government: Collaboration and Conflict*, edited by Elizabeth T. Boris and C. Eugene Steuerle. Washington, D.C.: Urban Institute Press, 1999.

———. "Social Services." Pp. 149–86 in *The State of Nonprofit America*, edited by Lester Salamon. Washington, D.C.: Brookings Institution Press, 2002.

Smith, Steven Rathgeb, and Michael Lipsky. *Nonprofits for Hire: The Welfare State in the Age of Contracting*. Cambridge, MA: Harvard University Press, 1993.

Smith, Steven Rathgeb, and Michael R. Sosen. "The Varieties of Faith-Related Agencies." *Public Administration Review* 61, no. 6 (November/December 2001): 651–670.

Snavely, Keith, and Martin B. Tracy. "Collaboration among Rural Nonprofit Organizations." *Nonprofit Management and Leadership* 11, no. 2 (2000): 145–65.

Social Investment Forum. *2003 Report on Socially Responsible Investing Trends in the United States*. Washington, D.C.: Social Investment Forum, 2003.

Stegman, Michael A. "Comment on Jean L. Cummings and Denise DiPasquale's 'The Low-Income Housing Tax Credit: An Analysis of the First Ten Years': Lifting the Veil of Ignorance." *Housing Policy Debate* 10, no. 2 (1999): 321–32.

Steinberg, Richard. "Should Donors Care about Fundraising?" Pp. 347–64 in *The Economics of Nonprofit Institutions*, edited by Susan Rose-Ackerman. New York: Oxford University Press, 1986.

———. "Nonprofits and the Market." In *The Nonprofit Sector: A Research Handbook*, edited by Walter W. Powell. New Haven, CT: Yale University Press, 1987.

———. "Taxes and Giving: New Findings." *Voluntas* 1 (1990): 61–79.

———. "The Economics of Fundraising." In *Taking Fundraising Seriously: Advancing the Profession and Practice of Raising Money*, edited by Dwight Burlingame and Lamont Hulse. San Francisco: Jossey Bass, 1991.

———. "Does Government Spending Crowd Out Donations? Interpreting the Evidence." Pp. 99–125 in *The Nonprofit Sector in the Mixed Economy*, edited by Avner Ben-Ner and Benedetto Gui. Ann Arbor: University of Michigan Press, 1993.

———. "Economic Theories of Nonprofit Organization." Pp. 117–39 in *The Nonprofit Sector: A Research Handbook*, 2nd ed., edited by Walter W. Powell and Richard Steinberg. New Haven, CT: Yale University Press, 2006.

Steinberg, Richard, and Burton A. Weisbrod. "Pricing and Rationing by Nonprofit Organizations with Distributional Objectives." Pp. 65–82 in *To Profit or Not to Profit: The Commercial Transformation of the Nonprofit Sector*, edited by Burton A. Weisbrod. New York: Cambridge University Press, 1998.

Stiglitz, Joseph E. "The General Theory of Tax Avoidance." *National Tax Journal* 38, no. 3 (September 1985): 325–37.

St. Louis Gives 2003. Center on Philanthropy at Indiana University, 2003.

Stocks, Bonds, Bills and Inflation: 1998 Yearbook. Chicago: Ibbotson Associates, 1998.

Swanson, Stevenson. "Field Museum Art Sold for $17 Million." *Chicago Tribune Online Edition*, December 16, 2004.

Tiebout, Charles. "A Pure Theory of Local Expenditures." *Journal of Political Economy* 64 (1956): 416–24.

Tobin, James. "What Is Permanent Endowment Income?" *American Economic Review* 64, no. 2 (1974): 427–432.

Treynor, Jack L. "How to Rate Management of Investment Funds." *Harvard Business Review* 43 (1966): 63–75.

Troyer, Thomas. "The 1969 Private Foundation Law: Historical Perspective on Its Origins and Underpinnings." *The Exempt Organization Tax Review* 27 (January 2000): 52–65.

Trussel, John. "Revisiting the Prediction of Financial Vulnerability." *Nonprofit Management and Leadership* 13, no. 1 (2002): 17–31.

———. "Assessing Potential Accounting Manipulation: The Financial Characteristics of Charitable Organizations with Higher Than Expected Program-Spending Ratios." *Nonprofit and Voluntary Sector Quarterly* 32, no. 4 (2003): 616–34.

Trussel, John, and Janet Greenlee. "A Financial Rating System for Nonprofit Organizations." *Research in Government and Nonprofit Accounting* 11 (2004): 105–28.

Tschirhart, Mary. "Membership Associations." Pp. 523–41 in *The Nonprofit Sector: A Research Handbook*, 2nd ed., edited by Walter W. Powell and Richard Steinberg. New Haven, CT: Yale University Press, 2006.

Tschirhart, Mary, and Jon Johnson. "Infidels at the Gate and Rebels in the Ranks: Protection from Takeovers in Nonprofit Membership Organizations"(paper presented at the ARNOVA Annual Conference, Seattle, WA, November 5–7, 1998).

Tuckman, Howard P. "The Various Stages of Development of a Non-profit Organization and Their Implications for Its Financial Health." Rutgers University, unpublished paper, 2006.

Tuckman, Howard P., and Cyril F. Chang. "A Methodology for Measuring the Financial Vulnerability of Charitable Nonprofit Organizations." *Nonprofit and Voluntary Sector Quarterly* 20, no. 4 (1991): 445–460.

———. "Nonprofit Equity: A Behavioral Model and Its Implications." *Journal of Policy Analysis and Management* 11, no. 1 (1992): 76–87.

———. "Commercial Activity, Technological Change, and Nonprofit Mission." Pp. 629–44 in *The Nonprofit Sector: A Research Handbook*, 2nd ed., edited by Walter W. Powell and Richard Steinberg. New Haven, CT: Yale University Press, 2006.

Tullock, Gordon. "Information without Profit." *Papers on Non-Market Decision Making* 1 (1966): 141–59.

Under One Roof Project. "The Under One Roof Project: Benefits and Challenges of Co-Locating Nonprofit Organizations." Website hosted by University of Michigan School of Social Work. 2004. <www.ssw.umich.edu/underoneroof/> (16 July 2004).

U.S. Census Bureau. *Statistical Abstract of the United States: 2002.* Washington, D.C., 2002.

U.S. General Accounting Office. "Tax Credits: Reasons for Differences in Housing Built by For-Profit and Nonprofit Developers." Report to the Chairman, Subcommittee on Housing and Community Opportunity, Committee of Banking and Financial Services, House of Representatives, GAO-RCED-99-60, March 1999.

Vesterlund, Lise. "Why Do People Give?" Pp. 569–90 in *The Nonprofit Sector: A Research Handbook*, 2nd ed., edited by Walter W. Powell and Richard Steinberg. New Haven, CT: Yale University Press, 2006.

Wedig, Gerard, Mahmud Hassan, and Michael Morrisey. "Tax-Exempt Debt and the Capital Structure of Nonprofit Organizations: An Application to Hospitals." *The Journal of Finance* (September 1996): 1247–83.

Weisbrod, Burton. "Toward a Theory of the Voluntary Nonprofit Sector in a Three-Sector Economy." Pp. 171–95 in *Altruism, Morality, and Economic Theory*, edited by Edmund S. Phelps. New York: Russell Sage, 1974.

———. *The Voluntary Nonprofit Sector.* Lexington, MA: D. C. Heath, 1977.

———. *The Nonprofit Economy.* Cambridge, MA: Harvard University Press, 1988.

———. "Tax Policy Toward Nonprofit Organizations: An Eleven-Country Survey." *Voluntas* 2, no. 1 (1991): 3–25.

————, ed. *To Profit or Not to Profit*. New York: Cambridge University Press, 1998.

————. "The Pitfalls of Profits." *Stanford Social Innovation Review* (Winter 2004): 40–47.

Weisbrod, Burton, and A. J. Lee. "Collective Goods and the Voluntary Sector: The Case of the Hospital Industry." In *The Voluntary Nonprofit Sector: An Economic Analysis*, edited by Burton Weisbrod. Lexington, MA: Lexington Books, 1977.

Weitzman, Murray, Nadine I. Jaladoni, Linda Lampkin, and Thomas H. Pollak, eds. *The New Nonprofit Almanac and Desk Reference*. San Francisco: Jossey Bass, 2002.

Werther, William B., and Evan M. Berman. *Third Sector Management: The Art of Managing Nonprofit Organizations*. Washington, D.C.: Georgetown University Press, 2001.

White, G., A. Sondhi, and D. Fried. *The Analysis and Use of Financial Statements*, 3rd ed. Hoboken, NJ: John Wiley & Sons, 2002.

Wilhelm, Mark. *The Distribution of Giving in Six Surveys*. Mimeo. Indianapolis, IN: IUPUI, 2003.

Wilhelm, Mark, Eleanor Brown, Patrick Rooney, and Rich and Steinberg. "The Intergenerational Transmission of Generosity." Working paper, Center on Philanthropy, Indianapolis, IN, 2004.

Wilson, James Q. "Religion and Public Life." Pp. 160–70 in *What's God Got to Do with the American Experiment*, edited by E. J. Dionne Jr. and John DiIulio. Washington, D.C.: Brookings Institution Press, 2000.

Wilson, John. "Volunteering." *Annual Review of Sociology* 26 (2000): 215–40.

Wing, Ken, Thomas Pollak, Mark A. Hager, and Patrick Rooney. "Getting What We Pay For: Low Overhead Limit Nonprofit Effectiveness." 2005a. <www.coststudy.org>.

————. "Donating to Charity: A Guide." 2005b. <www.coststudy.org>.

————. "The Quality of Financial Reporting by Nonprofits: Findings and Implications." 2005c. <www.coststudy.org>.

————. "The Pros and Cons of Financial Efficiency Standards." 2005d. <www.coststudy.org>.

Wondelleck, Julia M., and Steven Yaffe. *Making Collaboration Work: Lessons from Innovation in Natural Resource Management*. Washington, D.C.: Island Press, 2000.

Wuthnow, Robert. *Saving America?* Princeton, NJ: Princeton University Press, 2004. <www.naeir.org>.

Wuthnow, Robert, and Virginia A. Hodgkinson, eds. *Faith and Philanthropy in America: Exploring the Role of Religion in America's Voluntary Sector*. San Francisco: Jossey Bass, 1990.

Yetman, Robert J. "Tax-Motivated Expense Allocations by Nonprofit Organizations." *The Accounting Review* 76, no. 3 (July 2001): 297–311.

———. "Nonprofit Taxable Activities, Production Complementarities, and Joint Cost Allocations." *National Tax Journal* 56, no. 4 (December 2003): 789–799.

Young, Dennis R. "Entrepreneurship and the Behavior of Nonprofit Organizations: Elements of a Theory." Pp. 135–62 in *Nonprofit Firms in a Three-Sector Economy*, edited by Michelle White. Washington, D.C.: Urban Institute Press, 1981.

———. *If Not for Profit, For What?* Lexington, MA: D. C. Heath and Company, 1983.

———. "Commercialism in Nonprofit Social Service Associations." Pp. 195–216 in *To Profit or Not to Profit*, edited by Burton Weisbrod. New York: Cambridge University Press, 1998.

———. "Complementary, Supplementary, or Adversarial? A Theoretical and Historical Examination of Nonprofit-Government Relations in the United States." Pp. 31–67 in *Nonprofits and Government: Collaboration and Conflict*, edited by Elizabeth T. Boris and C. Eugene Steuerle. Washington, D.C.: Urban Institute Press, 1999.

———. "Organizational Identity in Nonprofit Organizations: Strategic and Structural Implications." *Nonprofit Management and Leadership* 12, no. 2 (2001): 139–57.

———, ed. *Effective Economic Decision-Making by Nonprofit Organizations.* New York: The Foundation Center, 2004.

———. "Social Enterprise in Community and Economic Development in the United States: Theory, Corporate Form and Purpose." *International Journal of Entrepreneurship and Innovation Management* 6, no. 3 (2006a): 241–55.

———. "Wise Economic Decision-making for Nonprofits in Uncertain Times: An Overview." In *Wise Economic Decision-Making in Uncertain Times: Using Nonprofit Resources Effectively*, edited by Dennis R. Young. New York: The Foundation Center and the National Center on Nonprofit Enterprise, 2006b.

Young, Dennis R. and Richard Steinberg. *Economics for Nonprofit Managers.* New York: The Foundation Center Press, 1995.

Zimmerman, Shannon. "Sizing Up Socially Responsible Funds." 2003. Chicago: Morningstar. <www.morningstar.com> (5 September 2005).

Zodrow, George R. "The Property Tax as a Capital Tax: A Room with Three Views." *National Tax Journal* 54, no. 1 (March 2001): 139–56.

Index

Page numbers in *italics* refer to tables or text boxes.

failure, market/government:
theory of, 7, 15, 41
fair market value (FMV), 230–31
Faith-Based Initiative, 85, 86–87.
See also White House Office of
Community and Faith-Based
Initiatives
Fannie Mae Corporation, 106
fees. *See* dues/fees
Field Museum, 234–35
File, Karen, 39–40
finance, nonprofit: bankruptcy
risk and, 318; concept of, 3;
crowd out for, 98;
design/adjustment for, 371;
diversity of, 5, 7, 13, 17, 170,
176, 179, 284; endowment for,
276, 366; free cash for, 255; as
healthy, 6–7, 318; monitoring
of, 6–7, 316–18; prediction
models for, 318, *319*; ratio
analyses for, 318; risk
management for, 169, 177, 322,
356, 364–67; stability of, 7, 17,
31, 43, 277, 365; theory for, 15,
17, 20, *343*, 350, 351, 361, 362,
364, 369
financial ratios, monitoring of, 17
financial solvency, 356, 361–64
financing, alternative, 14, *353*
fiscal stress, 7, 10, 11
501 (c)(3) organizations:
grants/assets of, 45, *48*, 315;
income for, 292; municipal
bonds for, 5, 74–75, 162, 167,
243, 244–45, 246–47, 251–52,
260; program service revenue
for, 97; revenue from, 125;
sector comparison for, *327*;
sector risk for, 325–26; tax code

for, 28, 47–48, 131–32;
valuation of, 321
501 (c)(4) organizations, 292
509 (a)(3) organizations, 276
fixed cost: collaboration for,
13–14, 210, 212–13, 225, 226; for
NPOs, 13–14, 210, 212–13, 225,
226, 284–85, 366; overhead as,
284–85; real estate and, 284–85,
286. *See also* overhead
fixed revenue/income, 284
FMV. *See* fair market value
food bank, 228, 230
Ford foundation, 59–60, 180n4,
288n11
for-profit organizations:
bankruptcy for, 180n6, 323;
bartering with, 221–22; cash
liquidity for, 243; in
competition with NPOs, 74,
104–5, 109, 189; financial health
of, 319–20; as lender, 258–59,
260–62, *262*; price
discrimination by, 101, 102,
109; slack and, 171–73, 174;
supply side theory for, 111–14;
surplus for, 283
Foster, Mary K., 209
foundation(s): administrative
costs for, 52; asset retention by,
51–52; behavior of, 58–63, 65,
111; charitable giving through,
4, 5, *8*, 16, 28, 52; collaboration
with, 225; consulting service
by, 63; distribution
requirements for, 51, 52, 53,
58–59, 61, 65, 66–67, 68n4;
donor restrictions by, 12, 30, 61;
endowment tax rate for, 51;
establishment of, 39;

organizational risk, 6–7, 17, 105,
129, 152–53, 164–65, 166–67,
178–79
Oster, Sharon, 89, 99
overhead: collaboration for
savings on, 225; as fixed cost,
284–85; for organization, 135,
173; staff as, 135, 173, 220
ownership, 271, 287n2
own-price elasticity, 142, 144.
See also membership
Oxford Dictionary/Thesaurus, 3

Panas, Jerry, 39
Panel Study of Income Dynamics
(PSID), 24, 40, 184, 196
partial responsibility theory. *See*
theory
partnerships, corporate:
American Express for, 105–6;
intellectual property for, 106;
for international relief,
105–6; MBNA for, 105; with
NPOs, 105–6, 211–12, 218,
353–54; for revenue, 99, 105–6,
117
patents, 106–7
payments in lieu of taxes
(PILOTs), 79, 90
Payne, Abigail, 36–37
Payne, James L., 158
PBS. *See* Public Broadcasting
Service
pecking order theory, 253, 259–60.
See also debt, nonprofit
perceived value, 136–37
Permanent Fund, 288n8
PGI. *See* Philanthropic Giving
Index
Philanthropic Giving Index (PGI),
32–33

philanthropy: as corporate, 227;
GIKI for, 227; as informal, 3, 28;
as institutional, 4, 5, *8*, 16, 28;
methodologies for
measurement of, 40; as private,
34–35, 41, 357
philanthropy, strategic, 348
PILOTs. *See* payments in lieu of
taxes
plan, strategic, 11
pledges, to NPO, 9, 123, 272
Pollak, Thomas, 31, 32, 78, 79, 168,
284
Ponzi scheme, 181n9
portfolio, management of: for
community support, 298–99,
307; diversification for, 5, 7, 13,
17, 170, 176, 179, 284, 291, 297,
312, 365–66, 368–69;
mean-variance model for, 297;
objective-maximization theory
for, 297–98; systematic risk for,
178–79, 297, 356, 365;
unsystematic risk for, 178–79,
297, 365
portfolio, nonprofit income: as
balanced, 5, 17, 160–61, 291;
components of, *311*, 343, 368;
diversification of, 5, 7, 13, 17,
170, 176, 179, 284, 291, 297, 312,
365–66, 368–69; marginal
adjustments for, 361;
multiattribute utility analysis
for, 301–2; NPO mission and,
291–92, 299, 300, 356, 361–64;
Prudent Investor Rule for, 163;
risk in, 6–7, 17, 105, 129,
152–53, 164–65, 166–67, 178–79,
356. *See also* investment
income; revenue
portfolio theory, 368

subsidies: as direct, 70, 71, 72–73,
88; as indirect, 69, 71–73, 88, 90;
for investment capital, 172
subsidies, government:
comparison of, 71; as direct, 70,
71, 72–73; for NPOs, 14, 70–71.
See also Medicaid; Medicare;
Social Security
substitute, service as, 110–11, 190,
360–61. *See also* pricing
supply side funding. *See* funding,
supply side
supply side theory. *See* theory
supporting organization:
foundation *v.*, 45
surplus: for for-profit, 283; for
NPOs, 316; revenue as, 111
sustainability, 330–33
symphonies: earned income for,
96, 99; price discrimination by,
100. *See also* arts/culture,
nonprofit
synergy, 214, 215, 215–16. *See also*
trade benefits
systematic risk, 178–79, 297, 356,
365

tax, disincentives, 6
taxation: avoidance *v.* evasion for,
73; bartering for avoidance of,
222; on capital gains, 68n5; cliff
effect for, 54; contributions
and, 72, 73; corporate tax as
neutral, 75; cost-shifting for,
75–76, 77, 97–98; deductions
under, 253; fairness in, 137, 138;
for 501 (c)(3) organizations, 45,
48, 131–32; for foundations,
45–46, 51–54, 59; by
government for public goods,
34–35; on investment income,

45–46; local choice in, 34; for
membership, 131–32, 140–41;
for NPOs, 5, 73; for private
foundation, 45–46, 51–52, 53,
59; reform in, 87; sales tax as,
222; UBIT for, 74, 75, 76–78,
97
tax credits, sale of, 80–81
tax incentives: for charitable
giving, 16, 73; for donors, 7, 11,
16, 46, 69, 71–73; dual tax rate
system as, 59; for 501(c)(3)
organizations, 5, 28, 45, 47,
74–75, 162, 243, 244–45, 246–47,
251–52, 260; for NPOs, 112;
property tax exemption as, 69,
78–79, 90; subsidies as, 69,
71–73; variety of, 7.
Taxpayer Bill of Rights 2, 328
tax price of giving, 73
Tax Reform Act, 280
TFA. *See* Tubman Family Alliance
theater, 96. *See also* arts/culture,
nonprofit
theory: of cooperative game, 139;
of market/government failure,
7, 15, 41; of partial
responsibility, 139–40; of
public/private goods, 15,
33–34, 107–14, 357; for supply
side, 111–14
St. Theresa's, *8*, 11. *See also* Roman
Catholic Archdiocese of
Brooklyn
toll goods, 109
Torous, W., 318
Tracy, Martin B., 217, 220–21
trade benefits: bartering as, 222,
353–55, 354, 358–59; NPO/
corporate partnerships for,
105–6, 211–12, 218, 353–54;

About the Contributors

Woods Bowman is Associate Professor of Public Services Management at DePaul University and editor of ARNOVA Abstracts.

Arthur C. Brooks is Professor of Public Administration and Director of the Nonprofit Studies Program at Syracuse University's Maxwell School of Citizenship and Public Affairs.

Joseph Cordes is Professor of Economics, Public Policy, and Public Administration in the School of Public Policy and Public Administration at George Washington University, and an Associate Scholar in the Center on Nonprofits and Philanthropy at the Urban Institute.

Charles M. Gray is Professor of Economics at the University of St. Thomas and President of the Association for Cultural Economics, International.

Estelle James is Professor Emeritus at the State University of New York, Stony Brook, former Lead Economist at the World Bank, and currently a consultant to the World Bank and other organizations.

Kevin Kearns is Professor of Public and Nonprofit Management and founding director of the Johnson Institute for Responsible Leadership in the Graduate School of Public and International Affairs, University of Pittsburgh.

Elizabeth K. Keating is Assistant Professor of Public Policy at the Kennedy School of Government at Harvard University.

Janet Greenlee is Associate Professor of Accounting at the University of Dayton.

Mark A. Hager is Director of the Center for Community and Business Research at the Institute for Economic Development at the University of Texas, San Antonio.

Renee A. Irvin is Director of the Graduate Certificate in Not-for-Profit Management Program and Associate Professor of Planning, Public Policy, and Management at the University of Oregon.

Anne E. Preston is Associate Professor of Economics at Haverford College.

Patrick Rooney is Director of Research at the Center on Philanthropy at Indiana University and Professor of Economics and Philanthropic Studies at Indiana University–Purdue University, Indianapolis.

Michael Rushton is Associate Professor at the School of Public and Environmental Affairs at Indiana University in Bloomington, where he teaches in the program in arts administration, and is coeditor of the *Journal of Cultural Economics*.

Richard Sansing is Associate Professor of Business Administration at the Tuck School of Business at Dartmouth.

Richard Steinberg is Professor of Economics, Philanthropic Studies, and Public Affairs at Indiana University–Purdue University, Indianapolis.

Howard P. Tuckman is Dean of the Graduate School of Business Administration and Dean of the Faculty of Business at Fordham University, and consultant to corporations, attorneys, and public agencies.

Robert J. Yetman is Associate Professor of Management at the University of California, Davis.

Dennis R. Young is Bernard B. and Eugenia A. Ramsey Professor of Private Enterprise, Andrew Young School of Policy Studies at Georgia State University, and President of the National Center on Nonprofit Enterprise.